A Closer Walk

∼∼∼∼∼∼∼∼∼∼∼∼
Day by Day
∼∼∼∼∼∼∼∼∼∼∼∼∼

**A Daily Devotional
by
Les Wheeldon**

All scripture quotations, unless otherwise indicated, are taken from the New King James Version®. Copyright © 1982 by Thomas Nelson, Inc. Used by permission. All rights reserved.

Scripture quotations marked (NLT) are taken from the Holy Bible, New Living Translation, copyright ©1996, 2004, 2015 by Tyndale House Foundation. Used by permission of Tyndale House Publishers, a Division of Tyndale House Ministries, Carol Stream, Illinois 60188. All rights reserved.

Scripture quotations marked MSG are taken from *THE MESSAGE*, copyright © 1993, 2002, 2018 by Eugene H. Peterson. Used by permission of NavPress. All rights reserved. Represented by Tyndale House Publishers, a Division of Tyndale House Ministries.

Scripture quotations marked ESV are from the ESV® Bible (The Holy Bible, English Standard Version®), copyright ©2001 by Crossway Bibles, a publishing ministry of Good News Publishers. Used by permission. All rights reserved.

Scripture quotations marked KJV are from the King James (Authorized) Version of the Bible.

Quotations designated (NET) are from the NET Bible® copyright ©1996-2018 by Biblical Studies Press, L.L.C. http://netbible.com All rights reserved.

Scripture quotations marked NIV are from the THE HOLY BIBLE, NEW INTERNATIONAL VERSION®, NIV® Copyright © 1973, 1978, 1984, 2011 by Biblica, Inc.™ Used by permission. All rights reserved worldwide.

Scripture quotations marked NASB are taken from the New American Standard Bible®, Copyright © 1960,1962, 1963, 1971, 1972, 1973, 1975, 1977, 1995 by The Lockman Foundation. Used by permission.

Copyright © 2019 Leslie John Wheeldon
All rights reserved.

Cover Photo by Adrien Tutin on Unsplash

ISBN: 9781671899612

Foreword

I am delighted to recommend Les Wheeldon's second volume of daily readings. As the title suggests, it will truly inspire a closer walk with God. This book will remind all who read it that God is here, God is able, and God is love. The author has brought out of his treasury " things new and old" that will strengthen and equip each individual in their walk with Christ.

Mary Seaton.

DEDICATION

To all the friends who have shown me by their loving example the beauty of a closer walk with Jesus.

ACKNOWLEDGMENTS

My heartfelt thanks to Mary Seaton, Kathy Bunten, Hugh Burney and most of all my wife Vicki for their patient encouragement to keep writing and their editing and improving of this book.

Les Wheeldon

January 1

Therefore do not worry about tomorrow, for tomorrow will worry about its own things. Sufficient for the day is its own trouble. *(Matthew 6:34)*

At the beginning of a new year it is vital that we do not carry tomorrow's burdens today. Every day has burdens of responsibility for ourselves and others, praying, counselling and caring. These can crush hope out of the heart if they are heaped up, stretching into the future. Each servant of God need only focus on the next few hours.

Yes, we plan for the future but no, we must not carry all the responsibilities that stretch out to the horizon. Sufficient for the day is the evil we have to confront. It is right to carelessly cast aside the burdens of the future, but we must never be frivolous about the souls we meet in our daily walk, and we must be dismissive and even laugh at the thought that we can prepare to help people by worrying about them.

Let a chuckle of content sweep across your soul about the future. Don't miss the humour in the Lord's declaration that "tomorrow will worry about its own things". God made us in His image, and that means He has a sense of humour. Laugh at your attempts to sort out the future by concentrated fretting. Commit it all to Him and know that He is able to plan each day perfectly. All our tomorrows are in His hands, and the less we care about the future, the more strength we will have to fight the battles of today.

January 2

And you He made alive, who were dead in trespasses and sins…. and raised us up together, and made us sit together in the heavenly places in Christ Jesus. (Ephesians 2:1 & 6)

The heart of prayer is to develop a consciously open-faced relationship with God. That is our throne in the heavenlies, to sit in that wonderful presence and be conscious of Him, His glory, His smile, His rule. We must learn that prayer is not only an activity that we engage in, it is a place to be entered into. When we pray, it is as if we poke our heads over the clouds and behold the undimmed glory of His presence. That is our real home.

True, His face may be clouded in times of temptation, and we fret and worry as we find our hearts are leaden and our steps heavy. We cast around in ourselves for the reason why we have lost the beauty of His presence, but when the time of temptation lifts, our joy knows no bounds. On other occasions we lose this place through neglect or sin and our seat in the heavenlies is vacant. But when we return there, there is no rebuke, merely welcome and joy that we are back in our place.

We may feel unworthy, but we have to throw off our beggar's garments and put on the dignity and majesty of the Son, not because that is better psychology but because it is the truth. We are not only in the heavenlies in imagination. We have the inner poise and faith of the risen Son of God at our disposal. Christ is in us and we are no longer slaves, no longer wretched spiritual failures, but dignified sons and daughters of God with the risen Christ as our inward life. We have a heavenly life that gravitates upwards to our Father and it is the Spirit of God that constantly draws us to sit there and learn to view the world from that wonderful angle.

~~~~~~~~~~~~~~

January 3

All the inhabitants of the earth are reputed as nothing; He does according to His will in the army of heaven and among the inhabitants of the earth. No one can restrain His hand or say to Him "What have you done?" (Daniel 4:35)

Nebuchadnezzar is speaking in this verse, after he had been through his terrible mental breakdown and had been restored to full health. He came to true and living faith in the God of Daniel. These and other similar verses communicate the sense of the awesome sovereignty of God. Truly God is sovereign and rules over all. Such a truth, if proclaimed to extremes, would produce the awful fatalism of eastern religions. But passivity is never the result of meeting the sovereign God of the Bible.

The effect on Nebuchadnezzar was manifold: he feared God, he worshipped God and trusted Him. God assures us that He is in ultimate control of everything. He is Lord of all and of all that ever shall be. God communicates in other places His invitation to be co-workers with Him, both in prayer and in faith. God invites us to participate in His rule by asking Him to use His sovereign power to save and to heal. Just think of the most impossible situation, the most blocked heart to God, the most entrenched habits of sinners, the most unbelieving of minds. God says: invite Me into that person's life and I will change it.

God will never violate the human will and force people to believe in Him, but He does present us with the unmistakable sense of His majesty, which challenges us to submit and surrender to Him. Think of proud politicians, philosophers, relatives, drug addicts etc... and pray for them. Remember that no-one can restrain His hand once He has risen to act.

January 4

"But will God indeed dwell on the earth? Behold, heaven and the heaven of heavens cannot contain You. How much less this temple which I have built!" (1Kings 8:27)

God is immeasurable in His infinity. His greatness is in one sense so vast that to imagine that we could comprehend it sounds like the deepest folly. Yet God has made the human heart and mind with this unique quality: we yearn to grasp the infinite. There is a restless longing in every human being to discover something beyond the horizon. Explorers journey on and on conquering deserts, mountains and rivers, but their discoveries do not satisfy the quest, the thirst for the infinite.

It is only when we come face to face with God that we realise what we were made for. Worship is the very essence of man's destiny. Worship is the soul set free to be what God made it to be. Worship is the heart of man soaring into the glory of God's presence and for a brief moment grasping the infinite and comprehending it. We seek to pin down our experiences of worship, to define them, to repeat them, but they are as unrepeatable as every sunset. All we can do is marvel at the beauty that is imprinted on our souls as we behold God.

It is as if we sit before God like individual grains of sand at the side of a mighty ocean and the ocean talks to us as if we were its equal. In that moment each tiny grain of sand contains the greatness and fullness of the ocean. This is the wonder that Christ lives in us and is the very doorway to fellowship with God.

January 5

Now no chastening seems to be joyful for the present, but painful; nevertheless, afterward it yields the peaceable fruit of righteousness to those who have been trained by it.

(Hebrews 12:11)

Suffering is not in itself an agent for the cleansing of the soul and it can in fact lead to bitterness and awful pollution. This is because suffering presents us with **a revelation, a choice and a challenge.** The most common and human reaction to suffering is "Why, Lord?" The answer to that question is quite simply that God wants us to face up to our heart's real state. It is in suffering that our most basic selfish instincts surface. We get angry, petulant and may even begin to accuse God of not caring, not loving.

The revelation of the awful attitudes of our own hearts makes us realise how deeply we need God to give us a new heart. We may pray for the pain to be taken away, for the suffering to stop. But how awful to have these sufferings stop and then we continue through life with an inner spiritual attitude that robs us of all the beauty and power of deep fellowship with God. Suffering leads us to know our own hearts and in response to humble ourselves before Him. Hebrews 12 teaches that God is a loving Father who chastens His sons, and that if He did not chasten us, we would not be true sons. Suffering is the rod, the staff that keeps us close to the shepherd, and that comforts us because we are kept in close fellowship with Him. There will come a day when we will bless God for the dark days for we will understand better that they were as much a part of His grace to us as the bright ones.

The choice is either to look at suffering as a bothersome distraction or to see it as a door to deeper fellowship with Jesus.

The challenge is to rise and praise God in the midst of the suffering and to sing in the night awaiting the coming dawn. This is the way of faith. Those without faith scorn the idea that any good can come out of suffering, but the deepest pain of the human heart is to suffer without hope. To turn our back on God in pain is to open our hearts to a gulf of darkness that is the pathway of despair.

~~~~~~~~~~~~~~

January 6

Jesus did this as the first of his miraculous signs, in Cana of Galilee. In this way he revealed his glory, and his disciples believed in him. (John 2:11 NET)

At the wedding in Cana in Galilee Jesus did His first miracle. It was a first for Him and for His mother and His followers. His mother had known Him for all these thirty years and had observed the beauty and wonder of His life. But now something new was to happen. Mary did not know what it would be, but she was the one who triggered the miracle by telling the servants that He had the answer: "Whatever He says to you do it." Perhaps there had been little moments of crisis in the home and she had discovered that He was always there with serenity of heart and mind to still the storms of life. But still this was a new beginning.

Since the dawn of time God is and has always been the God of miracles, from creation and through all His redemptive dealings with the human race. As believers we are familiar with the miracles of Jesus in the gospels just as Mary was familiar with the miracles in Israel's history. But still there is a beginning of miracles in every individual's life. What was the first miracle in your life? The miracle of Cana was the transformation of water into wine, and the only miracle that is guaranteed to us all is precisely that.

He will change the nature and atmosphere of our hearts and we will know the rich quality of life that comes from knowing Him. Mary understood more than all the people at the wedding that if the problem were laid at the feet of Jesus, all would be well. That is precisely what we must do. Put Him in charge of our lives and our eyes will open wide in wonder at the matchless favour of His presence.

∼∼∼∼∼∼∼∼∼∼∼∼∼∼

January 7

His mother said to the servants, "Whatever He says to you, do it." ... Jesus said to them, "Fill the water pots with water." And they filled them up to the brim. And He said to them, "Draw some out now, and take it to the master of the feast." And they took it. (John 2:5, 7, 8)

There were three stages to this first miracle and we do well to notice their order and their scope:

Stage one: make Jesus Lord. Obey Him, lay the matter at His feet. Don't try and imagine what He will do, simply spread it before Him, make it His problem and let it cease to be yours.

Stage two: let Him fill you with His Spirit, His presence, His love. When Christ fills us with His Spirit, we receive power to live, power to pray and power to overcome temptation, but this is still only the potential for a miraculous life.

Stage three: pour out the wine.
It is this third stage that we most often miss. We have felt the burden of need, there is a drought in our lives, we are dry and empty and we have been driven to fall at His feet by the pressure of that need. Then we have been touched, changed and refreshed by His grace. But though we know all this, there is another stage: that beautiful water of the Holy Spirit must deeply transform us so that we do not know the Spirit only as an addition to our lives, but as the very source. We need to have the beauty of love in the very fibre of our being. That miracle will only take place when we are poured out. The flow of the Holy Spirit will only be released as we love others and direct our lives to loving and serving others. Only then does the Christian life become the sweetest most miraculous wine of all.

~~~~~~~~~~~~~~

January 8

When we heard this, both we and the local people begged him not to go up to Jerusalem. Then Paul replied, "What are you doing, weeping and breaking my heart? For I am ready not only to be tied up, but even to die in Jerusalem for the name of the Lord Jesus." Because he could not be persuaded, we said no more except, "The Lord's will be done."
(Acts 21:12-14 NET)

Here we find two completely contradictory opinions about what Paul should do. Both sides felt that they were guided by the Holy Spirit. A closer examination reveals that the difference lay in their motives. Paul's friends were horrified at the realisation that Paul was about to suffer and their perception of the future filled them with dismay. They were concerned about their friend and this was a noble sentiment. However, Paul's vision was greater. He was concerned about the glory of God and His will.

When we look for the will of God, we may not realise how much we are swayed by our affections and our desire for things to go smoothly. Paul was not a masochist. He did not seek suffering, but he did not judge the will of God according to the easiest path that would open up. Nor did he place the feelings and opinions of his friends above his desire for God's will and plan to be fulfilled. We are not to seek the path of suffering, but we are to allow the vehement devotion of the Holy Spirit to the glory of God to fill our hearts.

Most of us sail under the flag of convenience. Our agenda is directed by how things will affect us and our friends. We may not even realise how subtly we have relegated Jesus to just one of the factors in our lives. But we are to develop a fixed and steady devotion to Jesus as the master passion of our lives. Those who follow this path will perplex others because they are marching to a different drum beat. Jesus perplexed His followers because of His steady and fixed determination to go to Calvary. He was not devoted to success for its own sake - He loved and served His Father.

~~~~~~~~~~~~~~~

January 9

Be being filled with the Holy Spirit. (Ephesians 5:18 author's translation)

I once had a beautiful car, a British Rover. It had a wooden dash board and air conditioning. The engine purred beautifully even though it was well over 15 years old. I bought it for a very good price, but realized very quickly why: the fuel gauge did not work and the Rover company had gone bust some years before so the parts to repair it were not available. So sadly, I ran out of fuel on two occasions and when I used to fill the tank I had to mark the distance covered very carefully so that I do not run out of fuel again. It was a great car, and without fuel it was still beautiful ... but totally useless. It could carry me comfortably for long distances but it was a terrible burden if I had to push it.

The Holy Spirit is the fuel of the Christian life. It is through the presence of God in us that we can pray, believe, love and pursue holiness. We might have the most admirable doctrines, the most detailed understanding of theology. We might boast of knowledge of the original languages in which it was written. But the great need is for that supernatural, empowering and transforming Spirit of God to bathe our heart, mind and will. Paul in Ephesians starts a very practical section on marriage and work with this exhortation to be continually filled with God's spirit. Take time and receive the loving supply that comes from His promise. Keep on asking, and He is faithful to keep on filling us.

∼∼∼∼∼∼∼∼∼∼∼∼

January 10

Blessed be the God and Father of our Lord Jesus Christ, the Father of mercies and God of all comfort, who comforts us in all our tribulation that we may be able to comfort those who are in any trouble, with the comfort with which we ourselves are comforted by God. *(2 Corinthians 1:3-4)*

There is a perplexing side to this verse. Paul says that he went through suffering in order to be able to comfort others who also go through suffering. But would it not be better if God ordered both our and their circumstances so that we did not have suffering at all? This would be true if the comfort that God gave us were just a pat on the back and an exhortation to keep going. But the comfort God gives us is of a totally different order to mere human sympathy.

Strangely we need to reach out to God in such a deep and radical way if we are to experience this comfort. It is only tribulation that shapes and positions our soul to receive this help from God. When we receive the comfort of God, our hearts are ennobled and purified in a positive way. We partake of the breathtaking love of God that is poured into our souls. We sense that we are partaking of a life that is so far above our former narrow little world, and yet this life is even more at home in the dust and ordinariness of human life. It is through suffering that we have a doorway into heaven, its atmosphere, its perspective and its purpose. God has to bring certain souls there, with such a clear understanding that they can declare to others the things that God is doing through these baffling moments of their journey.

Let the matchless comfort of the Holy Spirit bathe your life as you pass through valleys of weeping, and to your astonishment you will find that you have become another person through the tears and perplexity. Learn the lesson well, for there is a suffering world that desperately needs to hear you tell what God has done for you so that He may do it for them too.

January 11

Arise therefore, go down and go with them, doubting nothing; for I have sent them. (Acts 10:20)

Doubt and unbelief are the sin that so easily besets us (Hebrew 12:1). There may be good reasons that we can present to God as to why we should stop believing Him. After all, we can point to many prayers that were not answered as we would have wished. Our lives have not always been easy, and we may have assumed that having Jesus around meant that we would no longer be subjected to many of the sufferings that afflict the human race.

It is good to pin down this complaint for what it is: a selfish whimper that things have not gone our way. Faith is not a self-seeking lament, the selfish whine of a petulant child. We have to throw off that suffocating cloak of unbelief and rise up and believe that God is faithful and in control of our circumstances. God is answering our prayers far more fully and comprehensively than we ever realised. Faith is the joyful determination to praise God and to keep praying for things that are glorifying to God and not at all about our comfort and blessing.

We slowly realise that God is not going to answer our petty cries for an easy life. Yes, God does indulge those who are new in His kingdom, just as parents will wrap a new-born baby in warm blankets. But we quickly feel the challenge of His Spirit to lay aside the selfish grumbles, robustly dismiss our little discomforts and determinedly press on to intercede for others, praying for situations that demand the intervention of God. Doubt nothing, for God is with us and is faithful to renew us in our thinking and introduce us to the dignity and vigour of the mind of Christ.

~~~~~~~~~~~~~~~

January 12

Rejoice in hope, be patient in tribulation, be constant in prayer. (Romans 12:12 ESV)

The human heart thrives on hope. Hope is the foundation of joy, peace and faith in the heart. We need hope. Without it the heart sinks into depression and deep sorrow. Hope is the inner assurance that God sees us, hears us and despite all our weaknesses and faults, we know that He loves us. Because of this we know that we have a secure future. We may not have a clear plan or vision, but we know that God does. Hope is to burn brightly through the darkest days. We are tempted to lose hope when we make a mess of things or when our plans are dashed either by some unforeseen event or by our own foolishness.

When Jeremiah stood among the ruins of Jerusalem, he must have been tempted to utter despair. The ruins symbolized the lowest point that the nation of Israel had fallen to. The temple was gone, the people were scattered. But there in the midst of the ruins Jeremiah found hope:

"This I recall to my mind, Therefore I have hope. Through the LORD'S mercies we are not consumed, because His compassions fail not. They are new every morning; great is Your faithfulness. "The LORD is my portion," says my soul, "Therefore I hope in Him!" (Lamentations 3:20-25)

Nothing can stop the determined strategy of the love of God. No matter what has gone wrong, God steps in and picks up the pieces. God wastes no time grieving over spilt milk. He steps forward with His song of hope. Human beings grieve and regret, but God comes to lift up our faces and to breathe into us the assurance that all will be well because God is with us.

∽∽∽∽∽∽∽∽∽∽∽∽∽

January 13

Why are you cast down, O my soul? And why are you disquieted within me? Hope in God; For I shall yet praise Him, the help of my countenance and my God. (Psalm 42:11)

The Psalmist talks to himself here and challenges his own heart to give the reason for its sadness and melancholy. The reason is the loss of hope. We lose hope when we lose perspective. We forget so quickly the good things that God has already done. The Psalmist is here like a preacher challenging his own heart.

A good preacher addresses first the reasoning faculties of his audience. Then when he has laid out good reasons for his question, he shoots his arrow at the bull's eye. He challenges the will by a question that uncovers the seat of the problem. Why are you depressed? Why are you easily so sad? Face it: our dejected state is because of rank unbelief. God is with us and His unchanging grace flows into our circumstances as a river of fragrant refreshing. Preach to yourself, talk to your own will and rouse it by the plain facts of the amazing promises of God. Then frog-march yourself to the cross and take a long look at Calvary. Remember the incredible love of God that impelled Him to die for us. Every time we look there, we remember that God's love is written in indelible ink on the history of mankind, and most importantly on our history.

God cannot change. He loves us that much, and will always love us that much. Why do we have hope? Because the God we know cannot be invented. A god made by human imagination would give up and walk away. But the God of the universe has declared Himself by coming to live in this world and dying for our sins. Now in the face of this blazing light, how dare we be depressed?

~~~~~~~~~~~~~~

January 14

And they shall take some of the blood and put it on the two doorposts and on the lintel of the houses. (Exodus 12:7)
So the children of Israel went into the midst of the sea on the dry ground, and the waters were a wall to them on their right hand and on their left. (Exodus 14:22)
And you shall hang the veil and it shall be a divider for you between the holy place and the Most Holy. (Exodus 26:33)

These three verses describe three doors in the book of Exodus:
The first door is the door of the blood of the lamb, by which we escape the wrath of God and the destroying angel.
The second door is the door of baptism with the Spirit, pictured by the miraculous crossing of the Red Sea.
The third door is from the Holy place to the Most Holy place.
The first two doors are from guilt and the dangerous powers of the world and the flesh that seek to destroy us. But the third door is not a door of escape from something, it is a door from one degree of holiness to another. We might well be able to label the first two doors and say "this was my day of salvation," or "that was the day I was baptised with the Holy Spirit." But the third door is a door of fellowship, and as such it represents a constant choice before the believer whether to go deeper in our walk with Jesus or to live in the shallows. It is not a question of a choice between sin and holiness since both places are holy. It is rather a question of the hunger and thirst of our hearts. Jesus said that the believer that has a deep thirst for God will experience a deep inner transformation and deep fountains will be released and flow out of them (John 7:37). Holiness is ultimately to know a person. Jesus is not "in" the Holy of Holies, He "is" the Holy of Holies. All that God does in us is to bring us to this door, so that we may calmly choose Him, without the pressure of pursuing enemies or the inner yapping of the hounds of guilt. These things cannot take us into real holiness. That is something we must choose and continue to choose till it becomes a habit of life to dwell there with Christ.

January 15

Peace I leave with you, My peace I give to you; not as the world gives do I give to you. (John 14:27 NASB)
These things I have spoken to you, that My joy may be in you, and that your joy may be made full. (John 15:11 NASB)

Jesus promises His followers that He will give them His peace and His joy. He contrasts the way He gives with the way the world gives. He acknowledges that the world can give peace, but this is a false peace. It is peace on the surface, the peace of being distracted from the storms that are never far away. Jesus goes right into the centre of our storm and commands peace to descend. Peace is not found by pleasant green pastures or tropical beaches. It is a state of heart that belongs to all who have rested their hearts in God's almighty hands.

It is the same with joy. The world gives pleasures and amusements but these are all only substitutes for real joy. It is a strange fact that only those who turn their backs on the passing pleasures of sin will then know the deep wells of contented joy that sweep over the heart that is right with God. The word "amusement" is made up of two Greek words that mean "not thinking". This reveals the very emptiness of the world's pleasures. These are passing, fleeting moments that overlay a heart that is troubled or uncertain.

The joy of Jesus is not dependent on circumstances, and it is a constant background to the life that loves God. It is the joy of being. It is a state of heart. This peace and joy are His gifts to those who turn to Him in full surrender. So why wait? Turn and drink from the wells of everlasting life!

January 16

He saved us from so great a death, and he is saving us. We have set our hope on him that he will still save us.
(2 Corinthians 1:10 Author's translation)

Paul expresses in this one verse the way salvation affects our past, present and future. The scope of redemption is to fill our thinking with the brightness of grace in every dimension of our lives.

The past is blotted out and our personal history of sins is erased as we believe in Him and fellowship with Him. Nothing that we have done can ever be brought against us. We have been saved from the dreadful curse of condemnation.

The present is filled with His wonderful love. We have access to partake of His spiritual atmosphere. We have access to His faith and we do not keep holding before God our best struggles to believe, but drink in the waves of His faith to swallow up and replace our poor efforts. We are empowered to live for Christ each day.

The future is filled with boundless hope. We have a destination, a goal, a vision and it is all contained in the certainty of His coming.

In Ireland during the Depression of the 1930s, a story is told of some labourers who were employed to build a road. Their skill was undoubted, and they were pleased to work until one of them asked the foremen where the road was going, as they could all see that it was in a rural area. When they were told that the road was simply linking up a few remote homes, but actually going nowhere, the men were so disheartened that many left the project and those that remained lost all interest in it. We must keep the end in view because once we lose sight of the journey, we will also lose heart for the present and may even forget the achievements of the past.

Fellowship with Jesus, thank Him for past sins forgiven and for power to walk in the Spirit today, and look forward eagerly to His coming again.

January 17

And in the middle of the lampstands I saw one like [i]a son of man, clothed in a robe reaching to the feet, and girded across His chest with a golden sash. His head and His hair were white like white wool, like snow; and His eyes were like a flame of fire. (Revelation 1:13-14 NASB)

The revelation of Jesus described in these verses is overpowering. It is no surprise that John fell at His feet as one dead. What is surprising is that Jesus is like the "Son of Man" whereas it might seem more appropriate to say the "Son of God". In using this phrase, God draws our attention to His ultimate aim to glorify humanity in His Son. We often think that if we are to be like Jesus it means that we will have a measure of His peace and joy, but here we are given a glimpse into the astonishing revelation that we are to be like Him in His glory and His pulsating, infinite holiness.

How can this be? The answer is that human beings are like a glove that is made for the eternal God. When God has washed and redeemed us Christ fits into our lives like a hand into a tailor-made glove. Christ is at home in our hearts and we were created to bear His image, to show forth His glory and be His dwelling place. True, a glove has no will of its own and it does not cooperate with its owner to fulfil its function. But we are made in God's image. We have a will and a mind, and we must present them and surrender them constantly if we are to fulfil our destiny.

This earthly life is all about preparing us to share in His glory. How breathtaking it is that believers can surrender their lives, walk in faith with God and allow Jesus to be the life that is lived through them! Humanity was created to bear His image, not a static, colourless, cardboard cut-out of Jesus, but a living, breathing, loving manifestation of God through our weak frail humanity.

∾∾∾∾∾∾∾∾∾∾∾∾∾∾

January 18

I am the Light of the world; he who follows Me will not walk in the darkness, but will have the Light of life. (John 8:12 NASB)

A hundred years ago in the frozen wastes of northern Canada, the most important object in the cold homes of the Inuit was a lamp called a Qulliq. It was an oil lamp with a wick about 6 inches wide. This lamp was literally the light of their life. It gave them warmth in their tiny dwelling. If it went out, there would be anxious waiting till it was relit. Without it no snow could be melted to provide water to drink. Without it there was no means of cooking food. Without it darkness and cold would descend on their homes until these produced the stillness of death.

The presence of Jesus does not only give intellectual clarity - He warms our hearts and He releases the water of life for us to drink. The darkness that descends when we neglect Jesus is deathly cold and brings with it all the horrors of a spiritual wasteland. The wise virgins trimmed their lamps and had plentiful oil, simply because they realised their lamp was their sole guide when the bridegroom returned. The lamp is symbolic of a life filled with the oil of the Holy Spirit and burning with love for Jesus.

It takes but a brief time to trim the wick and top up the oil, but it is astonishing how quickly Jesus is crowded out of our daily schedule. Let it dawn on you this day that He is not just a pretty ornament in our busy lives - He is the Light of the world and he is the Light of our life. Without Him no day is worth living. Turn to Him, love Him, thank Him, enjoy Him and let your heart burn brightly with His loving, heart-warming light this day!

January 19

And we have known and believed the love that God has for us. God is love, and he who abides in love abides in God, and God in him. *(1 John 4:16)*

"God is love" and this means that is what we always find when we turn to Him. He cannot be unkind or petty and He cannot turn us away without hearing our cry. God is a warm welcome, with outstretched arms eager to hold us and shield us.

Our mind can feel it is trapped as in a bird cage, and we feel imprisoned behind bars made up of our doubts, our hurts, and our fears. But the Lord has opened the door of the cage and waits to coax us into His loving arms. Birds are hard to catch, they are cautious and hesitant. Our souls are more timid than any bird, and it takes the matchless patience of God's untiring love to persuade us to open our souls to Him and believe fully in His love. We sit and observe the world from within our prison and all the time the door is open.

The power of God to heal is His love - the winds on which we soar on eagles' wings are the winds of His love. To be loved by God is to be made whole. We are slow to grasp that it is in the arms of love that we can best understand God, and accurately present Him. "No-one has seen God at any time. The only begotten Son, who is in the heart of the Father, He has declared *Him*." (John 1:18) God is made known by those who have gone into those arms of love and been made whole. There are many "sane" people who have organized their lives and have a rational, even religious, pattern of life, but they are inwardly desolate and sick. Spiritual health includes a rational grip on life, but it is infinitely more than that. It is to know His favour, His joy, His embrace. He will not force us to know His love - He will coax us steadfastly until, inch by inch, we yield our inner life by faith into His arms.

∾∾∾∾∾∾∾∾∾∾∾∾∾∾

January 20

On that night God appeared to Solomon, and said to him, "Ask! What shall I give you?" (2 Chronicles 1:7)
Delight yourself also in the Lord, and He will give you the desires of your heart. (Psalm 37:4 NASB)

God is not like the genie in the lamp who gives us only three wishes. We can ask and keep on asking. But God reaches down into the depths of our souls and asks us what it is that we most ardently want more than any other thing. It is in this light that we understand how important our prayers are in our relationship with God.

We human beings can be so superficial that we often find ourselves praying for the most trivial of things. Oh Lord, let me find that bargain in the sales today... or, help me find a parking spot. Then we find our minds dwelling on things that will pass away, such as money, houses or possessions. It is not that it is wrong to lift up our hearts to God at all moments and in all circumstances, but God wants to know what it is that we really want from Him. It is good to take time to settle our hearts in prayer, to look steadily at Jesus and begin to understand what it is we are to pray. Jesus taught us to pray for God's glory: "Hallowed be your name, Your kingdom come, Your will be done on earth as it is in heaven." That is His passion and it is to be ours. It is in seeking His face and His presence that we begin to pray in line with the Spirit of God. God is working to form great prayers in our hearts, worthy of Calvary. "Be glorified in my life, make me to be love as you are love, lead me to serve others, to wash their feet and to touch them with your love."

Prayer is an adventure, because it opens doors in our hearts and in our circumstances. Praying for our small needs is not wrong but if it is all we pray about it is like walking in tiny circles. Once we launch out to pray great prayers for the glory of God, we find ourselves in full flow in the exciting river of God's interventions in this world, which is desperate for touches from His eternal power.

~~~~~~~~~~~~~~~

January 21

Therefore, brethren, having boldness to enter the Holiest by the blood of Jesus, by a new and living way which He consecrated for us, through the veil, that is, His flesh, and having a High Priest over the house of God, let us draw near with a true heart in full assurance of faith, having our hearts sprinkled from an evil conscience and our bodies washed with pure water. (Hebrews 10:19-22)

It is a simple fact that God has done everything to allow sinners to enter the Holy of Holies. Moreover, it is in entering there that we are changed, for it would be madness to believe that we could ever make ourselves clean enough to enter that blessed place. Many will hold back feeling that they are unworthy. Others will simply not believe that it can be that simple.

There are many excuses not to go to God, but they are all invalid. God has removed every excuse that people use to stay outside of His loving embrace. The fact is that as we come, we must lose not only our sin but our pride. We fear to lose face, or we feel that somehow we ought to make a contribution to earn our acceptance. These barriers that stop us are all in our own mind and imagination. God has broken down the real obstacles of guilt and condemnation. He has removed them forever by the death of His Son.

But the hurdles of shame and the fear of losing face with friends are as strong as ever, and God cannot remove these walls. We must throw our arrogance at His feet or stay outside in the cold and bitter winds that blow upon our lives outside of His presence. A man who falls into a cold river clutching a bag of gold must either let go of the gold or sink with it. The appeal of the writer in these verses is the warm and tender entreaty of God's own heart, and we have no excuse to hesitate.

January 22

Peace I leave with you; My peace I give to you; not as the world gives do I give to you. Do not let your heart be troubled, nor let it be fearful. (John 14:27 NASB)
And the peace of God, which surpasses all understanding, will guard your hearts and minds through Christ Jesus.
(Philippians 4:7)

It is a staggering thought that nothing has ever disturbed the peace of God's heart. God cannot worry nor is He ever afraid for He cannot fear anyone or anything. When Satan rebelled in heaven, when Adam sinned, when all manner of disasters occurred in the world He created, God grieved but never flinched. God's peace passes all human understanding and is based on His unassailable being dwelling in a power and authority that cannot be usurped or threatened.

God alone is Lord, and nothing can alter Him or His purpose. "You will keep him in perfect peace, whose mind is stayed on You, because he trusts in You." (Isaiah 26:3) God shares His being and His heart state with human beings because that is why He created the human race, to share in His life. Sharing in God's peace is God's will and plan for us. God opens a door for us in the Spirit and we become aware that peace is ours if we will simply believe and receive. We have a choice to either let our hearts be troubled and afraid or to allow the peace of God to rule in our hearts.

It may even seem wrong to our troubled minds to allow peace to fill our hearts. How can we be at peace when others we love are in pain or distress? But it is the only way we will ever be useful to God and to man. Peace can never be obtained by perfect circumstances, it can only be obtained by partaking of the perfect rest in God's heart that tells us that all is in His hands.

∾∾∾∾∾∾∾∾∾∾∾∾∾∾

January 23

He has shown you, O man, what is good; and what does the LORD require of you but to do justly, to love mercy, and to walk humbly with your God? (Micah 6:8)
For this is the will of God, your sanctification. (1 Thessalonians 4:3)
In everything give thanks; for this is the will of God in Christ Jesus for you. (I Thessalonians 5:18)

Christians go through many tense moments when they are deeply anxious to find out God's will and they will often go to someone hoping to find that little key that unlocks their future. It is a daring thing to tell someone "this is God's will for your life." But that is precisely what Micah and Paul do in these verses. They confidently declare to us all what God's will is. God's will for us is not primarily about where we live, but how we live. We might be engaged in a great project for the kingdom of God and yet be living in a manner which grieves God and shows to all the world that we are out of His will. It is as we pay attention to the way we live that we are in the right frame of mind to know the other bits and pieces of His will. Even if we make mistakes in our career choices, or even in more serious matters, yet we can still do His will by reacting to those around us in a loving, godly manner.

Notice the different dimensions in the three verses: acting righteously, showing mercy to others, humility, holiness and a thankful heart. All of these are attitudes that will enable us to do the most important of all, to walk with God. That is the foundation of His will that each day we take as part of a journey with God. The destination is incidental; the walk with God is His delight and His will. We may feel we are doing a good job in our preaching, our serving, our family, but the centre of His will is to develop these precious qualities that are the very heart of His own being.

January 24

Then He said to Abram: "Know certainly that your descendants will be strangers in a land that is not theirs, and will serve them, and they will afflict them four hundred years… Now as for you, you shall go to your fathers in peace; you shall be buried at a good old age." (Genesis 15:13 &15)

Abraham was deeply concerned about his pressing need for a son and heir. His eyes were on the immediate future. But God here speaks to him calmly and authoritatively about the next four hundred years, even giving a few details about the future of Abraham's seed. God also assures him that he will be buried in a good old age. This kind of prophetic utterance is rare, and we must drink from it and learn its lesson well. God is not in a hurry. His purposes are best served by people who have begun to walk with the Ancient of days.

Sin is a disease that has put us out of step with God, and one of our difficulties in dealing with sin and all its effects is the short termism of "the quick fix". We have to realise that our problem is not just in our passions and lusts, it is in our whole rushed perspective on life. Taking a step out of the pressure of the moment will give us a calm and a faith that are on the one hand much slower, but on the other hand much more real.

It dawns on us very slowly that God is not in a rush. It also dawns on us incredibly slowly that all our fuss and haste actually get us nowhere at all. So although God's leisurely pace is slow, it actually gets somewhere! We are to walk in the steps of our father Abraham and that means we are to get in step with God. Take time to meditate on His word and hear His voice, to reach out and hold His hand and to know His friendship. There is nothing quite like the false hollowness of human zeal, and there is equally nothing quite like the thrill of genuine, unpretentious spiritual life.

~~~~~~~~~~~~~~~

January 25

Catch us the foxes, the little foxes that spoil the vines, for our vines have tender grapes. (Song of Solomon 2:15)

Our attention is sometimes drawn to the larger difficulties of life, and that is not wrong, but the truth is that our big problems are sometimes just a crescendo of little ones. A bucket with a hundred pin pricks is as useless as a bucket with no bottom. There are little sins that cause the sky to cloud over in our walk with God.

Sometimes we pray for a fresh outpouring of grace or a vision or a dream that will relaunch us in our walk with God. In fact, the problem lies not in receiving fresh outpourings but in keeping them. The Holy Spirit whispers in our hearts to correct little things, while all the while we think He should be telling us great things. He tells us to stop being careless with our words. Negative words come easily to our lips, but must be stopped at source. Generosity must become a habit of life, and we must not wait till we have an abundance to give from. Sometimes the Holy Spirit tugs at our hearts because of some unkind attitude to a person. Once we lose this dimension of the Spirit's ministry, we are broken cisterns that can hold no water.

He that is faithful in that which is least will have the inner strength to be faithful in big things. He that neglects the little things and then seeks to be faithful in big things is probably just a showman with an empty heart and a desolate inner sanctuary. Pray that God will help us catch the little foxes that are spoiling the vines, hindering the growth of the rich fruits of the Spirit and spoiling the atmosphere in God's kingdom symbolized itself by a vine. If the vine is damaged, the loss will be incalculable.

January 26

Then God opened her eyes, and she saw a well of water. And she went and filled the skin with water, and gave the lad a drink. (Genesis 21:19)
Therefore I also ... mention you in my prayers: that the God of our Lord Jesus Christ, the Father of glory, may give to you the spirit of wisdom and revelation ...the eyes of your understanding being enlightened; that you may know ... the exceeding greatness of His power toward us who believe, according to the working of His mighty power.
(Ephesians 1:15-19)

Hagar was dying of thirst beside a well of water. God did not need to create this well for her, He just had to open her eyes to its existence. Revelation is the most pressing need and has the most powerful results. The believer does not need God to make him more powerful, he rather needs God to open his eyes to see how powerful he is through the power of the indwelling Spirit.

The believer is more than he knows, and God is infinitely greater than we can conceive. So it is right for us to pray the prayer of the apostle Paul for ourselves and others. When we think right, we live right. The mind does not have any power to make us better people, but it does have the power to align us with God's truth. Hagar simply did not know that a well of water was right beside her. Believers may struggle with powerlessness simply because they do not know what incredible power lies within their grasp.

The story is told of billionaire Howard Hughes, who was leafing through a book of paintings and saw one which captivated him. He ordered his agent to locate it and buy it whatever the cost. The agent set out and searched for several months before locating it in the basement of Hughes's home. He already owned it. God has bestowed His infinite love on us and endowed us with inexpressible grace and favour through His Son, and a brief moment of lifting the veil will open a vast future of spiritual power and blessing.

∾∾∾∾∾∾∾∾∾∾∾∾

January 27

"Do not sorrow, for the joy of the LORD is your strength."
(Nehemiah 8:10)

There is a vast ocean of joy available to the believer. This joy will come in two waves. First, when we obey God, a ripple of joy passes over God's heart. God Himself is filled with joy when we worship Him and love Him. His delight wells up and He allows us to witness that joy. We need to see what true joy is and like all noble human qualities, joy is in the image of God. His pleasure wells up from pure springs in His being, a being unclouded by any darkness at all.

Secondly, that joy overflows to us and becomes our joy. We experience and know what God is feeling, and that is the basis of the fellowship that He wants us to know. That fellowship is eternal life. This is not at all like the superficial passing pleasure that comes from good food and drink or from riches and possessions or the telling of a funny story. Those joys are all spoilt by the aftertaste of earth. They are short-lived and turn to dust in our mouths. True joy becomes the underlying atmosphere of life to those who love and obey God. It does not vary in days of hunger and loss, in days of storm and so-called "disaster". Walking before God in a good conscience gives the sense that all is right, even in the darkest night, because we sense His smile on His child, as we focus our hearts on pleasing Him.

It is not our joy that is our strength, it is His joy, and we do not have to make ourselves happy with false rejoicing, but simply walk and watch Him rejoice. Paradoxically, when we have this inner joy, we find that food never tasted better, skies never looked so beautiful. The greatest things in life are free and they cannot be bought for a treasure house of gold. They are gifts and the poorest and most deprived citizens of earth can feast on them.

January 28

Blessed is he who does not take offense at me.
(Matthew 11:6 NASB)

Jesus spoke these words as part of a message to John the Baptist in his prison cell. John was no longer able to preach and was in the hands of a volatile and unrighteous king. Shortly after this he was executed. Is it possible that John was feeling disappointed and let down? He had stood for righteousness and served God faithfully, denouncing sin and pointing to Jesus as the Messiah. But now the kingdom seemed to be delayed in its coming and unrighteous men still held power in Israel.

It is a fact of spiritual life that at some point we will be able to point to difficult situations which we prayed about but received no answer to our entreaties. What is the basis of our disappointment? The answer is that we have entertained ideas about God that were not true. We may well have allowed unworthy concepts of God to shape our relationship with Him. So many believe that God is like a big Santa in the sky waiting to distribute presents to those who ask for them. There is offence and disappointment when we discover that we were wrong.

John had to face the fact that Jesus was the Messiah with all the miracle power that was so evident, and yet He was not going to get John out of prison. In most cases when someone causes offence, they ask our forgiveness. But with God, we must ask forgiveness for our wrong view of Him. As we do so, the icy hardness of offence will melt, and we will begin to relate to God once more. When you feel God has let you down, humble yourself, quieten your heart, walk in patience and slowly you will realise that God is with you in your prison cell and has a purpose that will be understood if only you will trust Him.

~~~~~~~~~~~~~~~~

January 29

And He gave them their request, but sent leanness into their soul. *(Psalm 106:15)*

"So I say to you, ask, and it will be given to you; seek, and you will find; knock, and it will be opened to you." (Luke 11:9)

Of all Bible truths, the simplest is that God hears and answers prayer. He does not answer the petulant whine or the sudden flight of fancy, but He does listen to the steady prayer that rises from the heart. The Israelites longed for meat and at last God gave it to them to show them how empty their prayer was. The principle is firm: we shall obtain what we steadily seek. This is at the same time wonderful and appalling.

Why does God share these facts with us in Psalm 106? It is so that we may search our motives and ask God for a pure heart as we pray. Our prayers will change as we seek Him and not blessings for their own sake. The German evangelist Jonathan Paul was once praying for a sick man, and asked him "For whose glory do you want to be healed?" The question is right because it is ultimately the direction our prayers are to take. We are to pray for His glory, and if the desire I am pursuing is selfish then I will only bring sadness and leanness to my soul. Once my focus is on God and His glory then my prayers become a channel for God's plan and will to be performed. God desires to make human beings a setting for His amazing qualities of life. So many of the things we pray for are about making our life easier. Once we abandon that line of praying, we are liberated to pray for the things in our circumstances that truly glorify God.

January 30

the tree of life also in the midst of the garden, and the tree of the knowledge of good and evil. (Genesis 2:9 NASB)

The fruit of the tree of the knowledge of good and evil is presented at some point to every human being. It can be summed up as the path of self-realisation, or the quest of happiness for its own sake. The awful fact about the fruit of this tree is that the cost of eating it is so very high. Following our own desires and preferences, building our own world, is a downward path. For this is the tree of death. Those who pursue this course know a brief taste of pleasure, but then deep within comes the awareness that it is a hopeless path leading nowhere. The inner emptiness of life without God is so awful because at its heart is a life without foundations, without an anchor, without a future.

The tree of life is also presented to every human being. It is the path of fulfilling the will of another, of fulfilling the plan of God, following His desire and obeying His wisdom. The cost of eating this fruit is also high, since we must deny ourselves, laying down our lives, our preferences and our selfish desires. In the short term there may be hardship and a sense of loss. But though the price is high, the prize is unspeakably great. The reward is unspeakable joy, the realisation of God within us. Following the cross is not the exaltation of pain and suffering, it is the exaltation of God's will whatever the cost. The resulting delight is a joy that never decays but grows stronger. Relating rightly to God plants a well of joy in the soul. It is the delight of a pure conscience. Paradoxically, following God's ways never leads to sadness and misery, but always to ever-increasing fellowship with the life that has resources and bliss far beyond the wildest imagination of human beings.

January 31

Then He came and found them sleeping, and said to Peter, "Simon, are you sleeping? Could you not watch one hour? Watch and pray, lest you enter into temptation. The spirit indeed is willing, but the flesh is weak." (Mark 14:37-38)

In Mark 14:37-40 Jesus took His three closest disciples and asked them to watch while He prayed. The result was that they fell soundly asleep. The hour was dark and the danger real. The effect on their spirits was to make them lose focus and allow sleep to steal over them. Of all the lessons in brokenness, this is perhaps the most important. Christians too easily become spiritually dry and give up praying. It is easy to substitute reaching out to God with dusty rituals of praying through lists. Prayer is the most revealing exercise of the soul, and few will claim greatness in this area.

Our deepest brokenness is before the throne of God, as we reach out to understand and commune with the eternal God. It is in such moments that our souls are forced to their deepest honesty before God. Human beings can pretend and bluff their way through many things, but our masks nearly always slip when we are praying. Even children can tell when someone is insincere, and insincerity in prayer is a poison. Of all the trials they passed through, as the apostles reflected on their prayer life, they would have realised they were not just slow learners, they were completely ineffective and powerless.

If someone had said that the future of the church rested on their prayers, they would have either laughed in derision or sunk in despair. The apostles could not pray, and this consciousness was the vital antechamber to the discovery of the incredible power centre of the kingdom. It is in our weakest moments that we are on the verge of the greatest discoveries in the kingdom of God. Sometimes when we feel furthest from our goals, we are actually nearing the moment of their most stunning fulfilment. If you are feeling weak and are passing through deep trials, take heart, for you are in the very forecourts of eternity.

∾∾∾∾∾∾∾∾∾∾∾∾∾∾

February 1

And behold, one of the rulers of the synagogue came, Jairus by name. And when he saw Him, he fell at His feet.
(Mark 5:22)

Jairus was in great distress facing the deepest calamity – his beloved daughter was sick and near to death. Whenever we face a crisis, our perception of the world and our priorities change. Jairus would never normally have thrown himself publicly at the feet of Jesus. He may even have been reserved towards Jesus when He visited the synagogue in Capernaum and cast out a demon from a troubled man (Luke 5:31-37). He may have been among the group of scribes in Capernaum who questioned how Jesus could have the authority to forgive sins (Mark 2:1-12). Whether his reservations were mild or deep, they all vanished in the face of the awful tragedy that threatened to engulf him. His pride was broken in the maelstrom of suffering. His sense of religious dignity collapsed and he cast himself down at Jesus feet.

Though he could not have been aware of it, this was the primary purpose of the circumstances through which he was passing. His daughter was raised to life and that was a major miracle, but Jairus was also a changed man. He had reached out and touched the living God in a manner which released God's love and compassion upon himself and his family. It was the opening of a door for Jairus to walk with God through His Son from that moment.

When suffering and grief come into our lives a deep cry is released in our hearts. Our priorities change and we move from an elemental instinct to find God. The crucial matter is not to lose this moment and let it fade from our souls, but rather to treasure it and guard it, so that it may be as a seal that is stamped on us and changes us forever.

~~~~~~~~~~~~~~~~

February 2

And the people spoke against God and against Moses... So the LORD sent fiery serpents among the people, and they bit the people; and many of the people of Israel died... Then the LORD said to Moses, "Make a fiery serpent, and set it on a pole; and it shall be that everyone who looks at it, shall live." So Moses made a bronze serpent, and put it on a pole; and so it was, if a serpent had bitten anyone, when he looked at the bronze serpent, he lived." (Numbers 21:5-9)

This event is a parable of Calvary as Jesus Himself taught in John 3:14-16. The astonishing thing is that the sin of the people, for which the death of Christ became necessary, was the sin of complaining and unbelief. Subtly and unconsciously, we grade sins and come to believe that some sins are not that serious. Complaining is a disease that ruins our life as a worm makes an apple inedible. Complaining is the contagion of Satan that poisons our minds. Calvary is all about neutralising the serpent's venom. Complaining is the sure sign that the atmosphere of our hearts is joyless and irritated. It is a problem of the condition of our hearts, and is sometimes manifest in words, thoughts and facial expressions alone.

This state of heart is a fountain that wells up bitter streams of spiritual pollution that are the opposite of Christ and His kingdom. Jesus said, *"abide in Me"* and at its simplest level He meant abide in joy, in love, in kindness - let these be the atmosphere of your heart. How wonderful that the blood of Jesus Christ cleanses us from all sin, and especially these deeply troubling impulses.

The people thought that their circumstances were their problem. It was the inner outlook of their soul. God will not often change our circumstances but He will always change our inner attitude towards the little things that so irritate us. As we are washed in His wonderful love, we will burst into songs of praise and thankfulness to God for all the wonderful grace and provision that are ours.

February 3

"You shall love your neighbour as yourself."
(Matthew 19:19 NASB)

This is both a command but also a principle. It is a fact of life that the way we view ourselves shapes the way we view others. If we hate ourselves, then we will have a very low view of those around us. If we view ourselves as worthless, we will put very little value on those we live amongst. Our estimation of our own worth is itself shaped in our youngest years when parents and siblings either loved us or ignored us. Some have grown up with a damaged self-image, while many see themselves as unremarkable, simply nothing. They don't expect to do well, achieve anything or find deep joy and satisfaction in life. Survival is the bottom line. The untouchables in India were so despised that when they walked through a village, they had to drag a leafy branch behind them to wipe out their footsteps, so that no-one would ever know they had been there.

God's answer is to show us that He loves us as He loves His Son. When we know the love of God, we are liberated inside, melted and changed. The deepest change is the way we now see ourselves. We may not realise it but God has elevated us not to a position of importance, but of matchless worth. He presents us with boundless joy and pride before the Father (Matthew 10:32). He speaks our name before the hosts of heaven (Luke 12:8). The result is that we love ourselves, and we are free at last to love others. In the Vietnam war a wounded girl needed a blood transfusion. The girl's brother had brought her to the hospital, and the Doctor asked him if he would give his blood. The boy grew very quiet and thoughtful, and finally agreed. The Doctor drew some blood from his arm and thanked him. The boy's eyes opened wide with relief, "You mean I won't die?" he gasped. He had thought the Doctor wanted all of his blood. Let God's love bathe your mind and change the way you feel and think about yourself. It will launch you into the current of His love that will wash those around you with that same love.

∾∾∾∾∾∾∾∾∾∾∾∾∾

February 4

I resemble a pelican of the wilderness; I have become like an owl of the waste places. I lie awake, I have become like a lonely bird on a housetop. *(Psalm 102:6-7 NASB)*
The heavens shall perish but You shall endure, they will be changed but You are the same. *(Psalm 102:27)*

The Psalmist is in great distress of soul because he feels far from God. The range of emotions through which we pass is very wide. Here he expresses his feelings of being alone, cut off, misunderstood and a misfit. We can easily get distressed when we become aware of the strange feelings and places in which we seem to find ourselves. Put simply, we long for certainties that we can build on, but on occasions the very earth seems to move beneath our feet and all the things we took for granted disappear.

It is precisely at these moments that we must flee to the cross. When our world becomes a waste, howling wilderness, we must run to the one anchor which will never change: the love of God in Christ manifest for us when He died on the tree. It is as if a terrible blast is smiting the earth and sweeping everything aside, and the only place of safety is the cleft of the Rock, the place where we can shelter in His love. Wesley described this place with these words:

> "Hide me, O my Saviour, hide
> Till the storm of life is past,
> Safe into the haven guide,
> O receive my soul at last."

God has promised to shake everything so that only what cannot be shaken will remain. We must go to the cross and there find our shelter in His open side. He has reached out His hand to hold us and welcome us into the safest place of all, where we will be for ever secure. Run there and find rest in His love.

February 5
"I will make three tabernacles here, one for You, and one for Moses, and one for Elijah." ... and behold, a voice out of the cloud said, "This is My beloved Son, with whom I am well-pleased; listen to Him!" ... they fell face down to the ground and were terrified....and they saw no one except Jesus Himself alone. (Matthew 17:4-8 NASB)

The disciples on the Mount of Transfiguration were overwhelmed in the presence of Jesus and two of the giants of Israel's history. Their response was to offer to build three tabernacles. Their catastrophic error was to place Moses and Elijah on the same level as Jesus, the Son of God. This is easily understandable since when God uses human beings, it is easy to believe that those people are not just vessels of His power, but the source of it. This is a common mistake and believers revere preachers, authors and missionaries from the past and the present. But this is idolatry. Moreover, some believers revere special doctrines such as the Second Coming, Anointings, Israel, Creation or the New Covenant. Subtly we give to men and doctrines things that uniquely and solely belong to Jesus Christ.

At the transfiguration the cloud overshadowed them and Moses and Elijah faded into the background until only Jesus could be seen. God then spoke from the cloud, "This is My beloved Son, hear Him."

We might have an idea of what we want God to say to us; to provide us with explanations of some difficult Bible passages, or perhaps some fascination about future events at His coming. But God spoke directly and disarmingly simply to the disciples' hearts: 'Focus on my beloved Son, concentrate on Jesus.' There is nothing new here to satisfy curiosity. There is only the persistent, insistent theme that runs through the whole Bible: look long and hard at Jesus, look into His love, His serenity, His perfect holiness and see what He can make us, for as we look steadfastly at Him, we shall be like Him. We are always changed into the image of what we worship, and the power and centre of God's message is always the same: "This is my beloved Son, hear Him."

~~~~~~~~~~~~~~~

February 6

"The Lord, whom you seek, will suddenly come to His temple."
(Malachi 3:1 NASB)

In the early part of the 20th century, a farmer from the mid-western United States was leafing through a magazine and saw an ad for a barometer. He filled in the form and sent it off with his payment. A week later it arrived. He eagerly unwrapped it and admired the beautiful instrument with brass fittings and a beautiful dial. Then he noticed that the needle was stuck pointing at the word "hurricane"! He tapped it and fiddled with the instrument to no avail. With a sad heart he wrote a letter of complaint and wrapped the device in neat brown paper. He had just finished writing the return address when the hurricane struck....

It is a sad fact that many Christians read the Bible with little expectation of any immediate impact. The answer is that the Bible must be read with faith for it contains sure and certain promises that will be fulfilled. Some will only be fulfilled in us if we receive them in faith. Others will be fulfilled whether we are expecting anything or not. The Bible speaks of visitations of Christ, culminating with the final great coming of Christ to rule all nations. James even tells us that the Judge is standing at the door ready to intervene. (James 5:9)

The Bible is a spring board into the unseen world of God and His promises. Once we have this expectation, we will read the Bible not as a book of general information, but as a door for God to come through. God has promised that all who seek Him shall find Him (Luke 11:9). Look again with faith and expectation at "the exceedingly great and precious promises" (2 Peter 1:4) and lift up your eyes to see that they are about to be fulfilled.

~~~~~~~~~~~~~

February 7

Even though I walk through the valley of the shadow of death I fear no evil, for You are with me. (Psalm 23:4 NASB)

When we lived in Cameroon, West Africa, we had an enclosed garden with a secure gate and a high wall. It was therefore a huge shock when one day a deadly venomous snake (a Gaboon viper) was disturbed from its lair under a shed. It was swiftly killed by a friend and we felt safe once more. But then I began to have retro-active fears, remembering all the times I had walked through the garden at night (this type of snake is nocturnal). I also realized that my lack of fear in the past was misplaced, because I simply had been ignorant of the dangers all around.

Fear is not overcome by mere logic. Nor can it be overcome by assuring ourselves that there is nothing to fear. The person who is afraid of death will one day die. The person who fears they will fail an exam or a job interview may well have to cope with some bad news (especially if 2 Christians apply for the same job!) No, death and danger are all around us, but they are not the enemy. As Roosevelt said, "the only enemy we have to fear is fear itself." It is fear that paralyses us and robs us of that joy and peace that are to be ours today.

When David wrote Psalm 23 he may have been thinking of his encounter with Goliath. On many occasions David was in the thick of battle or pursued by bitter enemies. The answer to his fear was the presence of God, the knowledge that nothing could touch him without the knowledge and permission of God. His presence must be believed and received. We know His presence by experience and then we are armed to keep on believing when we feel nothing. God is with us and therefore we have nothing to fear from any source.

∽∽∽∽∽∽∽∽∽∽∽∽∽

February 8

You did not choose Me, but I chose you. (John 15:16 NASB)
With fervent desire I have desired to eat this Passover with you before I suffer. (Luke 22:15)

It is astonishing to realise how much God loves us and desires our company and our friendship. It is a breath-taking fact of life that God thinks we are simply wonderful and amazing. The love of God is far greater than we can ever grasp. When we meet with God and share our hearts with Him, He is so delighted that He is overwhelmed with pleasure. We often think that we are the ones driving our relationship with God, but the truth is the efforts of our hearts are weak at best, and our warmest thoughts are cold compared with the lava flow of God's love.

God is the driving force in our relationship with Him. True there are seasons when we ardently seek Him, but as we reflect we will realise that it was God who stirred us up to seek Him. If God did not love us we could never persuade him to. The Bible speaks of God as a father with His beloved children, or of a young man in love. Yet His love is stronger than any human love of mother or father. God did not give His son because of a sense of duty or responsibility but from the river of love that He is.

In the parable of the pearl, the merchant found one pearl of greatest price, and gave all that he had to buy it. The merchant is Jesus, who looks at us and is moved with love to give everything. God's love cannot deny his holiness, and His holiness can never slay His love. The result is Calvary where God's great dilemma is laid to rest for ever. There He is true to His holiness, but equally true to His love. For our part, all we can do is respond to His love surrendering ourselves to discover the beauty of inseparable love and holiness.

February 9

Therefore, brethren, having boldness to enter the Holiest by the blood of Jesus, by a new and living... (Hebrews 10:19-20)
I am the Way, the Truth and the Life. (John 14:6 KJV)

Jesus came to announce this new and living way. He was declaring to the world that all the old patterns of approach to God were passing away, and He had come to show another way to live, to be holy and to pray. Jesus showed this new and living way by example, He taught it by His words, and He opened it up for us by His death and resurrection. The simple fact is that Jesus IS this way, and the secret of a new and living way is to let Him live through us.

The old way is to do things **_for_** God. We labour for Him with commitment, consecration, zeal and sacrifice. God in His mercy still accepts these things even though they fall short of His plan and provision for us. The new way is to realise the power of Christ **_in_** me. For this we must enter into stillness of heart, ceasing from our own strivings, and enter into the full blessing of union with Christ, through communion in His Spirit. Christ is in us and it is the realisation that we can live as He lived that so baffles the mind and makes our hearts miss a beat. For this we must put off the old as we would throw off a heavy, suffocating coat. We lay aside the old ways and put on Christ as a new coat, yielding to Him in full surrender. In Him every aspect of our natural gifts and abilities will be suffused with a glory and a power that makes us more alive than ever before.

The old way was to harness our powers and make them serve God and His cause. The new way is to discover the delight and wonder of Christ in us, and to let the glory of Christ rise and fill our lives with His beauty and splendour. The discovery of Christ in us is as amazing as our first discovery of Christ. He is wonderful, amazing and full of majesty, but He is also in us, in our hearts, in the web and weave of our personality. This discovery is the new and living way that He made for us when He died on that cross.

~~~~~~~~~~~~~~~~

February 10

This is the day which the LORD has made; let us rejoice and be glad in it. (Psalm 118:24 NASB)

There is every reason to believe that this is the Psalm that Jesus sang in the upper room before he went out to the Garden of Gethsemane and on to His trial and crucifixion. The Jewish day begins and ends with sunset, not at the stroke of midnight, and Jesus sang these words at the beginning of the twenty-four hours of His suffering and death. He proclaimed the faith that this day was ordained of God and that therefore He would rejoice and be glad in it, knowing fully what lay ahead of Him. This was the day of His greatest sorrow, but also of His greatest victory. Well might we also sing and remember that day with joy when all the power of evil was comprehensively destroyed.

Let us also learn the lesson of joy in the face of adversity. Whatever a day may bring, it is a day made by the Lord. Nothing can happen that will take Him by surprise. A day may bring suffering and trials or abundant joy. And we will rejoice in Him. Jesus sang these words and by them embraced the Father's will, as He did when He prayed "Not my will but yours".

Jesus also sang the words "Bind the sacrifice with cords, *even* unto the horns of the altar." (Psalm 118:27) Within a few hours, He was bound in Gethsemane and led forth to the altar of Calvary. Few Christians will literally die for their faith, but all Christians are to allow the Holy Spirit to bind us to the altar, making it the central compass of our being. This altar is not a place of pain, it is a place of yielding to the Father's will. The words of this Psalm have their greatest application to Christ on the road to Calvary, but they were meant to be sung every day by believers who follow gladly in the steps of their Saviour.

February 11

Key to Power 1: The Scriptures.

Now a Jew named Apollos, an Alexandrian by birth, an eloquent man, came to Ephesus; and he was mighty in the Scriptures. (Acts 18:24 NASB)

Apollos had become wedded to the Scriptures and had found them to be a source of power. The farmer prays for rain but it would be foolish to do so if he had not first sown seed on his land. In the same way the Holy Spirit works in our hearts to activate and fulfil the seed of God, which is His word. It is vain to pray for outpourings of the Holy Spirit unless we are sowing the wonderful life-giving seed of His word into our lives. The word of God will give us power to overcome temptation when we are in trials of any kind. The word will lead us in the path of salvation. The word will give us understanding of the unseen world. Faith will come to our hearts as we listen to the word. The Bible is an explosive book that will give the Holy Spirit access to our lives to destroy sin and create holiness. Think of the Bible as a book of vouchers that must be redeemed. There are promises of a new heart, a new spirit, of the gift of joy unspeakable and of intimate friendship with God.

In the American war of Independence, George Washington was greatly aided by a North American Indian, who spied for him behind the British lines. When the war was over, Washington gave him a letter guaranteeing him a pension in old age. The spy folded it and kept it in a leather pouch around his neck. As he lay dying in poverty in old age, a doctor asked him what it was. The doctor opened the letter and was astonished to find that the man could have been wealthy if only he had understood the power of the letter he was carrying in his leather purse. The Bible has amazing power but it will only aid us if we claim it as the firm and unwavering promise of God to whoever will believe it.

February 12

Key to Power 2: Fervency

This man had been instructed in the way of the Lord; and being fervent in spirit, he was speaking and teaching accurately the things concerning Jesus, ... for he powerfully refuted the Jews in public, demonstrating by the Scriptures that Jesus was the Christ. (Acts 18:24-28 NASB)

Apollos was not yet filled with the Holy Spirit at the point referred to in these verses. Yet he was fervent and excited about the things he already knew. Probably he "only" knew that Jesus was the Messiah, that his sins were forgiven and that he would go to heaven when he died! But this message had so gripped him that he shared with a confidence and assurance that reached the hearts of those who heard him.

So often we wait for God to do something that will make us on fire for God. We believe that when the Holy Spirit has filled us, we will be enthusiastic and eager to pray and serve God. But in truth this has more to do with our attitude to the things we already know. Zeal has more to do with the choices we make, and the approach we develop to the things God has already shown us. Paul exhorted Timothy to stir up the gift of God which was in him (2 Timothy 1:6). Jesus commanded the church at Laodicea to be zealous (Revelation 3:19). Peter exhorted the believers to desire the word of God (1 Peter 2:2). God cannot command us to do something that is impossible. It is as we turn to the Lord and stir ourselves up that God will meet us and change us. Many believers who have received great promises and had many spiritual encounters with the Lord are weak and ineffective, waiting for some further sovereign intervention from God. Joshua was told to be strong and very courageous, for only with such fervency could he ever hope to lead others to inherit the promised land. So, pause for a moment, rejoice in the amazing things that God has done for you and serve the Lord this day with fervency and confidence.

~~~~~~~~~~~~~~

February 13

Key to Power 3: The Holy Spirit

"Did you receive the Holy Spirit when you believed?" And they said to him, "No, we have not even heard whether there is a Holy Spirit." (Acts 19:2 NASB)

These disciples in Ephesus had a breath-taking ignorance of the Holy Spirit. How is it possible to be believers and so out of step with God? The answer is simple: we are too strong and we drown out the gentle movings of the Holy Spirit. The Holy Spirit is the key to living the New Testament Christian life. We may be living a life of devotion to our Bibles and to the beliefs we hold. But we need a flood of heavenly power to fill us if we are to live the supernatural life of Christ. It is not only miracles we need, it is life on another plane, another kind of love, another depth of holiness. All of this is only possible through the person and work of the Holy Spirit. Have you ever given a present to a child at Christmas and then noticed with dismay the little label 'batteries not included'? A Christian who is ignorant of the Holy Spirit is about to have the most wonderful surprise as he discovers God's amazing promise to clothe us with power from on high.

The reason we are so ignorant is because we are too strong. The answer is to embrace the cross, to crucify our inner strength, our ability to get by on our own. As we learn this place of becoming weak, even becoming nothing, we are amazed to find that it is only as we die to self that we are filled with the Spirit. God can only fill what is empty. But the only way to empty ourselves of carnal things is to be crucified with Christ. This is not a path of pain unless we fight God. If we accept this sentence of death in ourselves, we will find that He bore the pain so that we might experience the joy of being filled to overflowing. God will not mix flesh and Spirit. One must die, and Jesus died to make a doorway for us to die by faith, lose our life and be swallowed up by another amazing life. Ask God to fill you now!

~~~~~~~~~~~~~~~~

February 14

Key to Power 4: Faith

God was performing extraordinary miracles by the hands of Paul, so that handkerchiefs or aprons were even carried from his body to the sick, and the diseases left them and the evil spirits went out. (Acts 19:11-12 NASB)

Faith is not an instrument in our hands that we can use at our whim. If so, Paul would have used this method on many occasions. This unusual miracle was the product of a liberated relationship with God that released Paul to do something completely new and fresh. It might be acceptable to imitate the venerable apostle. But if God did something so fresh and new in our churches today, many believers would question such unorthodox methods. Paul needed daring and boldness to do something that had never been done before. It is obedience to the Spirit that is the bedrock of faith. When Joshua was told to walk around Jericho for seven days, he might have wondered why God made him do it so many times. Why did Jesus spit on the ground and make clay to anoint the eyes of the blind man?

The truth is that the Holy Spirit rarely repeats His methods. This is so that we might develop a listening attitude to the Lord and so develop a close relationship of trust with Him. Faith comes by hearing and is outworked in obedience. Put simply: faith is the fruit of a close relationship with Jesus Christ. The result is that God will manifest His divine power through our lives as we pray and bear witness to His living reality in our lives. We must relate to God by faith - there is no other way. A.W. Tozer said: "The Bible recognizes no faith that does not lead to obedience, nor does it recognize any obedience that does not spring from faith. The two are at opposite sides of the same coin."

God is not challenging us to adopt methods, He is challenging us to act in obedient faith as we develop our relationship with Him.

February 15

Key to Power 5: Power in Prayer

But the evil spirit answered them, "Jesus I know, and Paul I recognize, but who are you?" (Acts 19:15 ESV)

This is one of the rare occasions when the Bible quotes a demon. Most often they were commanded to be silent (Mark 1:25). The demon knew Jesus since He was the One through whom all things were created, including the demons who had been angels in heaven before they sinned and fell. But here they also confess their fear of Paul. True, it was the presence of Christ in Paul that they feared, but Paul had allowed Christ to be master of His life to such an extent that the demons recognised and trembled at him. The challenge of these verses is to allow the Holy Spirit to so fill us and empower us that we become a threat to the powers of darkness.

Blessed is the city or country that has such Christians who have such intimate fellowship with Jesus that the powers of darkness are terrified when they pray. This certainly does not mean that we will have entered the blessing of a trouble-free life! Paul later describes this period of his ministry as one in which he despaired even of life (2 Corinthians 1:8). Paul was hated by the powers of darkness and he was a target for their anger and opposition. It is small wonder that Paul describes the Christian life of prayer as a wrestling match. For us to make progress in this realm, God must put the steely ruggedness of Christ into our souls. The Holy Spirit must produce in us the confidence that everything we go through will ultimately aid us in our pursuit of the triumph of Christ in our circumstances and in the lives of those we love. Don't waste a moment moaning about anything. Turn everything into confident prayer and praise, never forgetting that the Great Intercessor is in us, able to make us pray His prayers and shake the kingdom of darkness.

~~~~~~~~~~~~~~~

February 16

Key to Power 6: Radical Repentance

And many who had believed came confessing and telling their deeds. Also, many of those who had practiced magic brought their books together and burned them in the sight of all. And they counted up the value of them, and it totalled fifty thousand pieces of silver. So the word of the Lord grew mightily and prevailed. (Acts 19:18-20)

It is remarkable to notice that this verse refers to those who had believed, but were now deeply convicted and finished the work of repentance that they had started when they became Christians. It seems that they had hung on to their books probably because of their great value. Now they had come to realise that holding on to these objects weakened their spiritual life. Partial repentance leads to spiritual weakness. Radical repentance leads to spiritual power. The repentance led to a bonfire of destruction. There is always a release of joy when we truly repent and the result is the abundance of God's life in us. The verses tell us that the result was that the word of the Lord grew and prevailed. This means that the word preached is like a seed which can so grip the human heart, overthrow doubtful habits and break the addictions of the heart and mind. The word is of the very substance of the person of Christ, and He will grow in us, and we will become like him in love, holiness and spiritual power. It is time for believers to clean up their house to make room for the powerful presence of Christ and His word.

The famous preacher Gypsy Smith preached in Moody's tabernacle in Chicago. After the service a man approached him and asked him what the secret of revival was. Smith replied, "Go home, draw a circle of chalk around yourself, and pray that revival will begin in that circle."

~~~~~~~~~~~~~~~~

February 17

And they sang a new song, saying: "You are worthy to take the scroll, and to open its seals; for You were slain, and have redeemed us to God by Your blood out of every tribe and tongue and people and nation, and have made us kings and priests to our God; And we shall reign on the earth."
(Revelation 5:9-10)

Christians are singers. Singing is like poetry, it is the language of the heart. Many translations of the Bible mask the fact that God often speaks in poetry. God Himself is a singer (Zephaniah 3:17). It is with the mind that we grasp the great doctrinal pillars of the Christian Faith, and this provides the foundations of our mental and moral strength. And then we are to soar in abandoned songs of worship to God.

Worship is the dimension in which we grasp the infinite and touch eternity. God has created us with a capacity to embrace things of immeasurable height and depth. This explains why human beings look into the skies and long to grasp what is beyond our reach. No animal is ever found gazing at a beautiful sunset or looking up at the stars with longing and wonderment. The most beautiful and deepest place is found in God. Once we have been awakened to His matchless being, we discover the reason we were created. We analyse God, we explain Him, we handle Him with our minds, but in the end it is when we worship that we truly understand. It is when we let our spirits soar in song that the deepest faculties of our being are fully awakened. No-one can grasp the meaning of life simply by straining with their minds. We reach out in surrender and yieldedness to the love of God and find rest in His presence and fullness of joy. So stop pestering God for explanations at every turn of the path, and go to Him with a song. Pour out your being to Him and you will find Him pouring out His being into you.

∼∼∼∼∼∼∼∼∼∼∼∼∼

February 18

And when I saw Him, I fell at His feet as dead. But He laid His right hand on me, saying to me, "Do not be afraid; I am the First and the Last." (Revelation 1:17)

John is inspired with a vision of Christ in all His glory, with the result that he then falls as dead at His feet. John was in the conscious presence of God and this consciousness brought him to death. Death is so obviously a negative force in our normal experience, but dying in the presence of Jesus is the sweetest place of release that we can ever know. Death in His presence is not the death of positive things, but the death of all that is negative. There my selfish ambitions, my unbelief, my fretting and my hardness all die. The result is that I am His, supremely and totally His. I am free from using Him to my advantage and most of all free from self-consciousness unto God-consciousness.

The preciousness of all John's writings is the way in which we are conscious that John is both a beautiful disciple who loved Christ so deeply, and yet never parades himself or his ministry and devotion to Christ. Through all he is merely, *"the disciple whom Jesus loved"*. He demonstrates God's will for us that our lives should be a setting for Jesus Christ. As we become conscious of Him we communicate unconsciously the wonder of another world and of a matchless Saviour.

It is in this frame of mind that we are witnesses of Him. The believer is not merely a channel, like a pipe allowing water to pass through unhindered. A Christian is much more than that. We have a will, a soul and a personality that must be yielded to Christ. This means more than being a channel, it means conscious friendship and complete surrender to Him. The message of Christ is more than the communication of power, it is the communication of the most wonderful person imaginable. That person is Christ.

~~~~~~~~~~~~~~~

February 19

After these things I looked, and behold, a door standing open in heaven, and the first voice which I had heard, like the sound of a trumpet speaking with me, said, "Come up here, and I will show you what must take place after these things." Immediately I was in the Spirit; and behold, a throne.
(Revelation 4:1-2 NASB)

The spontaneous effect of hearing God speak was to take John within the veil. There John was consciously *"in the Spirit"* and he was immediately aware of the throne. The scene around the throne was of worship to God the Creator and then followed in chapter 5:9 with the new song of worship to the Lamb/Redeemer.

Why do we come to the throne? Every time we draw near, our conscience is cleansed. Then we become conscious of the infinite authority and power of God. We know He is in control, and that all is working for good. We may not know what the future holds, but we know who holds the future. It is this spiritual perspective that gives us power to live and pray. The peace of God is the calm that reigns in God's being. This supernatural tranquillity is imparted to us and deepened by our coming to the throne and surveying the world from God's perspective. It is so breath-taking that God sees all and is so unhurried in His majestic pace.

The Holy Spirit connects us with the throne and it is this atmosphere that produces faith that God will actively intervene and direct things as we fellowship with him and pray. It is this that makes us come alive with wonder at the person of Jesus Christ. If we neglect the throne, we sink under the clouds and become bogged down in the hopeless chaos that is in the world. We must rise above that and be shaped by what we see in the presence of God.

<div align="center">~~~~~~~~~~~~~~</div>

February 20

Or do you not know that all of us who have been baptized into Christ Jesus have been baptized into His death?
(Romans 6:3 NASB)

A certain man emigrated from Kenya to the USA in the 1920s. He had saved for over a year to buy his passage from Mombasa to New York on a steamship, but had no money left over. He quickly made many friends but whenever they went to eat he excused himself and went to his cabin to tighten his belt and avoid the mouth-watering smell of the food. As the ship neared New York, one of his new friends approached him: "Excuse me for asking, but you have never eaten with us. When do you eat?" The man smiled and explained: "I suppose since we are nearly in New York I can explain that I actually had no money to spare after buying my ticket." His friend groaned and said: "You mean you don't know! All meals are included in your ticket!"

Paul in Romans 6:3 exposes the danger of ignorance. Christians are so much more than they know. When Christ came to live in us, it was the same Christ who had conquered sin and death at Calvary, who is risen from the dead and rules the universe from the throne of God. All the power that is currently at Christ's disposal is also at ours. In Him resides all the fullness of the Godhead. All the riches that are in Christ, all His victory and holiness are ours. Once we have been made one with Christ through the baptism with the Spirit, it is the ceaseless work of the Holy Spirit to show us what we are in Him. The Spirit exhorts us to be what we are. The Christian with wrong thinking may actually starve to death, not knowing that in his pocket is a standing invitation to a continual feast. Be holy, because the Holy One is in you. Walk in power, because the powerful one lives in you. Be a praying person because the Intercessor is in you. Have a good long look at your ticket and remember there are no second-class sections on this journey.

February 21

Then He brought us out from there, that He might bring us in, to give us the land of which He swore to our fathers.
(Deuteronomy 6:23)
He has delivered us from the power of darkness and conveyed us into the kingdom of the Son of His love. (Colossians 1:13)

When we lived in Cameroon a missionary from Nigeria tried to visit us. He crossed the border out of Nigeria, but had no visa to enter Cameroon. After patiently trying to gain entry he was sent back, only to find that the Nigerians would not allow him to re-enter their country. He spent several days in their custody while his passport was sent to a higher authority, who eventually allowed him back in to Nigeria.

Christians are to leave the world, and that is a clear command and it is the foundation of being a true disciple. However, the most exciting part of being a Christian pilgrim is the discovery and exploration of a new kingdom, and it is tragic that many live in the rather dull no man's land between the world and the kingdom of God. This kingdom is a land flowing with milk and honey, or rather it is a land flowing with God's generous supply of spiritual strength and supply. There are wells of everlasting joy, fountains of worship and song that can carry the believer deep into this kingdom. The power to overcome all the habits and sins of our former life is in discovering the excitement of the new life. The chief activity of the Holy Spirit is to reveal to us our new place in the kingdom of God. We sometimes think His work is to keep condemning the practices of our old life. But the amazing truth is that Christianity is not a lifelong struggle to get out of the world and so be right with God.

We are out through an act of repentance and faith, and we are right with God. Now turn your face steadfastly towards the light of Christ, and step into the beautiful sunshine of His kingdom. This kingdom has another sun, which is Christ. We still sleep in the same bed and eat the same food. But we see everything in another light because we know Jesus, and we realise that we are in a completely different world.

February 22

We too were by nature children of wrath, even as the rest. But God, being rich in mercy, because of His great love with which He loved us, even when we were dead in our transgressions, made us alive together with Christ (by grace you have been saved). *(Ephesians 2:3-5 NASB)*

"But God..."

There are moments when we have made either such a great error or done something so foolish that we feel completely overwhelmed with the sense of hopelessness. There is no future, no possible solution and no remedy. It is at this moment that God steps in with this most astonishing affirmation. God does not allow anything negative to discourage him from stepping forward to take control and proceeding to introduce into the situation his fathomless love, his boundless creativity and his tireless hope. God approaches the worst of people and the worst of situations with an energy that is breath-taking, and yet makes the way forward seem so obvious.

The phrase, "But God" is the hinge on which everything turns. For our part we simply need to look up and believe, and the moment we do that, there comes into the mix of our circumstances the most beautifully unexpected confidence that all will be well. Once the door is opened to God, everything changes. Whether it be sickness, sin or just the baffling disappointments of life, God changes the atmosphere and the future is immediately totally different. God sets about in a brisk cheerfulness clearing up all the messes that came from our waywardness. God holds no grudges and wastes no time by going into a huff. He delights to turn night into day and darkness into light. He has the power, the will and the eagerness to help us when we are at our weakest and our worst.

~~~~~~~~~~~~~~~

February 23

The righteous shall live by his faith. (Habakkuk 2:4 NASB)

Faith in God is to life what petrol is to a car or electricity to a light bulb. It is the very heart and centre of living with poise and sanity. Without faith life is like a chair with uneven legs, like a guitar without strings. It is impossible to be righteous without faith. Faith sorts out our motives by connecting the heart to a source of purity that inspires and humbles us. Righteousness without faith has such confused motives that in the end it is as filthy rags (literally "menstrual cloths" (Isaiah)).

In the same way, unbelief is the root and heart of all sin. Our lives go wrong when we withdraw from believing. We need that inner leaning on a greater one, that continual surrender to the love of God in Christ. Faith is not the result of logic, though it is not unreasonable. It is the persuasion that God is there and is the source of inner strength to all who will pray and trust in His goodness. We sometimes pout and posture because we feel we should have some dramatic divine visitation that will make everything simple and clear. We long for supernatural words or signs and yet all the time God is there, reliable as the bed-rock.

The moment we surrender and believe, we sense relief, an inner rest. We have to commit our ways, our future and our loved ones to Him in faith, and then find the rest and joy that flow from that surrender.

~~~~~~~~~~~~~~

February 24

Therefore I urge you, brethren, by the mercies of God, to present your bodies a living and holy sacrifice,...so that you may prove what the will of God is, that which is good and acceptable and perfect. (Romans 12:1-2 NASB)

Paul in this verse draws the attention of his readers to the altar that is at the centre of the kingdom of God. This is not a literal altar where things are burnt and consumed but a spiritual altar, symbolising the way the kingdom of God works. Everything functions by the laying down of one's life in surrender to God. We are to lay our lives down on this altar continually and thereby find the power to live in God's will. As we learn to fall continually on this altar, we discover that this is in itself the will of God.

There are many Christians, including ministers and missionaries who serve God, who have given up careers and live in difficult circumstances. But it is possible to live in the place that God has chosen, and still be out of God's will. To be in God's will, we must live in the place of constant surrender of our lives to God, as an act of inner worship that leads to the transformation of our whole life. Israel functioned round the altar, and when Elijah led the nation back to God, he rebuilt the altar on Mount Carmel.

Wherever God refreshes His work in a life, He begins by bringing us back to the altar, where we surrender our all as a living sacrifice. This is the key to power to live and be holy. Note too that Paul beseeches Christians to do this. It is not Paul alone, but God through Paul who pleads with us to return continually to this place. God longs for our good and has given us the Holy Spirit, who is called the Comforter. This word is exactly the same word Paul uses, and could be translated 'the beseecher.' The word could be translated 'I implore' or even 'beg'. It is a strong word and communicates God's heartbeat, drawing us continually to the place He lives. It is a place of gain not loss, of strength through weakness, and there we discover the joy of the Godhead, living to serve and minister to others.

February 25

Hezekiah's tunnel

Hezekiah trusted in the LORD, the God of Israel, so that there was none like him among all the kings of Judah after him, nor among those who were before him. (2 Kings 18:5)
This same Hezekiah also stopped the water outlet of Upper Gihon, and brought the water by tunnel to the west side of the City of David. (2 Chronicles 32:30)

Hezekiah was one of the greatest kings of Israel because of his deep faith in the Lord. He walked with God through difficult days, comforted and encouraged by the words of the prophet Isaiah. Yet at the same time Hezekiah worked hard. He initiated a major engineering project that tunnelled through 533 meters of solid rock. This tunnel has been rediscovered and fully excavated so that tourists visiting Jerusalem can walk its entire length. The lesson is simple: the farmer prays for rain but also sows his seed. The builder may ask God's blessing on his labours but he digs a deep foundation and chooses the stones he uses carefully. Christians pray that God will save their loved ones, but will scour the bookshops for just the right publication for them.

There is no contradiction between praying and working. It is right to pray as if everything depended on our prayers, and work as if everything depended on our work. God is the God of the impossible, but he expects us to keep acting and living with the expectation that He will do His work at the right time. As Christians we pray for God to speak to us, but we study His word with eager devotion. We pray for Him to show us His will, but we work steadily and patiently at the thing He has given us today. The biggest tragedy is passivity, believing that we can develop an inward life and do nothing practically. Trusting God does not shrivel our ability to live, it makes us more alive than ever.

~~~~~~~~~~~~~~~~

February 26

Then Simon Peter, having a sword, drew it and struck the high priest's servant, and cut off his right ear. The servant's name was Malchus. (John 18:10)
Death and life are in the power of the tongue.
(Proverbs 18:21 NASB)

How we all identify with impetuous, zealous Peter. How it comforts us to know that men of God are hewn from the same block of humanity that we ourselves are made of! At the same time we must be careful to learn from his mistakes, so that we may ask God for cleansing and wisdom in order to change as deeply and radically as Peter changed. If we do not learn from his example, we will have to learn from bitter experience. Look at Peter here. His Lord is in danger and Peter draws his sword and strikes, no doubt aiming for the man's head, not his ear! How wonderful that the wound Peter inflicted was not mortal! Even so, there must have been a lot of blood, not counting the shock and danger that he must have provoked.

Disciples do not carry swords, but we do have a tongue that can inflict just as much damage. When we open our mouths to censure, correct or even just advise we can easily cut off the ears of the person we are talking to. The result is that we remove all chance that the person will ever hear what we are saying. Words can wound and hurt, but the net result is that we make people unable to receive the truth and help that they need. We are sometimes so eager to promote our line, our insights, that we become unconscious of the damage we are causing by our zeal and impetuosity.

Jesus can heal the wounded and He did heal Malchus' ear, but He can also change the heart of the man who wields the sword. He can make our mouths to carry words of life that bring faith and comfort to the afflicted.

February 27

Jesus answered him, "Will you lay down your life for My sake? Most assuredly, I say to you, the rooster shall not crow till you have denied Me three times." (John 13:38)
And the Lord turned and looked at Peter. And Peter remembered the word of the Lord, how He had said to him, "Before the rooster crows, you will deny Me three times." So Peter went out and wept bitterly. (Luke 22:61-62)

When Peter denied the Lord, he reached rock bottom. Notice carefully that he did not reach that place till he had denied the Lord three times. Before this there was perhaps still some rationalisation of his actions that excused them or perhaps some lingering hope that he could still make up for his dreadful moral cowardice and failure. Peter touched the depths and his heart cracked open to face up to himself, to know himself in all his emptiness. This was the final step in Peter's self-emptying, so that he could be filled with the power of God on the day of Pentecost.

Note the look of love from Jesus that strengthened him to face himself. From this time on, Peter did not believe in the strength of his own commitment to Jesus, he believed in Christ alone. We avoid this process, seeking to point to our good points or our achievements, secretly believing that we are exactly the kind of person that God needs in his kingdom. We have the gifts and abilities that will make a difference. But then we realize that all of this is less than a vapour unless we touch the depths of our own weakness, and then touch the rock which is Christ. At that moment the strength of the rock brings peace and calm to a life that is storm-battered and bruised. We simply need to lean on the rock and all will be well.

~~~~~~~~~~~~~~~

February 28

If you abide in Me, and My words abide in you, ask whatever you wish, and it will be done for you. My Father is glorified by this, that you bear much fruit, and so prove to be My disciples.
(John 15:7-8 NASB)

With these words Jesus describes the simple plan of God for His children, that we should dwell consciously in the presence of Jesus and allow all His words to form our minds and our world view. If we do this, the result will be a steadily deepening relationship with God in prayer, resulting in constant answered prayer. The resulting fruitfulness is the goal of God and by this He will be glorified. The beauty of this is that the will, plan and intention are not ours, but God's. It is God who plans that we should have this life.

It is easy to think of the Christian life like a series of high mountains. In the centre is the spiritual equivalent of Mount Everest and alongside are other lower peaks that we can attempt. Here Jesus reveals that this is to completely misunderstand God's plan and by so doing to miss the rest and serenity of a life that is walking with God. We do not have to try and climb high peaks. All we must do is maintain a steady focus on Jesus and on His word.

To some it is an astonishing revelation that we are supposed to enjoy being Christians. We are to enjoy the delight of a life that is right with God. The Christian life is not a constant battle to get right with God. By God's grace, we have been given the assurance of eternal life. Now all we must do is enjoy the delights that flow from that deep revelation and fact of life. To become a deeply spiritual person, all we must do is keep loving Jesus and His presence and unconsciously we will reach the most wonderful stages that are simply a by-product of enjoying Him.

~~~~~~~~~~~~~~

February 29

Christ, through the eternal Spirit offered Himself without blemish to God.   *(Hebrews 9:14 NASB)*

For by one Spirit we were all baptized into one body, whether Jews or Greeks, whether slaves or free, and we were all made to drink of one Spirit.   *(1 Corinthians 12:13 NASB)*

The place of entire surrender is the place where we are baptised with the Holy Spirit. It is God's will that we continually return to this holy ground of yielding up our lives to God. Why is it holy ground? Simply because it is all part of the great transaction of Calvary. Christ offered Himself to God in absolute surrender and the same Holy Spirit works in us to produce the same attitude of heart.

This deeper work of the Holy Spirit releases us from our own plans and desires and is the basis of moulding us into one body. In the place of surrender and the baptism with the Holy Spirit, there is an elimination of the things that commonly divide human beings. There is racial unity, and harmony between rich and poor, old and young. It is the fulfilment of the prophecy in Isaiah that *"the lion shall lie down with the lamb"* and not eat it! This is a miraculous state of peace founded upon the death of self-centred living.

The kingdom of God is manifest in a church when all the members are laying their lives, their preferences, their careers, their whole selves on the altar. Though this is the place of surrender and death to self, it is much more the place of total joy and abundant life. God's ways lead to the freest life we can imagine because it is the freedom of loving others and being loved by God.

∾∾∾∾∾∾∾∾∾∾∾∾∾

March 1

And when the Queen of Sheba had seen the wisdom of Solomon, the house that he had built, the food on his table, the seating of his servants, the service of the waiters and their apparel, his cupbearers and their apparel, and his entryway by which he went up to the house of the Lord, there was no more spirit in her.   *(2 Chronicles 9:3-4)*

Waiting on God is the most important attitude of the believer, since it is in and through this relationship with Him that His rule is maintained and applied to our lives and sphere of influence. The most common mistake in this respect is to believe that this is waiting **for** God rather than waiting **on** God. The servants who waited on King Solomon were not waiting for him to show up! They were actively attentive to His every need. They did this with such joy and zeal that the Queen of Sheba was overwhelmed by the attitude of the King's servants. The most powerful force in evangelism is to make people hungry for that joy and inner poise that we relish as servants of Jesus.

Waiting on God is for those who are continually taking up their ministry to the King. Ministering to Him is the foundation of all our service to God and man. Churches exist to satisfy the heart of Jesus, to exalt Him, to know Him and to make Him known. The clothing of Solomon's servants is specifically mentioned, and those who wait on Him will be clothed with dignity and the touch of His glory reflected in their faces, whether they wear jeans or business suits! As we wait there is an inner anointing oil that flows from the King over us. It is the fragrance of His love and presence. The Queen of Sheba saw the glory of Solomon in the pride with which his servants served him. They enjoyed being with Him. This is the kingdom of God, to love and serve the King and to fully enjoy ourselves doing it.

March 2

It happened in the spring of the year, at the time when kings go out to battle, that David sent Joab and his servants with him, and all Israel; and they destroyed the people of Ammon and besieged Rabbah. But David remained at Jerusalem.
(2 Samuel 11:1)

This verse is the introduction to the tragedy of David's sin with Bathsheba. The implication of this verse is that if only David had been with the army he would never have fallen into temptation. It was from this little decision that David proceeded to break 6 of the 10 commandments. He coveted his neighbour's wife, he committed adultery, he murdered a godly man, he lied, stole Uriah's wife and finally he took the name of the Lord in vain. Yet none of these grievous sins was the root problem. His first sin was complacency.

David took a break from the pressures of life and withdrew into a state of mind in which he felt that he was owed a well-earned rest from all his exertions. He relaxed from the challenges of life and retreated into an attitude of self-indulgence. His 'fall' from grace might subsequently have taken another route. He might simply have become impatient and grumpy with his servants, or insecure and fearful like Saul before him. His sins might have flourished but been less dramatic and shocking, yet they would have been just as deadly.

The Bible is not a book to smooth our ruffled feathers with charming platitudes. It is a deeply disturbing book and so it should be, because the words that now disturb us will ultimately judge us. We do well to learn the lesson and allow the Holy Spirit to awaken us from soul sleep till we forsake the simpering sin of complacency as we would crush a scorpion under our heel. If we will only rise up each day and follow the Lord with all our hearts, we will never know the countless snares that we have avoided.

~~~~~~~~~~~~~~~~

March 3

For I know the thoughts that I think toward you, says the LORD, thoughts of peace and not of evil, to give you a future and a hope. Then you will call upon Me and go and pray to Me, and I will listen to you. And you will seek Me and find Me, when you search for Me with all your heart.
(Jeremiah 29:11-13)

Loss of hope is the moment at which all forward movement stops. It is the train reaching the end of the track. It is vital to attend to this vital organ of our inner lives or we may find ourselves in a spiritual backwater far from the flow of the river.

James was a ten-year-old boy when his father was struck down with a stroke that left him in a coma. (This is a true story but the names have been withheld.) The doctors worked tirelessly but concluded there was little more they could do. James asked if his father could hear him if he talked to him. The doctors assured him this was definitely the case and James asked if he could speak to his father alone. He spent a few minutes alone with his father, and the doctors were astonished in the following days and weeks to see a marked improvement in his father's condition until he was at last discharged from the hospital. His mother asked him what he had said to his father. James answered: "I just told dad I loved him and that we needed him at home."

Healing may sometimes be a sudden act of God, or it may be triggered by the rediscovery of a reason to live. Mark Twain said that the two most important days of our life are the day we are born, and the day we discover why. When we lose the sense of destiny and purpose, we will become spiritually sick, and we will drag our feet through life. God has amazing plans for our short-term and long-term future, and all his plans are good. It is this realisation that makes us seek Him and launch out in the quest for God and the reason we were created.

~~~~~~~~~~~~~~

March 4

But we see Jesus, who was made a little lower than the angels, for the suffering of death crowned with glory and honour, that He, by the grace of God, might taste death for everyone.
(Hebrews 2:9)

The phrase "taste death" might leave the impression that Jesus had allowed death to brush his lips so that he might perceive the flavour. But that would not be the case. It is common for all of us to have to eat something we do not like. As children, we are commanded to eat up our vegetables, or swallow the spoonful of sour-tasting medicine. As a traveller I have eaten crocodile, monkey, snakes and even scorpions, but none of these dainties did me any harm.

To grasp what it was like for Jesus to taste death, we need rather to imagine a bowl of rotting food covered with mould and teeming with maggots. To eat it would not be just unpleasant to the taste buds, it would have a catastrophic effect on our health. Jesus looked into the sickness of the human race with all its evil and he did not just dip His finger into the cup, He drank it to the dregs. He absorbed into Himself all the bitter, deadly power of sin and destroyed it.

Now He offers to us the cup of His life, so that we might taste the power of His victory and the reality of His holiness. This is the message of the gospel: Christ drank the cup of sin with all its sorrows and pain so that we might drink the cup of Christ, be cleansed and drink to the full of His joy. We honour Christ most when we drink in deep drafts of His life into our hearts, thus making His death effective in us. We made His sorrow necessary to pay for our sin, and we now have the power to fill Him with joy as we exchange our lives for His.

~~~~~~~~~~~~~~~

March 5

And Jesus stopped and called them, and said, "What do you want Me to do for you?" They *said to Him, "Lord, we want our eyes to be opened." (Matthew 20:32-33 NASB)

Faith, hope and love are the essential foundations of the Christian life. Each one must have a definite object in view. A young man does not come home starry-eyed saying he is in love but with no-one in particular. In the same way it is no more possible to hope for or believe in something than it is possible to sit on air. No, we need a chair to sit on, and faith must have an object in view. The question Jesus asks us may seem to have an obvious answer, but it is vital for us to express our faith in order to focus our eyes first on Jesus and then on the thing He will do.

Look at Jesus, contemplate for a moment His love, His sacrifice, His perfect holiness, and then tell Him what you want Him to do for you. Looking at Him will sift our motives and some prayers will shrivel and die before they reach our lips. Other prayers will rise with greater fullness and confidence because we will see His eagerness to answer them. "Lord, open my eyes to know you." This is a prayer for new eyes and then for clear vision of something we have never seen before. Our prayers need to be more daring than we have ever imagined: Lord, create in me a new spiritual capacity to perceive you, to know you, to understand you, in short, to walk with you and not stumble around in darkness. We pray "bless me, bless my family" and God challenges us to grasp the heart of the matter and focus on Him and our real need. We need a spiritual miracle that will enable us to love and serve Him.

March 6

"I will give you a new heart and put a new spirit within you; I will take the heart of stone out of your flesh and give you a heart of flesh." (Ezekiel 36:26)

God here reveals the natural state of man's heart as being as hard as stone. This hardness is common to us all and is one of the last things that we will confess as being the root cause of our problems. We may be warm and friendly in countless situations but as soon as we are aware of the demands of a Holy God, our inner reaction is to dig our heels in and set our jaw to argue our corner. We immediately raise our defences and take our stand behind an impassive expression. The rock-like inflexibility of the human heart is the hardest substance in the universe.

The gift of a soft, warm heart comes in two stages. First, we must lower our guard and admit we are wrong. Our rigid attitude has hurt us and many others as well. Secondly, we must surrender, and fall into the arms of our loving Father, who will immediately melt the ice of our inner lives in His tender embrace. As we let go in His arms, He will do His matchless work of new creation. He will make something in us that is completely new - the ability to be easily corrected. The jagged edges disappear and we learn to walk with a new humility and joy. Hardness returns as soon as we argue our case again.

Leonard Ravenhill was once approached by an aggressive critic, who said he didn't like Ravenhill's sermons. "Mmmm" said Ravenhill, "I don't think much of them either." Ravenhill had a tough, rugged character, but also a disarming openness and humility that revealed an inner sensitivity and tenderness to God and His ways. How we need to receive this blessing from the Lord and guard it jealously all our lives!

∾∾∾∾∾∾∾∾∾∾∾∾∾

March 7

Oh come, let us sing to the LORD! Let us shout joyfully to the Rock of our salvation…. Today, if you will hear His voice: "Do not harden your hearts, as in the rebellion, As in the day of trial in the wilderness." (Psalm 95:1 & 7-8)

What a contrast in these verses from the same Psalm: first a joyful exhortation to sing and praise the Lord, followed by a warning not to harden our hearts. The Psalmist is presenting us with the constant choice, either to praise the Lord or to allow our souls to become hard. It is difficult to praise the Lord in the day of trial, but it is also the most life-changing exercise at such times. Trials are sent from the Lord to teach us and to humble us and we are to trace the hand of God at such times and engage our hearts in praise. Praise and worship are the atmosphere of the Holy Spirit and as soon as we follow the inner promptings to exalt the Lord we are carried further into His life-giving presence. The atmosphere of darkness is negative and critical and if we allow our hearts to feed on negative thoughts, we will soon be in unbelief.

John Hyde (known as praying Hyde because of his commitment to prayer) was a missionary in the Punjab in the early 20th century. He tells of an occasion when he travelled with an evangelist to a village that was resistant to the gospel. On the journey in a horse-drawn cart, there was a gloomy atmosphere. But two of the evangelist's children were in the cart and they knew no such sadness but rather sang aloud for happiness. Their joy was so infectious that Hyde and the preacher joined in until they were carried away with singing on the whole journey. To their amazement there was a breakthrough and a totally new atmosphere in the village as they preached and shared the gospel. Praising God is the key to positioning our souls each day to believe God and see His wonderful grace poured out in the most perplexing of circumstances.

∾∾∾∾∾∾∾∾∾∾∾∾∾∾

March 8

When Jesus therefore saw her weeping, and the Jews who came with her also weeping, He was deeply moved in spirit and was troubled.... Jesus wept.   (John 11:33 & 35 NASB)

Jesus wept when He saw Mary weeping. He was not weeping because Lazarus was dead since He knew that Lazarus was in heaven and was about to be raised from the dead. He wept because of the shadow of death and hopelessness that lay upon Mary. It grieved Him so deeply to see such a depth of sorrow that was through Mary's unbelief. Mary had so wanted her brother to live, and somehow she had become persuaded that being close to Jesus would spare her and her family from all pain. The grief of Jesus was real and deep. The words indicate that He shook as He sobbed at the sight of Mary's grief. The world is full of a grief that is magnified by its rejection of God's word and His rule. Mary simply had a small view of things and was not sharing in the view of things from the throne of God. Mary was disappointed in Jesus and the outcome of her prayers and faith, which had previously given her a world that was ordered and safe.

What then were Mary's feelings when Lazarus rose from the dead? There would have been brief puzzlement as she made the mental leap from hopeless sorrow to bliss. There may well have been a shiver of shame as she realized how she had misrepresented Jesus to those around her by not trusting Him in the trial. But even shame would have been swallowed up by the smile of Jesus, a combination of His unwavering peace and majestic power. The fact is that the Resurrection changes everything. We shall live forever on a plane that is so exalted and victorious that no negative thing can cling to us once we have embraced this fact with all its implications. We are to let all our shame, our regrets and our disappointments be swallowed up in that soaring life of Jesus, and swap our garments of mourning for garments of praise.

~~~~~~~~~~~~~~~~

March 9

For as often as you eat this bread and drink the cup, you proclaim the Lord's death till He comes.
(1 Corinthians 11:26 NASB)
"In Communion, we have no past but the cross, no future but the coming." Sir Robert Anderson.

There are three dimensions to the life of a believer that are indicated in this verse. Firstly our past: we proclaim the Lord's death. As we look into our past, we have many memories, but the memories that are the strongest are etched by joy or pain. It is for this reason that our deepest negative memories are the scars of sins committed by us or against us. This verse indicates the believer's joy that there is something in our lives that has wiped out the bitter pain of our guilt. As we look in the past, we see nothing but the clear blue sky of God's love and forgiveness: "no past but the cross".

Secondly, our present: we eat and drink Jesus' body and blood. The body and blood of Jesus are the very essence of His being and God has nothing better than Him with which to nourish our hearts. As we seek God's face and spend time in His presence, we are introduced to the mingling of our lives with His matchless life. This is the communion of the Holy Spirit, the blending of our lives in one. As we do this, His love becomes the colour of our lives, the tone of our voice, the background of all that we are and do.

Thirdly, our future: we show His death and commune with Him in anticipation of His coming. The man without faith looks into the future with dismay. He fears disaster, pain or loss and finally he fears death. But for the believer there is one mountain peak that towers over all other future events, and that is the coming of Christ. He will come and establish His everlasting kingdom. Ultimately, He will usher in the New Creation, in which death, sorrow and pain are no more. The believer has the hope that all that is now seen will be swallowed up in that perfect kingdom in which love will reign for all eternity.

~~~~~~~~~~~~~~

March 10

Paul and Barnabas strengthened the souls of the disciples, exhorting them to continue in the faith, and saying, "We must through many tribulations enter the kingdom of God."

(Acts 14:22)

The little word "must" indicates a spiritual absolute such as: "You must be born again" (John 3:7) or: "The Son of Man must suffer many things" (Mark 8:31). There is no other way for us to be saved than through the sufferings of Christ and a deep change in our personality. Paul adds here in this verse that difficulties and troubles are necessary for us to position our souls so that we might fully enter into the power and the blessing of the kingdom of God. Peter also speaks of faith being tested and coming forth as purified gold (1 Peter 1:7). Faith is like a muscle that must be stretched and used or it will degenerate and become weak and ineffective.

A scientist was observing the process by which butterflies emerge from their chrysalis. He watched the insect struggle decided to speed up the process by a careful snip of his laboratory scissors. He cut away the tight, hardened shell and the butterfly rolled out and lay still and died. He discovered that far from being a hindrance the struggles of the butterfly enabled the wings to fully stretch and unfold till the creature could fly. In the same way we may inwardly rebel against the limits upon our lives and the difficulties we all pass through, yet it is precisely in the midst of these "light afflictions" (2 Corinthians 4:17) that truly Christ-like qualities of faith and endurance are formed in us. We may later find our souls soaring in love and worship and may never notice the connection between our unfolded wings and the sorrows and hardships that preceded this. The will of God is that we learn to keep trusting, praising and thanking God through the darkest night till the work is done and we can fly.

"Not till the loom is silent and the shuttles cease to fly,
Shall God unroll the canvas and explain the reason why
The dark threads are as needful in the Weaver's skilful hand,
As the threads of gold and silver in the pattern He has planned." (B.M. Franklin 1882-1965).

∼∼∼∼∼∼∼∼∼∼∼∼∼∼∼

March 11

And He answered and said, "It is not good to take the children's bread and throw it to the dogs." But she said, "Yes, Lord; but even the dogs feed on the crumbs which fall from their masters' table." Then Jesus said to her, "O woman, your faith is great. (Matthew 15:26-28 NASB)

The Syro-Phoenician woman had a terrible burden: a daughter who was "severely demon-possessed." Her cry to Jesus was the cry of desperation. The astonishing thing is that she found impossible obstacles to her faith. First, Jesus had said that He was only called to the lost sheep of the house of Israel. This was a recognition that if He once was drawn to preach to the nations, He would never have fulfilled His appointment at Calvary. Millions would have flocked to Him. Then Jesus reinforced this obstacle by distinguishing between the covenant people of God and the dogs of the Gentiles. Jesus literally called her a puppy dog, but no matter how gently He spoke, there was an underlying potential for offence. The reply of the woman is disarming and goes to the heart of true faith. She accepted His description of her without the slightest trace of affront or even surprise. The fact is that she had come prepared to cling to Jesus whatever the obstacles might be. She was disqualified and unworthy to receive an answer and she already knew this. But though there was no merit in herself that she could appeal to, she could appeal to His mercy. When we throw ourselves on God's mercy, God will always catch us.

The woman fought through the obstacles which were placed before her by God. She had to humble herself and press through to touch His heart and the result was an instant reward. If we will not fight by laying aside our pride and our dignity, then we will fall short of the faith that conquers. Jesus Christ leads the way. He laid aside His majesty, submitted Himself to cruel scorn and ridicule. He embraced the lowest path of all and drilled to the centre of the human problem and conquered it in the embrace of self-emptying faith that throws itself in total abandon into the unfailing arms of mercy.

March 12

Or do you not know that your body is the temple of the Holy Spirit who is in you, whom you have from God, and you are not your own? *(1 Corinthians 6:19)*

That the body of the believer is the temple of the Holy Spirit is central to our understanding of the life of faith. The word Paul uses here is the Greek word "naos" which is used only of the sanctuary containing the Holy Place and the Holy of Holies. The believer is the inner sanctuary of the Holy of Holies by the presence of the Holy Spirit. We are the ark of the covenant, the portable dwelling place of God, the place where His shekinah glory is to reside and the vessel for God's Holy Laws written on the tables of our hearts not on tables of stone. It is the mystery that God lives within us and that by this fact we are able to commune with God in the deepest union of heart and mind, sharing in conscious awareness of His awesome being. The Christian life is one of glory.

But at the same time, we can rise to incredible heights of communion or sink to terrible depths of selfishness. The key lies in the little phrase "you are not your own." Most often it is taught that we receive the Holy Spirit but the reality is that the Holy Spirit receives us. God does not give us the Holy Spirit, He gives us to the Holy Spirit. Grasping this change of ownership is the key to whether we discover the wonder of our heart being the Spirit's shrine or whether we push the Holy Spirit to one side and make Him our servant joy-giver. We either allow the Spirit to blend us in oneness with God or we grieve Him and beg Him to give us an occasional lift of elusive joy when we feel down. The Holy Spirit must expel our selfish life or we will never know the wonder that God intends us to have once the keys of ownership have been given to the Holy Spirit.

~~~~~~~~~~~~~~~

March 13

So when He heard that he was sick, He then stayed two days longer in the place where He was. (John 11:6 NASB)

When Jesus received the message that His friend Lazarus was sick, He waited till He knew that Lazarus was dead. He allowed him to get into a worse situation before He intervened. This is something that we human beings resist with all our strength. We want to avoid the difficult challenges that come to us. We want God to keep us going, but God has a much deeper purpose. He wants us to face up to the fact that we have a much deeper problem, deeper than we have ever been conscious of. Jeremiah declared that the false prophets had healed the wounds of Israel "slightly" or superficially. They had not exposed the underlying problems of the nation.

Jesus will not heal us slightly, and will allow us to get worse till we realise that He must do a deep work in our hearts. When Lazarus died and was raised again he demonstrated the deeper work that God wants to do. He wants us to partake of the power of the cross, which will purify the very person we are. When we embrace the cross, we receive into ourselves the end of a life that is stubbornly self-centred. Until we do this, we are concerned about our survival and our well-being. Through the power of the cross we are liberated to be carefree about all the things that once dominated our thinking. Our priorities, our plans, our prayers will all change in the light of this astonishing reality that breaks upon our souls as we let go of our life and find it again in Him.

Do we feel that God is delaying to hear our cry? Turn to Him. He is waiting for us to abandon our whole being into His loving hands and therefore discover the perfect freedom of being dead to self and alive to God.

March 14

But we all, with unveiled face, beholding as in a mirror the glory of the Lord, are being transformed into the same image from glory to glory, just as by the Spirit of the Lord.
(2 Corinthians 3:18)

The key to all life and growth in the New Covenant is given in this verse. The Holy Spirit is given to us to enable us to see beyond the veil and look at Jesus. When the believer communes with God, it is not merely a question of meditation and certainly not a flight of imagination. The believer sees the glory of Jesus with a clarity that makes him wonder, but with a mistiness that makes him thirst for more. Paul says that the presence of Jesus is known in the same way we see our reflection in a mirror. But he does not mean the modern mirror with its astonishing clearness, but rather a bronze mirror that only allows one to distinguish the shape and outline.

The power and centre of the Christian life is to commune with Jesus in the power of the Spirit. This will produce an inward leap of joy, and at the same time will produce an inner refining of our whole personality. The Christian does not grow in Christ by seminars, Bible schools or any other outward means. All these things have a role to play in our spiritual development, but they cannot replace the simple power of a minute spent in the presence of Jesus. The most powerful thing in the universe is the moments that we spend with Jesus consciously sensing His matchless personality and perfect holiness. Our breath is taken away as we gaze in wonder into His face and we are changed forever. It is this place of encounter that will astonish and convince others to follow Christ. The world is essentially empty of joy, of wonder and power to live. The Christian is connected to a most wonderful life beyond the power of pen to describe. This is why a Christian's joy is inexpressible and full of glory (1 Peter 1:8).

~~~~~~~~~~~~~~~~

March 15

Now He who has prepared us for this very thing (the Resurrection) is God, who also has given us the Spirit as a guarantee. (2 Corinthians 5:5)

Paul refers to the gift of the Holy Spirit as a down payment or a guarantee. The gift of the Holy Spirit is the supernatural experience of the power of God filling and transforming us. We all have different experiences of the Holy Spirit, some very vivid and some very quiet, but the outstanding mark of the Holy Spirit is the resulting deep change in our lives.

This down payment is the first part of our experience of Resurrection life. Once we have received this flood of life we know that we will rise one day with Christ. In fact once we have been changed by this beautiful fragrant presence of God, then we have the first step in every area of our faith. The fact that God is a Creator is obvious to those who have been inwardly re-created. The proof that the Bible is true is undisputable to those who have claimed this promise and found it to be all that the Scriptures describe. We know that all the unseen world of angels, God's throne, heaven and matchless holiness are real, because a taste of heaven has come into our souls. We know that God can do miracles and heal the sick because He has touched us with such deep healing power in transforming our hearts. To the one who has not yet experienced this guarantee, the unseen world is a matter of faith. But to the one who has received the down payment, faith has been transformed into certain knowledge. The man who has an experience is not at the mercy of a man with an argument. There are many intellectuals who can tie some believers in knots and make them look foolish, but these believers will in the end still cry out "One thing I know: once I was blind but now I see!" This does not mean that believing God is for those who have no education or are weak-minded. There are many intellectuals such as C.S. Lewis who could debate the strongest minds and win. But God wants to remove all doubt about Himself and eternity by simply making Himself known in power and love by giving us the Holy Spirit.

March 16

Blessed be the God and Father of our Lord Jesus Christ, who has blessed us with every spiritual blessing in the heavenly places in Christ, just as He chose us in Him before the foundation of the world, that we should be holy and without blame before Him in love. (Ephesians 1:3-4)

Religion invariably teaches that God is waiting for people to earn their blessings. If we do good, then God will do good to us in return. For this reason religion produces tension and strain as the attempt is made to accumulate sufficient reasons for God to do us good. The gospel teaches us that God planned to bless us and do us good before we were born. The astonishing news is that despite humanity's appalling rebellion, God holds firm to His intention to do good to us and give us not one but every spiritual blessing that He is able to give No-one can earn these gifts - they are all of grace.

Grace is God's love active to do good to every human being regardless of their merit or demerit. It is for this reason that grace completely changes the foundation of our relationship with God. He will bless us by His persistent positive activity to remove all petty selfish and mean thoughts from our souls. The gospel of grace exalts God and His goodness. God is a loving Father and is working out His amazing plans for His children.

The greatest revelation is that God is good and a Father to all who turn to Him. He is extravagant and generous and sweeps aside our failures in the great flow of His love and generosity. Understanding grace removes the tension and stress from our lives and we are able to keep coming to God to enjoy His love and companionship.

~~~~~~~~~~~~~~

March 17

But we all, with unveiled face, beholding as in a mirror the glory of the Lord, are being transformed into the same image from glory to glory, just as by the Spirit of the Lord.
(2 Corinthians 3:18)
For it is the God who commanded light to shine out of darkness, who has shone in our hearts to give the light of the knowledge of the glory of God in the face of Jesus Christ.
(2 Corinthians 4:6)

One of the foundations of life on planet earth is the process of photosynthesis. A leaf will just turn itself to the sun and absorb the energy that shines upon it. The result is growth and health. It is a picture for the believer of the way we are to grow in Christ. We are to focus on Jesus and let His loving presence penetrate our hearts and minds, thus giving us all that we need to grow in Him. This is not one method among many, it is the only way. There is no substitute for sunlight and there is equally no substitute for spreading our lives before the light that streams from Jesus, and allowing Him to shine on and through us.

The presence of Jesus burns up unbelief and impurities and creates faith and loving kindness. The astonishing thing for the believer is the realisation that everything that God asks of us will be produced in us by God if we will simply learn the secret of fellowship with Him. It is the light of His presence that produces in us the strength to know Him and to walk with Him. It is as we neglect His presence that our faith shrivels and grows weak.

Learning to sit in His presence is like learning to speak a foreign language. We stutter and stammer and are like babies again. It is as we realise how little we know about His presence that we become teachable. Reach out to Him in love and worship and He will take you by the hand and become to you the Light of the world.

March 18

"And if you do not do well, sin lies (crouches like an animal) at the door. And its desire is for you, but you should rule over it."
(Genesis 4:7)
For sin, taking an opportunity through the commandment, deceived me and through it killed me.   (Romans 7:11 NASB)
Some years ago I was visiting Zimbabwe and was privileged to stay for a few days at a safari park. One of the attractions was to walk with lions. I was reluctant but a good friend paid for me and so we set off walking a few hundred yards with these majestic creatures. The lions were mere kittens weighing some 50kg. We were a group of about 4 people, and one lady (who at a guess also weighed only about 50kg) walked with her husband a few steps ahead of me. Suddenly one of the lions leapt on her back, digging its claws in, and giving her a playful nip with its powerful jaws. The lady collapsed to the ground, while the guards beat the lion off with their sticks. The physical and emotional scars from that brief encounter were permanent.

It is remarkable that the Bible speaks of sin as a wild animal on the very first occasion it is mentioned. Paul in Romans continues in this vein, speaking of sin as a power that deceives and kills. Sin may seem weak and controllable at the outset, but it is a dangerous and powerful force that is constantly seeking to take over our lives. Once bitterness, lust, anger, envy or something as commonplace as alcohol have got our attention, they can weave a web of deceit until we are completely under their power. The remarkable thing is that God said to Cain that the first line of defence was simply his will to resist sin. Human beings are completely powerless on their own against the spiritual subtlety and power of sin. The question is whether we will grip God's hand and thereby let God give us the strength to overcome. Dallying with sin is like playing with snakes and scorpions. If we will not tread them down, they will bite and sting. God's Spirit echoes like a fire alarm, urging us to deal radically and clearly with temptations while they are in their early stages. Hear the urgency in God's voice and tread down the powers that would ensnare us.

~~~~~~~~~~~~~~~~

March 19

You are wretched, miserable, poor, blind, and naked ... To him who overcomes I will grant to sit with Me on My throne, as I also overcame and sat down with My Father on His throne.
(Revelation 3:17 & 21)

There are times in the lives of an individual or a church when the Lord calls us to account for our way of life. The church at Laodicea was in a pitiful condition and received a stinging rebuke from the Lord, that He was so displeased that He would vomit the church out of His mouth! But grace is never diminished by failure and rather seems to abound the darker the background. Jesus assures the church at Laodicea that He has reserved for them the highest honour of sitting with Him in His throne.

It is so easy to lose the wonder of God's grace to sinners. We may easily acknowledge His grace to a drug addict living on the streets, but do we realise how much His grace is extended to us when we are cold and worldly. Jesus Christ draws near to His people and assures us that no failure has ever weakened His grace, or diluted His firm intention to bless us and clothe us with all the grace and glory that adorn the Son of God. We share in His destiny, in His glory, and we must not allow anything to weaken our faith in His matchless love. The gospel describes the collision between the love and grace of God in Christ and the cruel depravity of sin. Christ encountered a fallen humanity on the cross and embraced the darkened and guilty soul of man till He had overcome it. We must never linger in the shadows of our shame, but step out boldly and receive the floods of grace that are ours in Christ, who works in ceaseless activity to present us before His Father with boundless joy.

∾∾∾∾∾∾∾∾∾∾∾∾∾

March 20

"Nevertheless, lest we offend them, go to the sea, cast in a hook, and take the fish that comes up first. And when you have opened its mouth, you will find a piece of money; take that and give it to them for Me and you." (Matthew 17:27)

The story of the coin found in the fish's mouth is remarkable. The coin referred to is a Roman "stater", equivalent to 4 drachmas, exactly the right amount to pay the temple tax for two people. So God was in the accidental dropping of a coin in the sea, guiding a fish to take it in its mouth, and then to be caught by Peter. The purpose of all this was to provide for a small detail of Jesus' and Peter's financial needs. In the weave of our lives, God is assuring us that He is in the detail. There is nothing either too big or too small for God. He is interested in the major and the minor needs of our lives.

Corrie ten Boom told the story about a miraculous event that happened to Corrie and her sister, Betsy, while they were in Ravensbruck, the Nazi concentration camp for women. Corrie had a bad cold, and her nose was constantly running. She burst out: "I wish I had a handkerchief!" With child-like faith, her sister immediately prayed that the Lord would supply Corrie with one. A few minutes later, a fellow-prisoner called out her name and came to Corrie with a handkerchief she had made that morning from discarded sheets in the camp's hospital. After she had made it, God had told her to give it as a gift to Corrie ten Boom. Corrie said that simple gesture was like God tapping her on the shoulder and saying, "I know your suffering, and I am here with you." God will not satisfy our every want, but He does know our needs and is watching over us in love.

~~~~~~~~~~~~~~~

March 21
But the anointing which you have received from Him abides in you, and you do not need that anyone teach you; ... the same anointing teaches you concerning all things.   *(1 John 2:27)*

John speaks of the inner anointing by which we know all things. This is the knowledge of things that cannot be known by any other means. Just as we learn to read through the help of teachers at school, so we know God's love and presence in us by the anointing. The voice of the Holy Spirit is the voice of a dove and is itself quiet and brings calm. Every human being longs for this quiet place of rest, where all worry and striving cease and we know that we have truly come home. The presence of Jesus is so majestic and beautiful that whoever gazes on Him forgets everything else and is lost in worship of that matchless One.

When we truly wait on God something happens deep in the soul that is indescribable and yet affects everything we do. In the soul that waits on God, there comes a fragrance that is the knowledge of Jesus. This is not merely spiritual indulgence, because the sight of Jesus to the eye of the soul delivers us from the smallness of self-seeking. Gazing on Jesus we become conscious of His greatness. Other things fade away, and most of all our own self-importance. We become incidental and all we want is to be allowed to be there and behold Him. Jesus is Himself the very definition of beauty and there is no greater joy than to be aware of Him. To touch the hem of His garment is to be healed, and to be conscious of His inner life is to be transformed. Eternal life is not only endless existence, it is to be joined forever to this fathomless fountain of love and purity. There are things that are taught and things that are caught. We may be taught the facts about Jesus but it is when we linger in His presence that we catch the majesty, the rest, the peace that adorn Him. When believers have been with Jesus, there are elements to their lives that awaken thirst to know Him. There are things communicated unconsciously and it is these things that make us true witnesses of Jesus Christ.

~~~~~~~~~~~~~~

March 22

Dear children, keep yourselves from idols. (1 John 5:21 NIV)

God is the Creator of the human soul. He understands us so perfectly and leads us with consummate wisdom. The Quakers, led by George Fox, began to meet regularly in silent waiting on God, waiting for the Holy Spirit to speak. After some time the Quakers began to worship the silence rather than God. They swapped the living God for the idolatry of silence. Christians who find God will discover that God does not allow them to control their relationship with Him by following methods.

This is the experience of all who love Christ for Himself, that they pass through periods when all their methods stop working. Mary and Joseph took Jesus to the Passover when He was twelve years old, and on the way back to Nazareth they assumed that Jesus was somewhere in the crowd of friends and relatives. They assumed He would be where He always was, but to their consternation He was not to be found. They had to retrace their steps and seek Him. It is amazing that it took them three days to find Him (Luke 2:41-50). There were aspects to their little boy that now astonished and amazed them. So it must be in our seeking of God.

In the Song of Solomon there are two occasions when the Shulamite bride of Solomon cannot find Him. On the first occasion she finds him quickly (Song of Solomon 3:1-4) but on the second occasion she is hindered and suffers wounds in the process of her seeking (Song of Solomon 5:6-8). The process of overcoming the obstacles leads her to deeper love for Solomon, the chief of ten thousand (Song of Solomon 5:10). It is when God withdraws Himself for a season that our souls are purged from mere religious habits of prayer. So many have a "quiet time" without knowing His presence. God is watching over you to stir you to seek Him and to know Him for Himself.

∾∾∾∾∾∾∾∾∾∾∾∾∾∾∾

March 23

You therefore must endure hardship as a good soldier of Jesus Christ. No one engaged in warfare entangles himself with the affairs of this life, that he may please him who enlisted him as a soldier. *(2 Timothy 2:3-4)*
For we do not wrestle against flesh and blood, but against principalities, against powers, against the rulers of the darkness of this age, against spiritual hosts of wickedness in the heavenly places. *(Ephesians 6:12)*

Christians are in a battle against the powers of darkness not against human beings. The believer is aware of this battle and knows that there are unseen forces of evil behind the visible world. Christians will experience resistance in their prayer life and sometimes there will be a wave of discouraging thoughts. It is in precisely this realm that we are to fight to maintain a positive attitude.

If a believer forgets he or she is in a warfare, then battles may be lost. We must not just shout slogans about our victory, we must knuckle down and fight. Yes the war has been won, but there will be many 'mopping up' battles before that victorious position has been fully realized. The sad truth is that Satan can get an advantage, but only when God's servants give up the fight. Giving up the fight may be for many reasons. Some grow tired and discouraged and just withdraw from prayer and witnessing. Others become superficial and worldly and simply begin to enjoy the passing pleasures of this world.

The axiom *"Evil triumphs when good men do nothing"* is never truer than in respect to the dimension of Christian warfare. Some Christians simply do not engage in warfare. Some polish their doctrines endlessly, always seeking to prove others are wrong or have some nuance of error. While sound doctrine is to be cherished, this must not be at the expense of giving up on the fight. Remember there is a battle and that as we pray and stir our hearts to faith, we are promised that victory is already ours.

March 24

"The lad and I will go yonder and worship, and we will come back to you." So Abraham took the wood of the burnt offering and laid it on Isaac his son; and he took the fire in his hand, and a knife, and the two of them went together.
(Genesis 22:5-6)

Abraham expressed the faith that God would raise his son Isaac from the dead when he said **we** will worship and **we** will come back to you. But look carefully. Abraham took not only a knife, but also wood and fire. He bound Isaac, laid him on the wood, and proceeded to offer him up in a process which would have resulted in a pile of dust and ashes. This demonstrates the magnitude of God's power in the death and resurrection of Jesus Christ.

The dust speaks of finality, and when sin has had its way in a life the result is always a pile of ashes, with no evidence of the former promise and hope. Frequently situations cry out the sheer impossibility of restoration. We human beings react in the smallness of our minds, sometimes adding condemnation to the unfolding disaster of moral failure in an individual. But God is the God of the impossible. It does not mean that God **can** intervene in dire situations. Every human life is descending into the crumbling decay of a heap of ashes. God **must** do the impossible in every life, and bring life and soaring hope.

Give God an inch of trembling faith, and He will take more than a mile! He will raise that broken life into the exalted height of His heavenly being. God moulded Adam from the dust of the ground, and God will do a new thing in the life that dares to believe He is the God of Resurrection. This is news to us, but to God it is His way of life. Resurrection is not unusual to Him. He is the Resurrection and the life, and to touch Him by faith is to initiate a process that will always finish in God's breath-taking glory.

March 25

But the righteousness of faith speaks in this way, "Do not say in your heart, Who?" (Romans 10:6)
If you confess with your mouth the Lord Jesus and believe in your heart that God has raised Him from the dead, you will be saved. (Romans 10:9)

Our life is the incarnation of the word that we are repeating in our hearts. We speak to many people, but the person we dialogue with most of all is ourselves. In this verse Paul expresses the challenge of the Holy Spirit to stop speaking unbelief but rather to speak faith to ourselves. Human hearts cry out in despair for a Saviour with a deep consciousness that there is no human answer. Our negative words may produce sadness and depression.

The Holy Spirit constantly challenges us to confess the truth of the gospel. Christ is immediately present to the one who simply believes. We are to confess Him as Lord of our lives and our circumstances, and then we will become the incarnation not only of faith but of the wonderful life of Jesus Christ. The life of Jesus is positive and purposeful and as we believe we will become like Him. Jesus Christ is never discouraged. Negative thoughts find no place in His mind. No matter how hard the situation, He knows that He can bring healing and salvation. There is an irrepressible joy in the heart of Jesus Christ because He has purposed to save the most hopeless human wrecks. He looks into our darkness and exhorts us to confess Him.

After we are saved, we must apply this same principle to all situations and speak the same confident joy to the most awful circumstances. If we will attend carefully to our inner speaking, we will find an uncontainable delight welling up and shaping our approach to each day and each situation. Within a short time this will become the deepest habit of our life.

March 26

Let each be fully convinced in his own mind.   (Romans 14:5)
But on Mount Zion there shall be deliverance, and there shall be holiness; the house of Jacob shall possess their possessions.   (Obadiah 1:17)

Uncertainty is an open door for confusion. Paul in this verse is referring to matters of personal conscience, but it also applies more widely to spiritual life in general. For example: if we are not convinced that God is the builder and architect of the local church, then our commitment will be weak. If we are not deeply persuaded of the importance of prayer, then we will pass days, even weeks without praying. If we are not persuaded of the danger of hell, we will never have a burden to warn anyone.

We must give serious attention to the things we believe and allow our hearts to pass from general belief to deep personal persuasion. Like King Agrippa we are "almost persuaded" (Acts 26:28) and so linger on the edges of prayer and of a deep commitment to an active spiritual life. Only with deep persuasion will a deep change in our conduct accompany the things we believe. Obadiah speaks of a day when the house of Jacob will possess their possessions. They will then discover the wonder of what they have.

The Christian is to believe his beliefs, and so enter into the electrifying discovery of the power and reality of the unseen world of the kingdom of God. It is not the power of persuasion in itself. It is vain to be persuaded of things that are not true. But that is the whole point: the gospel is true, and God has opened a door for us to pass into the real experience of the kingdom of God, where the Son of God's love reigns.

~~~~~~~~~~~~~~~~

March 27

He must increase, but I must decrease.   *(John 3:30 NASB)*

John the Baptist, like every active intelligent person, could expect his life to increase. Human beings reach full physical stature around the age of 18, but they keep on growing all their lives in other dimensions. There is intellectual growth and the accumulation of responsibilities and possessions, along with trophies of success. Our lives grow and extend like a huge tree that can be easily caught and toppled by a strong wind or storm. Most people exert themselves to achieve something in their life that will serve as a monument after they have left this world.

But there is actually only room for one remarkable person in a life, and that person is to be Jesus Christ. The more we increase, the less we are aware of Him. The more we want power, influence and praise, the less we will know the rule and the presence of Jesus in us, and the less we will praise and worship Him. John saw it clearly: "I **must** decrease." John decreased by a series of conscious decisions that kept his life simple and focused on the eternal purpose of serving Jesus. God has given us the power of the cross to keep our lives pruned from wild and excessive growth that will make the fruit on the tree become small and sour. The path of Christian discipleship is fixed in the opposite direction to mere worldly objectives. We must allow the Holy Spirit to make us hardy, determined followers of the Lamb. Our life will seem as nothing to some who do not realise that we are to serve as a setting for the most perfect life.

~~~~~~~~~~~~~~~

March 28

Is the seed still in the barn?   *(Haggai 2:19)*
Behold the sower went out to sow.   *(Matthew 13:3 NASB)*
But others fell on good ground and yielded a crop: some a hundredfold, some sixty, some thirty.   *(Matthew 13:8 NASB)*

No farmer can hope for a harvest without sowing seed. He may pray for good weather, for sun and rain, but these will of themselves produce no fruit at all. The ground will remain barren. In the same way it is vain for believers to pray for the outpouring of the Holy Spirit unless they first receive the seed of God's word. It is a fact that Jesus sowed His word into the lives of the disciples before He poured out the Holy Spirit upon them.

It is vital to understand that as we receive God's word, pressing it deeply into our hearts through meditation, we prepare the seed that can be made to bud by the action of the Holy Spirit. The presence of God acting upon His own word in our hearts produces an astonishing harvest of spiritual life. Prayers rise from the heart that surprise the one who prays. Praise and worship sweep across the soul with a power and a refreshing that are solid and yet uplifting. The Bible is a bag of seeds, producing all manner of fruit. As we read and meditate, our capacity is increased. Then as we receive the Holy Spirit, wonderful life rises in our hearts. God has put within our reach the very keys of a spiritual harvest that will be first in our lives and then in the lives of those around us.

The Christian life is a cultivated plant, and the believer does not have to produce it from his own will and intellectual strength. Rather, we are to sow the perfect seed of the word of God into our lives and nurture it through the presence of God. The seed is good and the Holy Spirit is astounding in His health and life-giving effect.

∾∾∾∾∾∾∾∾∾∾∾∾∾∾∾

March 29

The thief cometh not, but for to steal, and to kill, and to destroy: I am come that they might have life, and that they might have it more abundantly. I am the good shepherd: the good shepherd giveth his life for the sheep.
(John 10:9 & 11 KJV)

For the shepherd to sacrifice His life is a waste unless there is hope of restoring the lamb to life. Christ died for ruined sinners, who all have no human hope of healing. The astonishing power of the cross is to counteract sin, even when Satan has done his worst. When a human life is damaged beyond hope, as long as there is an ability to hear the voice of Jesus, and to respond in the heart, then He is able to restore that life to a perfect state. Every pastor/shepherd in the church must seek to receive from Jesus the courage to risk his life for the flock, and the hope that however bad a state he comes across, Jesus is able to heal and restore to the image of God.

The shepherd heart is the foundation of all ongoing ministry. Human souls are as timid as birds and will fly away and shut their door if frightened. It is the Christ-like quality of gentleness that convinces people it is safe to open up and entrust their inner secrets.

Ultimately there is no-one quite like Jesus Christ. There are some choice men and women who have touched deep wells of His love, but there is no-one else who can handle our inner lives like He does. It is for this reason God's Spirit constantly works in us to enable us to open up to the love of God and there to find the incredible healing touch of God Himself in our lives.

March 30

I wait for the LORD, my soul waits, and in His word I do hope. My soul waits for the Lord more than those who watch for the morning, yes, more than those who watch for the morning.
(Psalm 130:5-6)

How then do we enter into this ministry of waiting on God? The answer is that we are to find the place where all inner noise has been stilled. The enemy of Christ's rule in our hearts is the inner, ceaseless clamour of our minds. Inner noise does not vibrate the ear drum, it disturbs and distracts the heart. Inner noise is produced by lusts and desires that draw the concentration away from God. The attitude of the Holy Spirit is one of total rapt concentration on Jesus, and nothing has ever distracted this focus. This is in effect the atmosphere of heaven, where angels gaze on God to minister to Him and to do His will. Concentration on Jesus is the attitude of waiting on God. It is not achieved merely by hours of contemplative prayer, but rather by a turning away from lesser things that are not worthy of the soul. Concentrating on Jesus is not through mental strain, but through the directing of the soul. Just as a telescope can be focused on a star, so the soul needs to position itself and then focus on God. The result will be the inner connection to God and in this attitude we serve God. His authority clothes us there and we are endued with an authority that is not from our strength of personality, but from the absolute and infinite authority of Christ Himself.

The key then is to turn from ourselves in self-denial, and cultivate a quiet, listening heart. Hearing God is the chief faculty of the disciple. In fact, He imparts knowledge to the heart, which then dawns as the Psalmist says, like a morning sunrise. We should not wait on God for "words" or prophecies. This often leads to frustration and disappointment. We should direct our hearts to God and let the Holy Spirit bathe us in His love and purity. As we wait there, we will become aware of things that distil on our conscious mind. We become aware of the glory of Christ dawning on our inner life.

~~~~~~~~~~~~~~

March 31

And so it was, when they had crossed over, that Elijah said to Elisha, "Ask! What may I do for you, before I am taken away from you?" Elisha said, "Please let a double portion of your spirit be upon me." So he said, "You have asked a hard thing." (2 Kings 2:9-10)

Elisha was given a unique opportunity to ask whatever he wanted from a man who was close to God and was about to be caught up in God's presence for ever. It is a parallel of the ascension of Jesus Christ, when He commanded His disciples to tarry in Jerusalem to await the coming of His power upon them. Elisha did not hesitate, but instantly replied "a double portion of your spirit!"

God wants us to ask 'hard things' from him. He Himself yearns for us to be like Jesus and is working all the time to that end. So many of our prayers are for things that we can imagine, things that are easily possible. God challenges us to ask for the impossible, for the daring God-sized prayer. *"Create in me a clean heart, O God"* (Psalm 51:10). When God creates a new heart in us, He puts things in our being that were not there before and which no amount of strain could produce. God remakes the human heart and this is the power of Calvary.

Elisha's prayer is not a neat, logical petition and it seems to have taken Elijah by surprise. Elisha's prayer was the spontaneous cry of a man who realises he wants the spiritual substance and reality that made Elijah such a rugged, authentic man of God. God does not want to decorate our lives with blessings that are not an integral part of our being. He wants to change the depths of our being, and give us the same inner life as the Son of God.

~~~~~~~~~~~~~~

April 1

Then Elijah said to Elisha, "Stay here, please, for the LORD has sent me on to Bethel." But Elisha said, "As the LORD lives, and as your soul lives, I will not leave you!" So they went down to Bethel. (2 Kings 2:2)

This verse describes a fascinating exchange between Elijah and his successor. Elijah actively discourages Elisha from following him. It was as if God were saying to Elisha: "You are no longer needed. Rest, take things easy, you are not vital to the fulfilment of my plans." Such a realisation is a great shock to our pride and can easily result in a subtle retaliation: "Well, if I am not needed, then OK I will just accept that and settle down." There are many moments in our walk with God when we are liable to take a huff and sulk.

The word of Elijah was a real obstacle in Elisha's path, a real discouragement and it had the power to sift Elisha's heart and purify him. When our pride is offended because we are overlooked, because we are not recognised or because we are not given the thanks or rewards we feel we deserve, then we are being tested. Elisha rose to the test and threw his pride into the dust and confessed: "True, You don't need me to fulfil Your great purposes, but I need You! And I can't live without You!" In the dust of this humbling experience, Elisha proved that his goal was not fame or fortune but God Himself.

There will be times in all our lives when we realise that we are not really that much use to God, and the fact that He uses us is not because we bring such zeal and intelligence to His kingdom. God uses us despite our qualities, and at the centre of our lives we must be weaned away from thinking this is all about our usefulness. This is much more about our raw need of God Himself, and about our rugged determination that we will have Him at any cost. The true test of each Christian will be the point at which we could quietly accept the discouragements and settle for something less than God would give us, if only we would press through our selfish pride and pursue Him for Himself.

~~~~~~~~~~~~~~~

April 2

When I thought how to understand this, It was too painful for me- until I went into the sanctuary of God; Then I understood.
(Psalm 73:16-17)
Then, behold, the veil of the temple was torn in two from top to bottom. *(Matthew 27:51)*

The Christian faces a choice between two worlds, that of the fallen world of pain and sorrow or the world of God and His unshakable throne. The Psalmist describes the pain he felt trying to grasp why there is injustice and suffering in this present age. It was not an argument or a logical explanation that satisfied him, it was simply the act of stepping by faith into the immediate presence of God.

God's presence is open to us in a much deeper way through the cross, and we may step not merely into the outer sanctuary but into the innermost Holy of Holies. Stepping there is like stepping into the nuclear core of the universe. A nuclear power station has an inner hidden place where power is generated. When the reactor core of Chernobyl was exposed, vast amounts of energy were released into the atmosphere. Soldiers were ordered to run into the core and pour sand and cement onto the uranium rods. Those who did so suffered terrible burns after moments of exposure. Many died within six months.

The presence of God destroys unbelief and drives fear out of our souls. Moreover, God's presence is not merely destructive of sin and darkness, it recreates our hearts into the image of God. Love and power flow within us as we behold the matchless person of Jesus. Trying to understand this fallen world outside of God's presence is like a blind man trying to paint the Alps. Once we get into the innermost place of God's presence, we immediately understand that justice will prevail, that evil men will fail and fall and that good will triumph. Perplexity can keep us out of God's presence, but don't linger in the outer courts, press in, enter God's presence and the peace that passes understanding will flood your heart.

April 3

A bruised reed He will not break, and smoking flax He will not quench, till He sends forth justice to victory. (Matthew 12:20)

Human life is often compared in the Bible to the grass that springs up and is soon withered and gone and here we are likened to a reed that is essentially weak. Moreover, life deals out blows and the reed is bruised and hurt. While it is true that to feel resentment over hurts is a sin, it is also true that many are deeply wounded by the traumas of life even though we may forgive and escape the deeper pain of bitterness. These words are filled with the incredible tenderness of Jesus Christ to gently nurse a broken spirit back to hope and joy. He gently exhorts us to rise and forgive those who have bruised us and then He patiently heals and strengthens us. This verse indicates that God does not expect us to suddenly rise and be confident, happy people. He knows that for some this will take time.

The image of smoking flax is similar. The flame has gone out and there is just a smouldering ember. Jesus takes it and blows gently upon it, maintaining the glow and coaxing it back into a flame. His ministry is that of the High Priest who tends the lamps in the sanctuary. On occasions our love burns low and could easily be extinguished, but Christ is a skilful High Priest and will not allow it to go out. He ministers the right mix of words and the life-giving presence of the Holy Spirit that will make us rise up once more and love Him.

The final thought is that He will send forth justice to victory. Forgiving is not excusing. I once ministered to a survivor of Auschwitz who had lost so many loved ones in those dark years. When I spoke with her, she was an old lady who had recently come to Christ. I encouraged her to forgive but reminded her that this did not mean that evil men would escape God's judgment. The only way to escape judgment is personal repentance, and these words of Jesus perfectly describe the framework of the universe: a tender God of love who will save those who fall into His loving arms, but a God of perfect and fearful justice on those who spurn His love.

〜〜〜〜〜〜〜〜〜〜〜〜〜〜

April 4

You also be patient. Establish your hearts, for the coming of the Lord is at hand.   *(James 5:8)*

Whenever the coming of the Lord is taught, many shrug off the imminence of his return as unlikely in our lifetime. Yet the teaching of the Bible is that no individual has to wait longer than their life span. When my life on earth ends, that will be the coming of the Lord for me. In the light of this fact, it is obvious that no-one has ever had to wait longer than approximately 70 years, and the majority have had a much shorter interval to endure.

The end of earthly life is the moment that we will be ushered into the courts of eternity, and there we shall give an account of our life on earth. There we shall witness the great scenes of the judgement of the human race and the passing away of heaven and earth. We shall behold with our eyes the sights that were hidden: we shall gaze on God, worshipping in the midst of an innumerable company of believers and angels. The coming of the Lord is at hand and it will be upon us sooner than we imagine. The exhortation to live in the light of His coming is not dependent on whether we are in the last generation that shall see Him come in the clouds of heaven. It is an exhortation to lift up our eyes and anticipate all that shall happen when we step out of life on earth. We shall suddenly realise fully the emptiness of worldly possessions. We shall perhaps have a rush of intense regret at all the opportunities to pray, to give and
to love that have now passed away forever. Each day is filled with passing openings that will never return. The key is to be patiently found living in the light of His imminent return. Lift up your eyes for He is at the door.

~~~~~~~~~~~~~~

April 5

If you then, being evil, know how to give good gifts to your children, how much more will your heavenly Father give the Holy Spirit to those who ask Him! (Luke 11:13)

This is one of the greatest promises of the New Testament. Like many promises it is often interpreted very narrowly to refer to the gift of the baptism of the Holy Spirit. This includes that great promise but is far wider and fuller in its scope. When Jesus said "everyone who asks receives" (Luke 11:10) the verb is in the present continuous and can be translated "everyone who keeps on asking will receive". This is because the constant great need of all believers for the aid of the Holy Spirit. We need Him to repent, to believe, to have hope; then we need Him to pray, to preach and operate in the gifts of the Holy Spirit. But we also need Him to love, to be good parents and to do good works.

The Holy Spirit is to our spirit what air is to our lungs or water to our bodies. We need a constant fresh supply and Jesus has promised to give it if we ask. The great difference between the natural and the spiritual is that in the natural world we do not need to ask for air. But in the world of the Spirit, we need to keep a dependent, supplicating attitude. We wander and become dry or mechanical in our spiritual life and then we return and take a deep breath, a long drink of the fountains of living water. The sad fact is that many look back on an experience of the Holy Spirit and have little conscious enjoyment of Him now. Moreover, some are looking for a big experience and miss the fact that God is faithful to supply us with the Spirit right now. We are to ask in faith and we are to rest in His faithfulness and in His skill and ability to minister the Holy Spirit to thirsty souls. Jesus said it was easy to drink: we simply need to come to Him believing and the waters will surely flow (John 7:37).

~~~~~~~~~~~~~~~

April 6

And from the days of John the Baptist until now the kingdom of heaven suffers violence, and the violent take it by force.
(Matthew 11:12)

This utterance of the Lord is one of the most baffling things He ever said. It seems at first glance that He is commending strong-willed, forceful personalities. This is something that totally contradicts other words such as "Blessed are the meek, for they shall inherit the earth." (Matthew 5:5).

The focus in this verse is in the effect of John the Baptist's preaching, which was repentance. The violence that is needed is not to be directed towards God in prayer, demanding that He let us in! It is rather to be directed to the carnal and selfish habits of our hearts. The person who would make progress in the kingdom of God must be ruthless and merciless with sin and self. This is the kind of violence that Jesus meant when He said that "if your right eye offends you, pluck it out ... or if your right hand offends you, cut it off." (Matthew 5:29-30). No-one ever yet cut their hand off or plucked their eye out physically, but all who would make progress in their spiritual life have done this spiritually. John the Baptist was a rugged man who embraced the disciplines of the wilderness in order to get close to God. It is precisely that quality that made his preaching so authentic and effective.

Christians are not to be people who embrace a harsh life-style for its own sake. But we are to recognize the areas of our lives where we are sorely tempted. We must not exchange the matchless privilege of spiritual authority for the dulling, sleep-inducing pleasures of self-indulgence. Christians can be tempted to blame the devil for everything. But we must sometimes rebuke ourselves, give ourselves a good shake down and plunge afresh into the bracing, life-giving and invigorating atmosphere of the kingdom of God.

April 7

Noah walked with God. *(Genesis 6:9 NASB)*

I remember once hearing a man say: "When I've paid my mortgage and saved some money, I'll serve God and do missionary work." That man was walking with his mortgage. The great question each of us must answer is: with what or with whom are we walking? Many of us walk with our ministry, seeking how we may do things for God. Some walk with regrets and sorrow, some with pleasures and happiness. The truth is that all of us have made a companion for our journey, and that is what will determine the outcome of each day and ultimately of our life's journey.

Walking with God requires the discipline of listening. We must tune our hearts to please Him and obey Him. Walking with God puts God in the driving seat and dislodges all the ambitions that we may have and makes them secondary to this primary goal each day. Once while shopping in a busy supermarket, one of our daughters let go of my hand for a moment and then absentmindedly reached up and held the hand of a stranger. The man smiled and was pleased to receive this unexpected attention and waited for her to realise her mistake so that he could return her to her father. It is not always wilful rebellion that stops us walking with God, it can be spiritual absent-mindedness. We suffered a tragic loss, or something happened that made us focus on something else for a while. Then we gradually became aware that we were holding the hand of a stranger and that we had lost the joy and purpose that previously had carried us through life. Walking with God is to tap into the limitless sense of purpose that underlies the universe. God is not wandering, He is walking determinedly toward His goal and the climax of the ages, when He will perfect all things in Christ. Reach out each day and hold the Father's hand. It is the secret of power.

April 8

If then you were raised with Christ, seek those things which are above, where Christ is, sitting at the right hand of God. Set your mind on things above, not on things on the earth. For you died, and your life is hidden with Christ in God.
(Colossians 3:1-3)

Imagine what your first thoughts might be when you finally get to heaven and your life on earth is over. Billy Graham was asked what his first thoughts would be and he answered with one word: "Relief!" Perhaps our next thought will be: "Why did I believe so little, why did I live such a narrow life wasting so much time on things that were passing away? If only I could have had a few moments to experience heaven, I would have lived so differently."

In fact it is one of the most extraordinary privileges of the Christian 'to die before we die' and to live in heaven before we get there. We are enabled now to live with the remarkable capacity to see our life as if it were already over, retrospectively evaluating how we should live. The crucial factor in our right thinking is to grasp the significance of our union with Christ through His death and resurrection. If we have anything less than this as the bedrock of our thinking, we will be earth-bound, and we will live as the multitudes struggling to survive.

The Christian is to have the serenity of eternal life and the sanctuary of living beyond time in close relationship with God. We are to have the freedom from covetousness that comes from a world where money is irrelevant. We are to have the joy of access to the limitless power of God that we can bring to bear on earth's direst situations. We are to enjoy the peace that passes human, earthly understanding, because we live in the presence of the One who controls the universe and whose love and care watch over every sparrow. Once you get this right thinking, the preoccupations of earth seem so vain and pointless. Presidents fight for national prestige, sometimes even willing to go to war, while businessmen fight for more and more money to expand their possessions. All will pass away one day, but for the believer who grasps this secret place, all has already passed away, and we are living in the courts of eternity.

∾∾∾∾∾∾∾∾∾∾∾∾∾

April 9

And the Angel of the LORD appeared to Gideon, and said, "The LORD is with you, you mighty man of valour!" (Judges 6:12)

The Angel of the Lord addressed Gideon with honour and respect calling him a fearless warrior. In the subsequent chapters, Gideon demonstrated a rather fearful and cautious character. He destroyed the altar of Baal at night. He asked for several confirmations that God was calling him, asking for dew on the fleece and then asking for the fleece to be dry. He asked for yet further confirmations of God's good favour on him on the eve of the great battle with the Midianites. This reminds us of the time when Jesus called Peter, giving him that new name – a stone - indicating he would be a solid unwavering man. Later events proved that Peter was wobbly and unreliable.

The point is that God is not describing what He sees in us. Rather He is calling into our hearts and lives by His powerful creating word. He names us according to His marvellous ability to reshape our lives by speaking into us. When we read the Bible, we must let it speak into us, recreating our souls and imparting the very qualities that God is seeking in His people. The Bible assures us that spiritual life is a gift that comes through His word. Faith itself comes by hearing, and hearing by the word. We inevitably assume that God is asking great things from us that are hard to achieve. They certainly are great, but He wants us to receive these commands as prophecies, not as burdensome laws. *"Be holy, for I am holy" (1 Peter 1:16). "You are a chosen generation, a royal priesthood, a holy nation, His own special people, so that you may proclaim the praises of Him who called you out of darkness into His marvellous light." (1 Peter 2:9).* The astonishing fact is that we are a people full of faith, love and holiness. We are a people who know how to pray with passion and perseverance. And it is long overdue that we realised that we are more than we know! We may feel wobbly and fearful or even powerless to change anything. But God addresses us with honour and respect and bids us rise and truly be His people.

April 10

"But many who are first will be last, and the last first."
(Matthew 19:30 NASB)

Being the best is something we all aspire to. There are inevitably moments when we feel that we are above others in our understanding and in our sense of being blessed. We may have a happy family, a blessed ministry or a good church we attend. The subtle temptation is to then believe that we are actually better than others, or that there is something about us that has made us achieve this exalted state of blessing. When we begin our Christian walk, we are overwhelmed with God's goodness and grace, but as we walk on, we often begin to think we have helped God a lot along the way.

The result of this shift is that we cease to be as blessed and begin to taste of the dryness that results from the awful sin of pride. Pride is so deadly because it can dress itself up in robes of dazzling virtue. We sink to the bottom of the class and become the last but we still maintain the delusion that we are the first. We may even lament the awful lacks in those around us and secretly parade our past successes to ourselves. But we are digging a pit for ourselves.

The answer is to return to the grace of God. Everything good and blessed about our lives came from God from beginning to end. If we will deal firmly and radically with our pride, treating it as the deadliest of sins, then we will return to our first love and be refreshed and renewed. It is inevitable that we will pass through something of this process of passing from blessing to pride, but we must learn from the words of the Saviour. We simply need to cry again: *"For I know that in me (that is, in my flesh,) dwelleth no good thing."* (Romans 7:18 KJV) 'My flesh' is my natural life apart from God. Imagine what we would be like without grace, and turn again to marvel at the wonder of His goodness.

April 11

"Come to Me, all you who labour and are heavy laden, and I will give you rest. Take My yoke upon you and learn from Me, for I am gentle and lowly in heart, and you will find rest for your souls. For My yoke is easy and My burden is light."
(Matthew 11:28-30)

Of all the rules of Bible interpretation, perhaps the greatest is context. It is possible to take the words of Jesus in these beautiful verses and make them into a lullaby that soothes us and puts us to sleep. Yet the context is remarkable. In the preceding verses,
Jesus had given a searing condemnation of three cities: Bethsaida, Chorazin and Capernaum. Nothing is known of any visit of the Lord to Chorazin, little is known of Bethsaida, but much is known of Capernaum. But Jesus says that Capernaum was a worse city than Sodom because it had light but no repentance.

The context of these verses is the most sober warning that all the blessings of miracles of healing are as nothing compared with the wonder of repentance. If only we would change our attitude, our outlook, our lifestyle, then we would be able to approach Jesus and find unspeakable rest of heart. Peace and rest are offered as a path to heaven in some eastern religions. But with Jesus Christ, they are the fruits of repentance, leading to a deep change of heart by the grace and power of God. The context tells us that a heart resistant to change will be heavy-laden and bowed down with sorrows. The heart that throws off sin will be introduced to the wonder of partnership in life with Jesus. We will be enabled to get into step with God and find that He has not just blessed us at a point in our lives, but He has become the secret source of life and peace as we journey with Him. The cry of Jesus in these verses is the appeal to abandon our superficial and selfish ways and to get into step with almighty God. The results will be a steadily increasing participation in the heart states that are in Jesus Christ Himself.

~~~~~~~~~~~~~

April 12

Then He said to the disciples, "It is impossible that no offences should come, but woe to him through whom they do come!
(Luke 17:1)
And blessed is he who does not take offense at Me.
(Luke 7:23 NASB)

It is a simple fact of life that sooner or later we are going to suffer something that will offend us. The great snare of offence is that we feel we have been wronged, and that we are right to feel this resentment. The statement of Jesus also teaches that we are sometimes offended without a righteous cause. No-one could ever say that Jesus has offended them! This fact emphasises the underlying truth that there are two causes of offence, the one who offends, and the inner pride of the one offended.

The way to overcome the toxin that rises when we are offended is firstly to forgive those who have wronged us, and then to ask for forgiveness for the venom that has pooled in our soul. No matter how deep the wrong may be, we have to humble ourselves and find release from the poison of offence. The great example of this is Jesus Himself, who suffered injustice and cruel mockery, followed by torture till He died. The remarkable thing about Jesus Christ is that He was never offended. He suffered and did not retaliate in kind. It is startling that mockery and insults are mentioned as part of the sufferings of Christ:

"For He will be delivered to the Gentiles and will be mocked and insulted and spit upon." (Luke 18:32)

What nails are to the body, mockery and insults are to the soul. Sticks and stones do break our bones, but bones heal. When we are called names and mocked, the wounds are deep and sometimes never heal. Amazingly, Christ did not pass from inner offence to forgiveness, He remained steadfast in a forgiving, unoffended attitude throughout His whole life. We do not have to steel ourselves to be like Jesus, we have to humble ourselves and allow the Forgiver, the Unoffended One to be just that through us.

April 13

Then Jacob was left alone; and a Man wrestled with him until the breaking of day.   *(Genesis 32:24)*

Jacob was a man on the run for all his life and he was running away from himself. It was in this great crisis of his life that his past caught up with him and he was surrounded by people he had trampled over and hurt in order to get his own way. Jacob's problem was himself, and blaming others was all part of his escape from the reality of who and what he was.

Jacob wrestled with the angel of God and he realised that it was all the same as if he were fighting God. Of course, we cannot fight God and win. We may wriggle and squirm in God's arms but we cannot achieve anything by our striving. God is not fighting us or we would be instantly destroyed. God is allowing us to face up to the fact that my biggest problem is me. Yes, we are fighting ourselves and it was only when Jacob was left truly alone that he faced up to all the twisted logic of a selfish soul. It is only when we face up to ourselves in heart-searching prayer that we are truly changed.

It is the moment when we let go all our attempts to assert ourselves, to justify ourselves, that we discover the wonder of *"a noble and good heart"* (Luke 8:15). Truth is not found only in books, it is found pre-eminently when we turn to face God and ourselves in the marvellous searching light that streams from Him. Every time we turn into the light, we are changed, we shake off the tendency to be selfish and we are healed. Fight and overcome all the things that would keep you from God this day, and you will be surprised how God's master touch will release you from selfish, unworthy thoughts and usher you into His eternal courts.

~~~~~~~~~~~~~~~

April 14

Saul, Saul, why are you persecuting Me? (Acts 9:4 NASB)

Assuredly, I say to you, inasmuch as you did it to one of the least of these My brethren, you did it to Me. (Matthew 25:40)

It is astonishing the degree to which Christ is joined to the believer. It is possible that the word of Jesus to Saul of Tarsus was the flash of light that not only revealed Christ, but also the wonder of His church. Jesus said that He felt all the persecutions that the believers were suffering. There are two implications of this fact.

First, Christ is completely identified with us - with our joys, our pains, our victories and our defeats. He cannot cease to feel what we feel when we do something that grieves Him, and He is filled with joy when we position our souls to glorify Him. Whether we are conscious of His presence or not, He is with us at every step of our journey.

Secondly, we have a unique opportunity to minister to Christ by the way we treat our fellow-believers. Christ is the person sitting next to you in the assembly of God's people. It is true that we are not Christ and will never be Christ, but He is so completely identified with us that whatever is done to us is all one and the same as if it were done to Him. If we despise a believer, we despise Christ. If we are generous to our brothers and sisters, we are generous to Christ. We may wish we could have washed His feet with our tears or anointed His head with the most expensive fragrance, but the truth is that we can still do all these things. The Holy Spirit has created a body for Jesus Christ and it is time that we fully realised the limitless possibilities that this opens to us, to love and bless our Saviour Jesus.

~~~~~~~~~~~~~~

April 15

Jesus said to him, "If you can believe, all things are possible to him who believes." Immediately the father of the child cried out and said with tears, "Lord, I believe; help my unbelief!"
(Mark 9:23-24)

God is purposeful and affirmative and He longs for His children to partake of the same positive mind of faith. The sin of unbelief is to capitulate to what we conclude to be inevitable. Jesus here challenges all of us to rise up and ask for things that seem impossible. Note that Jesus did not say that all things are certain to him who believes. He did not teach that faith is a latent power of our human soul by which we can work miracles. That is a great error and makes us look to ourselves rather than to God.

The point is that faith is drinking of the joyful awareness of God's infinite power and goodness. When we believe, we simply stop drinking of the wells of foreboding or fear. We look up to God and begin to pray daring prayers that are in complete contrast to the evidence of our eyes or experience till that point. The God of the Bible is the God of history, but the same God wants to write new chapters of His great working in our lives. The prophets of old were people of the same weaknesses that we have in our lives, but they reached out in faith and saw God work. That is how the Bible came to be written. The Bible is a great book but it must not only be studied, it must be believed. Challenge yourself. Ask yourself if you are in danger of asking too little or too much. Are you in danger of resigning yourself to a natural life without God's supernatural interventions, or are you joyfully making requests to God and expecting Him to be the dimension to life that makes us look on the worst situations with hope.

April 16

Then I looked, and I heard the voice of many angels around the throne ... saying with a loud voice "Worthy is the Lamb who was slain." (Revelation 5:11-12)

John was on Patmos and was granted to pass into eternity and see beyond the veil of flesh into the kingdom of God, normally invisible to the physical eye. To John it was a taste of what it is to die and go to heaven, to see God, to see the mighty angels and glorified believers that surround Him and serve Him. The world John left behind him as he stepped into the throne room was a world of persecution and suffering. It was also a world defiled with immorality and strife that had polluted the churches that John had ministered to. John's faith and prayers changed forever as his perspective changed. He felt deep sorrow but he also knew soaring joy as he imbibed the triumphant spirit of heaven.

All this is a description of what can happen to us if we truly turn to God with all our hearts in believing prayer. Prayer is not just about changing things, it is most of all about changing the one who prays. As we pray, we are having a foretaste of heaven, and the wonderful fact is that we are enabled to think and pray as those who have died and risen with Christ. The secret is to turn with undivided heart and let the cords that tie us to earth be loosened and fall away. Our fears and worries about temporal things such as money will melt away and we begin to pray with the same priorities as heaven. Not only do we partake of heaven's agenda, but we also partake of heaven's joy and faith as we sense the sovereignty of God and the untroubled peace that is built upon the unshakable throne of God. Pray and pass into the everlasting courts of the Almighty and bring that whisper of eternity down to earth to your family, your neighbours, your church and your nation.

April 17

"But the very hairs of your head are all numbered. Fear not therefore, you are of more value than many sparrows."
(Matthew 10:30-31)
You number my wanderings; Put my tears into Your bottle; Are they not in Your book? *(Psalm 56:8)*

God watches over every detail of our lives, from the number of hairs on our head to the tears that we shed. It is astonishing that God should so love us despite His detailed knowledge of our sins and failures. It is not that God wants us to sort ourselves out and make our lives perfect. God simply asks us to stop fighting Him and surrender to His great Shepherd heart. Over and over again, we find ourselves fighting and resisting the streams of love that flow so ceaselessly.

God knows the details of our lives down to the minutest detail, but He is most intimate with our tears and with the things that cause us pain and hurt. Our lives are a complex weave of inner wounds and senseless fears. God knows that the only place where all this can ever be healed is the cross, where the Son of God suffered all the pain of sin, from the misery of abuse directed against Him to the absorbing and forgiving of all the anger and hatred of self-centred humanity. There is a capacity in God to skilfully absorb all that troubles our hearts and makes us weep. God numbers our tears and waits till we turn to sob out our hearts in His arms. That is what the cross is in our experience: the place where all the inexplicable injustices of this world are healed. At the cross, we meet the love that can hold us in our inner battles till all the fight has gone out of us and we are washed in His presence. One can analyse these things, but analysis does not replace the mystery of grace that teaches us to capitulate to Him. Our minds ask the question 'Why?'. But the answer is not in a logical survey of events but in the everlasting arms that hold us till our hearts are at rest in His amazing love.

~~~~~~~~~~~~~~

April 18

And we have known and believed the love that God has for us. God is love, and he who abides in love abides in God, and God in him. *(1 John 4:16)*

Of all the wonders of the revelation of the Scripture, the greatest is that God is love. We struggle to pray and please God. We sweat, we sacrifice and we strain, but it is only slowly that it dawns on us that the thing that most satisfies God's great heart is that we believe He loves us. Once we do that, we are turned inside out. We stop living a life of manipulation to get God and others to notice us. We are released from the self-centred life that is the opposite of love and we ourselves are liberated to abide in love.

Of all the complaints that one hears in the counselling chamber, perhaps the most common is 'No-one loves me.' The trouble with this plague on our souls is that it is sadly true that the world is full of selfish people who are only interested in their own happiness and welfare. So it is such a refreshing surprise to meet people who are truly liberated and free to love others. Such people have simply believed that they are loved. They are then immediately freed from hours and hours of religious struggles and self-pitying penances. They are infused with a brightness and joy that is the burning flame of God's love in us. God's love is deeper than the deepest hate of humanity; it has the capacity to swallow up and absorb waves of cold mockery and cruelty. It is renewed by its flow and multiplies the more it is poured out. For this reason love never fails - it never runs out. God loves us and it is only at the point when we stop trying to earn His love and simply believe, that the warm lava flow of everlasting love flows freely in us and through us.

~~~~~~~~~~~~~~~~

April 19

*Now He was telling them a parable to show that at all times they ought to pray and not to lose heart.   (Luke 18:1 NASB)
However, when the Son of Man comes, will He find faith on the earth?   (Luke 18:8 NASB)*

It is in these verses that we hear the longing of God that His children would truly believe Him. The characteristic of true faith is that it is praying faith. Once we stop praying for something, it is a sure sign that we have stopped believing that God hears and will answer. The moment comes when we are faced with a choice, either to shrug our shoulders and lose heart or to rise up with defiance and persistence and persevere in prayer.

In this parable of the unjust judge the widow is commended for her continual coming to a churlish and unrighteous man, who only responds to get rid of this pestering voice. There are two vital lessons here. First, that we must keep coming to God in prayer and faith for situations that are in desperate need of His power and grace. Secondly, the unjust judge is described in contrast with God. God is never churlish or slow to hear us, and we can be 100% sure that He hears our cry. He is eager to hear and swift to answer us, though the answer may take longer than our impatient souls are prepared to accept. When God seems not to hear, do not begin to imagine God as implacable, cold or indifferent to our cries. Persist in defiant faith that He hears and will answer more than we can ever ask or think. This is true faith: persistence in believing that God is loving and eager to answer our cries in the face of silence when nothing seems to happen. Never exchange the truth that God is loving, righteous and merciful for a view of God that is simply not the God that we know in the face of Jesus. He is coming again and He will be delighted to find that we have continued in this faith, whether through dark nights of loneliness or even prison cells. However long, however hard, let your faith rise and pray.

~~~~~~~~~~~~~~~

April 20

For I am not ashamed of the gospel of Christ, for it is the power of God to salvation for everyone who believes.
(Romans 1:16)

When Paul explains the gospel to the believers in Rome he begins by locating God's power in this message of salvation. It is a great error to locate the power in other things, such as the preacher who brings the gospel or in the feelings or intensity that we sometimes sense as the word is preached. We may sit in meetings where there is such a strong persuasion that we think the strongest wills must bow to the pressure of the arguments presented. We can then easily be disappointed that our heroes seem to have disappointed us. But the simple truth is that the gospel in its bare facts is a statement of truth, and whoever repents and believes that Jesus died for their sins will be saved.

The same is equally true of our prayers. We secretly believe that if our feelings are particularly intense, or our words very passionate, then God will surely answer such prayers. The fact is that God has promised to hear the prayers of His children, and it is that fact, and that fact alone, that is the grounds for our right to expect an answer. Once we shift the ground to subjective feelings, we are believing not in God but in ourselves, our spirituality or our passion. It is only slowly that we realise that God is sufficient and we are inadequate. It is a shock when it dawns upon us that when we are conscious of our weakness and unworthiness, it is precisely at those moments that we reach out in naked faith, trusting only in Him and His word. At the same time, it is a profound relief to the striving soul to realise that all God requires from us is our weakness.

April 21

Be anxious for nothing, but in everything by prayer and supplication, with thanksgiving, let your requests be made known to God; and the peace of God, which surpasses all understanding, will guard your hearts and minds through Christ Jesus. (Philippians 4:6-7)

When the Bible tells us not to worry, we immediately accept this with all its self-evident logic. After all, God is in control and allows problems to shape us and make us more Christ-like. But when a severe crisis looms, we instantly say to ourselves that this is different to the normal everyday concerns of life. Times of great danger are different: someone is dangerously ill; a loved one is turning away from the Lord; our work-place is full of discord and dishonesty.

It is precisely at such times that we are to allow this word to have its full effect: "Be anxious for nothing." The power of this word is only possible to the soul that will turn to the Lord and unburden itself in fellowship with Him. We are to pray, casting the burden onto Him, and we are also to proceed to thanksgiving, to praise God that He is faithful and true in all circumstances. Through prayer and thanksgiving, we can then drink of the ocean of peace that is totally illogical. It almost seems wrong to have peace when waves are battering our little boat. In truth it is only the one who has seen the utter futility of worry that can have such peace. Worry is a deep root of unbelief and will constantly bombard our minds with words of despair. Worry is itself the problem of our soul, and God desires to slay it. We must cast our distress on the Lord and then praise Him for His faithfulness. God cannot fail His children, and the sooner we embrace this fact and praise Him, the sooner we will find a supernatural peace that defies logic.

April 22

Do not become sluggish, but imitate those who through faith and patience inherit the promises. (Hebrews 6:12)

The message of the Hebrew writer is that believers should press forward and fully receive all the marvellous promises that are ours through the death and resurrection of Jesus. The word sluggish indicates a passive attitude that is without a forward impulse to carry the believer forward in the quest to discover the kingdom of God and all its spiritual riches.

One might think that the opposite of spiritual laziness is faith combined with passion. But the writer here indicates that it is the ingredient of patience that is essential. Faith rises spontaneously to lay hold of God's word. But often the thing longed for is not immediately received. At that moment, the crucial ingredient is patience or endurance. This is the opposite of 21st century culture, where everything is instant. Books, films and music can be purchased and downloaded immediately without even the need for a same-day delivery by special courier. But the things of the kingdom require patience. We pray for the baptism with the Holy Spirit, or for the conversion of loved ones, but the answer may be long in coming.

George Muller began to pray in 1844 for five individuals. He prayed daily for them and the first was converted after 18 months, and two more after six years. He prayed all his life for the remaining two and they were both converted after his death in 1898. The great work of patience is to never accept defeat, to never give up but to fix our eyes steadily on Christ, who is utterly faithful. Abraham received the promise after he had patiently endured (Hebrews 6:15), and the most precious things of the kingdom must be received with faith that endures through all obstacles and still presses on till the moment we are called home.

April 23

He will sit as a refiner and a purifier of silver; He will purify the sons of Levi, And purge them as gold and silver, that they may offer to the LORD an offering in righteousness. (Malachi 3:3)

God is described here as a silversmith and His people are the silver. The work of a silversmith is highly skilled and involves heating the silver to just the right temperature and then watching carefully till the process is complete. There are three stages in this process.

First, the fires bring dross to the surface and it is carefully removed and scooped away. When we are in the fires of temptation and distress, our attitudes may not be sweet and full of praise. But as we pray and press through, we abandon wrong thinking and are changed. Our complaints turn to praise and our distress is replaced by a sure and certain hope.

Secondly, the silversmith will not allow the process to go on a moment longer than necessary or the silver will be spoilt. In the same way, God watches over us in our trials and will not allow them to harm us but will end them at the perfect moment, when His purpose has been fulfilled. God's skill is matchless and is girded by His perfect knowledge of how much we can bear.

Finally, the silversmith knows the process is complete when he can see his reflection in the cup of melted silver. In the same way, God looks at our hearts till He can see His image reflected in us. His purpose is to produce the nature and character of the Son of God in us, and to produce a people that can love and worship Him with purity of heart and righteousness of conduct. In the midst of trials we are to look up and see the Father's watchful care and love. He is with us in our darkest hour and speaks to encourage us to persevere and receive the amazing rewards that will be ours.

~~~~~~~~~~~~~~~

April 24

And He cast out the spirits with a word, and healed all who were sick, that it might be fulfilled which was spoken by Isaiah the prophet, saying: "He Himself took our infirmities and bore our sicknesses." (Matthew 8:16-17)

It is remarkable the ease with which our afflictions can be dismissed by a word from Jesus. When Jesus spoke to the leper, his leprosy simply passed from him in a moment. When we bow before Jesus, He can lift the burdens from our lives as easily as blowing a feather away from a table.

The reason it is all so easy is given in this verse: Jesus Himself took our afflictions upon Himself and removed them when He died on Calvary. Imagine if someone had a headache and I was to pray: "Lord, give me their headache." Imagine if the Lord answered this and I was suddenly stricken with a fearsome migraine! Well, a headache is bad enough, but what of cancers, mental illnesses and all the moral addictions and depravities that plague the human race? When Jesus died on that cross, He took them on Himself so that He might take them away from us. There is a beautiful ease when we pray and a terrible price paid by Jesus Christ on Calvary. The best way to glorify Jesus is to let Him take our burdens away. It will cost Him no more to do so since He has already paid the price in full. Everything He asks from us has already been provided for. When a father sends his son to the shop to buy something, he always gives him the money. Whatever the Lord speaks into our lives He has already paid for in full. All that is required is the realisation that it is done, it is paid for, and faith is all that is needed.

April 25

A night and a day I have spent in the deep.
(2 Corinthians 11:25 NASB)

It is quite common for us to wish that we had the amazing faith of one of God's great apostles. Then when problems come, we would be able to pray and see our burdens disappear before the mighty power of God. But we must pause and consider what it must have been like for Paul in the circumstances described in this verse.

Firstly, the ship he was in struck a rock or went down in a storm. Perhaps some of his fellow-travellers perished in the disaster if they could not swim. Paul managed to cling to a piece of drift wood, and then, cold and in extreme discomfort, he prayed for help. The hours went by and tiredness would have slowly weakened his concentration. The long night passes and the day dawns with hope but no help in sight. Perhaps by the end of the day, he sees land or another boat, and at last he is safe, though exhausted.

The triumph of Paul's faith lay not in the ability to call miracles to save him from distress, but in the ability to praise and trust God in the darkest hour and in the most impossible of situations. To have this faith, we must lift our hearts to God and sing. Deliverance will come in one way or another, but our faith is revealed in our attitude as we wait. The night may seem endless, the taste of sea water in our mouths may make us nauseous, but God is faithful and watches over us to work in our souls things in these moments that nothing else can do. We know He is all powerful and can do amazing miracles, and we will not doubt, no matter how delayed the answer may seem. God is in the shipwreck and His hand is shaping the heart of those who will trust him through the long night till our captivity is turned and His plan is laid bare.

~~~~~~~~~~~~~~

April 26

Jesus commanded them: "Take away the stone." Martha, the sister of him who was dead, said to Him, "Lord, by this time there is a stench, for he has been dead four days." Jesus said to her, "Did I not say to you that if you would believe you would see the glory of God?" (John 11:39-40)

When Jesus prayed for the raising of Lazarus, the stench of Lazarus was in the air when the tomb was opened. The air was also heavy with the grief of Mary and Martha. But Jesus here demonstrates this unshakable assurance that His Father would hear and answer His prayer. Jesus directed His thoughts and feelings towards His Father and was influenced not by what He saw, heard and felt around Him, but by what He perceived in His relationship with His Father.

Dallas Willard said that "ultimate freedom is the power to select what our minds dwell upon." This is the power given to us through the Holy Spirit that if we will direct our minds to God, we will be filled with the consciousness of God. This is the awareness of the fragrance of God's love and power, which drown out every grief and woe of the human spirit and impart the perfume of the triumph of God's love in all things. We must resist the temptation to sink amid the tides of human distress that are all around us, and allow our thoughts to penetrate the throne room on high. There is a buoyancy in God that no disasters can discourage, no despair can weaken. If we are to bring hope to a dying world, we must rise above and bring the whispers of eternity to bear, first on our own souls and then minister them into the broken lives around us. God's thoughts are not mere imagination, they are anchored in a real world of light that will never be dimmed, and it is to that place that we are called to fix our hearts in steadfast gaze.

~~~~~~~~~~~~

April 27

And John tried to prevent Him, saying, "I need to be baptized by You, and are You coming to me?" (Matthew 3:14)

John the Baptist was a great prophet but cried out in astonishment, expressing his need that Jesus would baptize him. The greatest believer who has ever lived will be the one who is most deeply aware of his or her need of Jesus and His baptism. It can be embarrassing to parade one's need and God certainly does not wish us to be constantly wringing our hands over our need. But John was not wringing his hands; he was boldly declaring his deep personal need for Jesus to wash him in a mighty baptism of the Holy Spirit. Such a declaration is rare on the lips of the modern Christian, who is rather prone to parade his achievements and gifts rather than his need.

The greatness of Jesus Christ should at times overwhelm us till we bow with our faces in the dust in worship, adoration and wonder, coupled with prayer to be granted access into heart fellowship with this amazing person. Jesus Christ is the outshining of the Father's glory, and it is through Him that the exact image of God's person is presented to whoever would know God. Our need is to be impacted so deeply with the person of Christ in a way which changes our way of thinking forever. This was John's need and it is ours also. It is a cry that God will cleanse our reasoning faculties till all unbelief, worry, fear and negative thoughts are banished from our minds, and we begin to think like the matchless Son of God.

April 28

Then Jesus lifted up His eyes, and seeing a great multitude coming toward Him, He said to Philip, "Where shall we buy bread, that these may eat?" But this He said to test him, for He Himself knew what He would do. (John 6:5-6)

Jesus looked at the multitude with compassion and gently challenged the faith of Philip. Philip answered that 200 days' wages (200 denarii) would not be enough to feed them. It was impossible to do anything for them. It is illuminating to realise how often God's people find themselves in challenging situations, often much more demanding than hunger. There are situations where we despair and can see no positive outcome. But Jesus already knew what He was going to do.

This fact is not limited to this event. It is a foundation of His relationship with His universe and with the human race. He already knows how human history will end. He knows how this year will end in every nation. He knows the future of every family and every church in the whole world. Jesus said that the Father's foreknowledge was the cure for every anxiety. "Your heavenly Father knows" (Matthew 5:31) is the source of rest and peace and we need to savour this amazing fact over and over again. If we are troubled and anxious as we pray in times of great stress and testing, we are to nourish our hearts in this certainty that God already has a plan and a purpose that He will work out. There will be moments when we will feel that things are spinning out of control, but then we need to remember that God is sovereign and that nothing can happen without Him. This should not make us passive, but motivate us to prayerfully commit situations continually to Him with thanksgiving. Our minds are small and weak and we can easily be intimidated, so we need to nourish our hearts on the unshakable rock that Jesus already knows what He is going to do.

∾∾∾∾∾∾∾∾∾∾∾∾

April 29

And when Jesus came to the place, He looked up and saw him, and said to him, "Zacchaeus, make haste and come down, for today I must stay at your house." (Luke 19:5)

It is an astonishing fact that when Jesus calls us, He is invariably lower than we are. We entertain lofty notions of God that He is distant and remote, and then He taps us on the shoulder and invites us to come down from the exalted perches we have constructed to survey the universe. God is still holy, but He is humble and breathtakingly approachable and available. If we can only humble ourselves, we will understand and find Him. A good dose of humility will itself cure a whole raft of evils that beset us. We will immediately see difficult relationships and problems in a new light.

The truth is that pride is not an easy tiger to tame. We puff and blow, we pout and put on airs, all to mask the deep inner knowledge that we are quite simply wrong. It is so refreshing and liberating to simply let go of our self-importance and get down to touch the feet of Jesus. Jesus is exalted and holy but He has no trace of arrogance. He shrugs off the belittling mockery of conceited human beings without the slightest trace of hurt. Faith and repentance are easy to the humble and so hard for anyone who withdraws into the castle of self-justification. Zacchaeus was a guilty man but He found cleansing and relief by simply going down to meet Jesus on His level. We need to take time to humble ourselves as we pray. We will soon find the quiet joy of relief rising in our hearts because once we have touched the feet of Jesus, it dawns on us that all will be well.

~~~~~~~~~~~~~~~

April 30

For it was fitting for Him, for whom are all things and by whom are all things, in bringing many sons to glory, to make the captain of their salvation perfect through sufferings.
(Hebrews 2:10)

Christ is the captain of our salvation. Other translations say He is "the pioneer" or one who takes the chief lead in a matter. Christ does this by being the one who has gone ahead of us, but it means much more than that, since not only has Christ shown the way, He is our Shepherd to guide us in the way of salvation.

Some time ago I was driving through the palm plantations of Cameroon, looking for an American missionary who lived deep in the rainforest. There were no road signs and it was late afternoon so that I completely lost all sense of direction. As dusk descended, I noticed a lone cyclist making his way through the lush plantation. I stopped him and asked him if he knew where the missionary lived. His face took on a worried expression as he summoned all his powers of English to explain to me the road I must take. I soon discovered that he could only say a few words such as "You go so!" He repeated this phrase with enthusiastic pointing of his fingers indicating when the phrase meant "go left" or "go right." He then found another couple of words and he finished by declaring: "You go far, far inside so, and you go see 'em." He sank back with a sigh of a man who has accomplished a great work. I shook his hand and thanked him warmly, but I left with no idea at all which way to go.

The New Testament has many complex concepts that can easily baffle us. But the most beautiful truth is that Christ will be our personal guide, He will be my captain. If only the cyclist could have ridden ahead of me, he would have led me safe and sound to my desired goal. Christ has gone ahead, but He does more than that, He gets into the car and directs us at each cross roads. Jesus is the way, the truth, the life, my Shepherd, my sense of direction, my food and drink for the journey. I follow not a thick book of complicated instructions, but obey simply the step-by-step instructions that will guide me through all of life till I reach my home in heaven.

May 1

"Then he will show you a large upper room, furnished and prepared; there make ready for us." (Mark 14:15)

For we are His workmanship, created in Christ Jesus for good works, which God prepared beforehand that we should walk in them. (Ephesians 2:10)

God is waiting for us to respond to His love and grace. But that does not mean that He is not making extensive preparations for our future. We often think that we are responsible for planning out our future, carefully designing how we will serve God and how we will be useful in our ministry. Here God lifts the veil to show us that He has gone ahead of us and everything is ready and waiting.

This is to comfort us in the trials, knowing that in these, too, God has prepared each step for us. It is to give us faith in our service, knowing that God has gone before and had already been working in the lives of the people we minister to long before we ever met them. We often think that the world is simply waiting for us to show up so that at last God can begin to do something. The truth is that we are a very small part of a great plan for the salvation of multitudes of human beings. The foreknowledge of God should make us eager participants in the discovery of the surprises that God has already set for us to discover.

This will affect the whole way we live and work for God. We are to have our expectation lifted to see the hand of God in every circumstance of our life. This will comfort us in our sorrows and also allow joy to flow into our souls as we eagerly look for His hand in the unfolding wonder of His amazing grace. The universe is a place of order and design and the same is true for our lives. When we repent, we leave the confusing chaos of a disordered world with me at the centre, and enter the magnificent world of the kingdom of God where God rules in serene majesty.

May 2

But what things were gain to me, these I have counted loss for Christ. Yet indeed I also count all things loss for the excellence of the knowledge of Christ Jesus my Lord, for whom I have suffered the loss of all things, and count them as rubbish, that I may gain Christ. (Philippians 3:7-8)

The essential characteristic of the cross is the ability to let things go. Jesus began His long journey to Calvary when He let go of heaven and all its glories and privileges. We are inclined to think of the bad things we have given up, but there is nothing of the cross in giving up the world. That would be like renouncing a pit of snakes and boasting of what a great sacrifice we had made! The table of the world is furnished with sweet-tasting poisons in a room without oxygen that will suffocate the faith and love right out of our hearts.

The cross is to be measured rather by the good things that we let go of in order to make room for the true riches of knowing Christ. The messenger of the cross has cut back his life and is keeping it constantly cut back in order to remain true to the master.

Sir Stanley Matthews captained the England football team in the 1940s. He died on 23 February 2000. He was 85 years old and had jogged every morning and never eaten anything that would cause him to put on weight. He fasted once a week. He was a true athlete and let go all of these dainty morsels in order to keep physically fit. Christ had plenty of time in His 33 years to perfectly fulfil His calling with calm and serene focus on each day's purpose. We always have enough time to do what God requires without striving and stress. But to do this, we must let go of all the legitimate pleasures that compete for our attention. Simply let things go, cut back and the space created will be filled with the sweetness of Christ.

May 3

The Spirit Himself bears witness with our spirit that we are children of God, and if children, then heirs-- heirs of God and joint heirs with Christ, if indeed we suffer with Him, that we may also be glorified together. (Romans 8:16-17)

One of the keys to deepening our walk with God is developing a right attitude to suffering. We often do not expect to pass through deep trials, or we set out on a venture assured that God will bless it with success, only to have it descend into ashes.

This was literally the case with Horatio Spafford, who invested heavily in property in Chicago, only to lose it in the great fire of 1871. Moreover, he lost four children, one young son to scarlet fever, and three daughters drowned when their ship went down in the Atlantic in 1873. Spafford's direct response to these disasters was to pen the song "It is well with my soul."

Some of us retreat into a huff with God at the slightest whiff of discomfort. The root cause is that we have made God into a kind of benevolent figure who is always handing out nice presents. But God is rugged and has deeper goals than we do. His aim is to make us shine like His Son and to this end He will allow us to pass through fierce fires and deep waters. Jesus does not rebuke us for moments of confusion and wrong reactions, but gently coaxes us to see that the God we serve is greater than we have ever imagined. God is magnificent and we are invited to swallow our pride, press through the pain, and praise and trust the Lord, who will never leave us or forsake us. God has promised us that if we do this, we will be endowed with riches beyond measure, riches of character and Christ-likeness.

~~~~~~~~~~~~~~~

May 4

Let Us make man in Our image. (Genesis 1:26 NASB)
And they continued steadfastly in the apostles' doctrine and fellowship, in the breaking of bread, and in prayers.
(Acts 2:42)

When God created man, He could easily have referred to Himself in the singular, but He referred to Himself in the plural, indicating that God is a relationship of three persons. He was also indicating that humanity is created in the image of that fellowship and by implication for the companionship that is at the very centre and heart of the Godhead.

It is for this reason that it is only a person in relationship with others that can reveal God. It is where 2 or 3 are gathered in His name that the miracle of Christ and His body are revealed (Matthew 18:20). The reason for this is that God is love and only where people are loving one another can God be revealed. God has never been alone and it is the essential quality of His being that He dwells in eternal love and in the eternal harmony and beauty of love that serves others and seeks the good of others.

To dwell in love requires the constant renewing of the Holy Spirit and the result is homes and lives that are radiant with the divine blessing and presence. To give up on church life is easy, but it will always produce an inner dysfunction and lead to a spiritual wilderness. To hold back is to slay love, and to get involved is to be vulnerable and at risk. The Christian who loves is as defenceless as Christ before the crowds that bayed for His blood. Paul said "For Your sake we are killed all day long; We are accounted as sheep for the slaughter." (Romans 8:36) Love is not for the faint-hearted and will test every sinew of our spiritual life, but the reward is to be introduced into the very heart and centre of the glory of God, into the very fellowship of the Holy Spirit.

~~~~~~~~~~~~~~

May 5

"I have hope in God, which they themselves also accept, that there will be a resurrection of the dead, both of the just and the unjust. This being so, I myself always strive to have a conscience without offence toward God and men."

(Acts 24:15-16)

Offence is one of the biggest hindrances to the activity of the Holy Spirit in our hearts. Yet it is possible for this monster to lurk unnoticed in the human soul. Part of the reason for this is that we can so easily feel justified in our behaviour. It is not our fault that others have been offended. And if we in our turn are offended, then it is obviously the arrogant insensitivity of others that has hurt us. It is one of the clearest marks of a supernatural walk with God that we are able to stay free from offence.

But to stay free we must be ready to confess our faults and to ask for forgiveness. The children of Israel, passing through the wilderness, were offended at everything. They complained about the lack of water, the manna, Moses's leadership and the lack of tasty vegetables, which had been so abundant in Egypt. But they caused their own trouble through their selfish fussiness and insistence on their comforts and pleasures. Have we ever realised how damaging our fussiness can be to our spiritual progress? The truth is that self is our biggest obstacle in overcoming the sin of offences.

Peter had blindly and confidently affirmed that he would never be offended (Mark 14:29 KJV). But Jesus had told him that they would all be offended because of Him that very night (Mark 14:27 KJV). The truth is that we have huge wells of pride in our souls and every Christian is going to face many situations which will leave us with deeply-wounded pride and stinging shame. Offences will come, but we must strive to keep our souls free from this paralyzing force. To do this we must pray for those who have hurt us, forgiving them and seeking the blessing of God on their lives. The mark of the apostles was that they processed their failures quickly and with humility. This is the only way to be a continuous blessing and to be constantly refreshed in our walk with God.

May 6

Mercy rejoices against judgment.   *(James 2:13 KJV)*

On a bitterly cold night in January of 1935, mayor of New York Fiorello LaGuardia turned up at a night court that served the poorest ward of the city. Mayor LaGuardia dismissed the judge for the evening and took over the bench himself. An old woman was brought before him, charged with stealing a loaf of bread. She told the mayor that her daughter's husband had left, her daughter was sick, and her two grandchildren were starving. However, the shopkeeper, from whom the bread was stolen, refused to drop the charges. "It's a real bad neighbourhood, your Honour," the man told the mayor. "She's got to be punished to teach other people around here a lesson."

LaGuardia sighed. He turned to the woman and said, "I've got to punish you. The law makes no exceptions. Ten dollars or ten days in jail." But even as he pronounced sentence, the mayor was already reaching into his pocket. He extracted a bill and tossed it into his hat, saying, "Here is the ten-dollar fine, which I now remit; and furthermore, I am going to fine everyone in this courtroom fifty cents for living in a town where a person has to steal bread so that her grandchildren can eat. Mr. bailiff, collect the fines and give them to the defendant." $47.50 was turned over to a bewildered woman who had stolen a loaf of bread to feed her starving grandchildren. Fifty cents of that amount was contributed by the grocery store owner himself, while some seventy petty criminals, people with traffic violations and New York City policemen, each of whom had just paid fifty cents for the privilege of doing so, gave the mayor a standing ovation.[1]

Mercy is kindness in action when harsh judgment would be required. The ultimate act of mercy is Calvary, and we must allow it to soften our hearts and share this mercy with every human being we meet.

ᴎᴎᴎᴎᴎᴎᴎᴎᴎᴎᴎᴎ

---

[1] Brendan Manning, *The Ragamuffin Gospel,* (2000)

May 7

He who observes the wind will not sow, and he who regards the clouds will not reap. ... In the morning sow your seed, and in the evening do not withhold your hand; for you do not know which will prosper, either this or that, or whether both alike will be good. *(Ecclesiastes 11:4 & 6)*

One of the greatest temptations is to become passive in the face of difficult circumstances. Some are passive because of their belief in the sovereignty of God. But to be passive is to completely misunderstand God and His majestic rule of the affairs of men. God is purposeful and positive and expects His people to be the same, to engage with all their hearts in the great work of cooperating with Almighty God.

A man may shrug His shoulders and say God will save people whether I witness to them or not. Another will say that what is meant to be is simply meant to be and I cannot change it. But the child of God rises in the morning with boundless hope that God will be in the day, working and blessing his labours and directing his heart into hope and faith for the outcome of each day. To be passive is to ascribe to God the heartless indifference of a loveless power. God is active and involved with human beings far more than we will ever know. He longs for us to rise in joyous anticipation of the good things that His sovereign will has already planned for us. When God created the world, He knew what He would do each day, and He created His children to engage with all their hearts in the work that He gave them to do.

Anyone who has driven a car without power steering knows that it is hard to turn the steering wheel of a car when it is stationary. It is when the car is moving that the wheel can be moved. In the same way, it is impossible to receive guidance if we are passive and inactive in our hearts and minds. It is as we engage in the work of God, counting on the activity of the Holy Spirit, that we can be nudged and channelled into the paths that God has ordained for us. Rise up and be doing, and reach out in prayer and faith, expecting God to bless the work of your hands.

~~~~~~~~~~~~~~

May 8

When He had called the people to Himself, with His disciples also, He said to them, "Whoever desires to come after Me, let him deny himself, and take up his cross, and follow Me."
(Mark 8:34)

Jesus relentlessly places the cross before us as the starting point of all discipleship. Once this is established as the cornerstone of each day, of every relationship and of every enterprise, then things fall into place. If the cross is pushed to the margins, to the add-ons of Christian understanding then we are building on sand.

The cross must be central in three key areas: Firstly, it must be the centre of our doctrine. Once we have lost the centrality of the cross, we are forced to wander into fascinating journeys of discovery of the Bible that will ultimately prove fruitless. Only the cross will lead to power to live and power to overcome temptation and the darkness of this world.

Secondly, we must enter by the cross into the presence of God. The cross is a door in the Spirit, it is a new and living way to God through the blood of Jesus (Hebrews 10:19-20). The cross is the way to discover God by experience, knowing His presence as a powerful life-changing delight. The cross is a way of escape from the dry wilderness of self into the dynamic of a Christ-centred life.

Thirdly, we must embrace the cross as the key to our lifestyle. The teaching of Jesus is a tenacious insistence on servanthood, unselfish acts of kindness, loving the outcast and the neglected. The cross is a generous, giving heart living with an open hand to those around us.

As we take up our cross daily, it dawns on us that we have embarked on the path of incredible joy as we discover that we are becoming companions with Christ and tasting of the incredible power and joy of His life.

~~~~~~~~~~~~~

May 9

Jesus said to him, "Assuredly, I say to you that this night, before the rooster crows, you will deny Me three times."
(Matthew 26:34)

It is astonishing that Jesus knows our failures and has not been in the least surprised by them. It is not that He is indifferent to our struggles but part of the inevitable instruction of our souls is to lead us to see ourselves as we really are, and to see ourselves in our staggering spiritual ineptitude and weakness. Almost without exception, the great men of the Bible passed through deep waters of their own failure. In fact, three of God's greatest vessels were former murderers: Moses, David and Paul. What a message to preach to those who have made a mess of their lives and are languishing in prison!

These three men had seen themselves in the dazzling beam of their total bankruptcy and had been brought through deep waters to an even deeper appreciation of God's amazing grace. God made these men genuine by the crucible of facing up to their need of God and then to a realisation that God was completely undaunted and irrepressibly serene and even cheerful in His ability to bring them through.

We are to guard against preaching negativity to our own soul and we are to soar out of the ashes, rising on the realisation that God foreknew our weakness and is delighted that we can face it with faith in His amazing ability. Only the person who really knows themselves can really believe God. We all have a secret belief in God and ourselves, but as we progress we believe less and less in ourselves and have a joyful, carefree confidence in God.

~~~~~~~~~~~~~~~

May 10

Then He brought us out from there, that He might bring us in, to give us the land of which He swore to our fathers.
(Deuteronomy 6:23)

The distance between Egypt and the promised land is a short journey that can be covered in a few hours by car. On foot with thousands of people it can take several weeks. In truth the distance from a life of darkness to the kingdom of light is but a step. The fact is that we are always at first conscious of what we need to get out of, especially if we have been caught in the snares of a soul- destroying bondage. It is only slowly that we become conscious of what we need to get into.

Nevertheless, getting out and getting in are connected. No-one has truly escaped the bondage of Egypt until they have reached the promised land. Christ is our promised land. So often we are consumed with overcoming the problems of our past, when really we need to begin to receive the amazing benefits that are now ours. Of all the inward treasures, the greatest is to allow Christ to be our very life. It is not living for Him that is the mark of the overcoming life, it is in letting Him live through us.

Corrie ten Boom lost several family members in Nazi concentration camps and suffered herself the inhumane treatment in Ravensbruck, where dozens died every day. After the war she was preaching on forgiveness in Germany and recognised a man in the congregation who had been a Nazi guard at the camp. He approached her to ask if she meant what she said. He extended his hand and Corrie fought a temptation to reject it. But as she reached out to him, she was filled with the love of God and a profound consciousness that the Forgiver was in her. In Christ we are empowered to be all that He is as He prays, loves and believes through us. We are to enter into Him and let Him be our new life

May 11

Blessed be Your glorious name, which is exalted above all blessing and praise! You alone are the LORD; You have made heaven, the heaven of heavens, with all their host, the earth and everything on it, the seas and all that is in them, and You preserve them all. The host of heaven worships You."
(Nehemiah 9:5-6)

There is something so entirely focused on the majesty and greatness of God in this prayer. It is filled with the joy of a heart that is surrendered to one thing only, and that is the attitude that is to infuse our attitude to God at every step of our walk. We are not to be constantly looking over our shoulders at other issues and problems. We are to let the activity of the moment fill our hearts and take over our minds. When we praise God, we are to surrender our souls in doing it as if there were nothing else in the whole universe other than to praise Him.

Likewise, when we cry to Him in need, we are not to hold back but to let that cry take over our whole heart and being. When we love others, we are to focus on that person as if they were the only creature in the universe. When we wait on Him in silence, quieting our hearts before Him, it is to be with that totality of single-mindedness that is to be ours at every step. We are to love and serve Him with our whole being, strength, power and might. This attitude will instil in us such confidence and whole-heartedness that is to be the mark of God's people.

The song thrush will climb to the highest boughs of a tree to sing for extended periods. The nightingale will sing through the night, filling the air with melodies. God created them to sing. It is their purpose. We have the privilege of conscious choice to be what God has made us to be, and we are to do whatever our hand finds to do with all our hearts in glad surrender.

<div align="center">~~~~~~~~~~~~~~</div>

May 12

Let the little children come to Me, and do not forbid them; for of such is the kingdom of God. (Luke 18:16)
Behold I and the children whom God has given Me. (Hebrews 2:13 NASB)

Everyone has at some time or other seen the pride of a father in the first pictures his child has drawn. Dad will often place it in a prominent place so his child can see the pride he feels in their artistry. This is how God feels about our stammering efforts to pray and believe. Jesus stands in the midst of His church with swelling pride at us His followers, and the more child-like we are, the more delighted He is.

When Jesus commanded us to let the children come to Him, He was indicating the beautiful readiness of children to simply believe and follow their parents. We are never to allow the cynicism of years to hinder their response. But we are also to realise that there is a child in each of us that we are also to allow to rise up and be the attitude of our hearts to God. We may have to move a heap of rubbish from our minds, but we are to return constantly to the child-like delight in our heavenly Father. The rubbish will include theological sophistication and cynical attitudes to others who are so naïve in their expectation that God will bless and provide for them. We might even catch ourselves saying things like "Just give those people a few years and they will realise it's not that simple to follow Christ."

The greatest thing about being a Christian is that we are children and God is our amazing Father. Just the fact that Father knows all about us and our circumstances is enough to comfort a child and we must allow that child-like faith to prevail. No father is indifferent if his children are hungry or suffering and no father is critical of his children's weak efforts to please him. Just as a child cannot do bad colouring, so too, a child of God cannot pray bad prayers. In fact the only thing that grieves Him is when we suffocate the child in us.

~~~~~~~~~~~~~~

May 13

You shall not make for yourself an idol. (Exodus 20:4 NASB)
Dear children, keep yourselves from idols. (1 John 5:21 NIV)

We are inclined to think that idols are all to do with images carved in wood and stone. But in fact, like all sin, idolatry begins with a thought. An idol is simply a substitute for God, whether in part or in whole. An idol is that which seeks to share ground in us that belongs to God alone.

When we grant a friend, a counsellor, a pastor or a leader a place of honour, we are to make sure we do not give to that person the place that is to belong solely and entirely to Christ. We can do this with our doctrine, our leaders, our denomination or even spiritual exercises. Some people speak of their prayer life, or revival, or their systematic theology as if these things held the key to salvation. The moment we place our faith in something other than Christ Himself, then we mentally make of that thing a dumb statue that will block our spiritual life. The chief quality of idols is that they cannot communicate, they are lifeless. Idolatry leads inevitably to inner dryness and God Himself imposes this dryness because He refuses to share us with anything or anyone. God is a jealous God and is determined to destroy both gross secret sins and the more subtle idols we set up in our minds.

Breaking down idols is the first step, but the most important thing is to keep a focus on Christ Himself, reaching out to know Him and His life-changing presence. It is the discipline of realising that He is always beyond our control. We are to bow inwardly to the One who moulds us as we press into the awe and wonder of the One who alone is worthy of our worship.

~~~~~~~~~~~~~~~

May 14

For you have need of endurance, so that after you have done the will of God, you may receive the promise. (Hebrews 10:36)

That you do not become sluggish, but imitate those who through faith and patience inherit the promises.
(Hebrews 6:12)

The writer to the Hebrews identifies patience and endurance as vital aspects of faith by which we are able to receive from God. The Lord has infinite wisdom and leads our souls carefully to position us to be purified from all the things that trouble us. There is no doubt that ambition and pride are most slain when they are forced to wait. It is our sense of self-importance that is laid bare when we become impatient. As we embrace the Lordship of Christ and submit to His discipline, we are led to surrender everything to His loving care and we die to our self-will and our arrogance.

Abraham was one who learned the rugged path of patience and endurance. He wrestled with his desire to have a son and had to learn that God's timetable cannot be hurried by our intensity and striving. In fact, we delay God's blessings, we hinder them and hold them back.

"Love is patient" (1 Corinthians 13:7, New American Standard) and this is the first quality of love that Paul mentions and so it is also the first characteristic of God. We need patience when we pray for something and we are not to expect instant results. Patience is not the passive resignation of the eastern religions but the steadfast persistence of the pilgrim assured of reaching his goal. We are to nurture this attitude in our prayer life, and most importantly when we pass through trials. Patience teaches us that God is working through the delay and through the trial. As we trust in the Lord, we rest in His presence and come to realise that today is as important as the future goal. If we will only rest in trust, we will enjoy the moment, frustration will seep out and child-like faith will rise.

~~~~~~~~~~~~~

May 15

And He said to them, "Assuredly, I say to you that there are some standing here who will not taste death till they see the kingdom of God present with power." Now after six days Jesus took Peter, James, and John, and led them up on a high mountain apart by themselves; and He was transfigured before them. (Mark 9:1-2)
A voice came out of the cloud, saying, "This is My beloved Son. Listen to Him!" (Mark 9:7 NASB)

It was on the Mount of Transfiguration that the kingdom of God was revealed in its core. A worldly mind would want to see rows of mighty angels wielding flaming swords. Such things are also real but they are not the essence of the kingdom. There are two great revelations of the nature of the kingdom by which we may know how well we know His rule.
Firstly, there is the moral and spiritual radiance that is the nature of the King. Adam fell from the kingdom the moment he disobeyed and lost the inward light of the presence of God. A Christian is to be the light of the world by keeping an inner light of fellowship with God burning bright. We know this by the delight and wonder we sense as we pray and draw near to the King. We may not always sense the same degree of majesty, but we have sensed the glory of the king and we can never be the same again. The three disciples who went with Him up the mountain could never forget what they had seen, and though it was the pinnacle of His self-revelation, it would be the hardest to talk about. Moments when we are lost in wonder at the person of Christ are the heart and centre of the kingdom, and yet they are the hardest to adequately share with others.
Secondly, the heart of the kingdom is to listen to the King. We are not listening to catch prophecies or words of revelation of unknown things. We are simply to cultivate a quiet heart of looking up to Him that is to shape our mind. The kingdom comes in power to deliver us from all distracting voices, from our desires, our intense energy and our ambitions. To abide in the power of the kingdom, we must keep our mind's eye free from the clutter of a thousand other things and settle our hearts in quiet concentration on Jesus. Whoever knows the place of sweet communion with Christ has seen the kingdom come in power.

~~~~~~~~~~~~~~~~

May 16

For we do not have a High Priest who cannot sympathise with our weaknesses. (Hebrews 4:15)
Therefore, when Jesus saw Mary weeping... Jesus wept.
(John 11:33 & 35)

Jesus wept from His complete identification with Mary and the grieving friends of Lazarus. It is astonishing to realise the degree to which He feels what we feel. Jesus did not weep for Lazarus because firstly, Lazarus was in heaven in Abraham's bosom, having a good time, and secondly, because He was about to raise him from the dead. God knows that there is blessing about to flood our beings and He also knows that only faith will bring us to the anticipation of that coming joy. It was unbelief, disappointment and loss of perspective that caused Mary to grieve so deeply.

Jesus did not stand aloof from them in their grief but felt keenly their sorrow. This is the expression of Christ's unselfishness and His total identification with others. He could have attempted to reason with them in their grief by explaining why it was not necessary. But He simply allowed His soul to merge with theirs in their bewildered grief. At that moment in time, God in Christ expressed His compassionate identification with a hurt and grieving world.

The world is full of sorrow and all of it to do with sin and unbelief, but God still feels with us and shares our pain. There are two sides to God's caring heart: first to weep with those who weep, and secondly to make our problems to be His. He entered the tomb of the human race when He died on the cross and was buried. He entered the darkness and fear and destroyed them, raising all who will believe to sit with Him in His triumph. He identified with us and became a man of sorrows so that we could enter into who and what He is and partake of the joy that is the everlasting atmosphere of God's heart.

May 17

"Assuredly, I say to you, among those born of women there has not risen one greater than John the Baptist; but he who is least in the kingdom of heaven is greater than he."
(Matthew 11:11)

This bold statement from the lips of Jesus is startling. John was a rugged and fearless prophet who renounced the pleasures of the world in order to fulfil his calling to be a voice for God. He lived a life of sacrificial renunciation to be a sign-post pointing to Jesus. Few would ever claim to be equal to him, let alone greater than he.

In order to understand this assertion, one must insert one word into the sentence, namely that he who is least in God's kingdom is 'potentially' greater than John. The key difference between John and the believer is the covenant under which we live. John was himself of the tribe of Levi, like his father Zacharias. But they served God before a door that was closed and firmly sealed. They could enter the Holy Places of the tabernacle but the inner sanctuary of the Holy of Holies was barred to all.

Now, because of Calvary, that veil has been torn and the door is wide open for believers to pass into intimate heart fellowship with God. Old Testament saints would have been amazed to hear this familiar truth, but to the New Testament saint it is the deepest challenge since it means following the heart's desire right through to deepest heart union with Christ. The choice is now not merely between the world and holiness, but much more between holiness and most holiness. It is the choice between the first steps in salvation and then pressing into the all-consuming fire of God's inner being that is now laid bare for believers to know by experience. The courts of the Lord are to be known in inward reality as we allow the Holy Spirit to illuminate our inner life with the inner glories of Christ Himself that are becoming our inward state.

<div align="center">~~~~~~~~~~~~~~</div>

May 18

Assuredly, I say to you, inasmuch as you did it to one of the least of these My brethren, you did it to Me. (Matthew 25:40)

From 1964 to 1980 there was a brutal war in Zimbabwe against white rule. Many remote farms were attacked and many died. One farm in particular remained untouched throughout the troubles. After the war on one hot afternoon, a large black limousine rolled up to the farmhouse. Out stepped one of the former freedom fighters, now a government minister. He asked the farmer, who was a devout Christian, if he would like to know why his farm had been spared. The farmer was curious and listened intently as the minister asked him if he remembered an old woman who had come to the farm begging food. "You not only gave her food, but you gave her a place to stay for as long as she wished. That woman was my mother, and I gave orders that your farm was never to be attacked."

So much may hang on one small act of kindness. It is not only the government minister who noticed the love of God expressed in a spontaneous act of mercy, but all heaven recorded it and rejoiced. It is far more common to assert that God hears our prayers than that He reacts to deeds of love, but it is actually love that draws God's attention to the heart that prays from a wellspring of love.

Opportunities to love come at unexpected moments and we are not always ready for them, but we must take them and open our hand to those in need. God bears witness to loving kindness by surrounding such people with His favour, smiling on His loved ones who do His will and express His heart.

May 19

Saul said: "All of you have conspired against me ... and there is not one of you who is sorry for me." (1 Samuel 22:8)

And David was greatly distressed; for the people spoke of stoning him, because the soul of all the people was grieved, every man for his sons and for his daughters: but David encouraged himself in the LORD his God. (1 Samuel 30:6 KJV)

The difference between Saul and David was simply their faith in God. Saul believed everyone was against him though he was completely wrong and no-one was conspiring against him. David, on the other hand, was dangerously unpopular among his followers at this moment. Yet David did not wait for any encouragement but rather stirred himself up to remember that God was with him.

Faith always causes us to focus on God, not on ourselves. Unbelief looks with dismay on our inner resources and gives up. If only Saul could have lifted up his eyes and turned away from self, he would, like David, have found all the positive help he needed. The truth is that there is a conspiracy behind the scenes, but it is not a plot to harm us, it is a heavenly strategy to do us good. When we are tempted to discouragement, it is simply a temptation to look on our circumstances without God. Once God is included in our perspective, we cannot lose, for if God be for us, there is simply nothing and no-one that can effectively oppose us. Saul's gloom was entirely of his own making, and one is left to wonder how he would fare when the danger was real. Certainly he was paralysed with fear and dismay at the taunts of Goliath (1 Samuel 17:11). David, on the other hand, could see that Goliath was finished. The power of encouragement is great and will change everything, but it begins when we rise up inside and believe God. It comes down to a simple question: "Will I believe in God to be with me in these circumstances?" Once I declare my faith to myself, to God, to the powers of darkness and to anyone else who is listening, then the battle is won at that moment. For it is a battle for the hearts and minds of God's people, so once my heart rises in faith, the battle is won in my heart and in my mind.

~~~~~~~~~~~~~~~

May 20

And as He was leaving Jericho ... a blind beggar named Bartimaeus, was sitting by the road. When he heard that it was Jesus the Nazarene, he began to cry out and say, "Jesus, Son of David, have mercy on me!" ... And Jesus stopped and said, "Call him here." ... he jumped up and came to Jesus. Jesus said, "What do you want Me to do for you?" And the blind man said to Him, "Rabboni, I want to regain my sight!" And Jesus said to him, "Go; your faith has made you well." Immediately he regained his sight and began following Him on the road. (Mark 10:46-52 NASB)

This event on the outskirts of Jericho teaches us the power of prayer. Bartimaeus was suddenly aware of the nearness of Jesus and began to cry out with all his heart for mercy. His cries intensified with the discouraging words of the crowd and at last Jesus stood still. It was in itself remarkable that Jesus paused and waited for this man to come to Him. God is touched by the cries of the needy and He hears their grief of heart; everything was suddenly frozen in time as God waited to hear the prayer of this broken man.

The question of Jesus seems initially to be superfluous since the man's need was obvious. But here is the point of the event: God wants to be asked, and has even ordained that He must be invited to help. God has sovereignly ordained that human beings have freedom of will and God will not violate His own ruling. God will thunder commands to demons, storms and Satan himself. But where human beings are concerned, He waits to be invited. Jesus waited for this man to spread his need before Him and He waits for us to do the same. It may seem superfluous but He requires it.

Prayer is opening the door to God, and when Holman Hunt painted Jesus as the "Light of the World", standing knocking at the door of the human heart, Hunt painted no handle on the outside of the door. It has to be opened from the inside. God's grace is persistent and powerful and without it, we would never even know God was seeking us. But God in His sovereign grace waits to be asked.

~~~~~~~~~~~~~~

May 21

And when Peter had come down out of the boat, he walked on the water to go to Jesus. But when he saw that the wind was boisterous, he was afraid; and beginning to sink he cried out, saying, "Lord, save me!" And immediately Jesus stretched out His hand and caught him, and said to him, "O you of little faith, why did you doubt?" (Matthew 14:29-31)

We inwardly smile at the thought that we might one day walk on water. It is the same inward laugh of unbelief that rose in Sarah's soul when God told her she would have a son before the year was out (Genesis 18:12). The sober truth is that we are to rise above the storms of life and walk to Jesus and then walk with Him.

The goal of God is that we should enter into the spiritual poise of an inner life that is calmly fixed on Jesus. That is what it means to walk on water. There are two options open to us: either to sink beneath the waves in the panic and distress that rise in the heart that has lost sight of Jesus, or to step out in faith and discover the hushed tranquillity that emanates from the person of Christ. Jesus didn't still the storm before Peter got out of the boat. Peter had to walk not on a mill pond, but on a boiling sea of instability. In the same way, God is not going to teach us the way of peace by giving us a cabin by a lake far from the hustle and bustle of real life. God is introducing us to another level of life and some of us have spent our years dismissing it as pie in the sky when we die.

God is inviting us to come to Him on the water, and not merely for our own good. There are multitudes drowning in distress and grief and they are waiting for someone who can walk above it all and reach out their hand as Jesus reached out to Peter. A Christian has the unique quality of knowing the centre of all things and dwelling there in a peace that is staggering to the carnal mind. Rise up and step out of the boat into the poise of walking with Jesus over the storms of life.

∾∾∾∾∾∾∾∾∾∾∾∾∾

May 22

Call upon Me in the day of trouble; I will deliver you, and you shall glorify Me. *(Psalm 50:15)*
Therefore the LORD will wait, that He may be gracious to you; and therefore He will be exalted, that He may have mercy on you. *(Isaiah 30:18)*

Some hikers walking in the mountains of Wales heard the frantic bleating of a sheep. Following the sound they found the culprit trapped on a ledge over a steep drop. They ran to the nearest farm house to alert the farmer. The farmer obliged their concerns by following them to the ledge. Seeing the farmer, the sheep raised its cries for help. The farmer paused and calmly declared to the hikers he would come back in the morning. Curious, they met him there the following morning and once again the animal began to bleat vigorously. To the hikers' astonishment, the farmer again said he'd come back the following morning. They all met again on the cliff top the next day. Now the sheep was exhausted and its cries were weak and desperate. The farmer calmly attached a rope to a tree trunk and climbed down to the sheep; he laid it on his shoulders, where it lay helpless and secure, and he carried it to safety. The farmer had waited till the sheep's cries had turned from a selfish, vigorous bleating, to a cry of weak surrender.

We are never to forget that God will intervene and hear us but He will wait till He may have us in His arms in full surrender to His love and grace. We want the trial to pass, but God wants a deeper outcome than we imagined. We are obsessed with getting off our precarious ledge and trotting off once more to vigorously explore the terrain. God wants us off the ledge, but much more fully yielded to His arms of love.

ᨁᨁᨁᨁᨁᨁᨁᨁᨁᨁᨁᨁᨁ

May 23

I do not cease to give thanks for you, making mention of you in my prayers: that the God of our Lord Jesus Christ, the Father of glory, may give to you the spirit of wisdom and revelation in the knowledge of Him, the eyes of your heart being enlightened. (Ephesians 1:16-18)

We live in an age of information. Facts and knowledge are all at our finger tips with the internet, online books and encyclopaedias. But the apostle is not praying that we will have ever more information, but rather that we would have revelation and wisdom.

Revelation cannot be obtained by force of intellect but rather by an attitude of heart. It is a gift of grace and so can only be received by the humble. Revelation leads to transformation in contrast to information. Revelation imparts more understanding in a second of time than years of study. It is the difference between learning how to swim from a book compared to the moment we actually get into the water. Then, all that we have learned comes alive and is relevant. Revelation touches springs in the heart that trigger the unfolding of long dormant faculties. Worship and singing rise up and flow out of the heart towards God. Depths of beauty are released as when a flower bud is opened up by the light of the sun. God in all His beauty impacts the heart and we are inspired to rise up and live with joy and anticipation of all the beautiful things God will yet do. We admire His handiwork - the flowers, the mountains, the rivers - but when we see Him we realise that we have only appreciated the beauty of God in the 3-dimensional world we live in. God is another dimension and we see in Him the source of all beauty in shimmering, unfathomable depths of personality and love. We will never tire of gazing at God, because His being is infinite in solemn profundity, heights of soaring joys and oceans of inexpressible peace and tranquillity.

With revelation comes wisdom. Wisdom is not knowledge but the ability to apply it to our daily walk. Wisdom is the foundation of a soul that is aware of God and lives in the awareness of His presence. Foolishness is to live as if God were not there, but once He is revealed, we are equipped to walk in the supreme mindfulness of God with us at every moment of our journey through life.

~~~~~~~~~~~~~~~~

May 24

My brethren, count it all joy when you fall into various trials, knowing that the testing of your faith produces patience. But let patience have its perfect work, that you may be perfect and complete, lacking nothing. *(James 1:2-4)*

James is here inspiring the believers to a right attitude to personal sufferings through various trials. He urges them to catch the joy that is surely coming in the future when the ordeal has had its full effect. No matter how deep the trial, it will have a good effect in the end and we are to fully absorb this as a settled and sure promise of God that no suffering will be void of meaning and reward. This is not fatalism. Atheists must inevitably be fatalistic since in their world-view there is no guiding hand that is protecting them. This is rather a positive challenge to fully grasp the message of Scripture that trials are like the first buds of spring that promise good things to come. God is not a cruel despot, ruling the universe with indifference to the griefs of the human race. God is loving and in His sovereign oversight of every life, He has committed Himself to use all things for good.

James challenges the reader not only to catch the coming joy, but to fully embrace the trial, to learn its meaning. God is here explaining to us that we can view the trial as a nuisance to be avoided at all costs or we can receive it with positive expectation that God is answering our prayers to save us and our loved ones. If we count the trial as a bothersome interlude, we may even have to repeat the lesson because we didn't get it the first time round! Joseph would never have chosen the hard path of suffering that God planned for him, but it led to a blessing for thousands if not millions of people. Through Joseph's suffering, God provided a way of escape from famine for all the surrounding nations including his own family. God has chosen paths for us to walk in and we must recognise that fact and embrace His will with eager anticipation of the blessing that will surely follow.

May 25

"Come to Me .. for I am lowly in heart ... and you will find rest for your souls." (Matthew 11:29)
"Zacchaeus, make haste and come down." (Luke 19:5)

It is a huge shock to realise that God has a depth of humility that far exceeds our grasp. God is always lower than us, which is why He is so full of compassion and understanding for the weak, and why He is never cynical or distrustful. He knows the pride and subtle ways of our hearts and He cheerfully bids us abandon our ridiculous high tower and come down.

We blow up a big balloon of moans and convoluted reasons why we are right to be depressed or fearful. Then God comes and with one word completely exposes our foolish pride, which has caused all the trouble. We put on airs and graces, we pout and we defend ourselves, and all the time God has seen through us and knows that we are much weaker than we have ever admitted and we are more flawed than anyone has ever seen. Yet all the time God is inviting us to join Him in His perspective of things. The moment we stop our childish bluster is the moment we are free. Zacchaeus was so full of self-importance that he probably didn't realise how ridiculous he looked to the crowds. The moment we grasp that God knows what we are like is the moment we are free to be ourselves and simply walk up to Him and receive Him.

When Zacchaeus descended from the tree into the arms of Jesus, he must have felt all the tension slipping away. He found at the feet of Jesus the power to be a new man and the power to throw off pretence and receive the love of God to be the new atmosphere of his life. "Come down" is God's constant command to His people, and He urges us to do it with haste, lest the moment pass and we find ourselves stuck on a perch that is blatantly precarious.

~~~~~~~~~~~~~~~

May 26

For if we have been united together in the likeness of His death, certainly we also shall be in the likeness of His resurrection. (Romans 6:5)
That I may know Him and the power of His resurrection, and the fellowship of His sufferings, being conformed to His death, if, by any means, I may attain to the resurrection from the dead. (Philippians 3:10-11)

Telugu is the language of Andhra Pradesh in India and their word for a caterpillar is 'gongalipurugu', which literally translated means "blanket insect." It perfectly describes human life with the heaviness of a body that is destined to grow weaker and one day die. The caterpillar weaves a chrysalis for itself and lies still for anything from a week to a winter. It then emerges, not as a caterpillar but as a butterfly. The Telugu word for butterfly is 'sitakokachiluka', which means a bird wearing the sari of God, or loosely translated: a bird with divine clothing.

Some think of the Christian hope as merely life after death, but it is infinitely more than that. The caterpillar is constrained by its heavy body, unable to fly, unable to lay eggs, unable to eat nectar. If the caterpillar has to travel even a short distance, it is faced with insurmountable obstacles. The butterfly, on the other hand, can rise above everything and cross even rivers and hills on the breezes that bear it up. The Christian hope is that one day we shall exchange this heavy blanket for the soaring wings of a heavenly life. It is impossible to grasp the change that will be ours at the Resurrection. The man who died beside Christ was given the assurance of being in Paradise by the end of that day, but that was still not the Resurrection. When we die, we are forever with the Lord, but one day we will be clothed with an amazing new body.

The teaching of Paul in Romans is that we can know the spiritual transformation of Resurrection right now in our inner life. We can embrace death to sin and unbelief and rise to a life of rising joy and victory. Once we have tasted the spiritual power of death and resurrection, we will be motivated like Paul to focus our whole being on this one great hope: to attain to the Resurrection of the dead.

May 27

And this is the testimony: that God has given us eternal life, and this life is in His Son. (1 John 5:11)

"One thing I do know: that though I was blind, now I see." (John 9:25 NASB)

Someone once said that a man with an experience is not at the mercy of a man with an argument. This is in the end the foundation of Christian testimony. Christians are not all clever debaters, though we thank God for those who are gifted in that realm. Christians are witnesses to something that they have experienced in their life or seen with their eyes. Paul affirms that he and all the apostles were eyewitnesses to the Resurrection and explains that anyone who denies the supernatural Resurrection of Jesus Christ has denied the Christian faith and made her founding apostles liars.

The truth is that Christian assurance does not rest only on the logic of Scripture but on the power of the Holy Spirit that has worked an undeniable work in our hearts. Lazarus did not rise from the dead because he had insight into a few scriptures. He rose from the dead because He heard the voice of the Son of God calling into his tomb and waking him from death. There can be no doubt that from that moment scriptures were flooding through his mind with breath-taking illumination.

The Bible and the Christian faith are under constant attack, but the final line of defence is that we were once dead in trespasses and sins but that God has given us eternal life. This is not an argument, it is a fact and the joy and wonder of the gift of eternal life is the strength of the soul when all hell is targeting us. Never forget the foundations of your assurance and put on the armour that protects against the fiery darts of darkness. Never forget the change that came over your soul like the sudden release of perfume that was the gift of life when you bowed and surrendered your life into the hands of Christ.

~~~~~~~~~~~~~~~

May 28

Be still, and know that I am God; I will be exalted among the nations, I will be exalted in the earth! (Psalm 46:10)

The greatest thing that can be said about God is that He is God. Worry and fear assail us when we think that God is less than God. God is the Creator and Sustainer of all things. He made the material and the spiritual world. He fashioned and sustains the measureless physical universe. He made the angels, both faithful and fallen ones, and He created all human beings, no matter how sinful. He sustains and permits all beings to exist in His infinite wisdom and works to a plan that is perfect and unstoppable. Peace will come to us as we grasp the significance of the being of God.

God is, moreover, majestic in His pulsating glory and goodness. God is beautiful in the unfathomable depths of a mind and imagination that produced an infinite universe, the eye of an eagle, the colour and magnificence of the orchid and the blend of green meadows, snow-capped mountains and the blue sky. Yet all of these are as nothing compared with the beauty of His love and grace. Earth seems dull when we grasp that God is Himself a fourth dimension, with a being that is not breath-taking because of size but because of unfathomable depths of life and character. Moments spent in the stream of God's self-revelation are transforming and empowering, uplifting and ennobling. Those who know God are robed in garments of wonder and brightness that are the reflected glory of His being. The work of man is to exalt God and enjoy Him forever. In truth exalting God is not the duty of the kingdom, it is the mark of it.

May 29

And from the days of John the Baptist until now the kingdom of heaven suffers violence, and the violent take it by force.
(Matthew 11:12)

This is at first sight one of the most perplexing things that Jesus said. It flies in the face of his earlier declaration: "Blessed *are* the meek, for they shall inherit the earth." (Matthew 5:5) It is inconceivable that strong, dynamic personalities should be able to force their way into God's presence and advance in the kingdom of heaven through the power of their will.

This is, nevertheless, an accurate translation, but the violence is not to be directed towards God but towards sin and self. It is easy for Christians to become weak and flabby spiritually, and here Jesus indicates that the kingdom must be taken with the exercise of radical action. We must be merciless with our whining, simpering self or we will one day find that we have lost our affinity with the "old rugged cross". We are prone to desist from prayer, from actively loving others because we don't feel energetic enough. There is a great danger that we will yield our lives to a reasonable and rational argument that rises from our love of comfort and an easy life. Churches may have many wooden crosses on their walls, but even more cushions in the pews. The words of Jesus are a constant challenge to follow Him in a life with no place to lay His head and a readiness to give up big and little things to keep our lives in the freshness of His wonderful companionship.

From prayer that asks that I may be
Sheltered from winds that beat on Thee,
From fearing when I should aspire,
From faltering when I should climb higher
From silken self, O Captain, free
Thy soldier who would follow Thee.

From subtle love of softening things,
From easy choices, weakenings,
(Not thus are spirits fortified,
Not this way went the Crucified)
From all that dims Thy Calvary
O Lamb of God, deliver me.   *Amy Carmichael*

~~~~~~~~~~~~~~~~

May 30

He who is not with Me is against Me, and he who does not gather with Me scatters abroad. (Matthew 12:30)

The Christian life is a war and here Jesus gives a most heart-searching definition of the terms of this war. If our hearts are lukewarm towards the things of God then we are God's enemies and are actively scattering and discouraging the people of God and the work of God. If we are not actively involved in helping, then we are making things worse.

This is shocking to most believers and means that many whose commitment to Christ is shallow are a barrier blocking the way of life to those who wish to enter. The famous Indian evangelist Sadhu Sundar Singh suffered terrible persecution. His family poisoned him and he nearly died. He was often fiercely opposed in his love for Christ and his bold witness to the gospel. But the only time when his faith wavered was when he went to Bible school and lived with students whose commitment to discipleship was weak and their lives were worldly and carnal.

'No man is an island' and there can be no doubt that our lives are a powerful force for good if only we will attend to the inner flame of first love for Jesus. The believer who has a real and consistent love for Him will build the kingdom of God whether they know it or not. The battle is intense, but it is incredibly personal and begins with the leaning of our inner affections. We may not be able to make ourselves outstanding Christians, but every day we decide which way our hearts incline, and the outcome is that we are either for Him or against Him. Rise up and receive the grace that will enable you to love the Lord with all your heart and soul and strength!

May 31

Go into the village opposite you, and immediately you will find a donkey tied, and a colt with her. Loose them and bring them to Me. (Matthew 21:2)

Billy Graham's son Franklin is a pilot and was flying in the USA when his 4-seater plane lost electrical power. All his instruments, including lights and communications, went dead. He turned the plane to the nearby Thompson airport in Jackson, but the small airport was in darkness and he had no means to get his bearings. Suddenly a green light was shining from the control tower and he was able to get a line on the airport. As he approached, the runway lights were suddenly switched on and he quickly landed, and then the lights went off. After they had parked, they found the airport deserted.

Some months later he was recounting this story and found out what had happened. An airport administrator Sydney MacCall had been demonstrating the airport facilities to a Baptist minister and his wife. He had briefly held a green light out of the control tower window demonstrating how he would guide a plane in. Then the minister had been allowed to switch on the lights for a few seconds. They had been astonished to hear a plane land but had thought no more of it.

It is staggering to think what apparently random processes led to these moments of miraculous intervention. Franklin Graham would have probably died if Sydney MacCall had not been at that small airport at that precise moment. In the case of the donkey that was waiting for the disciples to collect, it is fascinating to imagine what random decisions were taken that day to get everything in place. Things may seem random but there is an overruling loving mind that is closely involved with everything that happens.

When situations reach a crisis point and spin out of control, we are to remember that behind the scenes there is a guiding intelligence that has perfect timing. God is never too late or too early. A day is coming when all will be revealed and we will fall down and bless the hand that guided and the heart that planned.

June 1

For you were once darkness, but now you are light in the Lord. Walk as children of light. *(Ephesians 5:8)*

We all know what we were, but do we know what we have become? The Christian life is built on a deep transformation of our life by the grace of God in salvation and the power of the baptism with the Holy Spirit making us one with Christ. Then it is a process of discovering what we have become. We simply have to believe that we are who God says we are and that we have what God says we have.

When we put our trust in Christ God changed the whole foundation of our standing before Him. Before we stood condemned, now we stand before Him clothed in perfect righteousness. He sees no difference between us and His Son. What is more we possess all the power of victory that He won on the cross. The Bible does not tell us to attain power over sin, it says that we have it. The Bible does not tell us to try and be light, it tells us to let our light shine.

We are apt to judge our power in prayer or our standing before God by our feelings. Every Christian is more than he or she knows or feels themselves to be. We are a royal priesthood, a holy nation, seated with Christ in heavenly places. We are a new man but with an old way of thinking. We cannot evolve into a new man, we must simply put off the old every time we catch ourselves contradicting the word of God. We must simply start walking in newness of life. We need to put our hand on our chest and say "I am a man/woman of prayer," "I am full of the love of God," "I am righteous through faith." The chant of the enemy is to undermine everything God says about Himself and about us. The path of victory is to boldly confess what God has made me. I am a precious, beloved, righteous child of God and I'd better start walking and talking like one!

June 2

So Moses brought Israel from the Red Sea; then they went out into the Wilderness of Shur. And they went three days in the wilderness and found no water. Now when they came to Marah, they could not drink the waters of Marah, for they were bitter. Therefore the name of it was called Marah. And the people complained against Moses, saying, "What shall we drink?" (Exodus 15:22-24)

The children of Israel left the place of supreme victory and after three days they had completely forgotten what God had done. There is a terrible capacity in human personality to completely forget wonderful things that have happened in the past. Jesus commanded the church at Ephesus to remember the past blessings (Revelation 2:5), and the communion bread and wine are to stimulate the church to remember the cross.

The staggering fact is that no blessing of the past can be a substitute for faith in the present. We must simply never forget in the darkness what God has said and done in the light. Faith is not to have the constant beam of revelation filling our souls. Faith is to stir ourselves to remember and act in accordance with what we have seen and known in the past.

In Mark 6:44, Jesus fed 5,000 men plus women and children, but within a few weeks (Mark 8:4) the disciples found themselves in an identical situation and had forgotten what Jesus had done. When we are faced with impossible situations, the challenge is to stir our hearts to walk by faith, remembering that God never starts a thing merely to give up half way.

The simple truth is that blessings must be turned into a walk of faith. No Christian is powerful because of something in his past but only because of his present walk with the Lord. Walking with God requires stillness of heart to ponder His faithfulness and steadfast love. The greatest praise rises in the darkest night and the sweetest worship comes from hearts that pour out songs when there is yet no sign of dawn. Remember, rise and sing to God, for His help is on the way.

~~~~~~~~~~~~~~~~

June 3

And Moses said to the people, "Do not fear; for God has come to test you, and that His fear may be before you, so that you may not sin." (Exodus 20:20)

The Bible is not written in English, which is a bigger language than Hebrew or Greek. So English has 5 words for one Hebrew word. Fear may mean 'dread', which is the horrible feeling that bad things will happen. But fear also may mean 'reverence'. This is the loving respect of a son to his father.

God repeatedly charges us not to fear but at the same time instructs us to fear God. The lordship of Christ is not through any threats, it is through the willing surrender of loving children who delight to do His will. It is impossible to love God without reverencing Him, for love is the true foundation of the fear of the Lord. When Abraham had passed through the trial of offering Isaac on Mount Moriah, the Lord declared that He now knew that Abraham feared Him. One might have expected God to say "Now I know you love Me." By this, God was teaching all who follow Him that glad obedience from a heart full of awe is the mark of a truly loving heart.

We glibly say things like "I love ice cream" and it is true that some people love God on that level. It indicates that God is their latest fad or that God fits in well with their world. But the love of Jesus for His Father was that of One whose whole being was bowing in radical, uncompromising obedience to the Father's will. This is the atmosphere of heaven: love that inspires reverence and worship. It is by such reverential love that we take our seat in God's kingdom in the company of angels who have never disobeyed Him, and beside the Son of God, who lives to do His Father's will.

The fear of the Lord is the beginning of wisdom and without it we are prone to make foolish choices and fail to understand what God is doing in our lives. Once we fear God, we are pointing in the right direction, and in tune with the hosts that surround the throne.

∞∞∞∞∞∞∞∞∞∞∞∞

June 4

"We who are Jews by nature, and not sinners of the Gentiles."
(Galatians 2:15)

When Paul says that he is a Jew by nature, he does not mean that Jews are of a different genetic make-up. He is referring to the power of Jewish culture through the Bible to form their values. One might say that for a Jew, Sabbath observance is second nature since it is in the very fabric of their life. The truth is that all of us have a 'second nature', formed by the habits of a lifetime and by the words we heard from our parents in our earliest years. This is not the nature of sin that is common to both Jew and Gentile. It is simply the power of nurture as opposed to nature.

The Holy Spirit renews our hearts, setting us free from sin, but the habits of a lifetime must be renewed gradually as we meditate in the word and obey the truth. Peter writes about this and says that we have purified our souls through obedience to the Holy Spirit. It is vital to recognise the subtle leaning of our minds. Many have a very negative nature, which is easily sceptical and questions whether a thing is really true. Others have very low self-esteem, even hating themselves. It is vital to swim against the tide of our own minds and put on the mind of Christ.

The mind has the power to grieve and hinder the Holy Spirit in us, but also has the power to release the flowing of truth by the power of God in us. When we speak or think negatively, we are to catch ourselves and put that thinking aside. The Bible is to shape our minds and become our second nature. We are to make it personal and not treat it as an impersonal text book. It is describing how God thinks about us and we are to agree with God! "God so loved …." may be familiar to us but we are to put our name there and realise that it is God's attitude to me personally. If we really knew what God thinks about us, we would be ashamed of the way we have often contradicted him through negative words and attitudes. Prophesy to yourself by constantly making Scripture personal and bit by bit you will be amazed to find that Christ is being formed in you.

June 5

And Jacob their father said to them, "You have bereaved me: Joseph is no more, Simeon is no more, and you want to take Benjamin. All these things are against me. (Genesis 42:36)

The sad thing about Jacob's words is that they were completely untrue. Joseph was not dead, but even if he were, faith would still confess "the lad is not dead, he is asleep". Simeon also was alive and safe in the hands of his loving brother Joseph. Jacob's sorrow was self-centred and as such it was destructive. His sorrow was shaped by self-pity which made him the centre of his view of the world. His sorrow was bottomless because it lacked faith.

Faith affirms that God is in control in the midst of apparent disasters. Faith places God at the centre not me. The whole situation affects the Father in heaven much more than it affects any of His children. He can no more forget us in our distress than an earthly father can sleep while his child is crying out in pain. We are to decisively refuse the temptation that says that pain is meaningless. Jacob's anguish was mental, but Joseph's was real. Joseph was sold into slavery and was confined to prison in chains (Psalm 105:18), without hope of release. Yet he was blessed with abundant favour and all that he did prospered, even in the prison. Joseph kept a sweet spirit even when the whole universe seemed to be conspiring to harm him. This is the faith that made Paul exclaim "If God *is* for us, who *can be* against us?" (Romans 8:31).

We must jealously and zealously guard our hearts from any indulgence in self-pity, whether things are going well or badly. God is on our side and we must let the soaring faith of the Son of God shape our inner attitude. There is a sorrow that must be repented of lest we reckon without God. God is in control and we will one day see what He is doing behind the scenes.

June 6

Likewise you younger people, submit yourselves to your elders. Yes, all of you be submissive to one another, and be clothed with humility, for "God resists the proud, but gives grace to the humble." Therefore humble yourselves under the mighty hand of God, that He may exalt you in due time.
(1 Peter 5:5-6)

God is an implacable enemy of pride in all its forms. The chief ingredient of true faith and love is humility. Pride is the source of all hurts, jealousy and unbelief. Pride is the root of all evil. It is the poison of Satan that deceived humanity into believing we could stand alone and succeed without God.

God is faithfully cultivating true humility in us because He Himself is humble and completely devoid of every whiff of this deadly venom. The humility of Jesus Christ was not an unnatural act for Him, it was the most obvious path for God to take since that is precisely what He always does. At the same time, there is not a whiff of craven, abject humility about the Son of God. The dismal, hand-wringing humility of a Uriah Heap is a cloak for the worst fungus of human pride.

True humility is to take our proper place in utter child-like dependence on God. There is a cheerfulness and lightness about everyone who throws off their self-importance and stops taking themselves so seriously. Our days are to be full of joy and laughter because we have stopped carrying around the heavy load of pompous posing as important people. Humiliation is waiting around the corner for the proud, but truly humble people are surprised that anyone would attribute any power or virtue to them, since they know it all comes from God. The humiliation of Christ simply revealed the dazzling brightness of a life that was utterly free from the Satanic disease of pride and was free to respond with a triumphant love that could absorb and destroy the worst that demons and men could throw at Him.

~~~~~~~~~~~~~~

June 7

And whatever you ask in My name, that I will do, that the Father may be glorified in the Son. If you ask anything in My name, I will do it. (John 14:13-14)

One of the most critical moments in the life of any believer is when our prayers seem to go unanswered. Some of us pout and posture as if we have been deeply let down or misled. Some withdraw into a protective shell of resignation and passivity. Some are angry and resentful. All these reactions are indicators that our hearts were not right when we first prayed.

Prayer is not the exercise of sovereign free-will. It is our appeal to the only truly free will in the universe. God waits to be asked and has promised that all those who come before Him in the right frame of mind will find the sceptre of royal favour extended to them. God's sovereignty does not deny free-will, it defines it. Free-will is real but is a gift of grace, not an absolute right.

Modern man has reversed the role of God and man. Some treat God as if He were a waiter in a restaurant ready to spring into action at the flick of our fingers. Anyway, God should be grateful that we back Him since He isn't very popular these days and needs all the support He can get. After all, we are successful, educated, wealthy and enlightened and we are just the kind of people He needs on His team. Celebrities especially show considerable grace and favour to God because they are busy people facing heavy demands on their time...

The heart that truly loves God will praise Him for His wisdom and kindness in the way He gives us what we ask <u>and</u> when He declines. Job expressed it best:

"And he said: "Naked I came from my mother's womb, And naked shall I return there. The LORD gave, and the LORD has taken away; Blessed be the name of the LORD." In all this Job did not sin nor charge God with wrong." (Job 1:21-22)

Prayer enthrones God in my life and dethrones my foolish pride.

June 8

Then Joshua spoke to the LORD in the day when the LORD delivered up the Amorites before the children of Israel, and he said in the sight of Israel: "Sun, stand still over Gibeon; And Moon, in the Valley of Aijalon." So the sun stood still, And the moon stopped. (Joshua 10:12-13)

These verses describe one of the most incredible moments in the Bible narrative. The science behind this miracle is so breath-taking that one hardly dare think about the implications. One day all will be explained and we will understand how it happened.

This massive event has a parallel in our lives, because when we get into the direct presence of God it is as if time stops. Watch Jairus walking with Jesus as the news is brought to him that his little girl has passed away. Jesus turns to him and speaks:

"Do not be afraid any longer; only believe." (Mark 5:36 NASB)

At that moment, the world stopped revolving and Jairus was lifted out of time into a confrontation with the absolute, limitless sovereignty and power of God in the person of Jesus Christ. It was at that moment that Jairus's grief ebbed away and a sense of the majesty and control of Jesus Christ replaced his turmoil with peace. It is in the hushed, unhurried calm of His being that we discover that He can do whatever He wants and no-one is able to stop Him. There is only one sovereign will in the universe and though that will can never break the laws of science and nature, it can override them because God is above them.

God intervened on the cross, turning back impossible levels of corruption and decay and healing a fallen humanity. When God raised Lazarus, He demonstrated that nothing is too hard for Him. No-one is too far gone that He cannot redeem them. Enter the hushed calm that is Jesus, let sun, moon and stars and racing time stop and all hurry cease. Let the commanding presence of Jesus banish unbelief and watch Him do His good pleasure.

~~~~~~~~~~~~~~~

June 9

Abraham believed in the LORD, and He accounted it to him for righteousness. *(Genesis 15:6)*

The Hebrew word for faith is also the word for trust. Abraham trusted his life into the hands of God, surrendering his life and his future into God's care. God's response was to treat Abraham as a perfectly righteous man. The Bible does not say God forgave Abraham, though that is included in what God did. God saw Abraham as possessing the same qualities as His Son, who is the only measure of virtue that He recognises. God henceforth received Abraham's prayers as equal to the prayers of His Son.

All who believe in Jesus are partakers of this spectacular and daring act of grace. Grace L. Fabian, a missionary to Papua New Guinea called it "Outrageous Grace". It is as if God receives us into His primary school and gives us the highest doctorate degree the moment we sit down to learn the alphabet. We are certain to make mistakes and even blunders on our path but God never flinches from His set goal to present us one day as actually perfect as He ascribed to us the moment we started.

God ascribed righteousness to Abraham on day one and then set about the long task of shaping his character into the image of Christ. Abraham's greatest errors still lay before him, but underlying everything he did was a simple child-like trust that God meant what He said no matter how impossible it seemed. Abraham had still to grasp the enormity of God's power to fulfil His word, and tried to help God along the way. But through it all, God's unswerving plan was unfolded. Our salvation glorifies God because it is all of grace from first to last. Our contribution is to trust and even that is a love gift from God.

June 10

Teach me Your way, O LORD; I will walk in Your truth; Unite my heart to fear Your name. *(Psalm 86:11)*

But He, knowing their thoughts, said to them: "Every kingdom divided against itself is brought to desolation, and a house divided against a house falls." *(Luke 11:17)*

It is common wisdom that a nation divided must fall. The same is true of a church and in that case the consequences are deep and cause much harm. But by far the worst and most common form of division is a divided heart. If our inner life is pursuing two opposite goals, then it is certain that we will miss both. The prayer of the Psalmist is a cry for a deep work of the Holy Spirit to so purify the desires of his heart that he will be enabled to walk steadfastly in the way of the Lord.

This is the constant prayer of the pilgrim as he realises the paralysis of being one's own worst enemy. The prayer for a united heart is answered by the cross as our selfishness and pride are slain by the Lord. Jesus Christ is a master surgeon of the human heart and able to cut out attitudes and tendencies that are causing us to be uncomfortable in our own skin. Whenever we are tempted to blame others for our inner disquiet, we must pause and look within. We must lay bare our inner being to Jesus and pray that He will cut the disease out of us and give us a single eye that looks up to Him.

There is boundless joy when we discover the peace and power of a heart at rest in the Lord. There is such positive power when a church is united in energetic pursuit of one goal. The same is true of us when our heart is focused without distraction on Jesus. Watch out for the small ambitions that stubbornly resurface whenever we set our hearts on prayer or committing ourselves to serve God. We are to release the flow of the commanding presence of God as we are united with the heartbeat of God. Then we discover the incredibly unhurried and steady focus of the Holy Spirit on glorifying Jesus Christ. Without a whisper of condemnation, all heaven leaps for joy when we are back on track.

June 11

In this you greatly rejoice, though now for a little while, if need be, you have been grieved by various trials. (1 Peter 1:6)

Beloved, do not think it strange concerning the fiery trial which is to try you, as though some strange thing happened to you.
(1 Peter 4:12)

One of the most common temptations during times of suffering is to believe that these trials are somehow an indication that things are out of control. We panic because we believe we have put ourselves outside of the sovereign plan and will of God and are subject to random forces and influences. We may even blame ourselves and seek the source of our problems in our conduct, believing we have brought these disasters on ourselves. This is what Peter meant when he said we are not to think it strange when we find ourselves in deep trials.

It is precisely at times like this that we need to remember that God is faithful and will never leave us. Yes, we may feel a strangeness about the path we have to take but God is still in control and directing things for our good. Nothing has taken God by surprise. Peter was prophesying their coming day of trials so that they would know that God was aware of them long before they came. Equally, God planned what He would do to strengthen His people through this period and also has prepared a banquet of celebration at the end. If we knew what God will do at the end of it all, we would be filled with joyous anticipation. This is why James exhorted the believers to "Count it all joy when you fall into various trials." (James 1:2).

We are to guard our hearts above all things when we are tempted to lose hope, or to blame ourselves or to believe that God has changed. God is the same. His love and mercy never end. He is with us and sends touches of comfort and encouragement when His children are in distress. We must look up and sing in the storm and boldly assert that all these things are part of a great and perfect plan that will bring glory to God and unspeakable blessing to us His people.

June 12

But we see Jesus, who was made a little lower than the angels, for the suffering of death crowned with glory and honour, that He, by the grace of God, might taste death for everyone.
(Hebrews 2:9)

Christ was made a little lower than the angels that He might die our death. Many of us will have tasted unpleasant things in our lifetime. I myself have eaten several kinds of snakes, scorpions and many strange exotic dishes, but none of them made me ill. What Jesus tasted was the decaying mass of human evil, more akin to putrid food that has attracted maggots and poisonous bacteria. The word 'taste' may also mislead us into thinking that he simply dipped his finger into the bowl of human corruption. The truth is that He absorbed into Himself the full and awful power of sin and destroyed it.

The answer to sin is Jesus and when He agreed to take sin away, He bore it away in Himself. What happened on Calvary is a mystery but it is the greatest news that can ever be proclaimed: no-one need remain a slave of sin any longer.

The only power greater than sin is Jesus and for this reason we must receive Him into our darkness, into our unbelief, and let Him be Himself in us. It is not the power of human will nor the degree of our zeal for Jesus that will set us free. It is simply the action of receiving Him to be my life and continuing to walk in heart union and fellowship with Him. It is not something that God does in us that sets us free and keeps us free. It is simply what He is. For this reason, the most important thing I ever do is to build a relationship with Jesus of constant surrender to His wonderful, triumphant life. He destroyed my darkness so that I might have His light, His holiness and His inner life. This is not surrender to tyranny, this is surrender to the loving arms of our best friend, who wipes away our tears of shame and failure and imparts the poise and joy of a Christ-centred life. The Christian life is not striving and straining, it is the simplicity of delighting in Jesus.

June 13

You prepare a table before me in the presence of my enemies; You anoint my head with oil; my cup runs over. (Psalm 23:5)

The image that is conveyed by this verse is of a table furnished with abundance, but lurking all around in the shadows are a host of enemies. At the same time, God is ministering, anointing and filling our hearts with His life.

As an image of spiritual warfare, it is remarkable that God is bidding us look not at our enemies but at the ample provision set before us. The table is set with the body and blood of Jesus, the very essence of who and what God is. There is no cup of fear or condemnation, no bread of curses, no taste of worry in the food that God provides. In fact, all these things are the enemies around us. The power to overcome is to keep feasting with Jesus at God's table.

The contrast is stark: there is joy and fullness set before us, and terrible darkness all around seeking to distract us. Our lives are shaped by the things we do and the things we neglect. Feast on joy and neglect your enemies. The joy and peace of the Lord are unconscious weapons of great effect and by them our enemies are scattered.

Just look again at the table: it is not set with a dry crust but with the abundance of God's gifts of joy and peace as we fellowship with Him. He welcomes us and anoints us, thereby honouring and empowering us. No-one but He would pour and pour until our cup is full and then overflowing. Delight yourself in the Lord and whether you know it or not, you are conquering unseen enemies all the time.

~~~~~~~~~~~~~

June 14

I will instruct you and teach you in the way you should go; I will guide you with My eye. Do not be like the horse or like the mule, which have no understanding, which must be harnessed with bit and bridle, else they will not come near you.
(Psalm 32:8-9)

Have you ever longed for God to give you some vision or dream or even grant you to see an angel or hear an audible voice? God does indeed grant all these blessings but they are rare and they cannot form the basis of a relationship with God. In some measure they are outward not inward forms of communication. If they were the only means by which God made Himself known, then we would be like horses or mules needing the occasional sharp pull on the bridle.

While many of us have been blessed with such extraordinary touches of grace, we will also readily acknowledge that the foundation of our spiritual life is the inner witness of the Holy Spirit. He grants that little gentle tug on the heart that alerts us to His will. He grants an inner disquiet if we are tempted to make a step in the wrong direction. Most of all, He reveals Himself as we wait on Him and as we rise up from communing with the Master, our hearts have been melted and changed. Without realising it, we know what to do without any misgivings or doubts. We are being guided by God's eye as He keeps watch over us.

The most precious possession of the Christian is our inner witness, by which we perceive God and know His will. This faculty is our life-line, our anchor and our sure foundation. We are to keep a quiet heart and heed the whispers of His grace. We are also to rest secure in the assurance that we are His sheep and we do hear His voice. Even in the storm, His unmistakable tones will come clear, assuring us that we are His and He is in control.

June 15

I affirm, by the boasting in you which I have in Christ Jesus our Lord, I die daily.   (1 Corinthians 15:31)

Watchman Nee once placed an open coffin at the entrance of the meeting hall. The believers wondered who had died and looked into the coffin. They were shocked to see their own reflection in the mirror that Watchman Nee had laid inside.

Believers have the privilege of going to their own funeral and rejoicing over the fact that by faith we have passed through the gates of death and out in resurrection. We are to go to our funeral every day and remember that the power of the Christian life lies in the realisation that when Christ died, I died.

Jesus Christ was the deadest man who ever lived. He was dead to money, to sin, to reputation and the opinions of people. He responded to mockery no more than my car does or a dinner plate. Of course, He was at the same time the most alive man. He was alive to the presence of God, to the voice of the Spirit and to the presence of angels or demons. The truth is that it is not a question of whether we will die, but which death we will die. We can either die daily to self and sin or we will die daily to God and His kingdom.

Anger, frustration, impatience and lusts are all marks of being alive to the world and sin, and we must embrace our death with Christ and do it daily, even hourly if necessary. The cross is a door of escape and it is a perfect door. Beyond it lies the bliss of life, God's own peace and love imparted to those who lose their life and exchange it for a greater one.

~~~~~~~~~~~~~~

June 16

Therefore the LORD will wait, that He may be gracious to you; and therefore He will be exalted, that He may have mercy on you. For the LORD is a God of justice; blessed are all those who wait for Him. (Isaiah 30:18)

It was a cloudless sky over the mangrove swamps in Cameroon. A small group of pastors and evangelists had spent the weekend proclaiming the gospel in one of the most remote corners of the earth. They loaded their little boat and were ready for the three-hour journey back to the mainland. The little outboard motor refused to start and a note of frustration crept into the little band. Time passed and they sat around praying and longing for the engine to burst into life. Suddenly someone shouted "Tornado!" and they lifted their eyes in horror as a freak storm bore down upon them. They took cover in the little huts of the village as the gale passed over them. After an hour the wind had subsided and the boatman returned to start the engine. He had hardly touched it before it sprang into life. It took only seconds for the whole group to realise that this delay had saved their lives. If they had been on the open sea when the storm struck, they would all have perished.

It is not every day that we have such a stark lesson before our eyes of the benefits of waiting for God's timing. It is one of the supreme facts of life that we are to learn patience and trust that God is in the delay and that we are to praise Him and thank Him in the midst of a thousand things that frustrate us because we have so little awareness of the majestic foresight and sovereign rule of God.

Mary and Martha had to wait seemingly in vain for the Lord to come and heal their brother. But God is never late and He knows what is happening in our hearts. He longs for us to look up in trust and turn the waiting into a deepening of our faith as we raise our voices in praise. Catch yourself next time you are tempted to complain because of heavy traffic, or a cancelled flight or prayers that have been prayed for years without an answer. Turn the moment into a declaration of trust and praise to God, who will pour out His abundant grace in due season.

∼∼∼∼∼∼∼∼∼∼∼∼∼∼∼

June 17

Fear not, for I am with you; Be not dismayed, for I am your God. I will strengthen you, Yes, I will help you, I will uphold you with My righteous right hand. (Isaiah 41:10)

One of the everyday realities of life in many African countries is the police checkpoint. I was once driving through a city called Loum in Cameroon and as I was leaving the last check point, I heard a shrill police whistle. I assumed it was for someone else and kept driving. A friend in the car commented that he thought they had been trying to stop me. I kept driving but my imagination began to work overtime and by the time we reached our destination I was convinced that the police had my number plate and would be calling round to see me at any moment.

That night I couldn't sleep and I tossed and turned in the grip of fear. I woke up exhausted and tried to pray but I couldn't concentrate. It suddenly hit me what had happened. Fear had become my master and I was paralysed by it. Now fear is a merciless master and will whisper into our ears all the dreadful outcomes that are awaiting us. I turned and faced my fears. I accepted that the police might come and they might take away my driving licence and give me a stiff penalty. There were indeed many possible bad consequences that could transpire. But none of them was the problem. The problem was that fear had become my master. I surrendered my heart to Jesus and fear melted away.

The truth is that we are all going to die. But if we live in the fear of death, then our life is ruined by our obsession with that unchangeable fact. Through fear we are under the lordship of other powers, such as sickness, pain or disaster. In truth, we may pass through many trials but we are to fear none of them. God will be at our side and we will conquer everything by resolutely bowing to Jesus alone. David passed through the valley of the shadow of death more than once. He fought many battles and passed through many dangers, but through it all came the clarion call "I will fear no evil."

June 18

So I prophesied as He commanded me, and breath came into them, and they lived, and stood upon their feet, an exceedingly great army. (Ezekiel 37:10)

It is remarkable that the valley of dead bones was the remains of an army and as soon as life came into them they immediately became powerful warriors. That is precisely what God's life produces in everyone who receives Him.

The world is made up of three groups of people. On one extreme end are people who have sold themselves to do evil, including witches, Satanists and many other practitioners of spiritual wickedness. This group of people are terrified of the Bible, of praying people and of those who live lives yielded to God.

The second group is precisely those who have yielded to the Spirit by a deep transaction and have transferred their ownership from self to God. They are deeply conscious of the limitless and explosive power of the Bible. They open it with reverence and wonder, aware that it holds commanding sway over the destinies of all human beings.

The third group are the majority of the human race, who are completely unaware of this battle raging in heavenly places. Their lives are marked by a deep spiritual indifference. In short, they are anaesthetised to spiritual reality and completely passive in the conflict of the ages unfolding around them in the unseen world. Satan's plan is to keep people firmly in this group.

God's life has put the warrior within us and it is time for us to rise with supreme faith in our captain and engage heart, soul and mind in loving God and praying and proclaiming His word. Satan is terrified because the battle has already been fought and won. There is a great cry of victory in the heart of every Christian and we are to let it out and watch the enemy flee in terror.

June 19

One thing I have desired of the LORD, that will I seek: that I may dwell in the house of the LORD all the days of my life, to behold the beauty of the LORD, and to inquire in His temple.
(Psalm 27:4)

It is common to hear people talk of their 'bucket list', meaning the things they want to do before they die. Some want to parachute, see the Grand Canyon, fly in a helicopter etc... But no pleasure or exploration can be compared with the wonder of a moment in the presence of God. Whether we live in frozen wastelands or desert heat, the presence of God is merely a step away.

But though the step is small, it is only open to those who have renounced everything else to make it. Any pleasure seekers may tour the earth, but to enter the presence of God requires clean hands and a pure heart. This purity of heart is not perfection but has all to do with priorities. Once God is our one thing, then we are on track. God will not take second place, nor will He accept a place as an equal alongside other interests. He is either first or He is nowhere to be seen. Jesus said that the generation He lived in was spiritually adulterous because they loved religion more than God.

Yet if one could simply distil God's presence to a drink, it would be the most sought-after beverage on the planet. God's presence is exquisite and is the very definition of all beauty. After a few moments beholding God, we wonder how we could ever have seriously had any other goal. A glimpse of God has the effect of awakening all the spiritual senses which were previously dormant or even dead. Beholding God kills all the unbelief and hopelessness of the heart. God looks at us and in one moment it is as if He sees all the tangled complexity of our soul, calmly says: "Let me take that away from you" and it is gone in a moment. God is beautiful and it is not the 3-dimensional splendour of mountains or waterfalls that we see. He is life on another plane and we cannot access that life except by being with Him. He is no fool who abandons a diet of dust and narrows all his goals down to knowing God. For truly, all life's pleasures without God are vain and empty. Knowing God is eternal life and is the only life worth living.

June 20

From that time Jesus began to show to His disciples that He must go to Jerusalem, and suffer ... Then Peter took Him aside and began to rebuke Him, saying, "Far be it from You, Lord; this shall not happen to You!" But He turned and said to Peter, "Get behind Me, Satan! You are an offence to Me, for you are not mindful of the things of God, but the things of men."
(Matthew 16:21-23)

Jesus gave this stinging rebuke to Peter that he was mindful of the things of men not the things of God. The things of men are all to do with the short-term view. For this reason we are mindful of self-preservation and eager to maintain our comfort and personal security. But God has a larger view of things and His view contains fathomless depths of suffering and pain that lead to resurrection and immeasurable victory.

It is at this point that we realise that Satan is not seeking to draw people into debauchery or witchcraft. His plan is to encourage us to build our little comfortable world and push out the bigger, more challenging issues of eternity. There is a big ocean of life in which we will be tested to the limit, in which we will be exhausted and stretched beyond what we thought possible. But through it we will catch the unfolding eternal plan of the ages: to create humanity in the image of Christ, who lives on the altar of eternal living sacrifice to the will and plan of God. We will catch the upward current of purpose that would empower us to be participants in the conflict of the ages for the souls of men and for the glory of God.

Peter loved the teaching of Jesus, but he wanted to limit the Master and contain Him in the pattern of familiarity that all human beings treasure. But the Master is not to be tamed. He is ever pressing forward on the great call of the ages to partake of an astonishingly extraordinary life. God has created an amazing humanity. The outstanding qualities of this God-filled life will only be proved as we launch out on the adventure of the ages in fellowship with this incredible love- filled person called Jesus.

June 21

Who is wise and understanding among you? Let him show by good conduct that his works are done in the meekness of wisdom. (James 3:13)

Knowledge puffs up, but love edifies. (1 Corinthians 8:1)

James is writing his short letter to expose the danger of a decline into merely intellectual Christianity. If this corruption has taken place, believers will assume that someone is wise because they understand difficult theological concepts or are able to explain difficult passages of the Bible. But James here shows that this a great error.

True wisdom is not found in knowledge or in the accumulation of facts. It is found in the application of that knowledge to daily life and practical living. Wisdom is therefore to be measured by acts of kindness that are done in secret. A wise person will have kind words for troubled souls. A wise person will be aware of the needs of others around them and reach out to meet that need, either by praying for them or by giving generously of their substance.

The true foundation of wisdom is therefore love. The greatest fool who ever lived is one who never loved. The wisest person of human history is not the quick-witted or the one who parades their knowledge. Such things are signs of the awful heart malady called pride. Paul said that knowledge puffs up but love builds people up. Intellectualism most commonly leads to pride, which is the exact opposite of love. We often think that hatred is the opposite of love but this is flawed thinking. Pride is obsession with myself, while love is found in those who are freed from self and have abundant room to be conscious of others. Intellectualism stuffs the mind with ideas and the soul becomes a crowded room stuffed full of furniture that is never used. Wisdom frees the soul to be adapted to meet the needs of those around us.

If we would be wise, we must ask how we can bless others with acts of kindness, not how we can display our superior knowledge. Once this is understood, the heart will abandon all illusions of grandeur and humbly seek to be a tool in the hands of God to express His amazing love.

June 22

And when you pray, do not use vain repetitions as the heathen do. For they think that they will be heard for their many words.
(Matthew 6:7)
And Moses would return to the camp, but his servant Joshua the son of Nun, a young man, did not depart from the tabernacle.
(Exodus 33:11)

One of the most important lessons in prayer is to distinguish different kinds of prayer. Golf and football are both types of sport but are completely different in every imaginable way. To confuse the rules of each game would be disastrous in the extreme. The same is true of different kinds of prayer.

The first kind of prayer is to present our supplications to God. When we come to God with a deep burden, we are to unload that burden by asking for God's intervention with all the passion and desire of our heart. However, we are never to slip into the error of thinking that God is somehow affected by our many words. He hears the cry of our heart and will answer our plea.

The second kind of prayer is to reach out in communion with God. Joshua did not spend hours in the prayer tabernacle of Moses repeating and repeating his petitions. Joshua was enjoying the communion of heart-to-heart fellowship with God. It is in such times of prayer that our hearts reach out to know God, to drink in the wonder of His matchless being. As we linger in the presence of God, our hearts begin to beat in time with God's heart. Often, we ask for nothing as we simply absorb the atmosphere of life that awakens us to be more alive than we could ever have imagined. It is in fellowship with God that our sense of need is transformed. Many things we might have prayed about simply vanish from our minds. Other things are written so large across our hearts that we know that God is aware of the currents sweeping our inner being in a way that words could never communicate.

Prayers of petition are common to all humanity. Even people who don't believe in God will say a prayer as they enter an examination hall or go under the surgeon's knife. But prayers of communion are precisely what God Himself is longing for. As we wait before Him, we realise that He is reaching out to us much more than we are for Him. We are often in danger of fussing over things in prayer rather than resting in the wonderful arms that sustain the universe.

~~~~~~~~~~~~~~~~~

June 23

"Assuredly, I say to you, if you have faith as a mustard seed, you will say to this mountain, "Move from here to there," and it will move; and nothing will be impossible for you."
(Matthew 17:20)

The difference between a grain of mustard seed and a mountain is colossal. The power of this truth lies in the self-evident fact that a mountain cannot be moved by any human effort. But once faith is operating, the door is open for God to step in. For God, a mountain is no harder to move than a feather.

The answer to the weightiest problems and the most grievous circumstances is simple faith. A mountain of cares or an ocean of griefs are heavier on the human heart than Everest. The good news is that there is a faculty of the human heart created and activated by God that can dislodge the deepest fears and the most impossible of obstacles. Whether our problems are small and trivial or mountains with 'impossible' written all over them, in the end we are faced with a simple choice: "Will I believe God or not?"

The moment I choose to believe, the tranquillity of God's infinite power and majesty begins to seep into my mind and soul. A consciousness begins to form that the problem is over, the sorrow is passing and the dawn of a new day is appearing. The evidence of the new thing God is doing is not a change in my circumstances but the simple beauty of faith. Faith precedes the miracle. Jehoshaphat did not command the priests to praise God once they saw God begin to work. They were to praise God before the battle had even begun. David declared that Goliath was in trouble before he got anywhere near his giant-sized enemy. God's people are not in trouble, Satan is in trouble and, moreover, he has lost from the moment we dare to believe God. It is not the size of faith that is key, it is the fact of faith. Look up and praise God with the quivering voice that rises from mustard-seed faith. Faith is not an option, it is the only path available. A grain of faith is by its very nature stronger than mountains because it is the bond that establishes partnership between an individual and God.

~~~~~~~~~~~~~~

June 24

I have written to you, young men, because you are strong, and the word of God abides in you, and you have overcome the wicked one. (1 John 2:14)
Therefore submit to God. Resist the devil and he will flee from you. (James 4:7)

I once had the privilege of staying for a week with the Masai in Tanzania. The young men pass the test of manhood by killing a lion. An evangelist proudly showed me the teeth marks of the lion on his arm which he had suffered when he and a group of about 5 young men had passed the test. Fighting physical lions seems like madness but the truth is that the world is full of predatory beings - some human, some demonic - and these are equally if not more dangerous than the animals that roam the African plain.

While we may not wish to engage in battle, yet there is no other way to attain spiritual maturity. There are battles we must fight alone and we will have to face the tempter and overcome him. It is remarkable that in order to overcome him all we must do is persistently and determinedly repulse him by rejecting his lies and confessing the word of God. When Jesus fought Satan in the wilderness, He quoted the Scripture three times, and it is vital to catch the rising joy and authority that fills the soul that affirms the truth of God when our backs are to the wall.

We must gird ourselves with the belt of truth, take up the shield of faith and fight. The astonishing thing is that Satan's boldness is all noise. He has been rendered powerless by the blood of Jesus. As soon as we fight, we are conscious that Satan is a defeated foe. The Bible bids us "Ascribe greatness to our God." (Deuteronomy 32:3) It is to fall into the devil's snare when we acknowledge any greatness of power or skill to Satan at all. This is the path of maturity: to stand our ground and purposefully and steadfastly resist the enemy of our souls.

~~~~~~~~~~~~~~~

June 25

When you give to the poor. (Matthew 6:3 NASB)
And when you are praying. (Matthew 6:5 NASB)
Whenever you fast. (Matthew 6:16 NASB)

Jesus in His teaching on spiritual life assumed that His followers would regularly engage in all three of the above exercises. He did not say 'if' but 'when' you give, pray and fast. The fact is that true faith gives, prays and fasts. Fasting includes the relinquishing of all things that weaken the inner life of fellowship with God. We are to let go of indulging in anything that distracts us from the primary source of life which is God's presence. Some need to fast from television, others from social media. Modern life clamours for our attention and we are to realise the battle that is raging to keep us from walking closely with God.

The soul that does not pray is trusting in his own power and wisdom to get him through life, through trials, through crises. Often when deep trials come, we are awakened to seek God's face and we are to keep these habits of relying on God when the trial has passed.

The truth is that these things are not means to an end. They are the end itself. Prayer is not just a lifebelt to rescue us from the waves, it is to be the boat into which we climb. The prayers of desperation are to turn to prayers of deep communion. God sometimes allows troubles to get our attention, and when they pass, we are to make sure that we learn the deeper lessons that God will always be there for us when we need Him, but, most of all, He is longing for undistracted times of friendship when we make Him know that He is more important to us than anything. All the trees of Eden offered delicious fruit and all but one were permitted. The tragedy of Adam and Eve is that, as far as we know, they neglected to eat the tree of life. If only we would eat His flesh and drink His blood, we would be strengthened to overcome all temptations. The way to the cross, the tree of life, is open again. Let us turn from every other tree and feast on undisturbed fellowship with Christ.

June 26

Now I say this, that each of you says, "I am of Paul," or "I am of Apollos," or "I am of Cephas," or "I am of Christ."
(1 Corinthians 1:12)

Paul wrote to the Corinthian church concerning their divisions and it is easy to identify their error of following a preacher such as Paul (Calvin? Wesley?), with his amazing revelations, or Apollos with his intellectual depth and grasp of the Bible. But how could it be wrong to say "I am of Christ." Don't we all belong to that party?

The answer lies in the subtle shift from truly spiritual love for Jesus to the Pharisaical sense of superiority that looks down on others and that has nothing in common with Jesus. It is astonishing how easily we slip from deep gratitude for the matchless grace of God to self-righteous despising of others. We might think we understand some part of Scripture better than others but we disqualify ourselves when we look down from our perch on others who have not attained our lofty heights of spirituality. The purer our doctrine,
 the greater the tragedy.

The Corinthian church had lost the anchor of the cross in Christian conduct. Perhaps the most supernatural mark of spirituality is when we genuinely esteem others better than ourselves without a whiff of affectation. When a Christian is truly a messenger of the cross, it will always mean that they have found the power of the supernatural love of God that inspired the cross. This love is a healer of hearts, a cure for divisions and a well-pleasing fragrance of Christ that melts all obstacles and disarms the confrontational.

To be truly of Christ means that we are filled with love for others. It indicates that we are currently actively engaged in washing the feet of our fellow disciples. It means that we have truly grasped the heart of Jesus and joined him in the sacrificial love for those with whom we have little in common. Love breaks down walls, builds bridges and is full of kindness and gentleness. Love builds no cliques, never condemns the failing and never slights or belittles holiness. Love draws all to the feet of Jesus, where all hearts are healed and everything wrong is put right.

June 27

Now when they heard this, they were cut to the heart, and said to Peter and the rest of the apostles, "Men and brethren, what shall we do?" (Acts 2:37)

Peter's sermon was very powerful and convicted the hearers of their need to act. It is remarkable that the preacher had omitted to tell them what to do and it was the dismayed cry of the listeners that made Peter continue to tell them the most important instruction of all.

All teaching, preaching and Bible study must ultimately lead to a change of conduct and action or it will simply harden our hearts. To hear without action is to become dangerously familiar with the most challenging truth we could ever encounter. If we can read the Bible and not be disturbed, then we are not reading it in the right way. "Leave all! Sell all and give to the poor! Love your enemies! Pray without ceasing!" The flavour of the Bible is to challenge every person to the roots of their being and provoke a heart response that results in action.

If the gospel is merely internalised, it will lead to intellectual excellence but moral mediocrity. We must constantly ask what we must do and we must act quickly. We know that we are saved by faith, but that faith must be the kind that changes our conduct. Scripture teaches that judgment day will be on the basis of whether we have visited the sick, clothed the naked and fed the hungry. Jesus taught that those who build their house on the rock are those who hear His word and do it (Matthew 7:24).

The Holy Spirit is called the Comforter, which is a selective translation of the word 'paraklete'. It can also be translated 'exhorter' and exhortation is the cry of the Spirit to bring our lives into line with what we know. The Holy Spirit will teach us many things but He will always end in beseeching us and even begging us to turn faith into action. The Holy Spirit is not a beggar, but He may beg us, as a father will plead with his son, to do what is right and abandon a path that leads astray. Listen to the exhorter and catch the urgency of His voice and the passion of His pleading.

June 28

Furthermore King David said to all the assembly: "My son Solomon, whom alone God has chosen, is young and inexperienced; and the work is great, because the temple is not for man but for the LORD God." (1 Chronicles 29:1)

The title of a book "How to be my own best self" reveals the trend in the 21st century to construct a world that revolves around me. The Bible teaches that such a mindset will lead to sadness, not to joy and fulfilment. Often we may have the impression that the gospel is all about our forgiveness and cleansing through the blood, and this is largely true. But there is a greater underlying purpose to the cross and to the work of salvation, namely that God is glorified.

Everything from the stars to the birds is for the glory of God. All things find their calling and well-being when they are focused on God and exalting Him. When an alcoholic bows before Jesus, that individual is set free and blessed, and most of all God is glorified. Everything that takes away from God's glory will ultimately weaken the work of God. Pastors may sometimes bask in the praise and appreciation of their congregation but in so doing they have occupied a seat that is reserved for God alone.

Praise and worship may subtly shift the emphasis from glorifying God to feeling good. When God is glorified, we are most at ease with ourselves because we are free from self-obsession. Finding the place of praise and worship is not about flattering God, but about steadfastly looking away from all other things and getting gripped with the beauty and majesty of holiness that pulsates and streams from God. Worship opens a window on the soul that heals us of our deepest malaise, mainly because we cease to be concerned with how we feel. We are joining in the song of all creation that is repeatedly nourished by God's delight in His people.

June 29

And the God of peace shall bruise Satan under your feet shortly (literally: quickly). The grace of our Lord Jesus Christ be with you. Amen. (Romans 16:20)

There is a calm confidence expressed by Paul in his final greeting to the believers at Rome that they shall quickly prove full victory over the powers of darkness in their walk with the Lord. Paul in Romans had surveyed the vast power of the cross to neutralise guilt and destroy the rule of sin, thus liberating believers to a life of holiness through the power of the Holy Spirit. But what may surprise many readers is that this is the first and only time in the whole book of Romans that Paul mentions Satan. Moreover, he has not one word to say about demons.

It is indeed liberating to realise that God does not direct us to focus our attention on our enemy but rather on our walk of faith in the finished work of Christ. In truth, the arch-enemies of the human race are sin and self and as we believe in the love and forgiveness of Jesus and the cleansing power of the cross, we will find ourselves having swift triumph over the attacks of the wicked one.

Satan is terrified of Jesus Christ and is powerless to stop a person being liberated and transformed as soon as they bow to the crucified and risen Saviour. The cross is a place of immeasurable conquest of all the enemies of the human race. Make it your habit to bow with heartiest surrender to Jesus. Then let the peace and calm assurance of God's promise renew your mind and impart the relief that all the hosts of darkness cannot touch the weakest believer that trusts in Christ. Satan cannot touch those who love Jesus, and he fears the faith that rises in us and prays for those still in darkness and have not yet heard that the reign of darkness is over.

~~~~~~~~~~~~~

June 30

We have the mind of Christ.   *(1 Corinthians 2:16 NASB)*

Let this mind be in you which was also in Christ Jesus.
(Philippians 2:5)

Imagine if someone suggested you had the mind of Einstein or Michelangelo. We would surely laugh at such an impossibility, but God tells us that through the indwelling Spirit we do have the mind of Christ. The mind of Christ is of course infinitely greater than any human intellect, since He created and designed the human race. His mind has huge resources of artistic and intellectual ability, but the greatest qualities of His mind are not intellectual but moral.

Winston Churchill, with razor-sharp wit, said of Clement Attlee: "Attlee is a very modest man, and he has a lot to be modest about." That could be said of every human being, but it could never be said of Christ. He has nothing to be humble about: He is the infinite, almighty, everlasting God and yet with all these breath-taking qualities, He is humble. He treated every human being with respect, especially identifying with the poor and the outcast. He was indifferent to comfort and wealth and was completely at ease in the company of sinful, hurting people. There is no whiff of a religious 'holier than thou' approach. The Queen of England might stoop to have tea with a lowly subject of her realm, but Jesus would abandon His palace and live in the poorest part of town.

The astonishing truth is that a Christian has access to this mind. We are able to embrace the lowest lifestyle, letting go of position, reputation, comfort and privilege to serve those around us. We are called to serve others with joy, not to be served. When we pray for God's will, we will always be challenged not merely to find an activity that pleases God, but most of all an attitude. God's will is not where I live, it is how I live, and God gives the astonishing intellectual and moral power to be clothed with the mind of Christ.

~~~~~~~~~~~~~~~

July 1

And Moses placed the rods before the LORD in the tabernacle of witness. Now it came to pass on the next day that Moses went into the tabernacle of witness, and behold, the rod of Aaron, of the house of Levi, had sprouted and put forth buds, had produced blossoms and yielded ripe almonds.

(Numbers 17:7-8)

The rod of Aaron that Moses placed before the Lord in the Holy of Holies was a dead piece of wood that had been cut from a tree many years before. It represented Aaron himself and the life of all believers. We are as dead and fruitless as that staff and completely incapable of producing even the smallest evidence of life. It is a complete and utter impossibility for any person to produce a loving heart in themselves, though we may occasionally do a good deed that vaguely resembles love.

Love is a fruit of God's own presence acting on the dead wood of our lives. God's holy presence – the Holy Spirit - activates something deep within the core of our being and the result is the stirring of life. Aaron's rod budded, produced beautiful flowers and even yielded edible fruits in the short space of one night. When God commands us to love one another, He is commanding us to cooperate with Him to produce the conditions in which love can grow in our hearts. Love is a fruit, not a work. Imagine the most fragrant blossoms and the sweetest oranges and we can begin to imagine the wonder of what it is to love. Love is not a means to an end, it is the goal itself. Love is God's blueprint for humanity. It is the reason we exist and the reason God persists in drawing us back to His presence.

Love is more beautiful than the most stunning orchids, and sweeter than the sweetest fruits. Yet none of God's created flora and fauna ever loved anyone. Love can only grow in a human life. It must be cultivated with care and attention, keeping ourselves firmly in the pulsating life-giving presence of God. God's presence burns off disease and destroys the selfish attention-seeking which is so contrary to love. Love has a depth and a mystery that are as unfathomable as God Himself. Only the one who has discovered the grace of loving can ever grasp the depths of joy and peace that adorn the soul that truly loves.

~~~~~~~~~~~~~

July 2

They complained against the landowner, saying, "These last men have worked only one hour, and you made them equal to us who have borne the burden and the heat of the day."
(Matthew 20:11-12)

"Now his older son was in the field. And as he came and drew near to the house, he heard music and dancing. So he called one of the servants and asked what these things meant."
(Luke 15:25-26)

In these two parables, a note of complaint enters the heart of the long-serving faithful servants and of the son who had remained faithfully serving at home while his brother wasted his life. The cause of this grievous state of heart was the loss of delight and wonder at serving such a great master, of being sons of such a great father. The gift of salvation is so beautiful but years can tarnish our appreciation of the unspeakable gift of grace. Familiarity may make us even begin to think we have earned some special reward.

The older son asked the hired servants the cause of the joy in his father's home. He had lost the delight of being a child and had begun to acquire the mind of a hireling. He related to paid workers more than to his father. The switch is subtle and gradual and may not be noticed until the flame of love has burnt so low that it is almost extinguished. The depth of his fall is revealed when he rebuked his father with the words: "You never gave me…" (Luke 15:29).

The reward of being saved is that we are children of God. Our inheritance is to sense the father's smile and joy and to bask in His radiant love. The moment we want some payment from God, we take a step into the shadows. The way back is to rediscover the simple fact that there is no higher calling, no greater joy, no higher achievement than being a son or daughter of the living God. We are to find sheer delight in doing the will of God – yes, we are to enjoy being Christians! Turn your back on the dreary path of hirelings and let the burdens roll away. God's great arms of love are open to all his children - those who get lost in distant lands and those who lose their way in the midst of faithful service. Let the music of God's love and the delight of His dancing heart be yours today and every day.

~~~~~~~~~~~~~~~

July 3

That your days may be multiplied, and the days of your children, in the land which the LORD sware unto your fathers to give them, as the days of heaven upon the earth.
(Deuteronomy 11:21 KJV)
Your will be done on earth as it is in heaven.
(Matthew 6:10 NASB)

It would be easy to interpret these verses in terms of material prosperity since our minds so quickly relate to conditions full of comfort and security. But is that a right view of heaven? Certainly heaven has no cruel guards or barbed wire, but heaven on earth is to find God in any circumstances.

Corrie ten Boom was in Ravensbruck concentration camp for women during World War II. Conditions were so bad that approximately eighty women died every day. One cold, frosty morning they were woken by the head of their barracks at 4 am, an hour earlier than normal, and called to assemble in the camp square. They were cold, with their ragged dresses hanging loosely on their gaunt bodies. Corrie walked with her sister Betsy and they talked to the Lord. They could see the crematorium, the gas chamber and the towers where the guards looked on with their machine guns. The presence of God drew near, making Betsie exclaim: "Isn't this a bit of heaven? And Lord this is a small foretaste. One day we will see You face to face, but thank You that even now you are giving us the joy of walking and talking with You."

Heaven on earth must always have an element of paradox since this earth is so full of shadows and snares. But this is precisely the greatness of this promise, that God will bring heaven into the most hellish corners of earth, into the vilest settings. Whether it be a bed of sickness, a difficult working environment or even a concentration camp, we can discover the kiss of heaven and the smile of God. As amazing as it may seem this paradox has a profound logic to it. It is so often in distress that we turn from the shallow best bliss that earth offers and drink deeply of the fountains of living waters in the true paradise of God.

∽∽∽∽∽∽∽∽∽∽∽∽

July 4

Thus says the LORD: "Let not the wise man glory in his wisdom, let not the mighty man glory in his might, nor let the rich man glory in his riches; but let him who glories glory in this, that he understands and knows Me, that I am the LORD, exercising lovingkindness, judgment, and righteousness in the earth. For in these I delight," says the LORD.
(Jeremiah 9:23-24)

The key to all of life is to know Jesus. Through that knowledge we have salvation, power to live and the strength to overcome sin and darkness. This knowledge is not gleaned from books alone but is primarily imparted through life's events. It is through the convicting power of the Holy Spirit that we open our hearts to Jesus and are saved. It is as we spend time with Him that we learn to walk by faith.

The believer is to learn the art of asking in all of life's circumstances what God is teaching us about His Son. When the disciples battled to cross the sea of Galilee through a fierce storm, Jesus came walking over the waves declaring "Be of good cheer! It is I; do not be afraid." (Matthew 14:27) After the resurrection, when they had fished all night and caught nothing, Jesus stood on the shore and suddenly John exclaimed "It is the Lord." (John 21:7) Whatever circumstances you are passing through, it is certain that the Lord is in them. He is in the storm and in the moments of testing and trials in the wilderness. He is at the wedding and the funeral. He is surrounded by children and questioned by austere rabbis. He cooks a breakfast and serves His disciples with a smile of contentment. He is on the mountain-top bathed in blinding glory.

Whenever we think we know Him, God takes us into fresh circumstances where we feel out of our depth. And so it must be because Jesus is so easy to know and yet always beyond our grasp. He is so deep and vast that it will take an eternity to know Him. Don't rush through life so fast that you miss His voice calling in the situation you find yourself in right now. Thank God for the things that bring you up with a jolt and make you look around to ask with fresh wonderment "Who are you, Lord?"

~~~~~~~~~~~~~~

July 5

Now it came to pass, in the days when the judges ruled, that there was a famine in the land. (Ruth 1:1)

The period of the judges was one of the darkest in all the history of Israel. There was spiritual and moral chaos as everyone did that which was right in their own eyes (Judges 21:25). But in the midst of a confused and unruly nation, God was still working His great purposes out in the lives of individuals. The book of Ruth focuses on three people - Naomi, Ruth and Boaz - and their gentleness and kindness to one another.

This is of enormous significance because it teaches us that the events in the so-called corridors of power are often irrelevant. What really counts are the words and attitudes developed in the closest relationships around us. We may have great programmes and plans for our churches, our families, our businesses and our communities. But all of these are of no importance compared to the love we express to one another. Ruth was kind to her mother-in-law. Boaz was thoughtful and caring towards this impoverished foreign woman who was gleaning grain from his fields.

Human life is a constant process of sowing and reaping. Programmes are like cold inanimate machines. The only seeds that will multiply and change the world for good are the beautiful prayers and actions that rise from lives that have stepped back from the rat race and grasped the eternal power of love. We are often tempted to exalt the fact that we are busy people. In fact the Bible exhorts us to the opposite, to take time for the only two things that matter: God and people. If we rush past either of these on our headlong pursuit of success, we shall one day find ourselves surrounded by lifeless things and weep great tears of regret. Every day is another opportunity to live for eternal things by simply reaching out and touching lives with that infinite love that has shaped us.

July 6

Though He slay me, yet will I trust Him.   *(Job 13:15)*

The greatest joy a human being can bring to God is to love Him for who He is, rather than what we get from Him. The greatest reward for one who loves God is to know Him. Jesus Christ was at complete ease as He passed through life because He had attained His goal of companionship with God. All other pursuits were secondary to this one great inward passion.

The apostle Paul came to the same inner poise which he expressed when he said that he counted everything but loss for the excellence of knowing Jesus Christ, esteeming other achievements as rubbish compared to Him (Philippians 3:8). Job had this same focus and it was proved when blessings were withdrawn. In his sickness, bereavement and loss of material wealth, Job remained unmoved. Job loved and trusted God for Himself.

Horatio Spafford lost nearly all his substantial investments in the fire of Chicago in 1871. Two years later he lost 4 daughters when the ship they were travelling in sank on its voyage across the Atlantic. Spafford then penned the amazing hymn "It is well with my soul." It is precisely in the darkest moments that our hearts are sifted and we make our deepest life choices. This was the faith of Meshach, Shadrach and Abed-Nego when they chose to be burnt alive rather than deny their faith. This was the faith of Jesus when He died for the sins of the whole world. It was God's will and plan that brought Him to Calvary. It was the Father who offered up His Son. This was demonstrated in a prophetic action when God led Abraham to offer up his son.

We are invited by God to choose Him above all other things, to allow Him to take things away as well as give them and to praise Him in sickness and in health. We may pass through many trials but their purpose is to produce the pure gold of a faith and love that is triumphant though it be in desperate weakness. Whatever our circumstances, let everything that has breath trust the Lord and sing His praises.

∼∼∼∼∼∼∼∼∼∼∼∼∼

July 7

But the fruit of the Spirit is... faithfulness.
(Galatians 5:22 NASB)

There was once a factory foreman who was responsible for the sounding of the klaxon that indicated the finish of the working day. He knew he must be 100% accurate and took comfort from a watchmaker whose shop he passed every day on his way to work. In the window was a clock and he always set his watch by it. One day the watchmaker was standing in the door of the shop and he stopped to thank him. "How do you get it to be so accurate?" he asked.
"That's very simple" he replied. "I listen every day for the klaxon in the factory since I know the foreman there must be very careful to keep good time."

It is often true that we judge our faithfulness by comparing ourselves with other Christians. When Daniel the prophet was exiled in Babylon, he was offered unclean food from the king's table. Later he was threatened with death if he would not desist from his habit of praying three times a day. Daniel may have seen thousands of compromising Jews around him who may have argued that it would do no harm. But Daniel set his watch by what he discovered in the secret place with God.

The nature of God is the very bedrock of the universe. God, like the sun, runs His course with totally predictable regularity. God has never broken a promise, never uttered anything that was not true and He has never disappointed anyone who believes in Him. God is faithful and that quality is imparted to everyone who loves and receives the oxygen of His being. The faithfulness of God is the characteristic of all who love His living presence.

Daniel was a man of prayer, holiness and clear witness in his working environment. But the quality that undergirded all of these was his faithfulness, which was of such depth that even his enemies knew that no matter what the consequences he would never stop. We must be faithful in our love of His presence and set our spiritual clocks by what we see there.

July 8

But the fruit of the Spirit is self-control. (Galatians 5:23 NASB)

Self-control is essentially the power to say "No." It is most manifest when we have the strength to withhold from saying something. It is also the ability to refrain from some desire of the body, be it for food, drink or in the sexual realm. As soon as we mention the word self-control, we think of the exercise of an iron will in the face of fierce temptation.

Paul here reveals that this most godly quality is a fruit of the conscious presence of God in us. The great implication of this is that our failures rarely have to do with our weakness of will to abstain from something. The source of our sin is precisely that we so easily neglect the pursuit of the conscious presence of God. Adam and Eve ate of the tree of the knowledge of good and evil, the tree of self-realisation, but it is also certain that they never tasted of the tree of life. If they had eaten of that tree, it is possible they would have been strengthened inwardly to resist the temptation to satisfy their desires.

God is here revealing to us that the power to overcome lies in the positive things that we indulge in. Paradise has many trees: the tree of prayer, the Bible and the fellowship of God's people, to name but the most obvious. All of these trees work in us because they are intended to be the means of discovering the life-sustaining divine atmosphere.

The tree of life was planted on earth on Calvary and the crucified body of Jesus is a torn veil back into the presence of God. The door is low, and all who enter in must do so humbly confessing their need. But the door is wide open, giving access to God's holiest presence. If we will only press in to breathe that air, we will be amazed that without realising it, we are empowered to overcome all the temptations that come our way. We are able to say "No!" because we have uttered a resounding "Yes" to Christ in us, who is the power of holiness.

~~~~~~~~~~~~~~

July 9

Five of you shall chase a hundred, and a hundred of you shall put ten thousand to flight. (Leviticus 26:8)
If two of you agree on earth concerning anything that they ask, it will be done for them by My Father in heaven.
(Matthew 18:19)

There is great power in fellowship and unity. The Bible here teaches that there is not an addition of power but a multiplication of it. If a person can find another with whom they are one in spirit and prayer, then their faith and effectiveness shall increase exponentially.

Take first the negative implications of this. One gossip can do some damage, but two gossips who unite to freely indulge in negative words can destroy a church or a ministry. Whether we realise it or not, there is a plan to recruit people to negative thinking in matters that are harmful to our spirit and to our fellowship with others. The word 'devil' is a Greek word 'diabolos', meaning slanderer or gossip. The activity of negative speaking is the work of the devil and must be heartily renounced by every believer. The enemy's work is to divide because he knows there is power in the unified fellowship of believers.

Take now the positive implications of this principle. When two or three join in the name of Jesus to pray and fellowship, His presence will be manifested. Where intercession is made from hearts united in purpose and passion, that prayer will bind forces of darkness and loose captives. Where love is joined with love, it will grow from strength to strength in influence on all around. God's plan is to gather to Himself a community of love from which He can rule and spread the fragrance of the gospel to every corner of the planet. This is a principle underlying the power and influence of a Christian marriage, of Christian friendship and most of all of the power of local assemblies. As with all things, we must set our mind and will on treasuring the unity of the Spirit and enjoying the sweet benefits that flow from it.

July 10

For what great nation is there that has God so near to it, as the LORD our God is to us, for whatever reason we may call upon Him? (Deuteronomy 4:7)

The human race is God's greatest creation. The brightest star in the universe is without the power of will or conscious expression. The sweetest orchid is blind and cannot interact with anyone. But a human being can appreciate beauty and express its wonder and delight.

The church is that part of the human race that has begun to recognise our amazing calling, to be God's companions through all eternity. This privileged status is not exclusive. It is God's original plan for all people. But once we believe, we become His people. This means that we have entered the courts of the Lord and have become His friends and companions.

God loves His people more than any earthly father ever loved his children. When a child is hungry, the parents can never rest till they have answered that cry. When God's people turn to Him, they have an exclusive avenue to the deepest part of His heart. Archimedes said: "Give me a lever and a place to stand and I will move the (planet) earth." God has given us a place to stand before His throne, not as mere supplicants but as beloved children, and from that place we have more power and authority than we can ever imagine. An American citizen must go through many channels if he wishes to have an audience with the president, but the son of John F Kennedy played with his toys in the Oval office.

To be a member of the church is not to be part of a bureaucratic institution but to be His beloved family. We have God's ear and whatever we are going through, we have the promise that all heaven's resources are ours through Christ.

~~~~~~~~~~~~~~

July 11

The fruit of the Spirit is love. (Galatians 5:22 KJV)
God is Spirit. (John 4:24 Author's translation)
God is love. (1 John 4:8 KJV)
God is light. (1 John 1:5 KJV)

The Bible reveals that God is Spirit. Spirit is uncreated being and not of this material universe. Spirit is the substance of another world and it is eternal and immortal. We are given the unspeakable privilege of spiritual life, by which we sense God in the deepest part of our being. Intellect alone cannot feed the spirit, nor can emotion. The heart longs for manna from another world and it is God alone who can feed us.

God is light and the Holy Spirit impacts our beings by revealing what is in us and leading us to repentance. The light is not physical but of the substance of Spirit, shining not on our faces but on our hearts. The light of God warms our hearts and transforms us into the image of God. His light is like radiation, destroying unbelief and sin and imparting faith and holiness.

God is love and the presence of God impacts the heart of the believer with waves of love, producing a deep peace through the consciousness that we are loved. While arguments may convince us of God's love, it is through the inner bathing of the heart in God's presence that we are settled in that love. Love removes all fears and anxieties and founds us on the unshakable rock of God's eternal love. Love is the strongest, most stable force and produces deeper foundations than we ever imagined possible. The person who is loved is granted an inner stability that can outlast the severest storms and goes far deeper than the anger and malice of Satan and men. Love is the power that conquered at Calvary, and it is that very love that clothes and girds everyone who believes and has received that love.

The deepest part of Christian experience is to believe and receive that love. It is in this that we are freed from lesser things and are empowered to love others. The effect of love is a serenity, an inner calm and an unquenchable hope that God will triumph over evil and turn all things to good.

July 12

But the fruit of the Spirit is... peace. (Galatians 5:22 KJV)

The source of war is the heart of man. Man is in conflict with himself and he can never attain inner harmony until Christ is the focus of his life. The conflict is extinguished by the miracle of a new birth placing Christ as the source and centre of the life. From that moment the Holy Spirit's activity is to maintain this relationship of giving Christ His rightful place in us. The Christian life is the school of learning to build our life around Him. He is the hub from which all things proceed.

Once this is understood, peace is no longer something to be attained but rather to be maintained. Peace wells up within the heart of the person rightly related to God. Christ is our peace for He is untroubled by the storms that afflict the world. He is unthreatened by any enemy, whether human or demonic. He is the unshakable rock on which the whole universe is built, and He is to be the centre of all things and not only my life. He is the centre of a harmonized universe.

We are not to strain to produce peace but to hold fast to Christ and then let peace arise through our mind, heart and will. This is then conscious salvation. The Christian who is at peace with God and himself will find that this is the place of power. This is the inner state of Jesus Christ, and the place from which He worships the Father. This is the place of true worship and victory, the calm clarity that enables us to overcome when we are tempted and make right decisions with true priorities. God's peace is to be the light in which we survey a troubled world. It is also the most powerful means of winning souls because the hearts of sinners fail with fear and longing for a place of refuge.

~~~~~~~~~~~~~~~

July 13

But only speak a word, and my servant will be healed. For I also am a man under authority, having soldiers under me. And I say to this one "Go," and he goes; and to another, "Come," and he comes; and to my servant, "Do this," and he does it."
(Matthew 8:8-9)

The centurion was in a community of authority. He was in submission to his commanders and consequently had genuine authority himself. If a person bought the uniform of a general in the army and began to issue orders to soldiers, he would be a laughing-stock because he has no place in the chain of command. A real general receives orders from those above him and he is backed by the full authority of the state. No soldier dare disobey a real general.

In the same way Jesus lived in the community of spiritual authority by being in entire submission to His Father. He also embraced the disciplines of living in the kingdom of God while in the place assigned to Him in the family of Joseph and Mary. Once we make authority a nebulous thing, we get into unreality. We must take our place in the ranks of God's servants. The moment we do, we sense that we are backed with all the authority of heaven. We may be tempted to take short cuts but the truth is we must learn to relate to God and those around us in simple submission.

Jesus was astounded at the simple but extraordinary faith of this man. He had not found such childlike faith in any Jew, whether among the Pharisees or among His chosen apostles. The centurion was conscious of the power of a word spoken by a man in genuine submission. Take submission away and words become meaningless. Those with genuine authority do not need to shout to demonstrate their power. A whisper is sufficient. The closer we get to God and to His people, the more we are clothed with faith and are conscious of the backing of Almighty God and all the armies of heaven.

July 14

For none of us lives to himself. *(Romans 14:7)*
It is good neither to eat meat nor drink wine nor do anything by which your brother stumbles or is offended or is made weak. *(Romans 14:21)*

Paul celebrates our freedom from sin (Romans 6:7) and our freedom from the law (Romans 7:6). But he does not by this mean absolute freedom from everything. He means we are now under the lordship of Christ through the Holy Spirit. The lordship of Christ is the lordship of love personified. Love is the great power that moves and directs a Christian.

Absolute liberty is the enthronement of self, but we are now joyous slaves of Jesus and of the love that flows through Him. We are not to think of what pleases us but rather what pleases Him and the people around us. The proof of this freedom is that we are no longer seeking to assert our own opinions and preferences, but we are free to give up things that may cause offence. No-one can claim to be free until they have given up some cherished opinion or indulgence for love's sake.

Hudson Taylor caused uproar in the expatriate community of Shanghai when he gave up his western hairstyle and wore a Chinese queue along with Chinese clothes. He not only gave up his western tastes, he also lost dignity in the eyes of his fellow Europeans. He was a laughing-stock at first but he was quickly followed by dozens of missionaries who followed his example. Hudson Taylor embraced the lifestyle of the people he wanted to win for Christ. In this he was an example to every Christian, since none of us is to live for himself but rather to please Christ and win others to follow and love Him. Apart from the gospel we are to let go of all our leanings, whether to do with our nationality, politics, food or culture. We are to identify with all we meet and to serve them with the fervent love of Christ. Jesus Christ laid aside His majesty, His conscious divine attributes and became a servant to fallen human beings. He so loved us that He became one of us. Love comes at enormous cost, and God paid the price in full on Calvary.

~~~~~~~~~~~~

July 15

Do you not say, "There are still four months and then comes the harvest?" Behold, I say to you, lift up your eyes and look at the fields, for they are already white for harvest!
(John 4:35)

Jesus told His disciples to lift up their eyes for the harvest when they had only just begun to walk with Him. To say they were ignorant and inexperienced is an understatement. Yet God bids all His children be ready to share the few crumbs we have gleaned with those around us.

It is one of the most common errors to think that I am being prepared for something in the future. J.O. Frazer prepared himself for the mission field by attending Bible school, learning the language and finally arriving among the people he wanted to reach. But it hit him while still at Bible school that he was to reach people around him and not to wait for the perfect circumstances in which he could serve God. God is here and now and there are multitudes around us who know nothing of the ways of God.

We tend to think that we are on a journey and the great day will one day come when we reach our destination. But God continually taps us on the shoulder and bids us forget about the future and live in the joy of the present. He is declaring to us that the journey is the destination. Travelling with God through life will never end. Eternity itself will not be motionless, like some scene frozen in time. Eternity will be the continuation of a voyage of discovery and of sharing with others the delight of knowing God. In this life we walk among lives shattered by tragedy and marred by sin. We will never have a greater opportunity to serve God than now. Never will there be a whiter harvest.

Lifting up the eyes is to realise that the gospel is not 'wait for special circumstances' it is rather 'repent and believe now!' The same principle is true for us. Walk with God and spread the fragrance all around. Love all and share generously the joy of the things you are receiving by your expedition into the uncharted territory of discovering God.

July 16

If you love Me, keep My commandments. (John 14:15)
Assuredly, I say to you that there are some standing here who will not taste death till they see the kingdom of God present with power. (Mark 9:1)

The kingdom of God is one of order and harmony whereas the hallmark of Satan is chaos, disorder, self-will and rebellion. In the ranks of saints and angels surrounding the throne of God, there is not one discordant note. The great mark of this order is obedience motivated by love. To kneel beside the mighty archangels Michael and Gabriel is awe-inspiring because they are strong, intelligent and totally obedient. The most awesome of all is Christ Himself, whose qualities shine with such radiance, and yet all the facets of His person are coloured and held together by the gold of complete obedience to the Father's will.

Believers display the kingdom of God by their glad surrender to the will of God and their complete submission to Christ and to one another. This is what makes the church a display of another world where love reigns supreme. The mark of this kingdom is unity.

The greatest display of the beauty of Jesus is in His total submission to the Father's will on Calvary. There Jesus destroyed the heart of rebellion and made it possible for sinners to be redeemed and clothed with the same love that motivates all of heaven. By the blood of the cross we have the same heart as Jesus. Yet this love is never robotic or mechanically automatic. We must follow the instincts imparted to us by the Holy Spirit and so joyfully and deliberately take our place, blending in with the hosts that love and adore the Lamb. Redemption is the building of order out of the chaos of a sin-wrecked universe. The mark of it is the laying down of my life for the glory and enthronement of Jesus. This is the kingdom of God come in power.

July 17

How lovely is Your tabernacle, O LORD of hosts! My soul longs, yes, even faints for the courts of the LORD; my heart and my flesh cry out for the living God. Even the sparrow has found a home, and the swallow a nest for herself, where she may lay her young - even Your altars, O LORD of hosts, my King and my God. (Psalm 84:1-3)

The call of the Lord is to dwell in His courts and know the delight of His presence. Our bodies are the temple of the Lord and this means that we are the inner holy place where He lives in holiness and transforming glory. Yet we are not to neglect our conscious fellowship with Him or we will lose the power of the place into which we have already been brought. We are not called to attain the glory but to allow the glory to shine within us. The Christian dwells between two worlds and we are to be shaped by the majestic presence of God within us. If we neglect the courts of the Lord, we will lose the brightness and our love will burn low. The world may crowd in upon the Christian and make the courts of the Lord seem distant and hard to attain, but if we simply turn, by faith, the fragrance of His being will rise like perfume in our hearts.

It is an astonishing fact that though the Lord dwells in the majestic authority of the supreme Ruler of all, yet the courts of the Lord are not austere and there is even a special welcome there for sparrows and swallows. The courts of the Lord ring with the praises of children and the pure song of delight from those who love Him. How could timid little birds feel so at home nesting on His altars? The answer is that there is a perfect love that casts out fear and makes shy children come alive with confidence. There is nothing to harm or frighten anyone. It is the home which all are longing to find. There is no substitute for that cheerful, loving welcome that reigns in the Holy of Holies. Nowhere else can we feel as much at home or experience the freedom from self-consciousness. This is our inheritance and we must keep turning through the doorway of faith into the inner room, where we meet the God of grace.

~~~~~~~~~~~~~~~

July 18

If God will ... then the LORD shall be my God... and of all that You give me I will surely give a tenth to You.
(Genesis 28:20-22)

Jacob's prayer in Genesis 28 was intensely selfish. He had received great revelations from the Lord and yet he saw everything in the light of how this could profit him. It was as if Jacob saw himself as doing God an enormous favour by following Him and worshipping Him. Jacob's vow to give a tithe to God was all part of his scheming to get blessing from God. Jacob means deceiver and he somehow even believed he could deceive God.

Later Jacob had his life-changing encounter with God and he received a new name: Israel – prince of God. His huge ego had been broken and he was free from the millstone of a self-centred life. Now he looked up to God to see God in His own light. God is magnificent and He is the very definition and source of all that is beautiful. To look on God without thinking about what is in it for me is the most blessed place to which we can attain. The filter of selfishness is capable of blocking out the sun, of turning paradise into a wilderness. The moment we realise we are not saved for our own benefit is the most liberating in our walk with God. We are saved for God's pleasure and delight, and the best thing we can ever do is fixedly turn our eyes on Him.

Like all spiritual transactions, this will begin in the will as we determine in our hearts to forget all the clamouring needs of our circumstances. As we train our minds to look on Him, we will realise that the action of looking on Him releases us continually from thinking about ourselves. He burns with such majesty and holiness that we actually forget about ourselves and become enthralled with the perfect light in which He dwells. We worship until we become true worshippers and are unconsciously transformed into a royal priesthood as we do so.

July 19

Ye are of God, little children, and have overcome them: because greater is he that is in you, than he that is in the world. (1 John 4:4 KJV).
There is but one God, the Father, of whom are all things, and we in him; and one Lord Jesus Christ, by whom are all things, and we by him. (1 Corinthians 8:6 KJV).

I remember being approached by a lady asking for prayer to be delivered from a demon. In my spirit I had no sense that she was demon-possessed and instead of praying I asked her two questions: "Is Satan everywhere and does he know everything?" "Yes!" she firmly replied. I explained to her that only God is everywhere and only God knows everything. Her problem was that she was convinced that Satan was some powerful being almost equal to God. In her mind Satan was powerful and consequently her view of God was too small.

It is remarkable how little the Bible speaks of Satan. The Bible deals with the heart of man, challenging us to repent and believe the word of God. It is in that simple response that Satan's power is broken. The chief enemies of any individual are sin, pride and self. Our greatest need is to simply believe God's word.

Satan is terrified of God and unable to cross any line that God sets for him. The moment we turn to Jesus, the powers of darkness are paralysed. In the presence of God we have peace and through that peace we have victory. God's grace is granted to the soul that ceases striving and believes that Christ is infinitely greater than the powers of darkness. Christ was never frightened of anything - neither death, powers and principalities, men, poverty or pain. The Bible bids us take our eyes off the threatening, lying boasts of the evil one and fix our gaze on Christ alone in His majesty and loving authority. Bow in sweet submission to the Lord, the conqueror of sin, death and Satan. At His feet is the place where we are safe and secure in the love of God. Dwell in that perfect peace and it will soon dawn on you that Satan is crushed beneath your feet.

July 20

*And when he had begun to settle accounts, one was brought to him who owed him ten thousand talents.   (Matthew 18:24)
But that servant went out and found one of his fellow servants who owed him a hundred denarii; and he laid hands on him and took him by the throat, saying, 'Pay me what you owe!'*
(Matthew 18:28)

10,000 talents is 750,000 lbs of gold. This is 375 tons or 12 million ounces. One ounce is worth more than $1,000, giving a total of $12 billion. The point is it is an impossible sum to even think of repaying. The debt of sin is the punishment that we deserve for the wrong we have done. It is an accumulated weight of offence that will crush our souls with an impossible load of guilt. Many people simply refuse to consider the wrong they have done, with empty logic such as 'I am not as bad as others.'

The king forgave the man freely. The forgiveness of sins is the great gift made possible because Jesus paid this impossible debt when He died in our place. God's grace is extravagant, even outrageous. It is the act of immeasurable love poured out on undeserving sinners. Just as Isaac was released from death because a ram was found to die in his place, so we too are released from the burden of guilt.

100 denarii is 100 days' wages for a manual labourer, which could be at most $100, giving a total of $10,000. It is a significant sum but far lower than 10,000 talents. The forgiven man did not pass on a single drop of the grace he had received from the king, so at the end of the parable the king cancelled his grace and the debt was reinstated. This is the law of reciprocity. God requires of us that grace should make us gracious and generous, so that we pass on the flood of grace that has been poured out upon us. Forgiving others is never easy, and it may require time spent in prayer as we search our hearts and pray for those who have offended us. But we have no choice. We must develop a mind of generous grace, being kind to some who have hurt us and caused us pain and loss. We are brought into a world of grace and we must take care to exercise our souls to act and think with the same amazing love that has reached us.

~~~~~~~~~~~~~~

July 21

You therefore must endure hardship as a good soldier of Jesus Christ. No one engaged in warfare entangles himself with the affairs of this life, that he may please him who enlisted him as a soldier. (2 Timothy 2:3-4)
"Follow Me, and I will make you fishers of men." They immediately left their nets and followed Him.
(Matthew 4:19-20)

Billy Graham held conferences for evangelists in Amsterdam. At one of the conferences Billy and his wife Ruth mingled with the delegates. They sat down next to a man who from his clothes seemed to come from a poor country. But his face had a gentleness and a joy about it that were immediately apparent.
"Where are you from?" Billy asked.
"I am from Botswana." He said he travelled, often on foot, from village to village, preaching the gospel of Christ to anyone who would listen. It was, he admitted, discouraging at times, with frequent opposition and very little response.
"Are there many Christians in Botswana?" Billy asked.
"A few," he replied. "Only a very few."
"What is your background? Did you go to Bible school or get any education to help you?"
"Well, actually," he said, "I got my master's degree from Cambridge University."
James Denny said, "There must be great renunciations if there are to be great Christian careers." This does not mean that everyone has to give up their job and become a great missionary or preacher. It means that the call of God must have pre-eminence in our lives above every other calling. We are on this planet for a purpose and once we have that great call of God echoing in our hearts, we must allow nothing to weaken it or compete with it. The call of God makes us rise each day with purpose and joy. If we lose the consciousness of the call, it is because something else has called to us, such as money, an easy life or even something as innocent as sport. Eric Liddell turned down the opportunity to win the 100 metres gold medal at the Paris Olympics of 1924 because it was run on a Sunday and was against his beliefs. Life can anaesthetise us and make us sleep our lives away on lesser things. Underneath everything, God has called into our spirit and we must rise, leave all and follow Him.

∼∼∼∼∼∼∼∼∼∼∼∼∼∼

July 22

This Book of the Law shall not depart from your mouth, but you shall meditate in it day and night, that you may observe to do according to all that is written in it. For then you will make your way prosperous, and then you will have good success.
(Joshua 1:8)

God spoke prophetically to His servant Joshua and directed him to the written word that had been given to the people of Israel. He was directed not merely to read but to meditate on it. Reading may be a fleeting skim over the surface, but meditation is the act of letting down our nets to catch the living treasures contained in the Bible. The calmer our minds, the more restful our approach, the finer our net will be and the larger the catch.
"Begin with reading or hearing. Go on with meditation; end in prayer... Reading without meditation is unfruitful; meditation without reading is hurtful; to meditate and to read without prayer upon both is without blessing." (William Bridge 1600-1670).
Meditation on the Scripture is to allow the words to have their full impact on our minds and our spirit. As we do so, we discover that the word becomes a door for faith to come to our hearts. Then the word becomes a door through which we pass into the presence of God. We may not always find it easy to lift our hearts to the Lord in prayer, but as we chew on the word, desire will come.
Many use the Bible as a book of information, like a text-book. But the Bible is a doorway to revelation and must be read with the heart as well as the mind. A text-book is like a picture in two dimensions, but the Bible comes alive when read correctly and the hand of God reaches out and touches us. It is a door, a window on the unseen world. Without the Bible, we only know what we can see with our physical eyes and hear with our physical ears. Faith will never come that way, but as we prepare our hearts by careful surrender to its message, we will be amazed at the power of the Bible to transform our lives into the image of God. Few people read the Bible, but as we meditate on it, we become living pages and we awaken hunger in others to discover the hidden secrets of those who have discovered this great key of knowledge and spiritual power. Joshua was not a great man by strength of personality- his life was a fruit of God's creative word.

~~~~~~~~~~~~~~~~

July 23

Honour all people. Love the brotherhood. Fear God. Honour the king. (1 Peter 2:17)
Honour your father and your mother. (Exodus 20:12 NASB)
Husbands, likewise... giving honour to the wife. (1 Peter 3:7)

One of the marks of Jesus Christ is the honour He gives to every human being. He spoke with respect to those who had fallen low, such as the woman of Samaria, or Zacchaeus the corrupt official. God does not talk down to people and when Jesus invited Zacchaeus to "Come down", it was an indication of His humility. It also exposed the ludicrous high perch that we human beings so frequently make for ourselves.

In one way these people did not deserve the respect that was given them. When Peter said "Honour the king", he was referring to Nero, who was a cruel despot, as were many of the kings mentioned in the New Testament. The point is that respect adorns the soul that respects more than the one respected. The moment I choose to honour another, I am clothed with the garments of Jesus Christ.

Yet this is not to be a mere pose, which would be a garment of falsehood. It all begins when a person opens their heart to be melted as they allow the Son of God to wash their feet. There is a reverse hierarchy in the kingdom of God, and the one who takes the lowest position, paradoxically, is in the highest station. This is the hierarchy of love and the person who cannot find it in himself to honour a flawed human being, is incapable of love. The heart of the kingdom is to be loved and so be empowered to love. It is love that breaks down the stoutest defences and shatters the hard-hearted bastions of selfish pride. The moment we withhold honour from someone, we join them in their coldness. We spread the frosty, cheerless atmosphere of a lost race. Without realising it, we lose our self-respect and we begin to slide into the mind of low self-esteem which ends in the dust of self-loathing.

Take the lowest seat and allow Jesus to clothe you with His majestic robes and place a crown upon your head and a ring of authority on your finger. Only those who love and are loved have genuine spiritual power and authority. Only those whose eyes have overflowed with tears of gratitude for the undeserved grace and honour they have received are able to reach out to others with genuine love.

July 24

Therefore it is also contained in the Scripture, "Behold, I lay in Zion a chief cornerstone, elect, precious, and he who believes on Him will by no means be put to shame." (1 Peter 2:6)

Christ is the cornerstone of all things. Without Him the stone arch would collapse into a heap of rubble. This truth may be a little abstract to us until we realise that this applies most of all to our own life, not some mystical imaginary building.

It means that He is the cornerstone of all spiritual and moral qualities. We may have dozens of things that bring us joy: a happy marriage, a special holiday, or even just a special meal with loved ones. Yet all joys are lacking something unless we have the joy of Christ's loving presence within. I am personally convinced that no-one enjoys life more than a Christian. No sunset is more beautiful, no food so good as when the heart is filled with the inner radiance of God's own pleasure.

God and love are joined as are God and peace and God and joy. Without Christ all our attempts to live in these things will collapse, leaving us with a sense of incompleteness, of emptiness. If Christ is the centre, a dry crust can be a feast and a prison cell becomes a palace. Richard Wurmbrand, Madame Guyon, Geoffrey Bull and countless others have told of their discovery of the power of Christ when imprisoned for their faith. They felt like dancing with the inexpressible joy that filled their prison cell.

All attempts to enjoy pleasures for their own sake will end in the dust and rubble of the dreariness of a life without inner depth. That Christ is the cornerstone means that we have surrendered our inner life to Him and that we maintain this inner structure by our daily surrender to His loving rule. Neglect this source of sweetest joy and the dreariness will return. Look up to Him in faith and instantly life and light will steal back into our parched hearts.

July 25

But before faith came, we were kept under guard by the law, kept for the faith which would afterward be revealed. Therefore the law was our tutor to bring us to Christ, that we might be justified by faith. But after faith has come, we are no longer under a tutor. *(Galatians 3:23-25)*

There are many spiritual lessons to be learned from the things we see in creation. The example below helps illustrate the difference between a life lived under the rules and regulations of the law and a life of grace freely given in Christ.

The animal kingdom can be divided into two main groups: creatures with backbones (vertebrates) and those without (invertebrates). Did you know that 96% of animal species are invertebrate? Many of these creatures, such as crabs and insects, have hard exoskeletons like suits of armour, a bit like the law or Old Covenant. This gives protection but growth is restricted as a hard, legalistic shell builds up. The shedding of its skin can allow an invertebrate to gain size rather like a person changing denominations, only to replace one list of rules for another!

Jesus Christ came as the first true spiritual vertebrate – warm and approachable and with inner backbone. There was no rigid inflexibility in his nature; rather, He came to show us the liberated life of one who is in relationship with the Father. He never built up a framework of rules and laws but instead promoted the free movement and growth that an inner backbone allows. The laws and moral standards are no longer worn on the outside, but are the promise of a changed inner nature governed by love.

The greatest need is not to shed our hard outer shell and replace it with another, but to receive a new nature and be born again as a person with backbone in the image of Jesus Christ.

~~~~~~~~~~~~~

July 26

Again He designates a certain day, saying in David, "Today," after such a long time, as it has been said: "Today, if you will hear His voice, do not harden your hearts." (Hebrews 4:7)

Behold, now is the accepted time, now is the day of salvation. (2 Corinthians 6:2)

The writer uses the word 'today' twice in this verse. He has already emphasised this on three occasions in the previous chapter (see Hebrews 3:7; 3:13; 3:15). This is a truth that the Holy Spirit is strongly underlining. It is the word of immediacy that quickens faith. The literal translation of 'now is the accepted time' is 'behold the now season is acceptable.' We are to live in the 'here and now'.

The favourite words of Satan are either 'yesterday' or 'tomorrow'. He is constantly reminding us of our past failures, or telling us that the conditions for God to work are not quite right today and we will have to wait for a revival or a special word or move of God. Yes, we may pray and yearn for revival, but at no time do we ever preach "repent and wait for the conditions to come to pass in which you might be saved."

Human beings love to procrastinate, putting off the things we know we should do right now. Sometimes we think nostalgically of past blessings and times when we knew greater blessing. But all these things detract from the glory of God. God the Father, God the Son and God the Holy Spirit are the same yesterday, today and forever. It is blasphemous to imply that God cannot fulfil His promises today. God can never disappoint anyone who believes in His word.

The force of this word is to rouse us to believe and enter in right now. Joy is not a faraway dream nor a pot of gold at the end of the rainbow. We certainly do not need to compass sea and land to find God. God is within reach and His power is a breath away. Rise up and enter now into the powerful righteousness, peace and joy of the kingdom!

July 27

You shall also make a lampstand of pure gold; the lampstand shall be of hammered work. Its shaft, its branches, its bowls, its ornamental knobs, and flowers shall be of one piece.
(Exodus 25:31)

The golden lampstand is a symbol of Jesus standing in the Holy Place and burning continually. The Light of the world is to shine upon us and then we are to receive that light into our inner being, so that by the activity of the Spirit our hearts become the Holy Place.

The mystery of prayer is that we are to enter by faith into that Holy Presence and so keep renewing our inward condition. Christ never grows dim but our hearts may become darkened if we do not turn and look on that warm radiance that is Christ in us. Jesus is love, joy and unceasing, unquenchable hope, and it is these things that shine within us and cause our hearts to be fresh and alive with the exquisite loveliness of Him. Prayer is not a means to an end, it is the action of our hearts to look upon the fountain of living waters and be a well-watered garden.

The sweetest, most attractive part of the life of faith is simply knowing Jesus by experience. Yes, we live by faith not by sight, but faith leads to knowing God, and that knowing is not intellectual, it is by spiritual experience. The tragedy of much Christian teaching is that it equates intellectual understanding with the work of the Holy Spirit. Meanwhile, the heart is gasping for the touch of the divine. Without the inner luminosity of Christ, we lose that skip and inward dance which makes our hearts run to prayer and which makes our hearts full of song. Still your mind, direct your inner gaze upon the unseen but real presence of Jesus and allow the Holy Spirit to make you to be love, joy and unquenchable hope, partaking of the same substance of the eternal Son of God. The open secret of the Christian life is Christ in me, and the discovery of all the riches that flow from that daring and seemingly outrageous claim that our bodies are the holy tabernacle of God.

July 28

Therefore I take pleasure in infirmities, in reproaches, in needs, in persecutions, in distresses, for Christ's sake. For when I am weak, then I am strong. (2 Corinthians 12:10)

The great paradox of the Christian life is that God only really requires that I be weak enough to rely on Him and not on myself. It is the mystery of the spiritual world that God doesn't turn to clever, influential or wealthy people but to the "foolish things of the world", so that no flesh should glory in His presence.

Hudson Taylor, the renowned missionary to China, was visiting Toronto in Canada. He was travelling on a train with a friend named Henry Frost. Frost had just read a magazine article that was deeply critical of Taylor and tried to hide it from his friend. But Taylor noticed and picked it up to read the stinging comments: "Hudson Taylor is rather disappointing... A stranger would never notice him on the street... Nor is his voice in the least degree majestic... He displays little oratorical power... He elicits little applause... launches no thunderbolts... It is quite possible that were Mr. Taylor, under another name, to preach as a candidate in our Ontario vacancies, there are those who would begrudge him his probationer's pay." Taylor's reaction was to smile at Frost and say "This is very just criticism, for it is all true. I have often thought that God made me little in order that He might show what a great God He is."

It is a foundational principle of spiritual life and ministry that God uses us in proportion to our consciousness of how powerless we are without Him. The weakness God requires is simply a profound consciousness of how deeply we rely upon Him. We depend on Him to be able to pray, to preach and to love and care for others. Paul was a highly educated man with formidable powers of intellect. Yet he had learned the secret that though God could use these abilities, he could not trust in any of them to do the work of God. God requires joyful humility that surrenders to God and allows Him to live and work through us.

ɴɴɴɴɴɴɴɴɴɴɴɴɴ

July 29

Therefore we will not fear, even though the earth be removed, and though the mountains be carried into the midst of the sea.
(Psalm 46:2)
Be still, and know that I am God.   *(Psalm 46:10)*

The Psalmist describes here on the one hand a world dominated by fear and on the other a world of quiet trust and faith. The world is frequently shaken by catastrophic convulsions. These may be in the realm of politics, finances or, worst of all, personal adversity and heartbreak. But no matter what troubles shake our lives we have a simple choice: to fear or to believe; to allow our lives to be tossed around by life's events or to live in the calm of God's presence.

The writer declared "we will not fear", expressing his inner determination, his firm resolve. As he turned to trust, he heard the voice of God: "Be still," and he entered into the untroubled, hushed calm of God's own being. Tranquillity is the essential bedrock of who God is. The moment we believe, that serenity is communicated and we know something of the wonder of what God is like. He is all-knowing, all-powerful and unthreatened. He is majestic in immeasurable depths of holiness, and the moment we believe it is as if time stops, the threatening noise of other voices vanishes and we know God by experience.

There is a peace that passes understanding that defies all the countless reasons to panic and give up. In the worst imaginable circumstances, God bids us to partake of His peace and allow His presence to drown every anxious thought, every cause for alarm. Logic may scream that we must do something, but God simply invites us to trust Him. God will still defend us, even if we do panic, but we will miss out on the indescribable blessing of sipping at the cup of God's own inner state.

~~~~~~~~~~~~~

July 30

"And again I say to you, it is easier for a camel to go through the eye of a needle than for a rich man to enter the kingdom of God." When His disciples heard it, they were greatly astonished, saying, "Who then can be saved?" But Jesus looked at them and said to them, "With men this is impossible, but with God all things are possible." (Matthew 19:24-26)

Jesus affirmed that it is easier for a camel to go through the eye of a needle than for a rich man to enter the kingdom of God. In so doing, He was teaching that it is humanly impossible. Rich men have too many resources to rely on, and will not easily come to lean on God with all their hearts. The disciples realised immediately that this had implications for everyone. There are those who have riches of intellect, others have strength of will and some have absolute self-confidence to the point at which they have no need of help or salvation at all.

Then Jesus shone the blazing light of hope on the impossible. When Jesus said "With God all things are possible", He was referring to the door that is opened when a soul bows in prayer. The word of God introduces an entirely new dimension into every human situation and suddenly the word 'impossible' vanishes from sight. As soon as Jesus is invited into a situation, everything changes.

God's world-view is totally unlike ours. We face impossibilities at every turn that are like granite walls that have never moved. But God views the hardest granite as candlewax that will melt and disappear at His breath. It is simply the act of inviting God into the situation that changes everything. For God, the word 'impossible' simply doesn't exist. There is no obstacle of sin or darkness or human stubbornness that will not yield to His power and authority. No-one can be saved without God in the mix. Simply open the door and the world suddenly changes forever. There is a world where God is not known and there is a world where He rules. The moment we bow and pray, the darkness vanishes and all things are suddenly possible.

∾∾∾∾∾∾∾∾∾∾∾∾∾

July 31

But know that the LORD has set apart for Himself him who is godly. *(Psalm 4:3)*
My beloved is mine, and I am his. *(Song of Solomon 2:16)*

God lays personal claim and ownership of all those who set their hearts on following Him. One can imagine how great care is taken in the royal kitchens to select only the best food for the king. No blemished fruit is allowed to touch the royal lips! In the same way, God Himself is constantly looking for those whose hearts lean towards Him in love and obedience. God is at work to foster moments when our supreme consciousness is that of belonging personally and uniquely to Him.

The highest experience of the believer is the astonishing realisation that God's love is not general but personal and selective. It is the fact that we are not only called by a common call but we are called by name - we have been chosen by the King.

President Eisenhower once received a letter from a sick boy and it was noticed by one of his staffers that the president was passing very close to that address the very next day. The family had no phone so there was no time to warn them, so the next day the motorcade stopped outside the house. The father of the boy opened the door in his vest and his mouth fell open in disbelief that someone so important had noticed him.

A president cannot care for all his people in that way, but God does. He has laid personal claim to your life and His greatest joy is to sit with you and declare His pride in owning you. The love of Calvary is universal, since Christ died for all, but it was above all personal because His goal was not to save an anonymous multitude, but to stamp His seal of ownership on every single believer. For God, the sweetest fruit of Calvary is the moment when in child-like wonder we express our joy in being simply His.

August 1

"Watch therefore, for you do not know when the master of the house is coming - in the evening, at midnight, at the crowing of the rooster, or in the morning- lest, coming suddenly, he find you sleeping. And what I say to you, I say to all: Watch!"
(Mark 13:35-37)

God promised He would send His Son to die on a cross for the sins of the world. He also promised He would send the Holy Spirit to apply this cleansing power and recreate human beings from the inside by the gift of a new heart. Both of these prophecies have been fulfilled to the letter. God has also promised that His Son will come a second time, not to suffer but to rule.

To watch is to persistently and patiently live in the light of the coming of Christ for it is as sure and certain as the sunrise. This fact is to shape our thinking. As it does so, we will be empowered to live in the most profound freedom from the influence of the world. Believers live in the world but are not of it. The world with all its burdens and cares often seems so permanent and strong but it is passing away, and it is as we realise this that it loses its grip.

The coming of the Holy Spirit is the down payment, the first instalment and taste of Christ's everlasting kingdom. Now we are to live keeping short accounts, without grudges and without baggage, ready to leave at a moment's notice and stand before the Master. This prophecy is not in one or two obscure verses but is the main subject of the book of Revelation. It was the subject of His teaching when He sat with His disciples on the Mount of Olives. It is the framework that undergirded all His teaching from the parable of the wheat and the tares to the parable of the wise and foolish virgins.

The command of Jesus Christ to watch is a solemn charge to all His followers to firmly establish this truth as the framework of their thinking and living. This will work as an antidote to morbid thinking about the future and will produce a joyful anticipation of the glory that is about to sweep across this world. Rejoice, He is at the door.

~~~~~~~~~~~~

August 2

Your word is a lamp for my feet, a light on my path.
(Psalm 119:105 NIV)

For the word of God is alive and active. Sharper than any double-edged sword, it penetrates even to dividing soul and spirit, joints and marrow; it judges the thoughts and attitudes of the heart. *(Hebrews 4:12 NIV)*

The Bible never invites us to introspection but rather to come to the light of God. There is a huge difference, because self-diagnosis is highly dangerous and unfruitful for two great reasons:

First of all, because no individual can understand his own heart until he comes under the searchlight of God's word. Without God's truth to guide us we will end up either in self-congratulation or more likely self-condemnation. The strongest human mind is a frail gleam and is as incapable of guiding us as a flickering candle could guide us through slippery mountain tracks. The result of following our own light is that we will fall into the precipices of hopelessness and gloom.

Secondly, because the word of God not only gives light upon our situation, it bathes us in a brightness that is warm and strengthening. By the light of the word we see our condition but we also see the solution to our problems. The word of God will never leave us in self-pity or despair but will lift us up and pull us out. There is no situation we can ever face that is too hard for God to resolve.

According to Greek legend, the Gordian knot was impossible to untie and whoever succeeded would be the supreme ruler of Greece. Alexander the Great wrestled with the knot until at last he drew his sword and sliced it through. We will wrestle in vain with ourselves until we place ourselves firmly under the light of God's word. It has a piercing clarity that gives instant understanding of our plight, but combines it with the razor-sharp power of the cross to cut us free.

August 3

God shall arise, his enemies shall be scattered; and those who hate him shall flee before him! (Psalm 68:1 ESV)
He raises the poor from the dust and lifts the beggar from the ash heap, to set them among princes and make them inherit the throne of glory. (1 Samuel 2:8)

When David penned these words he was stating a simple fact of the universe. God will arise and intervene in majestic power and authority in the affairs of the human race. This is the certainty that derives from the very fact of God. He will not remain silent and will not allow wicked men to triumph forever. Their day will come to an abrupt end and God shall rule.

In the same way, believers are united with the same Spirit of resurrection. God has given us a soaring Spirit that yearns to break free and worship with the hosts that lift up their hearts in joyful certainty that God will always prevail and reign forever. God is not asking us to be the power that rises above the darkness, He is simply telling us to catch the upward draught of His being and fly above the darkness.

The point about rising is that it is supernatural and far-reaching. We could compare it to the choice of climbing the stairs of the Empire State Building or taking the lift. The difference is that there are no stairs to rise out of darkness. There is only the uprising of God's being to take us up and out of the claws of the night and into the triumphant presence of God. The moment we grasp the ways of God, we realise that Christ could never lead us out of sin and the grip of Satan by mere teaching. He did it through a death and resurrection. He reached down to the lowest point a human being can ever fall to and rose from there to the highest throne.

This is the paradox of the cross: it is the place of escape from the deepest pit to the highest throne in blazing holiness and glory. Christ died and, rising again, has burst the gates of hell. Let us now soar where Christ has led and let His triumph be ours.

~~~~~~~~~~~~~~

August 4

But the day of the Lord will come as a thief in the night, in which the heavens will pass away with a great noise, and the elements will melt with fervent heat; both the earth and the works that are in it will be burned up. Therefore, since all these things will be dissolved, what manner of persons ought you to be in holy conduct and godliness...? (2 Peter 3:10-11)

There are two aspects of the prophecies of the end of the world. First, there are the uncertain details of how and when the prophecies will be fulfilled. The reformers were persuaded that the pope was the Antichrist while John Wesley thought the Ottoman empire heralded the end of the world. For many years we have heard of the coming computer chip that will be implanted in our hand and will replace cash. The truth is that the years roll by and every generation is convinced that it is living in the last of the last days.

The second aspect of these prophecies is why they were given, and this has not changed since the day that Peter wrote these words. So many great men of God have got it wrong in working out the details of the coming of Christ. But they got it right in interpreting why God has revealed the future. God teaches just enough for us to realise the end is coming and so produce a godly fear in the hearts of His people.

The purpose of prophecy is to stir up God's children to fervent love, to heart holiness and to steadfast endurance in the face of hardship and persecution. The expectation of the Lord's return is about shaping the thoughts of the heart. Christians must simply believe their beliefs. If we lose our mental grip on this truth, we will drift into a mindset that counts on the permanence of the world and its systems. We must hold the return of Christ before our eyes continually to keep us from drifting into a dangerous soul sleep. It is this blessed hope alone that can give us the power to rise above the downward current of this present age. It is this hope alone that cuts the final ties with sin and enables us to fellowship with Christ with a truly burning heart.

~~~~~~~~~~~~~~

August 5

*Write in a book what you see and send it to the seven churches which are in Asia.   (Revelation 1:11 NASB).
And the first voice which I had heard, like the sound of a trumpet speaking with me, said, "Come up here."*
(Revelation 4:1 NASB)

John was in a prison camp on the island of Patmos when he saw the risen Christ and heard the prophetic words for the seven churches. We don't know how much John already knew, but it must have come as a terrible shock and disappointment to hear about the state of the churches. His beloved Ephesus had forsaken the ways of love. Pergamos and Thyatira were defiled with immorality while Sardis was spiritually dead. Laodicea was perhaps the worst with a smug pharisaical attitude of spiritual superiority. John may have been close to despair when he heard the words: "Come up here!"

He was taken far above to see the throne of God and to hear the heavenly hosts singing ceaseless songs of joyous praise. There will always be pressure and difficulties but through it all the worship of God is unending. God's invitation is to rise and join the singing.

The songs around the throne are never superficial or trite. They are solemn, yet joyful. They are full of child-like wonder and depths of awe at the holiness and beauty of the Godhead. They are songs that are the spontaneous result of the impact of the divine radiance on the hearts of the redeemed.

Faith is all about perspective. It is essential to believe that the visible world is only temporary and passing away while the real world is in the Spirit. Moses 'saw' the invisible world by faith. It is as we become conscious of the rule of God far above the affairs of men that we are able to partake in the perpetual triumph of the heavenly hosts. 'Come up here, rise above the restless turbulence' of earth and partake of the exultant praise that is the reward of faith.

~~~~~~~~~~~~~~~

August 6

"Fill four pitchers with water and pour it on the burnt offering and on the wood."   *(1 Kings 18:33 NASB)*

Elijah challenged King Ahab and the prophets of Baal to a contest, which would prove who was the true and living God. It would be the God who answered by fire. This whole event on Mt Carmel was a picture of Pentecost. One of the most striking aspects of the event was that Elijah ordered water to be poured on the sacrifice.

This can only mean that God does not look to His people for any other fire than that of the Holy Spirit. There was nothing combustible about this sacrifice. We do well to accept that we do not bring any spiritual fire to this altar.

There are two great lessons from this image. First, for those who feel they are weak spiritually, there is encouragement. God is not asking us to build up natural enthusiasm for the things of God. He knows our lukewarm state and our selfish ways. He asks us to come as we are and receive the fire that will burn up all that is contrary to the fire of God.

The second lesson is for those who feel that they have the qualities needed to build God's kingdom. God will have to wean us from trusting in ourselves and lead us to trust in the power of the Spirit alone. "But God has chosen the foolish things ... the weak things ... the base things ... the things which are despised ... and the things which are not, to bring to nothing the things that are, that no flesh should glory in His presence." (1 Corinthians 1:27-29.) God delights to show that He can take the disqualified and thereby glorify His Son. So we no longer may boast in ourselves, nor may we grovel in our poverty. God will take us as we are and display His incredible grace.

~~~~~~~~~~~~~

August 7

Jesus said to him, "I am the way, the truth, and the life. No one comes to the Father but through Me." (John 14:6 NASB)

The gospel does not focus on paradise when we die but on Christ. Paul preached Christ, not heaven. The reason is simple: Christ is the light of heaven, He and the Father are worshipped and adored there. Anyone who doesn't love Jesus Christ will certainly not feel comfortable in that world of light and love.

Our focus is therefore not on the hereafter but on the magnificent person of Christ. Yes, we long for a world without sin and suffering but we also grasp that the gospel has brought us face to face with God in Christ. He is the power of an endless life and the constant challenge of the Spirit is to come to Him.

There is a constant cry for God to do something in our circumstances or in our hearts. The truth is that God cannot do a deep work, He can only be that deep work in us. Because of this we must continue to be in an attitude of living in Him. The fact of His indwelling is the foundation of Christian living. We already have within us all the resources of patience and love that we will ever need. Some speak of their resources as batteries that need re-charging. The truth is that the inner power of Jesus works by direct connection alone. It is to become the habit of our life to draw on Him.

As Christians we are more than we know. Christ is in us and the attitude of depending on Him leads from faith to faith, from deeper dependence to deeper dependence and from glory to glory. The incredibly simple message is that we are to receive Him and keep on receiving Him. We are to stop thinking of attaining some lofty heights which will make us automatically victorious. Relating to Christ will test the sinews of our inner life as we continually reach out to love and trust Him who lives within. The more we know Him, the more we bear His likeness.

August 8

No temptation has overtaken you except such as is common to man; but God is faithful, who will not allow you to be tempted beyond what you are able, but with the temptation will also make the way of escape, that you may be able to bear it.
(1 Corinthians 10:13)

In times of temptation, clouds cover the face of God. This is the very heart of temptation and God allows us to pass through moments of darkness when everything seems to contradict God's faithfulness. Think of Job, who longed for a word from God. Think of Joseph, who was sent to prison despite resisting temptation to sin with Potiphar's wife. Think of Moses, long years alone in the wilderness. How these men must have longed for some comfort or confirmation that they were not forsaken!

The path of temptation is common to all. There are deep breakings as we are forced to examine ourselves and hold fast to our faith. It is at this point that we need to hear loud and clear that God is faithful. God is the one who sets the limits of the trial. He is watching over every step we take and will allow it to humble us but not destroy us. God, who knows our capacities, will not allow the test to damage our personality. It was prophesied of Jesus Christ that on the cross His bones would not be broken (John 19:36 and Psalm 34:20). This means that the inner structure of His personality would remain intact. It is a remarkable fact and easily overlooked that in the Resurrection Jesus was at perfect peace. The trauma of the cross had passed and He stood in total perfect poise before His disciples.

God will do the same with us and will bring us through the deepest traumas of apparent desolation. He will faithfully watch over every step and as a master physician will both allow the trial to strengthen us and then cause the distress of the ordeal to pass from us, as if it had been a dream. Hold fast to His hand and let the words be emblazoned as a beacon of hope: God is faithful.

∼∼∼∼∼∼∼∼∼∼∼∼∼

August 9

Do not love the world or the things in the world. If anyone loves the world, the love of the Father is not in him.
(1 John 2:15)
Neither did anyone say that any of the things he possessed was his own.   *(Acts 4:32)*

When Adam sinned, it was an act of substituting that forbidden fruit into the place of God. Since that time, one of the great marks of fallen humanity has been the love of 'things'. A sure sign of the love of things is that we cease to get inspired when we worship God. If Abraham had refused to offer Isaac up to God, he would still have been a blessed man but there would have been a grievous dilution of his love for God. He would have loved God and Isaac, or perhaps even Isaac and God. We may be sure that God does not want Isaac to die. But we may be equally sure that God does not want Isaac to take His place.

Letting go of the love of things may in truth be as agonising as having a rotten tooth drawn. The difference is that we cling fiercely to our idols and argue and plead for them. All we do is prolong the pain till we realise that in letting go we will receive something that is far more precious than silver or gold. When God takes His proper place in our hearts and all rivals have been expelled, then we grasp why God is so insistent. Then there is peace that passes understanding. Then there is a careless indifference to 'things' and a realisation that all our loved ones are safer when they are committed to God.

Abraham was led to offer Isaac on Mount Moriah, a stone's throw from Gethsemane and Calvary. Jesus sweated drops of blood as He offered up Himself to God for our sins. To our shame, we sometimes sweat and agonise as we let go of 'things' till God is allowed to take the throne of our lives. It is the only way, there is no other path of progress in friendship with God and the rewards are profound and eternal: "He is no fool who gives what he cannot keep to gain what he cannot lose." Jim Elliot.

~~~~~~~~~~~~~~

August 10

"You seek Jesus of Nazareth, who was crucified. He is risen! He is not here... But go, tell His disciples- and Peter- that He is going before you into Galilee; there you will see Him, as He said to you." (Mark 16:6-7)

The women were amazed to find the tomb empty and two angels waiting to speak with them. Their message for the women was directly from the Lord and must have been carefully enunciated so that there would be no misunderstanding. They had been commanded to remind the disciples that He would see them in Galilee. But the remarkable thing is that they mentioned Peter by name.
The Lord knew that Peter would be sunk deep in despair and self-condemnation. He must have felt totally disqualified and believed that all the promises that had been spoken over his life were now null and void. He had made a mess of His discipleship and was in process of giving up. The disciples, too, were probably wondering what their relationship with Peter was to be like now. So the Lord made it abundantly clear: nothing has changed. His love was unmovable and Peter was still called to be among the apostles.
When we fail, we cannot erase the past. We cannot expect that all others will have the mercy and compassion of Christ. The more we know about people's weaknesses, the harder it can be to love them. But this is not the case with Christ. He is able to love us though knowing the worst about us. We can be sure of one thing: that Christ restores those who fall so completely that it will never be mentioned again. We will one day gather around the eternal throne and no-one will then remember our flaws or our failures. But Christ is not merely around that throne, He is on it! For those who have faith and love to perceive it, we may already grasp the wonder of God's immeasurable mercy and grace for all His people.

True, we live in a world where few have achieved this heart of kindness to those who fall. True, it will not always be possible for those who fail to continue in church government and ministry as if nothing has happened. But that is not to cause us to be cool to any brother or sister in Christ. We are to drink deep of the boundless love that is our only hope and make sure we pass it on to every person we meet.

August 11

I will meditate on the glorious splendour of Your majesty, and on Your wondrous works. Men shall speak of the might of Your awesome acts, and I will declare Your greatness.
(Psalm 145:5-6)

God is a safe house for the battered, a sanctuary during bad times. The moment you arrive you relax. You're never sorry you knocked. (Psalm 9:9-10 MSG)

These psalms are a great hymn of praise to the persistent love of God to humanity in all its need. The world is a dark place because it is without the knowledge of God. Human beings are never the source of the true understanding of the mind of the eternal God. It is common to hear people blame God for all the ills of the world. Behind these thoughts there is a concept of God that is totally false. As someone once said to an atheist, "I also don't believe in the God you don't believe in."

When once we entertain wrong thoughts about God, it will not be long before we become despondent. The prodigal son had his head in a pig trough imagining his father would reject him. The Bible says "he came to himself" (Luke 15:17), indicating that he was previously verging on insanity. He suddenly woke up to the fact that his father's house was bright and cheerful, and adorned with love, mercy and kindness.

We are to throw off the intimidating lies of darkness and open the window of the Bible and take a long, hard look at God and His kingdom. There are songs of joy, with feasting and dancing. There is abundance of forgiveness and power to wash stains of shame away. There are the Father's great arms of love to welcome us. There is a warm hearth with a place prepared with our name on it. We won't be given a random bunk but will be escorted to the place uniquely suited to make us feel at home. Unbelief is persistent mental self-harm. Faith is to enter the real world of God's exquisite kingdom of healing love.

August 12

As the Father has sent Me, I also send you. (John 20:21 NASB)
"Come in, wife of Jeroboam, ... for I am sent to you."
(1 Kings 14:6 NASB)

The wife of Jeroboam went to see the prophet Ahijah. He was an old man and blind and did not move from his house. Yet he said he had been sent to her. The force of this statement is that to be sent is first and foremost about who sends us and from what place. Ahijah was sent from heaven, where his spirit was communing with God.

The most important thing about any person is where they are coming from. Jesus said "You are from beneath; I am from above. You are of this world; I am not of this world." (John 8:23) By this He was indicating that His perspective on all of life was different, in the constant consciousness of the overarching sovereignty of God.

When we panic, we show that we have been lulled by this world's smooth talk into taking our eyes off the centre. There can never be a panic in heaven since God is never taken off guard by any event or decision of man. Those who would serve the Lord are to be His sent ones, coming continually from a consciousness of His majesty and supreme authority. We are to be ambassadors of peace with words of power. We are enabled to live between two worlds by the Holy Spirit and the Bible. For these two are the same on earth as they are in heaven. We are to soak in His presence and His word and so have a message of life and hope for a dying world.

We are not to go empty-handed to starving people but to have abundance of spiritual bread. We are not merely carrying words, we are conveying the atmosphere that surrounds the throne of God. We may never leave our house, but we are sent to all who we meet with the whisper of another world.

August 13

No one has seen God at any time. The only begotten Son who is in the bosom of the Father, He has declared Him.
(John 1:18)

Jesus Christ is God's way of self-disclosure. We would never have known God unless Jesus had come to declare Him. He did this by taking human form and expressing the amazing qualities of the Godhead. Those who met Jesus would have been arrested by things they had never seen before.

The greatest surprise would be to see the face of a person who had never sinned. This meant there would be no shadows or regrets from past actions or words. There was no guilt or shame. At the same time, there would be no fear of the future, no fear of death or judgment. There was the serenity of a person completely right with God.

There was also absolute authority revealed for He was subject to no other power than His Father. There was no acknowledgement of any threat, whether from Satan or from human government. Jesus passed through communities, knowing that demons trembled and fled and every authority was subject to Him. He was not clothed with kingly robes but inwardly was resplendent with the majesty of inner purity and holiness.

The most attractive quality was His mercy and compassion for sinners. It was the prostitutes and corrupt officials who noticed this most because they saw so little of it in themselves or others. It was also this aspect of His character that they needed. It touched the hearts of needy souls because of the consciousness that here was a man in perfect harmony with God. He knew God's heart and God's word and carried all authority, yet combined this with love and kindness. How awful that some spat on this same face and plucked out His beard! How more amazing that He did not react but loved and loved, proving that God's love is stronger than man's deepest hate! The light that shines in our hearts is not impersonal but is the very beauty of God revealed in Jesus.

~~~~~~~~~~~~~~

August 14

Some of the armed men marched in front of the priests with the horns and some behind the Ark, with the priests continually blowing the horns. "Do not shout; do not even talk," Joshua commanded. "Not a single word from any of you until I tell you to shout. Then shout!" (Joshua 6:9-10 NLT)

As the people of God walked around Jericho they kept silence. This is because they would have been tempted to give voice to their fears as they considered the high walls of the city. The walls were bristling with spears and arrows and the fierce faces of the enemy. In the same way, fear and worry can easily lift up their voices to intimidate us and destroy our faith. We need to silence our hearts and listen to the trumpet sound of God's word. It is as we keep silence that the word of God has a clear and unambiguous quality that produces a resounding echo of faith in our hearts.

If we can calm the voice of our fears and exalt God's promises, then a green shoot of faith will appear in us. It may take some time but we are to persist in listening and not speaking unbelief to ourselves and certainly not to the person marching next to us. Keeping a quiet heart is the essential movement that will lead to faith. This is not an empty-headed silence but a deep and calm attentiveness to the written word.

The walls stood firm for seven days and our problems will not disappear immediately as we meditate on the word. Faith is not needed when our problems have vanished but when they rise up to defy us. Faith is to be joined with patience and persistent obedience. The faith required to conquer Jericho was faith to be silent and look up to God. Faith will give way to a firm assurance and the walls will suddenly collapse. It took seven days for the people of Israel, and for some situations it may take seven years but the answer will come and God will be glorified.

~~~~~~~~~~~~

August 15

Our friend Lazarus... *(John 11:11 NASB)*

Lazarus had no great title such as apostle, bishop, pastor or evangelist. Yet he is here given the greatest and highest position any person can ever hope to attain. Jesus said of him that he was "our friend".

The whole purpose of the gospel is to reconcile sinners with a holy God. This reconciliation is so profound that we are taken from the alienation of inner darkness to close friendship with Jesus Christ. The gospel can be reduced to one great exhortation: 'Make friends with Jesus.'

We are not set free from sin by a doctrine and certainly not by a creed. These important things undergird our thinking but they cannot save us. Everyone who is saved has met Jesus and entered into a loving bond with God through Him. Because we are saved by a relationship, the most important thing we ever do is simply talk to Him and allow Him to influence and shape us by His transforming presence. The place where I meet God is the most empowering and liberating that I will ever enter. Church meetings are of no value unless they bring us face to face with God, to know, love and worship Him.

The second dimension of this verse is that Jesus did not say 'My' but 'our' friend Lazarus. Jesus was a frequent visitor at this home in Bethany and loved to stay there, but He hardly ever turned up alone. He always brought a crowd of 12 or more! Not all twelve were spiritual and the Bible says that several were critical when Mary anointed Jesus while Jesus and Lazarus were eating together (John 12:1-5 & Matthew 26:8). But Lazarus loved both Jesus and the disciples who followed Him. It is certain that one cannot be a friend of Jesus if we reject those who also love Him. Salvation produces the same friendliness towards all. That is the hall mark of Christ Himself.

~~~~~~~~~~~~~

August 16

The day you die is better than the day you are born. Better to spend your time at funerals than at parties. After all, everyone dies - so the living should take this to heart. Sorrow is better than laughter, for sadness has a refining influence on us. A wise person thinks a lot about death, while a fool thinks only about having a good time. (Ecclesiastes 7:1-4 NLT)

On June 26 1993 Billy Graham preached on these verses at the funeral of Patricia Nixon, the wife of President Richard Nixon. The Nixons had had their fair share of controversy and grief. It was a bold choice by Billy to preach on this text but it was also incredibly appropriate for the Nixons and for the whole world watching.

When politicians argue heatedly and sometimes lead their nations to war, one is forced to ask what their view of eternity is. The answer of course is that most people never think about the really important questions that affect us all. It is the privilege of being a reader of the Bible that eternal issues are constantly held before our eyes. This is not to make us morbid but to make us have a solemn, deep hope of life beyond the grave. If we can attain to that hope, it will make us have better priorities as we live our lives on earth. We will live for things that really matter and, hopefully, we will be more caring, more forgiving and more loving.

Solzhenitsyn wrote a book called 'Cancer Ward'. He was a devout Christian and described the differing reactions of the patients to their imminent demise. Important bigwigs from the communist party couldn't let go of their self-importance. Everyone had to give up small ambitions that were now unattainable and trivial. People who are dying often write letters they should have written years before. They make phone calls, say prayers, give hugs and gifts that were long overdue.

Of course, the Bible is right. Take a long, hard look at your mortality and let it purify you of all the petty things that have taken too strong a hold. Then let it dawn on you that you actually have a lot of time left to make your life count.

August 17

And the devil said to Him, "If You are the Son of God, command this stone to become bread." But Jesus answered him, saying, "It is written 'Man shall not live by bread alone, but by every word of God.'" (Luke 4:3-4)

Eleazar (one of David's three mighty men) arose and attacked the Philistines until his hand was weary, and his hand stuck to the sword. (2 Samuel 23:10)

Temptation is a moment of conflict between darkness and light. The question at stake is what we believe. The target of the devil is our faith and our relationship with God. The devil loves to speculate about things that are firmly established. God had just declared from heaven that Jesus was His beloved Son, and now that statement was being challenged.

It is a fact of God's being that He does not speculate. Jesus never encouraged His disciples to speculate about the nature of God. He constantly urged them to believe in Him and the unchanging word of God. The moment we respond to the devil's speculations, we are off the ground of truth. So the answer of Jesus is powerful on several different levels.

Firstly, He was declaring that beyond every thought and feeling He was trusting in the written word of God. Secondly, He was declaring that He loved and honoured the word more than life itself. Despite His incredible weakness through fasting, He chose to put the word over every other appetite and priority. Thirdly, He was speaking to the powers of darkness from an unshakable conviction forged in the heat of temptation.

The sword of the Spirit is the word of God, and it is through the heat of temptation, through the battle for faith, that we either let it slip or it becomes our very life. It says of Eleazar that in the heat of battle his sword stuck to his hand. That is the positive outcome of temptation: that we cling to God's truth till it becomes an inseparable part of our life.

~~~~~~~~~~~~~~

August 18

For those who live according to the flesh set their minds on the things of the flesh, but those who live according to the Spirit, the things of the Spirit. For to be carnally minded is death, but to be spiritually minded is life and peace. (Romans 8:5-6)

The art of living and walking in the Spirit is the centre and key of New Testament Christianity. There are spiritual aspects to this, including the conscious pursuit of God and His presence. There are also quite down-to-earth and practical dimensions to this heavenly art.

To be spiritually minded is quite simply to think as God Himself thinks. When we enter a room and meet people, we are to think about them with the mind of Christ. By this we don't measure situations and people in the way they affect us, but rather in the way they affect others. We become quite simply dispensable and unimportant. The purposes of Christ become central and our function is simply to allow Him to love people through us.

To be spiritually minded is to mark each situation out as a subject first for praise and secondly for intercession. God is great and is to be found wherever we go. God is powerful and able to touch lives with a transforming breeze that blows from eternity and changes the most impossible situations into opportunities for the glory of God.

Carnal thinking is trapped in a negative spiral of impossibilities. We must throw this whole way of thinking off, just as we would throw a disease-ridden blanket into the flames. The spiritual mind is fundamentally positive and rises to meet each moment with hope and joy. Watch your thinking, for it is a step that leads you deeper down a path either of life and peace or death and disquiet. God's mind is refreshing and knows no weariness and no despondency. God's mind is ever new, like the river of clearest crystal that flows from the throne on high. The Bible tells us we have the mind of Christ (1 Corinthians 2:16). We are to allow our thoughts and attitudes to be informed by another greater mind than our own. As incredible as it may seem, "let this mind be in you which was also in Christ Jesus." (Philippians 2:5.)

August 19

"A voice was heard in Ramah, lamentation and bitter weeping, Rachel weeping for her children, refusing to be comforted for her children, because they are no more."
Thus says the LORD: "Refrain your voice from weeping, and your eyes from tears; for your work shall be rewarded, says the LORD, and they shall come back from the land of the enemy. There is hope in your future, says the LORD, that your children shall come back to their own border."
(Jeremiah 31:15-17)

The first part of this prophecy is well-known. Herod the Great slaughtered the innocents in Bethlehem, believing that by doing so he would kill the Messiah and maintain his few remaining years on his throne in Jerusalem. Such was the outrageous arrogance of that inhuman monster. Rachel was weeping, indicating the mothers whose infants had been murdered. The streets of Bethlehem were filled with their anguished cries.

But the prophecy continues in Jeremiah to give the eternal perspective on these events. God bid them refrain from weeping because there was hope for their future beyond this life. In the midst of total darkness, a shaft of light appeared. These precious children would rise again and stand in their place because the arm of the Lord does not only punish evil doers, He rights the wrongs and protects and restores what was lost. It is to be wondered if someone shared these precious words with the grieving mothers in Bethlehem.

But it is also time to share these words again. There are so many situations that are full of deepest darkness. There are so many grieving and rightly refusing the superficial comforts that are offered to them. The God of hope comes with a magnificent promise of things yet to be revealed in eternity. The last word has not been spoken yet. The darkness of this world shall never have the last word on any life. God who is kind and merciful will yet bare His arm and reveal His righteous judgments. Do not refuse the comfort of God, who alone knows all things and will rescue many that we thought were impossibly lost. Never give up hope. Speak the sure words of God through Jeremiah: "There is hope."

<div align="center">~~~~~~~~~~~~~~~~</div>

August 20

Now when Mephibosheth the son of Jonathan, the son of Saul, had come to David, he fell on his face and prostrated himself. Then David said …. "Do not fear, for I will surely show you kindness … and will restore to you all the land of Saul your grandfather; and you shall eat bread at my table continually."
(2 Samuel 9:6-7)

Mephibosheth was of the family of Saul, who had doggedly tried to destroy David. He was a cripple with nothing to offer the new king by way of service. His grandfather had been killed in the turbulent years preceding David's accession to the throne. His name means 'from the mouth of shame'. In truth, this man had nothing to expect from life but loneliness, hardship and rejection. And now he was summoned by the new triumphant king.

Imagine then his shock as he heard the words of grace that came from the lips of David. 'Kindness', 'restoration' and elevation to friendship with the king were the three gifts of the king. Mephibosheth might have expected prison, banishment or death, but instead he found mercy and compassion. The man without hope was given privilege and high honour. Of all the gifts bestowed, the greatest was continual access to the king at his table. He was elevated to the same status as David's sons. Through this gift he could be sure that none of his needs would ever go unnoticed.

It takes us a long time to be convinced that we are not going to be treated as second-class citizens. It may be that we have always been secretly fearful of rejection, of shame. We like to hide in the anonymity of the crowd, to be unnoticed and suffer our fate with endurance. But Christ has prepared us a kingdom, a throne and a victor's crown. Christ has prepared for us a continual feast. It matters not how disqualified we are, nor whether we are mildly or severely disabled. We are greeted at this table with joy and smiles every time we take our place. The reception is as beautiful and clear as a trumpet fanfare or a full-blown orchestra of soaring musical welcome. We were enemies of the King, we did Him harm and we mocked Him, but His love will hear none of it. He receives us into His loving embrace to be His forever.

August 21

Then He brought him outside and said, "Look now toward heaven, and count the stars if you are able to number them." And He said to him, "So shall your descendants be." And he believed in the LORD, and He accounted it to him for righteousness. *(Genesis 15:5-6)*

Abraham was old, along with Sarah, his wife. Their hope of having a child had faded away. But God caused him to lift up his eyes and consider that He was able to do something so vast that it was as great as the stars in their beauty and expansiveness. Then Abraham simply believed what God said. God's response was to take that faith as Abraham's perfection. God counted him as a righteous man.

This action of the heart to believe God is what makes us children of Abraham. It makes us one of the stars that he saw when he lifted up his eyes. For God, the culmination of His hopes and dreams is the moment when we simply trust Him and believe His promises. It is at that moment that we are in tune with the eternal and infinite God of the universe.

God speaks and will always fulfil what He says. His word is before all things. Human beings believe in the primacy of the physical world. In the beginning was a swirling cloud of dust, or a bit of slime and bacteria. But for the believer, the first thing is the Word. "In the beginning was the Word." It is for this reason that we must become like Abraham and look away from our impossible situation and condition to the promises of God. We can never find peace and inner poise till we agree with the Creator and Redeemer of the human race. It is a choice given to us as soon as we know what God has said. Faith is a response and a choice and by it our hearts beat as one with God's heart. Our minds begin to think as God thinks. Unbelief is like living on a north face slope of a mountain where the sun never shines. It is cold and dark with lingering patches of snow and frost. The moment we believe, we are in the brightness of God's faithfulness and in the everlasting warmth of the sure and certain hope that He will do exactly as He has said.

∾∾∾∾∾∾∾∾∾∾∾∾

August 22

To him who overcomes I will give to eat from the tree of life, which is in the midst of the Paradise of God. (Revelation 2:7)

The Lord spoke searchingly to the seven assemblies of Asia and ended each message with a promise to those who would overcome. This is the stirring appeal to every believer to conquer in the fight. Each of us must fight with temptations to sin, to stop loving or to give up hope.

The fiercest battle is against the dread power of self and pride. This is also the sweetest victory, when we at last shake off its dreadful suffocating influence and are free to keep loving, worshipping and praying. The point of overcoming is that we are either defeated by our circumstances and problems or we are maintaining a life of praise in the midst of our conflicts.

Our goal is often a life without conflict but that is not the world we live in. There is no retirement from the battle of the ages to exalt Christ and to present Him to a fallen world. To be passive or unengaged is to allow the enemy to prevail. The battle is not fought by shouting or posturing, it is won by fervent, persistent love. Christ conquered the very heart of darkness by love. *"Having loved His own who were in the world, He loved them to the end."* (John 13:1.) It is often taken for granted that Christ bore with patience the carnal reactions of His followers. They were slow to grasp His teaching and they argued who among them would be the greatest. They were unable to watch with Him and pray and abandoned Him at His arrest. But none of their weaknesses affected His calm determination to love and keep them to the end. Let us rise up and follow our captain in the triumph of the ages and make it ours.

~~~~~~~~~~~~~~

August 23

And the LORD God caused a deep sleep to fall on Adam, and he slept; and He took one of his ribs, and closed up the flesh in its place. Then the rib which the LORD God had taken from man He made into a woman, and He brought her to the man. And Adam said: "This is now bone of my bones and flesh of my flesh." (Genesis 2:21-23)

This event was the first time blood was shed as God cut into the side of Adam and removed part of him. It is remarkable that this blood was spilt as an act of loving-kindness. It is the first picture of Calvary when God allowed His Son to be cut by the hands of men. The huge difference was that Jesus Christ suffered with no anaesthetic to lessen His pain.

The purpose of Christ's sufferings was that God would take of His spiritual substance and plant it into human hearts, building a companion to be at His side for all eternity to love and serve Him. Believers have the Spirit of God within them and the very life of the Son of God. Christ looks at His own and declares, "This is now love of my love, purity of my purity and joy of my joy." We have within us the very character traits of our Saviour waiting to be outworked.

The cross is the place where God identified with a fallen human race, so that we in turn might identify with God in His matchless love and mercy. We must also receive 'surgery' in our hearts by faith as we let go of our lives and are united with Him in the love that is the reason for everything. It was love that conceived the human race in eternity and love that carries out that plan in time. It was love that designed us and love that redeemed us to bring us back to the original blueprint.

The cross is a surgical operation on the human race to remove the defiling distortion of our fallen nature and replace it with the love of Jesus. To see the cross from God's perspective is to realise that it is to gain and not to lose. We lose the irritating discomfort of pride and self-will. We gain the life of the Son of God and embark on an eternal journey as His closest friends.

~~~~~~~~~~~~~~~

August 24

The wilderness and the wasteland shall be glad for them, And the desert shall rejoice and blossom as the rose.
(Isaiah 35:1-2)
Immediately the Spirit impelled Him to go out into the wilderness. *(Mark 1:12 NASB)*

No-one would normally choose to go into a wilderness. There is no life there, rather a slow dying. There is no stimulation for the senses, neither food nor entertainment for the mind. There is no internet connection and no phone signal. The wilderness is a place of great loneliness and the result is a deep stillness of soul.

As the craving of the senses fades and dies, there appear new longings and hitherto unknown desires for God, for the eternal and for the world beyond our physical senses. It is at that point that the desolate place becomes a doorway into another world. God may use sorrow or any kind of setback to introduce us to another world. It is a remarkable fact that some of history's greatest prophets were nurtured by long spells in prison or lonely exile. This is true of Moses, David, Jeremiah and Paul, to name but a few. To that list can be added Watchman Nee, Richard Wurmbrand, Madame Guyon and Geoffrey Bull, who all spent years in prison and found that to be a door into a deeper relationship with God.

As the world fades away, the desert begins to blossom with spiritual delights and the result is unspeakable joy and singing. When the time comes to return to the world, everything is seen upside down. The world is a wilderness with cheap and superficial pleasures. There is a dreadful absence of meaning that is tinged with deep tragedy. People with amazing minds and a spiritual capacity for the infinite and the eternal are seen dabbling in empty pursuits. Once we have truly been alone with God, we can never give ourselves to the passing pleasures of this fading and broken world. Make a conscious choice and let the Spirit guide you far away to another world. Astonishingly, the doorway to the greatest discovery is right beside you, waiting for you to forsake lesser paths and embark on the quest for God Himself.

August 25

But we preach Christ crucified, to the Jews a stumbling block and to the Greeks foolishness, but to those who are called, both Jews and Greeks, Christ the power of God and the wisdom of God. *(1 Corinthians 1:23-24)*

The most astonishing fact about the Christian gospel is the message of a crucified Messiah. The Jews could grasp their need for anther Gideon or another Moses. They could certainly hope for another David, who would slay their Goliaths and drive their enemies out of the land of Israel. But the Christian message would be as if David went into battle and simply stood and allowed himself to be hung on a gibbet.

If the cross had not been prophesied for centuries, Christians could easily be accused of making the best of a bad outcome. But the prophecies of the cross are of equal prominence in the Old Testament to the prophecies of Messiah. Christ must suffer His heel to be bruised as He crushes the serpent's head. Joseph had to be rejected by his brothers and sold into the lowest dungeon before he could save the world from famine. Moreover, Isaiah boldly prophesied the mystery that Messiah would be despised and rejected, and that the Lord would lay on Him the iniquity of us all.

This groundwork for the cross was vital so that believers may fully grasp that the cross was the determined plan and will of God from the foundation of the world. The conflict between good and evil found its climax in the confrontation between love incarnate and unfettered religious and political evil. As foolish as it may sound to the philosopher, to the one who believes, there is immeasurable power in the cross to cleanse the heart and make people fit to be indwelt by a loving, holy God. This is God's amazing wisdom and is God's provision for a fallen world.

August 26

And when He (the Helper) has come, He will convict the world of sin, and of righteousness, and of judgment.   (John 16:8)

The word "Helper" is sometimes translated "Comforter." The Greek word "parakletos" can also be translated "Exhorter". He has a wide ministry but one of them is to apply the truth of God to the hearts of people. He is a preacher and in fact He is the only preacher. He uses human beings but He can also work spontaneously on the conscience of any person. No preacher can convict of sin, righteousness and judgment without the accompanying activity of the Holy Spirit.

This is true of the work of conversion and also true of the development of our walk with God. He will teach us, He will guide us and He will reveal Christ to us and in us. He is working on our consciences, challenging us to respond to the amazing facts of who God is and what He has done in Christ for the salvation of the world.

There is a whole world to discover of which we are completely ignorant until the Holy Spirit teaches us. Faith, hope, love, joy and peace are all imparted to us as we cooperate with Him. Walking in the Spirit is the foundation of New Testament Christian experience and behaviour. It consists of simply obeying His prompting on our inner conscience. He doesn't come alongside us to chide us but to plead with us as a best friend or a father would. He comes to encourage us to believe and not give up. He challenges us to love people with whom we have little in common. Not only does He encourage us, He helps and empowers us to do what He shows us. He comforts us in our weakness and will not leave us wallowing in need but will strengthen and empower us. Thanks be to God for the gift of the Comforter!

~~~~~~~~~~~~~~~

August 27

For in Him we live and move and have our being. (Acts 17:28)

The Holy Spirit brings the deep consciousness that we are living our lives in the constant presence of God. The more we realise this, the more we understand that the only audience we have to play to is God Himself. Most of us waste time and effort trying to please an earthly audience. We are to live to the glory of God alone.

Helen Rosaveare was a missionary to the Congo in the 1950s. In 1951 she went to the Mission headquarters for training. One day after breakfast she was told to go and wash the cement floor of the toilets in the women's quarters. She found a bucket and a brush and set to. Helen was a qualified medical doctor and this was almost the first time in her life that she had done a household chore. She scrubbed out the first toilet and started on the second. A candidate entered the first with muddy shoes. The floor was still wet. When she left, Helen returned and did the first again. Meanwhile, someone else entered the second. This continued some little time with a rising sense of frustration. Helen felt she had failed and as she kept scrubbing away, tears pricked her eyes.

Helen was being watched by a lady named Elizabeth, who was in charge and had given her the task. She gently asked her why she was so upset. Helen explained the cause of her frustration, that she felt she would never get the floor clean enough.
"For whom are you scrubbing this floor?" Elizabeth asked.
"Why, for you of course; you sent me here."
"No, my dear, if you are doing it for me you may as well go home. You'll never satisfy me. You're doing it for the Lord and He saw the first time you cleaned it. That now is tomorrow's dirt."

All things are for God and we are to live our lives unto Him and for His glory alone.

August 28

Jesus said to them, "He who is without sin among you, let him throw a stone at her first." And again He stooped down and wrote on the ground. Then those who heard it, being convicted by their conscience, went out one by one, beginning with the oldest even to the last. (John 8:7-9)

The conscience is the moral faculty of every human being. It is the inner awareness of standing before a final bar of justice. It is one of the evidences for the existence of a Holy God since there is in every person a consciousness that there must be a day of judgment. If not, then the universe is built on a fractured foundation and the wicked triumph.

Our conscience is sharpened when we receive Christ and it becomes an essential part of our relationship with God. It is by our conscience that we are guided to do good works and not just avoid wrong actions. The conscience takes us out of the clique we associate with and causes us to stand alone before God. We all too easily look for approval for our lives from the conduct of others. If we can convince ourselves that we are above average (not as bad as so and so), then we feel some measure of relief. But once the Holy Spirit has shone His searching light into our hearts, we must do something about it or die. The Holy Spirit will not allow us to walk in the dull fading standards of others. Conscience makes us feel as if we were the only person in the world.

God works to sharpen our inner faculties, to awaken us to a conduct that is divinely empowered. He will prompt us to acts of generosity and kindness and woe unto us if we suppress His inner touch! Others may not have the same conflicts but that is no excuse. God is looking for courageous souls who will be different and exhibit a love and righteousness that is not of this world. As we love and serve Christ, God will shine a light that will convict others. God is looking for pioneers who will explore the kingdom of God and bring back a report of a world of brightness and joy in the Holy Spirit.

August 29

For I consider that the sufferings of this present time are not worthy to be compared with the glory which shall be revealed in us. For the earnest expectation of the creation eagerly waits for the revealing of the sons of God.   (Romans 8:18-19)

Paul examines in Romans the tremendous power of God to set us free from the power of sin. But his gaze extends far beyond this life to the coming glory that is to be ours in the resurrection. He sees a great plan stretching from before the foundation of the world, interrupted by sin but fulfilled in the final transformation of all things.

We human beings are born in time, but we were conceived in eternity. God planned every individual who has ever lived on planet earth and His plan is that we partake of the eternal life and glory of God. We are to nourish this firm hope in our hearts by meditating on our future beyond the grave. Some have mistakenly said that so and so is so heavenly-minded they are of no earthly use. In fact the opposite is true, and our earthly use is determined by the clarity with which we have glimpsed the future.

Paul was not tired of living and he had no fear of the future. He lived in the forecourts of eternity, conscious of the tremendous joy and blessing that were his in leading people to eternal life, yet equally eager to enter the brightness of eternity with Christ. Amy Carmichael (1867 – 1951) was a missionary to India and worked tirelessly for the orphans she loved and served. Amy was once visited by a lady who explained to her that she was not in good health. Her doctor had assured her that she could die on the spot if she so much as stood up too quickly. Amy was taken aback and asked "How ever do you resist the temptation?"

The great tension of the Christian life is the desire to live and serve our generation combined with a desire to depart and be with Christ. The Bible bids us nourish our hearts with the hope of unspeakable blessings and then share this hope with those around us.

August 30

I will betroth you to Me forever; yes, I will betroth you to Me in righteousness and justice, in loving-kindness and mercy; I will betroth you to Me in faithfulness, and you shall know the LORD. (Hosea 2:19-20)

Hosea was declaring God's heart to Israel in a very dark period of their history. Yet his prophecy reveals God to be continually like a young man in love. The astonishing note of His message is the persistence with which God was pursuing a disobedient and rebellious nation.

God is not put off by our unattractive ways, our weaknesses or our quirks. He is not even put off by our indifference and rejection. He just keeps on loving and pleading with the hearts of human beings till we capitulate. Human love is towards those who love us. But God's love does not look for common ground. His love is for His enemies, for those who hate Him and wish Him ill. God loves those who are the opposite of everything He stands for.

God knows that He can turn our ugliness into beauty and our sin into holiness. Love is known by its actions and love can never be passive. It must explore every avenue to win over the object of its affection. Love is active, full of goodness and creative. Love will always spend of itself and pour itself out in hope of a loving response. Christ died to swallow up the last unloving gasp of selfish sinners and enable them to glimpse God and exclaim their love for Him. Love cannot wish harm to any person. By loving the unlovely, it will never be defiled but will grow and prevail.

The miracle of Calvary is that love has triumphed over evil. Men may still harden their hearts to love and ultimately reject it, but love has conquered by presenting the human race with a magnificent beacon of unquenchable love. Calvary will save the hardest and the worst, but it will also condemn those who harden their hearts to love and choose the dread darkness of selfish pride.

August 31

The voice of my beloved! Behold, he comes leaping upon the mountains, skipping upon the hills... My beloved spoke, and said to me: "Rise up, my love, my fair one, and come away. For lo, the winter is past, the rain is over and gone. The flowers appear on the earth; the time of singing has come."
(Solomon 2:8-12)

God removes the moan from the soul and replaces it with songs of joy. God takes meanness from the soul and replaces it with abandoned generosity. God is not mean or heavy-hearted. He comes as a bridegroom to win His beloved bride. The great power of the cross is that by it we have passed from shadows and darkness into light and joy.

The great question is, have we realised that this once-and-for-all transition has taken place? Why must we rise up? Because the long winter of sin and death has ended. It will never return. Once we have believed in Jesus Christ, we have begun a new life. Our history has been blotted out and we have a new future. Fresh new shoots are springing up in our souls and we have new avenues to explore, new gifts to discover and new songs to sing.

The Bible is a song book. God Himself and all the angels are singers. All His children are to join in with the melodies of heaven. We may not be great singers but it is not the vocal cords that God is listening to. He hears the love and joyous abandon with which we approach Him. To sing is to be carried away with inward unrestrained surrender to the one we love. To sing is to let faith release our souls from cautiousness and prudence. To sing is to become a child again and to express ourselves with delight and confidence that we will be received and never rejected. Darkness has passed away; it is time to sing and it is time to worship. There are things to be studied, but we cannot enter God's presence any other way than by letting our hearts soar in song.

~~~~~~~~~~~~~~~

September 1

My son, do not regard lightly the discipline of the Lord, nor be weary when reproved by him. For the Lord disciplines the one he loves, and chastises every son whom he receives.
(Hebrews 12:5-6 ESV)

It must be stated boldly that the difficulties we pass through are a proof of God's genuine, fatherly love. The Hebrew writer states clearly that no chastening seems to be joyful at the time we pass through it and it is only much later that we see the benefits (Hebrews 12:11).

What does the writer mean when he exhorts us not to regard our trials lightly? We might easily grit our teeth and go through looking eagerly for them to end. But rather, we must develop a fully positive attitude towards our problems. Spiritual life is a gymnasium in which muscles are stretched and tested to the limit. It is not a greenhouse with artificially perfect conditions.

To develop this positive attitude, we must praise God, even when it is a sacrifice to do so. We don't have to praise God for every problem but we certainly must learn to praise Him in the midst of them. We must also allow ourselves to be vulnerable, permitting the Lord to reshape our hearts in the furnace. The blacksmith heats the iron in order to shape it for use and he uses heat and hammer blows. The difference is that the iron has no say in the matter. It is inanimate and lifeless. But we have a will and mind that can cooperate with the Master and even kiss the hand that wounds us. It is as we surrender to God's love in the midst of the trial that it has its complete effect and produces full fruit in our character.

This time of testing is His love gift and it is as we recognise this and embrace His love, even through the tears, that God will be glorified and His purposes perfected. We are never to compare ourselves with others who seem to have an easier path. The choicest wreaths are bathed with tears and the purpose is yet to be fully revealed when the Master displays His trophies of grace.

September 2

The LORD said to him, "What are you doing here, Elijah?"
(1 Kings 19:9 NLT)

People have many questions that they wish to ask God, but the most important question is always the one that God asks us. Elijah was a mighty prophet and a fervent man of prayer. But at the moment God asked him this question, he was sunk deep in depression and fear.

When we wander from our path, whether it be a major departure from our calling or simply a neglect of our prayer life, God pursues us. He will speak right down to the root of our being and challenge us about the purpose that undergirds our life and activity. There is a restlessness about every person until they discover their calling. It takes just a nudge from God to awaken this deep longing to discover why we were created.

The tragedy of humanity is its escapism. Modern man lives for his leisure hours, to spend as much time as possible relaxing and forgetting the real world. Relaxation is right when it refreshes us and allows us to be strengthened to return to the fight with renewed vigour. But leisure must not be an end in itself. The human mind was not made to lose itself in endless pleasure, but to walk with God and stand for truth and righteousness. Elijah was in danger of losing his warrior spirit, of retreating into himself and fleeing the hazards of battle.

"Evil triumphs when good men do nothing" and this is most true when Christians retreat from the demands of spiritual life. There is a world to win, there is a truth to be proclaimed and great prayers to be prayed. When God asked Elijah what he was doing, Elijah answered with words of self-pity: "I alone am left; and they seek to take my life." (1 Kings 19:10) God's answer was to take him out onto the great stage of human life and send him out with the anointing and power to make a difference. The challenge of each day is to step out of the small things of my world into the bigger world of God and His kingdom.

September 3

Receive the Holy Spirit. (John 20:22)

Be filled with the Spirit. (Ephesians 5:18 KJV)

Believing a command is not enough, we must obey it. Yet it is one of the easiest snares that entangle the believer. We are commanded to love one another, to be holy and to be kind and tender-hearted to one another. At the heart of all the instructions of the New Testament is the command to be filled with the Holy Spirit. To disobey would be like buying a car, but declining to fill the tank with petrol. The Spirit is the power to do all God asks of us.

The fullness of the Spirit is known by experience. Jesus said that when the Spirit comes "you will know that I *am* in My Father, and you in Me, and I in you." (John 14:20) The work of the Holy Spirit can be summed up in the way He makes God real to us. The Holy Spirit communicates the deep things of God, not through emotions and not through books, but through the impact of the divine presence on our spirit.

Even a cursory comparison of the life of the disciples before and after Pentecost will conclude that their spiritual life was deeply transformed. Belief became unshakable assurance. Fear was swallowed up by boldness. Spiritual dryness was replaced by fervent worship and daring and persistent prayer. God has set before us the wonderful provision of power to live, power to love and power to esteem others better than ourselves. The Holy Spirit is the doorway to a supernatural life in God. We must be persuaded of these simple truths and then obey, surrendering ourselves and receiving God's amazing gift.

~~~~~~~~~~~~~~

September 4

To know the love of Christ which passes knowledge; that you may be filled with all the fullness of God. (Ephesians 3:19)
Father, I desire that they also whom You gave Me may be with Me where I am, that they may behold My glory which You have given Me. (John 17:24)

These two prayers are extraordinarily large, far-reaching and positive. The truth of the gospel is that it is not solely a call to leave something, it is a call to embrace someone. Freedom from sin is not only the absence of bad things - it is far more the presence of the living Christ.

Think of that fullness and glory of Christ. He dwelt in the deep stillness of the Father's presence through all eternity. This divine abundance is best described by the pulsating waves of love and holiness that emanate from His being. This is not a geographical place, but a spiritual place attained by entire surrender of one's being to the wonder of the eternal, infinite God. Christianity as described by Jesus and His servant Paul is not a set of beliefs but an open door into the limitless world of God. We are to have all of God and we can only have this if we are prepared to let God have all of us. These words are an expression of a whole-hearted manner of life that is God's earnest intention for every believer.

This is not merely a desire to live without too much trouble, it is a yearning, a raw hunger for God Himself. It is the desire to be united with Him in the centre of our wills and our emotions and to know His peace, His love, Himself. As we open up our being for these daring prayers to be answered, we will occasionally know the impact of the divine in moments of overwhelming bliss. The consequence is ever-renewed entire surrender to One beyond words to describe, and thus to discover the power of an endless life beating at the centre of who we are.

~~~~~~~~~~~~~~

September 5

For if you remain completely silent at this time, relief and deliverance will arise for the Jews from another place, but you and your father's house will perish. Yet who knows whether you have come to the kingdom for such a time as this?
(Esther 4:14)
Esther found favour in his sight, and the king held out to her the golden sceptre that was in his hand. Then Esther went near and touched the top of the sceptre. *(Esther 5:2)*

Esther was uniquely placed by God's grace to be able to intercede with king Ahasuerus. All Esther had to do was go boldly to the king and hope that he would extend mercy to her by holding out the sceptre. It is an astonishingly simple picture of the church and her unique place as the bride of Christ. Esther melted the heart of the king and God's heart is moved as He looks at the believer clothed with all the beauty of Jesus. Ahasuerus was wilful and unpredictable, while God is faithful and welcoming. Esther risked her life, knowing the king might be in a bad mood and reject her, but believers know that with God "there is no variation or shadow of turning" (James 1:17).

Esther held in her hands the fate of the Jews and believers hold tremendous power by the simple fact that God has promised to hear us when we pray. Governments, individuals and demonic strongholds all yield to the sovereign decrees of God in answer to prayer. It is for this reason that prayer is the one thing that Satan dreads and that he opposes more fiercely than any other activity. God has committed Himself to answer prayers that are according to His will and that are prayed from pure motives.

The phrase "such a time as this" can be written large over every phase of history. Church unity is maintained more by prayer than by committees. Conflicts are resolved, sinners are saved and ministries are blessed and flourish through prayer. There is no danger in approaching the King, but there is disaster if we hold back and neglect the place of prayer. Whatever our capacity, we are simply to boldly step forward and pray.

September 6

But then I will win her back once again. I will lead her into the desert and speak tenderly to her there. I will return her vineyards to her and transform the Valley of Trouble into a gateway of hope. (Hosea 2:14-15 NLT)

Immediately the Spirit drove Jesus into the wilderness.
(Mark 1:12 KJV)

God's spirit led even Jesus into the wilderness and the Greek word for 'drove' implies some exertion of force. It is understandable that we are apprehensive about the desolate places in which we are forced to enter. But God is here exhorting His people to be full of hope and without anxiety when such times come upon us.

There is a clear choice before us in every difficult situation. We will be tempted to moan and groan in self-pity like the children of Israel and go round and round in circles or we will allow deep blessings to distil upon our souls. If we will quieten ourselves and trust, we will find that the word of God will come alive in hitherto unimaginable ways. We will discover its relevance and power in our daily life. The word will stir our faith, inspiring us, strengthening us and making us as bold as lions.

It is also through the rigours of tough situations that our hearts are sifted, our motives purified and our life-goals are narrowed down. Our priorities change and we lose the fussy pettiness of our preoccupation with trivial things. There is an enemy to overcome and we had better gird up our loins, dig into the Word and resist the devil. It is in the wilderness that we most learn to fight. Part of the fight is the pruning and purifying that comes as we learn to let go of things that once seemed important. Every soldier who has been in combat situations has learned to let go of any encumbrance and so free himself to use his weapons.

So never fear the wilderness, but enter boldly, following your captain who has gone before. Know that the Spirit of God has brought you here to fully equip you to fight and win the battles ahead.

September 7

The water that was made wine.   *(John 2:9 KJV)*
I am the vine, you are the branches. He who abides in Me, and I in him, bears much fruit; for without Me you can do nothing.
(John 15:5)

There is a remarkable beauty about the structure of John's gospel and a consistency in the images and symbols. The vine is God's 'machine' for turning water into wine. As a tree it has no strength in its branches, unlike the mighty oak or the sturdy mango tree. This is the smallest and weakest of trees and needs a wooden structure to support it. Jesus was never a more fruitful vine than when He hung on the cross.

The cross was a visible and cruel outworking of a beautiful principle in God's very nature. To speak of a crucified life may sound horrific to many people but it is nevertheless the best way of describing life in the Spirit. Jesus was the most dead man who ever lived. He was dead to money, to sin, to pride and to self. At the same time, He was the most alive man: alive to God, to love and free to notice and love others. He lived quite naturally in the place of self-denial and God-consciousness. It is precisely this living consciousness of God that distinguished Him from religious people who had outward forms of knowing God, but had no conscious, experiential knowledge of Him and His presence.

Abiding in Christ cannot be a merely doctrinal position or it would be to make it an intellectual exercise, a mental posture. It is the surrender of the heart to the living presence of Jesus Christ. He permeates our being as we continually yield, drowning out the pitiful moans of an unloving selfish personality and infusing us with Himself. Fragrant, delicious fruits of His presence appear, as we maintain this inner exaltation of Him above our preferences, our choices and even our own lives. To know God's love is sweet beyond description. But to see love growing in our own hearts is sweeter still, because it is Him in us producing the very same life. It is to know the sweet-smelling perfume of love in the deepest fountains of our own life.

~~~~~~~~~~~~~

September 8

By faith Jacob, when he was a dying, blessed both the sons of Joseph, and worshipped, leaning upon the top of his staff.
(Hebrews 11:21 KJV)

Jacob was worshipping leaning on his staff, not merely because of old age but because he was a cripple. That staff had become an essential part of his life since his encounter with God at Peniel. He must have remembered that night of wrestling with God every time he stood up. The angel's appearance had been unexpected and he had fought with all his strength. Jacob had proved to have an inner citadel that resisted God and kept Him at arm's length. He must have wondered that night whether the angel was trying to kill him. But God had sent his messenger to break Jacob's inner bastion of self-reliance and independence from God. It must have hurt him when at last his hip was dislocated. Jacob was at last vulnerable and open to God. He was a worshipper at last, relying on the strength that God supplies.

Every worshipper has experienced an inner shift from a self-contained place to one that is deeply related to God as the source of all things. The apostles had had their good days when they had healed the sick and walked with Jesus. But the day came when they all forsook Him and fled. Their best was not enough. Thank God, He is not appealing to the best in us. He simply wants us to come and surrender to the cross as a door of power. Some put up a big fight and have to pass through some humbling experiences but some simply yield with sweet surrender to the lordship of Christ.

As we lean, Christ is formed in us. If we fight, we retain the prickly, manipulating ways of all who think they can live without God's help. It doesn't have to hurt. It simply requires a deep persuasion that this is the way we are designed. A caterpillar in its own strength will take years to cover a single mile and will never cross a river or a mountain. But once it has yielded to death and resurrection, it is given wings to fly in minutes where it never dreamt it could reach in its former life. Jacob was crippled that he might learn to lean and take flight in wonder and worship.

∾∾∾∾∾∾∾∾∾∾∾∾∾

September 9

Fear not, for I have redeemed you; I have called you by your name; you are Mine. When you pass through the waters, I will be with you; and through the rivers, they shall not overflow you. When you walk through the fire, you shall not be burned, nor shall the flame scorch you. (Isaiah 43:1-2)

Someone has counted that there are 366 occasions when the Bible bids us not to fear. That would be one for every day of the year with one spare for a leap year. It is certainly a constant refrain throughout the Bible and it comes to us on three different levels.

First, it is a command, because God is not merely suggesting that we should throw off fear. He is speaking with all His divine authority and power. God looks at fear as a surgeon looks at a cancer. He addresses it as a virus from Satan which deserves the full blast of His powerful rebuke.

Secondly, it is a plea. God knows that fear is the biggest enemy to faith, and is in fact negative faith, the belief that something bad will happen. He pleads with us as a father with a beloved child to look full into His wonderful face and feed our souls on His loving care and watchful protection over us. Fear will not be a conduit for bad things to happen, but it does rob us of peace and allows tension to take root in our body, soul and spirit. God keeps His promises and is especially tender to His fear-stricken lambs. He holds them in His arms with fiercely protective love. Jesus pleads with us not to let our hearts be troubled nor afraid, for He will never leave us or forsake us.

Finally, it is a prophetic word of power. When Jesus spoke to the leper, the disease disappeared. When He spoke to Lazarus, His word called into the realm of the dead and raised him to life. The word of God comes with the power to fulfil what He says. It is as we receive His word with faith that it will have its full effect in us. Love casts out fear and God is love, speaking tenderly and powerfully into the depth of our beings to raise us from the grave of fear into the warmth of His powerful, sheltering hands.

September 10

Then, when Mary came where Jesus was, and saw Him, she fell down at His feet, saying to Him, "Lord, if You had been here, my brother would not have died." Therefore, when Jesus saw her weeping, and the Jews who came with her weeping, He groaned in the spirit and was troubled…. Jesus wept.
(John 11:32-35)

The greatest pain and suffering is the loss of hope. Mary briefly lost her trust that Jesus was in command of her circumstances. This did not hinder the outcome, but it did plunge her into the unnecessary grief and pain of despair. Mary had convinced herself that Jesus would heal Lazarus and her world fell apart when he died.

Mary found it hard to relate to this marvellous all-powerful Saviour now that things had gone wrong. Such moments are dangerous and in times of affliction, we will be tempted to believe that God has forsaken us, stopped answering our prayers or, worst of all, is punishing us for some unknown reason. We may feel so alienated that we even begin to think of God as our adversary. We may also begin to blame ourselves that we didn't pray enough or have sufficient faith, or perhaps we are not holy enough.

Mary was the one who had spent hours sitting at the feet of Jesus and she should have known better when the crisis came. The same applies to us. When things take an unexpected turn for the worse, we must simply believe. It is a choice we must make, based on His abiding faithfulness in the way He has dealt with us all our lives. It is also rooted in His word, with numerous promises and examples for us to consider.

Jesus had no condemnation for Mary. He identified with her infinite sorrow and bewilderment. He did not weep for Lazarus since He knew that within a few moments, he would be raised to life. He wept for the deep sense of lostness that can engulf us if we stop trusting. God is not punishing us. He is not our adversary and He cannot leave us or forsake us. The answer is to boldly proclaim our trust. The fog will one day lift and then we will understand His perfect master plan.

~~~~~~~~~~~~~~~

September 11

Now as He sat on the Mount of Olives, the disciples came to Him privately, saying, "Tell us, when will these things be? And what will be the sign of Your coming, and of the end of the age?" (Matthew 24:3)

Matthew 24 and 25 are the record of Jesus' discourse on the Mount of Olives about the end of the world. It has been the cause of endless discussion and some arguments. The most important aspect of it is easy to miss. Simply look at the serenity of Jesus, surrounded by his confused disciples and yet able to comfort them and give them a perspective of peace and final triumph in the midst of trouble.

Jesus was facing crucifixion and death. His disciples had been completely out of step with Him regarding His approaching passion and resurrection. Jesus was the Man of sorrows and isolated in His awareness of what lay immediately ahead. He was about to be betrayed by Judas and abandoned by His closest followers. Beyond this He also saw the coming centuries, with the fall of Jerusalem and endless wars. He saw the church in all its ups and downs through persecution and internal strife. Yet Christ was not living under the fear of the darkness, not even of the shadow of His imminent suffering.

There is a majesty and tranquillity as Jesus lifted up His eyes and saw the ultimate triumph and accomplishment of the plan and will of God. He knew the resurrection was but three days away, and looking further, He saw His glorious return and rule and establishing of His everlasting kingdom. Believers may rightly discuss all the details of this prophecy, but the key lesson is much simpler. We are to sit with Him and drink of His peacefulness and calm as we face whatever the next three days may bring, or the next three hundred years.

~~~~~~~~~~~~~~

September 12

We are afflicted in every way, but not crushed; perplexed, but not driven to despair; persecuted, but not forsaken; struck down, but not destroyed; always carrying in the body the death of Jesus, so that the life of Jesus may also be manifested in our bodies. (2 Corinthians 4:8-10 ESV)

Paul is describing his feelings during a time of extreme distress. The remarkable thing is that though the trial was severe, Paul had an inner assurance that He was not forsaken. The worst moment in any life is precisely when a person feels that God has abandoned them. This was specifically what Jesus experienced at the height of the cross. He suffered the wretchedness of taking our place and suffering the horror of separation from God for us. He agonised in the anguish of identifying with us so that we might experience total acceptance. This is the worst of human suffering and Christ bore it for us.

Now we have the promise "I will never leave you nor forsake you." (Hebrews 13:5 ESV) It is the unshakable promise that we will never be abandoned by God. Even if we panic and forget this promise, it will not change the fact that He is faithful to His word. We may well be afflicted, perplexed, persecuted and struck down by life, but we will never be abandoned. This means that we have the everlasting arms of love to hold us. It means that God is suffering with us. He is not the enemy and so we have a strong wall of protection against despair.

The death of Jesus is the power working in us to remove sighs of simpering selfishness and to replace it with the robust confidence of unbreakable unity with God. Jesus Christ feels our burdens more than we do and stands in perfect empathy with us. What happens to us happens to Him. Those who are against us are actually defying God Himself. God is in us to lead us in triumph. It will not mean there are no problems or pain, but it does mean that an irrepressible light of hope burns unquenchably in our hearts.

~~~~~~~~~~~~~~

September 13

Take care of him; and whatever more you spend, when I come again, I will repay you.   *(Luke 10:35)*
You give them something to eat.   *(Matthew 14:16 NASB)*

These are the words of the good Samaritan to the innkeeper followed by the words of Christ to His disciples. Christ Himself has established an inn where hurting souls can be cared for. He has made us the householder to run His affairs till He returns. He has undertaken to give us daily bread, a home and everything we need. His will and purpose is that we will imaginatively engage in His grand venture of loving people into the kingdom of God in anticipation of His return.

It is obvious that Christ cannot bake a cake for a lonely widow. He cannot visit a prison to preach to the inmates and He cannot visit the sick. But we can, and He depends on His body to be His special people "zealous of good works" (Titus 2:14). True, our good works can never save us, but we are to glorify Him as we distribute the loaves and fishes and watch them multiply in our hands. He has given us abundant love and grace, and it will multiply in us as we pour it out. "Sell what you have and give alms" (Luke 12:33). "It is more blessed to give than to receive" (Acts 20:35). "Whatever your hand finds to do, do *it* with your might" (Ecclesiastes 9:10).

There is a great promise attached to these commands; that whatever we spend in this great will and plan of God will be given back to us in another form at the return of Christ. The resurrection will be a joyous reunion and it will also be a time of rewards. The Lord Himself has solemnly promised to repay whatever we have given to those who cannot repay us. As with all spiritual discipline, there is a measure of conscious choice combined with the enabling of the Holy Spirit.

Evan Roberts at the outset of the Welsh Revival prayed "Lord, bend me!" We must pray constantly for opportunities to fulfil the mission of the King by good works, by witnessing - in short, by loving people. It will take God's almighty power to bend our souls to be shaped and used so that we may open our hand to release the bread to a dying world.

September 14

Then Elisha prayed, "O LORD, open his eyes and let him see!" The LORD opened the young man's eyes, and when he looked up, he saw that the hillside around Elisha was filled with horses and chariots of fire. (2 Kings 6:17 NLT)

At Hyde Park Corner, an atheist boldly asserted that there is no God. He said "I have never seen Him, nor heaven nor an angel. They don't exist!" There were loud cheers of agreement. Then a man raised his hand and asked if he could say a word. He was escorted to the front by a friend. "There are no clouds in the sky," he began. "There are no trees in the park, and there is no sun in the sky. I have never seen them. You see, I'm blind."

Christians may defend their faith with powerful and convincing intellectual arguments. But in the end, we are witnesses of something we have seen by faith. The blind man in John 9 was humiliated by the Pharisees and their arguments. But in the end, he cried out: "One thing I know: that though I was blind, now I see." (John 9:25)

As sight is in the world of light, so is faith in the world of the spirit. The moment we believe, we understand and things fall into place. If God were a product of our intellect, we would never agree on anything, but God is real and we are blind till we believe. The wonder of having our eyes opened through faith is that the spiritual world is so amazing. There are majestic, powerful beings surrounding us and protecting us. When Dietrich Bonhoeffer was in prison awaiting execution, he penned some astonishing lines demonstrating an extraordinary serenity: "Wonderfully shielded by good powers, we await with inner comfort what the future holds. God is with us in the evening and in the morning, and quite certainly on every new day."

September 15

Then Jesus told Peter, "Follow me." Peter turned around and saw behind them the disciple Jesus loved…. Peter asked Jesus, "What about him, Lord?" (John 21:19-21 NLT)

Peter was enjoying the greatest privilege a human being can ever have: a personal audience with Jesus Christ. Yet in the middle of this life-changing conversation, Peter looked over his shoulder and saw John. It is the little distractions that make us look back while relishing moments of worship and the majestic self-disclosure of God to our souls.

The Queen was once in conversation with a visitor at one of her garden parties at Buckingham Palace. Suddenly their mobile phone began to ring. "You should answer that," said the Queen, "It might be someone important." In theatres, cinemas and other public events, participants are routinely charged to turn off their mobile phones. This instruction is normally followed, simply because people have often paid to be in that place and are eagerly awaiting the show. Imagine though if someone were waiting for a call regarding an important job interview. Think of someone waiting for some important results of a medical test. The list of important communications is endless. It is a strong person who can switch off their phone when they go to prayer, and even stronger the one who can switch off their flitting thoughts.

It is the backward glance that stops us entering into the fullness of His presence. It is the urge to just take a peek at someone else's situation that trips us up and distracts us from the full impact of Jesus Christ and His speaking to our soul and our situation. The power of Christ is unchanging but the channel for that power is an undisturbed gaze. The most blessed state of any person is to serve the Lord without distraction, not allowing any cause, whether big or small, to take their eyes off Him.

September 16

Because of the weakness of your human nature, I am using the illustration of slavery to help you understand all this. Previously, you let yourselves be slaves to impurity and lawlessness, which led ever deeper into sin. Now you must give yourselves to be slaves to righteous living so that you will become holy. (Romans 6:19 NLT)

The vainest pursuit is that of absolute freedom. Only God is absolutely free. His is the only sovereign free-will in the universe. Our freedom of will is real but derived from Him.

Democracy has deluded people into believing that if they have enough money, they can create their own world. Some have gone so far as to project this delusion into the after-life, claiming that we all make our own heaven or hell. Imagine telling the tax man that we should be allowed to create our own levels of taxation. We would meet the real world with a harsh bump.

There is no middle ground between being a slave of sin and a slave of righteousness. We are either under the power of darkness or of Christ. It is for this reason, too, that freedom from sin is not merely to lose something. It is, far more importantly, to gain someone. It is the positive pursuit of the rule of Christ in my life. Paul is here exhorting the believer to the same enthusiastic surrender to holiness as he once had to worldly things.

Paul is opening our eyes to the wonder of belonging entirely to Jesus. He never exalts liberty for its own sake. The moment we see our faith as a duty and not a delight, we lose our freedom from the world. Paul is revealing that only when we discover the joy of surrender will everything fall into place. The Christian life should be the heart-felt pursuit of God and righteousness, and only then will power flow into our spiritual veins and fill our souls with liberating joy and abundant life. To serve Christ is truly perfect freedom.

~~~~~~~~~~~~~~~

September 17

Pray without ceasing.   *(1 Thessalonians 5:17 NASB)*

All religions pray. Buddhists have prayer flags and prayer wheels, Catholics light candles at shrines. Many churches have liturgies or written forms of prayer that are repeated, often including the Lord's Prayer. However, in themselves these things are not prayer.

Prayer is talking to God. Prayer is reaching out to discover the living God and to meet with Him. Prayer is opening a door for God into our lives and circumstances. Prayer is the true exercise of the human soul, in cooperating with God so that His plans and purposes can be fulfilled in the earth.

Prayer is like the train tracks for a train. The train is powerful, but can only move if there are tracks. So God has ordained that unless human beings request Him to do certain things, He will not do them.

Prayer is the highest activity of the human soul, and involves the exercise of that faculty of our spirits that can commune with God. Prayer is a longing, a thirsting for God. Some say prayers for revival but do not thirst for it.

"Prayer is not the spare tyre on the car of our lives, it is the steering wheel!" (Corrie Ten Boon) Prayer is not for the strong who need no help, it is for the powerless who need a miracle. We have to be weak enough to pray.

Pray when you feel tired or refreshed, when you feel strong or unwell. Pray when you have much time, pray when you have but minutes to spare. Pray at set regular times of the day. Pray spontaneously when you have an unexpected opportunity. Pray alone or with others. Let prayer be so continual that it becomes the unthinking instinct, our second nature to lift up our eyes to God for help. Pray without ceasing.

September 18

Abraham obeyed when he was called to go out to the place which he would receive as an inheritance. And he went out, not knowing where he was going. (Hebrews 11:8)
But now they desire a better, that is, a heavenly country. Therefore God is not ashamed to be called their God, for He has prepared a city for them. (Hebrews 11:16)

Hebrews chapter 11 describes the Christian life as a great journey of faith. We embark on this voyage by repentance, leaving the world behind and fixing our eyes on a better world, not sure where it will all lead on our earthly course, but certain of an eternal, heavenly home.

We see the goal, the heavenly city, and we have right values because of this vision. We must not lose sight of our goal. Like those who have gone before, we engage in the work God has called us to do; we build, we sacrifice, we follow and we obey. We also meet significant obstacles and we endure hardship, overcoming persecutions and temptations to turn back.

The power to keep us on our journey is faith. Faith is the faculty that deals with the unseen and the future. Sin and unbelief make man live in the externals, and thus a person without faith is cut off from the source of life. All things come from God, the Creator. To live free from inner darkness, we must live a life of faith in touch with the invisible source of life and power – the Creator. Man is compelled to explain all by the visible until he believes. Then, and only then, he understands. The physical world is secondary; faith and God's word are primary. Faith is real substance (Hebrews 11:1). It is more real than the physical world.

The visible world can crowd out God and intimidate us. But the world offers hollow pleasures that disappear like a puff of smoke. Lasting joy is only found in the discovery of the unseen God, revealed through His unchanging word. Just as the eye cannot hear, so the heart cannot believe through seeing external things. It is only by hearing the word of God that we believe. Whatever trial or obstacle we may be facing, we are to rise up and believe the word and the testimony of a great crowd of witnesses, past and present, who are cheering us on our way.

~~~~~~~~~~~~~~~

September 19

For I am the LORD, I change not. (Malachi 3:6 KJV)
You thought that I was altogether like you. (Psalm 50:21)

God is immutable. He cannot change, for alteration would imply that He could improve or that there were some imperfection that would be ironed out through time or some outward influence upon Him. God is perfect and faultless. He is love eternal and will never change.

This has consequences, most of all that God will never allow Himself to be adapted to suit us. We can waste much time editing God to please the world in which we live. We tend to believe we understand best what people need, and we try and make God more like us. So we speak much of His love and little of His holiness. We spread out the hope of a new world without pain and suffering, but we speak less of the pressing need of radical repentance. We speak much of Him as Father and little of Him as judge.

We must stop trying to invent our own version of the God of the Bible and come with open hearts to discover Him. He will take us by surprise as we recognise that we have had a far too superficial view of Him. We assumed we were more personable than He, but we discover that we are the mechanical ones. Our warmest thoughts are frozen ice compared to His loving heart. He is more holy than we imagine, with depths of blazing purity. We are often slow to realise how much we assume God is like us.

It is a doorway of discovery when we grasp how different He is. One commentator speaks of the "otherness" of God. In all His qualities, He is more than us and we must change and be altered to become more like the radiant, amazing person that He is. That "otherness" is His incorruptible, radiant and holy love, which can never make peace with sin other than by destroying it. The appeal of the gospel to every hearer is to simply let God be Himself to us and in us. If we let Jesus be Himself to us and in us, we will begin to see things from His amazing standpoint and He will begin to be the power of our life.

September 20

And the LORD went before them by day in a pillar of cloud to lead the way, and by night in a pillar of fire to give them light, so as to go by day and night. (Exodus 13:21)
And when he putteth forth his own sheep, he goeth before them, and the sheep follow him: for they know his voice.
(John 10:4 ESV)

How wonderful that God always goes before us, whether by day or by night! God meets all the situations we will ever face ahead of us. He confronts the enemy first, so that He does not stand behind us, we stand behind Him. He will give us shade from the heat of the sun by the pillar of cloud, and He will give us light in the darkest night so that we may have comfort and know the next step. The shade and the light will always be sufficient. He has promised to supply all our need through all the rigours of the journey of life.

The journey of faith is precisely that. It is not by sight. We may not always know what our master is doing, but we know He will never leave us or forsake us. We may be surprised by a sudden turn of events, but God is ready and has prepared us for what we are about to face. We are to cultivate a consciousness that we are not our own, but rather we are servants of a great King. Whatever we meet is primarily His concern not ours. If we suffer lack, He will provide us with manna. If we lack water, He will break open the rock to quench our thirst. If we are attacked, He will give us the wisdom to overcome every situation.

When a head of state such as the Queen pays a visit to a town, an army goes ahead to prepare for her security and every other need she may have while there. Christ has gone ahead and is stepping out in front of us. We may lose the awareness that He is there but that does not change the fact. He has all the armies of heaven at His command and He sends them to keep us and our loved ones safe in His keeping.

~~~~~~~~~~~~~~

September 21

Look to Me, and be saved, all you ends of the earth! For I am God, and there is no other. (Isaiah 45:22)

The year was 1942 and it was the siege of Stalingrad. A young German soldier named Wilhelm Hufer was hit by shrapnel in the back and the neck. He lay badly wounded on the battle field. His eyes shifted from the battle to God and he prayed vowing that if God would bring him home, he would serve him forever. God changed Wilhelm's life that day as He met him in the mud of Stalingrad. Another soldier picked him up and carried him back to safety. He was transported out and made it back to convalesce in his home village. He kept his promise and served Jesus for the rest of his life till his death in 1980.

The marvel of this man's salvation was that he was able to believe in Jesus Christ in the most extreme circumstances imaginable. The Bible says simply "look to Me and be saved." The Bible is here defining faith as a steadfast look at Jesus Christ. There is a faculty of the heart that corresponds to the eye, and by it we can turn and fix our gaze on the everlasting God.

Looking is a perfect description of faith, because it is within the reach of every person. It isn't a long prayer of theological precision. It is not attendance at church or a series of good works. Faith, even as the eye cannot see itself, looks away to one greater and is not self-conscious. Faith is to look to Another, who alone has the ability to intervene on our behalf. Faith is ceasing to look to ourselves and it is ceasing to look down; it is the upward gaze to the face of God. Everyone who looks will find a face of love and authority looking back at them. The moment we believe, something changes in the soul and we get infinitely more than we expected. The whole life takes on a new shape as the substance of faith becomes the foundation of our life. There is peace, there is hope. Salvation has come and we have taken the first step on the journey of a lifetime.

September 22

Then He appointed twelve, that they might be with Him and that He might send them out to preach …. Simon, to whom He gave the name Peter; James and John ….   (Mark 3:14 & 19) When they saw the boldness of Peter and John, and discovered that they were uneducated and ordinary men, they were amazed and recognized these men had been with Jesus.
(Acts 4:13 NET)

It is remarkable that Jesus chose twelve men who brought very little to the kingdom of God. It is said of Peter and John that they were uneducated and ordinary. They were not deep thinkers nor were they wealthy. They were fishermen who probably had to live from hand to mouth. Moreover, Peter had some deep character flaws. He was very impulsive, often speaking without thinking. Sometimes he got it right (Matthew 16:16) and sometimes he got it completely wrong (Matthew 16:23).

So what was the quality that Jesus saw in these men? The most important thing was that when they were rebuked they did not go into a huff and sulk. They were not offended but took the reproof on the chin. They didn't make a great fuss but humbled themselves, picked themselves up and followed Him.

It could be said of these men that they denied themselves, took up their cross and followed Him. It might be said they had no reputation to lose, but that is not true. Everyone has some self-respect and dignity. So everyone must be willing to make themselves of no reputation. No-one can do this for us. Jesus humbled Himself (Philippians 2:8) and we must humble ourselves. Life deals out its heavy blows, but will not make us humble. That is something we do from the inside.

Peter and all the apostles forsook Jesus (Mark 14:50). But they were all there on the day of Pentecost, having turned away from their failure and believing in His grace and forgiveness to take them on. We may have many musical or intellectual gifts and talents, but none of them will keep us following. It is only that ability to be totally careless about our self-importance that will allow the Holy Spirit to take up our lives and show the grace of God through us.

September 23

For Christ is our peace, the one who ... destroyed ... the hostility, ... to reconcile the Jews and the Gentiles both in one body to God through the cross, by which the hostility has been killed. (Ephesians 2:14-16 NET)

For much of our lives we have been enemies of God. We were strangers to His love and His promises, living in the darkness of unbelief. But God has now reconciled us to Himself. We are now His beloved children. It is sometimes heard that believers have been urged to 'storm heaven' with their prayers as if God were still the enemy or at best the reluctant general. Nothing could be further from the truth.

The Christian is not caught in some grey territory between darkness and light. We are now ranked behind our heavenly Father and Jesus, the captain of our salvation. God is for us and therefore who can be against us? The battles we are facing are not ours, they are the Lord's. We must banish from our minds any thought that God is against us or even indifferent to us. Many tears are shed because of a feeling of abandonment. But those days of being forsaken are passed and gone.

We are God's precious children. We are a royal priesthood, a chosen generation. We may sometimes pinch ourselves and think there must be some mistake. But God knows who we are and He has adopted us into His family as co-heirs with Christ. We are not serving a probationary period to see how we do, nor are we second-class citizens. Our minds must simply catch up with the breath-taking reality that we are now, and ever shall be, the apple of God's eye.

~~~~~~~~~~~~~~~

September 24

For our momentary, light suffering is producing for us an eternal weight of glory far beyond all comparison.
(2 Corinthians 4:17 NET)
For I consider that the sufferings of this present time are not worthy to be compared with the glory which shall be revealed in us. *(Romans 8:18)*

One day we will die and we will open our eyes on another world. We will be swallowed up into a love that we cannot begin to imagine. One may ask why God does not cut out all the challenging steps that take us deeper into His love in this life. There is so much that tests our spiritual sinew as we pass through this vale of tears. But if God did not take us on this journey, the world would never have the slightest glimpse of that magnificent world of love.

There is a deeper level of union with God where His thoughts become our thoughts. Often we are a step away from this oneness because we have a lingering idea that God may be remote. We suspect He may be angry with us or just waiting indifferently on the side lines.

The truth is that God identifies with us, first in our fallen state, dying our death and sharing His life with us. Secondly, He identifies with us as His children, feeling what we feel, both our pain and our joy. But thirdly, He wants us to identify with Him, to let Him in and be the great positive power that sustains us. After all, we are not gaining the approval of a distant uncle. This is almighty God we are dealing with. He wants us to share His greatness. Yes, we may be suffering, but He is travailing with us and He wants us to partake of the serene assurance that He will turn it all to good.

We are a window on a great kingdom, and it is not a static tableau. God is shaping our lives and He takes His time as He brings us ever closer to deepest union with Himself. As we yield ourselves to Him in our deepest moments of struggling, we emerge like butterflies from a chrysalis and the effect is amazing. We are not putting on a show, because we are not even conscious that anyone is watching. But our lives are lived out on a grand stage, fulfilling a magnificent plan. All things work together for good for those who love God. This is the unshakable confidence that shines through our lives as we go steadily on with our wonderful Father.

~~~~~~~~~~~~~~~~

September 25

Let us run with endurance the race that is set before us, looking to Jesus, the founder and perfecter of our faith.
(Hebrews 12:1-2 ESV)

At the 1968 Mexico City Olympics, John Stephen Akhwari of Tanzania started the Olympic marathon with all the other runners but finished it alone, and in last place. Several miles into the race, Akhwari suddenly found himself trapped in the middle of some other runners. Unable to see well, he fell and hurt his leg horribly. He now knew he could not win a medal, but with great courage, he continued. Long after the winners had finished and received their praise, this final runner entered the stadium. Sirens blared as this lone weary and injured man entered. Only a few hundred spectators were left, but as they realised this was a runner who was finishing long after all the others, they began to applaud - quietly at first, but it grew into a crescendo. He took his lap around the track with his bandaged and bloody feet. Though suffering from injury, fatigue, leg cramps, dehydration, and disorientation, Akhwari finally crossed the finish line. When asked by a reporter why he did not just quit, he answered, "My country did not send me to Mexico City to start the race. They sent me here to finish."

It is an inspirational story and it illustrates perfectly the Scripture that describes faith as a race. Faith is a marathon, not a hundred metre dash. It doesn't matter how we feel about ourselves, it matters only that we keep our eyes on Jesus. If we look at ourselves, we may well give up, but we are not to trust in ourselves but in Christ. He is the one who planted the first seed of faith when we first looked at Him. He is the one who will keep us going and make our faith perfect on the final day. It is a marathon in which all who keep going win the prize. Heaven will erupt with praises as we finish the race. We must not regard the weakness we feel, nor the painful scars from conflicts fought and won. We conquer the dread power of self every time we lift our eyes to look on Him who pours His love and encouragement into our hearts.

~~~~~~~~~~~~~

September 26

My soul longs, yes, even faints for the courts of the LORD; My heart and my flesh cry out for the living God .... For a day in Your courts is better than a thousand. (Psalm 84:2 & 10)

The Psalmist estimated that one day in God's presence was better than a thousand. The average person lives seventy years or 25,550 days. So the Psalmist reckoned that to live just 25 days sensing God's nearness was better than to live out a whole life without that awareness. Many believe that the presence of God is accessible, but do not experience it.

The distinctive mark of all who pursue God in a deep way is that when they discover God, they seek Him till His presence becomes the dominant note in their life. God manifests Himself to all people in some degree. Unless God draws near to us, we could have no more hope of finding Him than a needle in a haystack. But God does want to be found and manifests Himself. He tugs at our hearts and we are awakened to another world we scarcely could hope existed. No- one has ever seen God, but God demonstrated His desire to be known by sending His Son and then the Holy Spirit.

God can be found. Once we have known even just a whisper of the matchless majesty that is God, we are to cultivate our spiritual faculties till knowing Him becomes the reason we live. Augustine said that our hearts are restless till they find rest in God. Once we have tasted God, we will be hollow shells till we have developed the habit of drinking long and deep at this well of eternal life.

God has brushed your heart with His presence. Now the question is: what will you do about it? The Psalmist was not suppressing his thirst for God but surrendering to it. He was allowing it to shape his priorities, his way of life. We often bemoan our lack of time. The truth is simply that we have not made time. Rise up in heart and pursue God, for to know Him is the only reason worth living for.

~~~~~~~~~~~~~~~

September 27

Let us draw near by a new and living way which He consecrated for us, through the veil, that is, His flesh.
(Hebrews 10:20)

For until this day the same veil remains unlifted in the reading of the Old Testament, because the veil is taken away in Christ. But even to this day, when Moses is read, a veil lies on their heart. Nevertheless when one turns to the Lord, the veil is taken away. *(2 Corinthians 3:14-16)*

These verses speak of two veils, the torn body of Christ and the proud religious egos of the religious self-righteous. The tearing of Christ from His Father is a mystery of divine love that we can barely understand. The indivisible perfect unity that is Father, Son and Holy Spirit was shattered for the hours in which Christ was made sin. The veil was rent in Christ and this was not merely a poetical thought. It was a terrible reality as Christ opened up His veins to make it possible for sinners to return as sons to a holy God.

The second veil of religious pride still cloaks the heart of many who study the Bible, both Jew and Christian. This veil speaks of an indescribable tragedy that God should pay such a price for us to fellowship with Him while human beings will pay so little to tear the veil of self-interest. This second veil is as real as the first veil. It may be that we whine and protest as our virtues and talents are all cast into the dust. But our whingeing is only delaying the moment when we turn in deepest repentance and humility. Then the veil simply disappears and we are ushered into the breath-taking presence of the Holy of Holies. The need for the crucifixion of our flesh is a fact and as we turn in faith, we discover that it falls aside as if a strong iron shield had been turned to dust and ashes.

Turning to the Lord is just a movement of the heart. But it may be that our heart is like an old rusted door that will resist and protest with creaks and groans. We may have a skilfully-woven veil of pride that we have patched up and repaired. We are to simply let it all go. Paul suffered the loss of all things that He might know Christ, and we must follow the same path and discover the beautiful life-giving presence of God.

September 28

God for whom are all things and by whom are all things.
(Hebrews 2:10)

The instinct of a baby is that everything revolves around it. It has needs that must be met. But the sign of maturity is an ever-increasing recognition that we only play a small role in a greater purpose. This is also true in our prayer lives.

The great question in the kingdom is "Who is serving whom?" Christians begin their new life with a true understanding that God is serving them, but quickly they must grasp that this is only temporary. If they remain the centre, then they perceive God as simply there to meet their endless needs. They will see prayer as a fire extinguisher to be used to put out all the fires that keep breaking out. Their prayerfulness will increase when they have problems and decrease when things are going well.

When Lazarus became ill his sisters Martha and Mary went into firefighting mode. When he died, their joy expired and their faith faltered. When he rose from the dead, they had the opportunity to go back to living as they had before. But now, they had a greater opportunity to take their place in the vast heavenly choir that worships God without ceasing. Prayer is for the glory of God. The centre of the kingdom is all about a priestly activity that goes on day and night and whose chief function is to bring God pleasure and delight.

The challenge is to sing in the darkest hour with the same joy as in the easy day. In the siege of Leningrad, the symphony orchestra kept playing and broadcasting their music day in and day out. They did so to show that their spirit was not broken by the evil of men and that there were better things to live for that would far outlast the Second World War. How much more should Christians lift up their hearts in defiance of all the schemes of men and devils and glorify the God of unchanging majesty!

September 29

And as Elijah stood there, the LORD passed by, and a mighty windstorm hit the mountain. It was such a terrible blast that the rocks were torn loose, but the LORD was not in the wind. After the wind there was an earthquake, but the LORD was not in the earthquake. And after the earthquake there was a fire, but the LORD was not in the fire. And after the fire there was the sound of a gentle whisper. (1 Kings 19:11-12 NLT)

The most powerful moment of our lives is when we hear the gentle whisper of the Holy Spirit communicating the deepest thoughts of God. There may be a lot of noise and bustle preceding this, but it is all a preparation for hearing God.

Earthquakes, wind and fire are impressive, but God is not in them, even though He sent them. God is in the still small voice. .That inner stillness is the moment before the sun rises in our hearts and we become conscious of God. The work of the Holy Spirit is always the opposite of the ways of man. This is why so little is known about Him despite the fact that He is omnipresent and all-powerful. Human beings are the opposite: noisy and boastful but weak and restricted on every side.

Isaiah pleaded with Israel to look to Him: "Only in returning to Me and resting in Me will you be saved. In quietness and confidence is your strength" (Isaiah 30:15 NLT).
But Israel loved the business of making alliances with Egypt, trusting in their armies. It was the fear of death that had suddenly gripped Elijah and had drowned out the still small voice. He had seen God work in power on Mount Carmel but even the drama of those events had caused Elijah to look to impressive things rather than to the inner whisper.
The person who knows the still small voice is invincible. From that voice, and from that voice alone, flows the indomitable power of God. Nothing can stand against the whisper of God. Death fled when Jesus called Lazarus. Sin, Satan and hell came crashing down when Jesus cried "It is finished." To hear the Spirit breathe through the word is to tap into the power that created an infinite universe. To overhear this quiet whisper is to dip one's heart into the redeeming love that healed a broken world. There is no more magnificent activity than to quieten one's heart and read the word with rapt inner attention to the Spirit of God.

September 30

And behold, a woman in the city who was a sinner, when she knew that Jesus sat at the table in the Pharisee's house, brought an alabaster flask of fragrant oil, and stood at His feet behind Him weeping; and she began to wash His feet with her tears, and wiped them with the hair of her head; and she kissed His feet and anointed them with the fragrant oil.
(Luke 7:37-38)

The tears of this woman were more fragrant than the bottle of perfume. Money can buy a fragrance, but only love can produce tears. God is never impressed with outward forms such as musical skill or fine voices. God looks on the heart and longs to be loved as He loves.

The extravagance of this woman was embarrassing. She was evidently a woman of bad reputation and she dared to touch Him, first letting her tears flow over His feet and then actually kissing his feet. There is no description of when she received salvation. It seems that she was melted and cleansed by simply seeing Him. Perhaps she had looked and listened from the back of the crowd and had suddenly grasped the full meaning of what she was witnessing. God was speaking to her through this man. God's presence was reaching out to her in waves of forgiving love. It hit her powerfully that this man was in perfect harmony with God and that therefore what He said would stand above every other voice and authority for all eternity.

It is not recorded that anyone ever washed the feet of Jesus other than this woman. We may wonder at the degree of darkness and hurt that had shaped her life to this point, but in a few seconds it had all been swept away and she was free. In the presence of Jesus, liars become honest men, drunkards become sober and a prostitute became pure. The result is that she was now able to minister washing to Him. He was never defiled, and this was not washing from uncleanness, it was the washing of refreshing, as tides will wash a beach or rain will rinse the sky. This woman had forgotten herself and her problems and was herself overwhelmed by an ocean of love. Her tears were not tears of sorrow, but of depths of wondering joy. The Father had sought out and found a woman who would worship Him in Spirit and in truth.

~~~~~~~~~~~~~~~

October 1

Come out of Babylon, my people, so that you will not share in her sins, so that you will not receive any of her plagues.
(Revelation 18:4 NIV)

"Now Daniel so distinguished himself by his exceptional qualities that the king planned to set him over the whole kingdom of Babylon." *(Daniel 6:3 NIV)*

The world in which we live is described as Babylon the Great by the apostle John in the book of Revelation. John Bunyan called it "Vanity Fair". It is therefore not surprising that the Bible bids us get out of Babylon. What is startling is that Daniel rose to be the first minister in that godless nation. The lesson is clear: we must leave Babylon in our hearts while remaining there geographically. Jesus prayed: *"My prayer is not that you take them out of the world but that you protect them from the evil one. They are not of the world, even as I am not of it." (John 17:15-16)* We are in the world but not of it. There is no teaching in the New Testament that holiness is attainable by monastic vows or an ascetic lifestyle.

Daniel demonstrated that we impact this world not by our politics, but by our personal integrity and faithfulness to the Lord. Daniel preferred to die a horrible death in the lions' den rather than give up praying for a single day. In 1977 President Carter proposed the return of compulsory military service. A university student protested with a poster declaring "Nothing is worth dying for!" Charles Colson commented: "If nothing is worth dying for, is anything worth living for?" The Christian has taken his place among a vast throng of witnesses who have counted their lives as expendable.

The church is not called to smooth the troubled conscience of the world but to cause a disturbance by being the pigeon that is thrown among the cats. The outcome may be painful but it will be a true beacon of hope. We may not be able to offer political hope to our generation, but we can certainly demonstrate a greater kingdom that is alone worth living and dying for.

October 2

So then each of us shall give account of himself to God.
(Romans 14:12)

Many years ago there was a wise old king who was severely troubled by a neighbouring kingdom ruled by an impetuous, angry young man.[2] One day the young man mustered his armies and attacked the old king. The old king had many skilled knights whom he commanded to capture the young man alive. After several weeks of conflict, the young man was brought in chains before the wise old king. The old man feigned anger and commanded his foe to be executed. The young man pleaded for his life, so the old man gave him a test. If he passed, he would be spared. He was to carry a jug full of water through the street that passed through the city and hand it to the old king without spilling a drop. The old king also ordered that the crowds on the left of the prisoner should mock and belittle him, while those on his right were to cheer and encourage him. The young man succeeded and handed over the vessel. Then the old king asked him what he had answered the cries of the crowds. "I had no time to consider insults or praise," said the young man. "All my concentration was on not spilling a drop of water."

Our attention to the state of our soul is the most important matter for any human being. Any garden neglected will soon be a riot of thorns and thistles. To cultivate flowers and fruits requires constant care and attention. Wesley wrote: "A charge to keep I have, a God to glorify, a never-dying soul to save and fit it for the sky." We must not allow vain flattery or bitter criticism to deflect us from obeying our conscience in the presence of the king. He watches us during every step of our walk and requires that we give account to Him, not our husband or wife, our pastor or board of elders. God said to Abraham, "I *am* Almighty God; walk before Me and be blameless." (Genesis 17:1.) Or in the language of our story: "Walk before Me and don't spill a drop."

~~~~~~~~~~~~~~~~

---

[2] Richard Wurmbrand, *Sermons in Solitary Confinement,* p 43. Hodder & Stoughton 1969.

October 3

*O LORD, God of our fathers, **are you not** God in heaven?... **Did you not**, our God, drive out the inhabitants of this land before your people Israel? ... O our God, **will you not** execute judgment on them (the attacking armies)?*
(2 Chronicles 20:6-12 ESV)

This extract is from the great prayer of Jehoshaphat for deliverance from a vast confederation of armies that were attacking Judah. He appealed to three things: who God is, what God had done in the past, and what He would do for them in the future. These three things undergird the faith of everyone who prays.

Firstly, God is flawless and perfect, the very definition of goodness. He is alone supreme, the Creator of all things, dwelling in highest authority over the universe both visible and invisible. He is all-knowing, all-seeing and all-powerful. Nothing is too hard for Him and He dwells in immutable, unhurried and undisturbed light, ruling over all the affairs of human beings.

Secondly, God has done innumerable great things, both in Bible times and throughout the history of the church. He delivered His people from Egypt, He healed the sick, raised the dead and delivered the afflicted from every power of evil. He raised up great men to turn the nations back to God and has transformed the lives of countless thousands of sinners.

Thirdly, standing on these two great pillars of who God is and what He has done in the past, we may bring our petitions to Him, knowing that He will never change. As He has been in the past, so He will be in the future. He comes to the aid of all who call upon Him. God has never broken a promise for He is incapable of doing so. It is the same God of believers in the past who will act on our behalf today. He is "Jesus Christ the same yesterday, today and forever." Hebrews 13:8.

∼∼∼∼∼∼∼∼∼∼∼∼∼

October 4

Make the heart of this people dull, and their ears heavy, and blind their eyes; lest they see with their eyes, and hear with their ears, and understand with their hearts, and turn and be healed. (Isaiah 6:10 ESV)

Parts of this prophecy in Isaiah 6 are quoted in all four gospels and also in Romans and Acts, thus indicating the importance of these words. It is at first astonishing that God should take away someone's ability to understand spiritual truth. The prophecy is that God will sometimes take away free-will from people. Why would God do this?

The answer is that free-will is a precious gift of grace from the sovereignty of God. We are used to hearing that we have rights. We may think that we have the right to pray and be answered. But the Bible teaches that this is a dangerous manner in which to approach the holy, sovereign Lord of the universe. Free-will is a privilege not a right. The doctrine of God's absolute sovereignty does not deny free-will, but it does define it. The only being in the universe with unqualified free-will is God. He in His wisdom has chosen to confer this faculty in some small but significant measure on His beloved creatures.

Free-will is part of what it means to be in the image of God and is the ability to choose to love and serve another. Tragically, mankind chose freely to love and serve sin. Now we are presented with the choice to deny ourselves and love and serve God. The constant misuse of free-will so damages our personality that God in His loving-kindness may take it away. It is His plan that human beings will then awaken to their folly and call on Him to restore this grace gift. Jesus said *"Walk while you have the light, lest darkness overtake you. The one who walks in the darkness does not know where he is going. While you have the light, believe in the light, that you may become sons of light."* (John 12:35-36 ESV.) It is as we exercise free-will in loving obedience that we are filled with light and understanding. Right use of our liberty will lead to joyous abundance of freedom and delight. We may make hundreds of tiny choices each day, but all of life can be reduced to one simple choice: God's way or mine.

October 5

Some were tortured, refusing to accept release, so that they might rise again to a better life. Others suffered mocking and flogging, and even chains and imprisonment. They were stoned, they were sawn in two, they were killed with the sword... of whom the world was not worthy.
(Hebrews 11:35-38 ESV)

Boris Talantov was arrested on Sept 3 1969 for dissent in Soviet Russia. His father and older brother had both died in prison for their faith. At his trial he reaffirmed his allegiance to his religious convictions and was sent to prison. Prison in communist Russia was not an easy place but involved cruel beatings, minimal food and poor conditions. He died in prison January 4 1971 of a heart attack. His last letter has been preserved, in which he wrote: "I am cheerful in spirit and with gratitude accept from God all bitter trials."

The problem with the tribulations of western nations is that there is no obvious enemy. The governments are not imprisoning, torturing or executing people. For many, the trials are trivial, such as poor service in a restaurant or difficulty finding a reliable mechanic. It is not rare to find someone bitterly lamenting their deep frustration at a computer crashing or how expensive it is to park their car. Then there are other religious trials such as uncomfortable seats in the church or the music is too loud.

Of course, it is wrong to compare our trials with those suffering tribulation. But we must address this issue head on. Our trials may be miniscule, but we are to triumph in them with the same spirit as Boris Talantov. We must throw off the consumer culture which makes me king, and adopt the patient, forgiving and gentle spirit of the Master Himself. Yes, our trials are trifling and petty. This is all the more reason why we should discard the moans and groans that are unworthy of God's children. Believers everywhere march to a different drumbeat than the world. It is this spirit of triumph that must make us refuse to lose our peace over the petty discomforts we face, and so show the joy and courageous spirit of another kingdom.

October 6

"Behold, a virgin shall conceive, and bear a son, and shall call his name Immanuel. Butter and honey shall he eat, that he may know to refuse the evil, and choose the good."
(Isaiah 7:14-15 KJV)

One might ask how eating butter and honey could ever help to discern evil and choose the good. The answer is simple: it is through constant familiarity with wholesome things that one quickly notices what is harmful. It is said that in order for agents to detect a counterfeit bank note, they spend hours studying the genuine article. They are then immediately able to spot the slightest deviation from the true.

Obsession with what is false can grip the mind. There are people who are constantly on the watch for what is wrong with this or that ministry. The problem is that we can easily sink under the weight of confusing voices. The answer is to go to the wholesome source of all things, to Christ and His word. If we partake of Him then we are eating the most nourishing food and our senses will be able to immediately discern when something foreign comes in.

Feasting on Christ is to eat and drink holiness and love. Jesus spoke of "living water", meaning that as we spend time with Him we will be refreshed and made alive. There is no-one remotely comparable to Him for He is life on another level. Christ is the exact expression of the brightness of divine glory. To know Him is to have the assurance of eternal life. It is the awesomeness of who He is that melts the heart. All the counterfeits are dry and lifeless in comparison with Him. The gospels describe Jesus and His ministry. He did not allow anything to dilute or cloud the directness of His appeal or His person. The reaction of the crowds was that no-one ever spoke like Him or had such authority. It is as we get to the source that we are transformed and sustained and our senses are awakened "to discern between good and evil" (Hebrews 5:14).

~~~~~~~~~~~~~~~

October 7

Howbeit in the business of the ambassadors of the princes of Babylon, who sent unto him to enquire of the wonder that was done in the land, God left him, to try him, that he might know all that was in his heart. (2 Chronicles 32:31 KJV)

It is in the exercise of free-will that we develop character. Many argue whether we even have free-will, but if our choices are all overridden by a higher power then we have no moral responsibility for our actions. Our freedom to choose is certainly limited and no-one is wholly free. We do not choose our parents, or when and where we are born. But it is in the use of our freedoms that we form our character.

Hezekiah was given a moment without divine pressure or guidance. He could do whatever was in his heart and he used this moment to parade his wealth before the visitors from Babylon. In many nations there is more free time than ever and yet it is astonishing to note that attendance at prayer meetings and Sunday worship has declined. To have a truly free evening is as much a test of character as a crisis. Often when the crisis comes, what we have done in our free time will determine how we react in the crisis. This is because our little decisions produce our character.

The great question is: what do you do when you are really left to yourself? When a person walks among market stalls, he will stop at the ones that attract him. In the same way, we may linger long in our Bibles, in prayer or in loving, unselfish acts. The easiest route would be to linger long at superficial distractions. Relaxation is not an end in itself but is for those who have spent their strength and are exhausted. Love should lead us to draw close to the Lord. Love is the supreme exercise of free-will, freely choosing to know, love and serve the Lord of glory above all other things. The challenge of Joshua rings as loud and clear as the day he said it: "Choose you this day whom you will serve." (Joshua 24:15 KJV.)

October 8

This was the appearance of the likeness of the glory of the LORD. So when I saw it, I fell on my face, and I heard a voice of One speaking. And He said to me, "Son of man, stand on your feet, and I will speak to you." (Ezekiel 1:28 - 2:1)

This verse describes the first vision that Ezekiel saw. It describes how God made him to be a prophet in four steps: "I saw, I fell, I heard, I stood." This pattern is repeated in all God's servants in one way or another. It takes but a moment of revelation for a person to become a servant of God. Each one has had a revelation of the greatness of God and is a witness of things that are unseen and unknown by the natural man.

The effect of God's glory is to cause us to fall as dead at the feet of the Lord. As we lie there, we discover that our whole world has changed in a moment of time. There are no more arguments when we have seen Him. In a second we become witnesses, not apologists. To lie prostrate in worship is the place of transformation of our thinking and our living. It is also the place where our ears are unblocked. As a radio is tuned to different frequencies, so our hearts must be tuned to hear the voice of the Lord. It is as we spread our lives before Him that we become aware of the voice of the Spirit.

The last step in Ezekiel's preparation was to stand before the Lord. Ezekiel was not to have revelations and spiritual experiences for himself. He was going to have to rise up and hear the word for others. Standing before God was the first step in presenting the Lord to His people and also of learning to intercede for them. Ezekiel was called in the darkest hour of Israel's history to be a beacon of hope to a fallen nation. He prophesied that Israel would return to the land and Messiah would come. The mark of every true witness is a burning hope that cannot die. Later, Ezekiel had the prophetic vision of the valley of dry bones. That vision sums up his experience in this chapter and his entire prophetic ministry. The person who has met with God has a message to speak to the dead and bring them back to life.

October 9

These are the nations the LORD left to test all those Israelites who had not experienced any of the wars in Canaan, (he did this only to teach warfare to the descendants of the Israelites who had not had previous battle experience).
(Judges 3:1-2 NIV)

"The LORD is a man of war" declares the Bible (Exodus 15:3 ESV). This does not mean that He delights in battle. It means that He will not watch indifferently as evil seeks to destroy the souls of men. Moreover, His people are "an exceedingly great army" (Ezekiel 37:10). The weapons of our warfare are not physical since swords and guns are of no effect against the hosts of darkness. The greatest weapon is prayer from a heart of love and we are to engage in the battle of the ages that is raging all around us.

Where there is no awareness of the seriousness of the conflict, believers may indulge in trifling pursuits. It was an unspeakable crime of Nero that he played his fiddle while Rome burned. If we have little experience of battle, we may have an attitude of unconcern about the devastation that is going on all around. We may be more concerned about our doctrines and our biblical accuracy than about those who are sinking into the grip of the powers of darkness. There are two extremes to be avoided: the first is having an unhealthy obsession with the devil and his legions; the second is being completely ignorant of the lies of Satan and his strategies to kill, steal and destroy.

When God looked in vain for a man to stand in the gap (Ezekiel 22:30), He was seeking someone who would take up the fight for the people of Israel. He found no-one and so poured out judgement. Intercessors are foot soldiers in this war. The warfare is in prayer and God allows enemies to break into our circumstances to wake us up to the battle. The church is a sleeping giant until she is roused to action. Sleep may be a conscious choice to avoid the challenge and strain of the battle. When the Bible commands us to wake up, it is an appeal to our will to take our place alongside our battle-scarred captain. We may be inexperienced but that should not deter us. The stakes are too high to remain indifferent. God is always recruiting, and there are always gaps to be filled in this, the greatest war of all.

October 10

"All of you have conspired against me." *(1 Samuel 22:8 KJV)*

The people spoke of stoning him ... but David encouraged himself in the LORD his God. *(1 Samuel 30:6 KJV)*

These two verses are first from the lips of Saul and then from David. The contrast could hardly be greater. Saul was mistaken, for no-one was against him. The problem was located in his own view of himself and the world around him. He was moody, suspicious and full of self-doubt. David's problems were real and he was on the brink of catastrophe. Yet just as Saul's imaginary problems lay with his thoughts, so, too, David found the solution to his real troubles in his inward attitude.

Some workers in a garage decided to play a trick on a fellow mechanic. When he arrived for work, they each in turn remarked how ill or how pale he looked. This continued until he left mid-morning to see his doctor! The inner attitude of our hearts will determine how we see the world. If we have developed a negative world-view, then we will feel that everyone and everything is against us. But even if it were true, it would not change the fact that we have the resources within our own hearts to rise up and defy the darkness.

There is a fighting spirit in faith; a calm defiance of the giants that are opposing us. It is not bravado that is needed, for our inner attitude will not always change the world around us. Meshach, Shadrach and Abed-Nego faced the fact that they might well perish in the act of boldly standing against the command of King Nebuchadnezzar. But they counted it better to die fighting than to compromise. If they had bowed down to the King's idol, they would have shrivelled up and died anyway. Because of their attitude, they made victory inevitable, either passing into eternity with joy, or experiencing a miracle of deliverance. Faith allows the light of God to shine into our world and it will always triumph, whether in life or death. Don't wait for someone to encourage you. Rise up and take your stand on the divine promise: "If God *be* for us, who *can be* against us?" (Romans 8:31 KJV)

∽∽∽∽∽∽∽∽∽∽∽∽

October 11

Now when these things begin to happen, look up and lift up your heads, because your redemption draws near.
(Luke 21:28)
Those also that love his appearing.   (2 Timothy 4:8 KJV)

In the New Testament there is a joyful expectation of the return of the Lord. This does not mean that they had a better understanding of the details of His return. Today, there are thousands of books that explain every facet of the last days. These books often contradict one another and many shed only short-lived light on the subject. The abundance of conflicting interpretations has contributed to the decline, in some quarters, of even studying the Scriptures that speak of the end of the world. But Biblical accuracy alone will never produce this sense of longing for the coming of the Lord.

This yearning for the second coming is based on an ardent love for Jesus. The Lord taught that the disciples would not fast and pray while He was with them, but that once He was taken away then they would seek Him (Mark 2:19-20). By this He meant that genuine, spiritual thirst is the result of missing His voice, His touch and His presence. The prophet pleaded: "And you will seek Me and find *Me*, when you search for Me with all your heart." (Jeremiah 29:13.) To live without the love of Jesus, having once known the gentle healing breeze of His love, is to live with a deep wound in the heart. It is an ache, even at times an almost physical pain. In the dark three days between the death and resurrection of the Lord, it was Mary Magdalene who carried the deepest wound and longed for something to bring back that majestic warmth, that indescribable magnificence that is Jesus. Those who long for His coming have also treasured His appearing in private times of prayer, or in exquisite moments when believers gather and sing, preach and worship.

Those who love His appearing have an equally deep dissatisfaction with the things this world has to offer. The abundance of possessions, amusements and pleasures, can easily dim our fervent longing for the end of this world. Possessions have a voice that is smooth-talking, fawning and hypnotic. We are to shake off the deceiving, sleep-inducing atmosphere that seeks to suffocate our faith. We are to lift up our heads with eagerness, awaiting the final step of liberation that will be ours at the coming of the Lord.

~~~~~~~~~~~~~

October 12

Yes, and all who desire to live godly in Christ Jesus will suffer persecution. *(2 Timothy 3:12)*

For Christians in the West this is quite a puzzling verse, since few, if any Christians, have been imprisoned or executed in the western democracies. Persecution in such nations often takes the form of social exclusion or derision. The Egyptian captivity involved hard labour and ethnic cleansing, as male babies were executed. The Babylonian captivity was much more benign, with absorption into the culture. Daniel and his friends refused to adopt Babylonian culture and preserved their unique identity as Jews. If they had watered down their devotion to Jehovah, they would never have suffered persecution. This is the great temptation of many cultures, to be reasonable, respectful and largely silent about our beliefs, in short: to blend in.

The Welsh revival began when Evan Roberts gave a message with four simple points: 1. Confess any sin and wrong done to another and put it right. 2. Put away all doubtful habits. 3. Obey the Holy Spirit promptly. 4. Confess your faith in Christ publicly. Living godly in Christ Jesus will involve wearing my faith openly in more than one way. This may be challenging but it is impossible to live for Christ and keep it private.

During World War II many Lutheran clergymen went along with the Nazi agenda by keeping their heads down. One of the most famous exceptions was Captain Niemoller, who had earned the iron cross for bravery as a U-boat commander in World War I. By the time Hitler came to power, he had become a Lutheran pastor. He was part of a delegation invited to meet Hitler and he openly opposed the Fuhrer. This so enraged Hitler that when Niemoller was at last arrested, Hitler wanted personal reports about 'his prisoner'. A chaplain who was visiting the prison expressed surprise to see Niemoller there and exclaimed, "Why are you in prison?!" "And brother, why are you not in prison?" came the reply.

October 13

Then the glory of the LORD departed.   (Ezekiel 10:18 NIV)

Ezekiel saw the moment that the glory of the Lord left the temple of Solomon just before it was destroyed in 586 BC. It is not surprising that the glory departed. What is astonishing is that it was still there after all the sin and disobedience of the nation. The same might be said of the 7 churches of Asia in Revelation chapters 2 and 3. Christ was still standing in their midst, still speaking and working despite the gross immorality of some.

The Bible tells us not to grieve the Holy Spirit. One of the ways in which we do this is to assume He is not active or present at all times. Not only is He active, but He burns unceasingly with the glory and holiness of God. Christians and churches are more powerful than they could ever guess. God's glory is upon us and we should simply rejoice, believe and allow the glory to shine through. We may have grown dull, but He is the same. We may be quite deaf to His speaking, but He persists.

Christians walk through life by faith, not by sight, nor by feeling. We are to stir up our hearts and believe in the promise of His presence whenever we gather. Jacob said at Bethel: "Surely the LORD is in this place, and I was not aware of it." (Genesis 28:16 NIV) There will always be more of God in our lives and assemblies than we know. Dare we believe what the Bible says about us? Gideon laid out a fleece and asked for it to be wet with dew while the ground was dry. The next night he asked for the fleece to be dry and the ground wet. (Judges 6:37-40) This could have gone on for weeks, but in the end he had to rise up in faith that God was with him as promised. The glory of the Lord is upon His church. Don't wait for a sign: "Arise, shine; for thy light is come! And the glory of the LORD is risen upon thee." (Isaiah 60:1 KJV)

~~~~~~~~~~~~~

October 14

Then Jesus said to his disciples, "Whoever wants to be my disciple must deny themselves and take up their cross and follow me... What good will it be for someone to gain the whole world, yet forfeit their soul? Or what can anyone give in exchange for their soul?" (Matthew 16:24 & 26 NIV)

In an extraordinary reversal of this statement, the philosopher Voltaire once exclaimed that he would sell his place in heaven for a Prussian sovereign. A Prussian officer startled Voltaire by replying that in Prussia a thing could only be sold if there were proof of ownership. Voltaire had simply demonstrated that he had no concept of the value of his eternal soul.

The truth is that Jesus Christ asks for our full surrender to Him as Lord and Saviour and there is a powerful logic behind this statement. If we yield only part of our being, then we are maintaining our independence as a bargaining position for future negotiations. We are staying outside of the kingdom, arguing the conditions on which we may enter. We are, in short, asserting our own lordship over our lives.

The madness of this, of course, is that we have no bargaining strength with which to exert any influence. We will never be able to bribe God or impress Him with gold or any academic or political achievements. In the awful siege of Leningrad in World War II, only food had any value. Gold and diamonds were exchanged for a few mouldy potatoes. In the light of eternity, all priorities change.

But more than this, only what God guards is safe. We cannot maintain our life, our possessions or our well-being without God. The moment we realise that we have an eternal soul, the value of every worldly treasure evaporates. Gaining the whole world for a few years becomes meaningless. The Lord appeals in crystal clarity to our will, our mind and our heart. He presents to us the uncompromising basis on which we may possess and keep eternal life. It may be uncomfortable, but it is the irrefutable logic that is to be drawn from the conviction that Jesus Christ is the Son of God and God in human form. We must yield everything to Him and maintain that place of entire surrender on our pilgrimage into eternity.

~~~~~~~~~~~~~~

October 15

How can you believe since you accept glory from one another but do not seek the glory that comes from the only God?
(John 5:44 NIV)
Woe unto you, when all men shall speak well of you.
(Luke 6:26)

It is at first glance odd that we should beware when we are praised by others. But it is in our moments of greatest success that our hearts are sifted. It is easy to detect the monster called self when we hear a boaster parading his own virtues. However, when others praise us, or when we have moments of personal achievement, we must be on our guard against the greatest enemy of our Christian walk: the flesh.

The NIV in its first editions translated the Greek word for flesh "sarx" in two very different ways. In Galatians 3:3, it is rendered "human effort" while in the whole of Romans 8 it is translated as "sinful nature". (More recent revisions have again simply used the word "flesh".) These two phrases demonstrate the breadth of this power. The best definition of the flesh is: 'living from my own resources rather than from Christ in me'. It can immediately be seen that it is only the Christian who can overcome the flesh by receiving and submitting to the indwelling presence of God.

The flesh can mimic spiritual life. It can pray and fast with appropriate humility. It can definitely preach well and can even speak in tongues. The flesh is skilled in all kinds of religious activities. Moreover, flattery speedily revives the flesh. The pursuit of happiness and pleasure for their own ends will also soon cause a Christian to wallow in the quick-sands of spiritual paralysis. The flesh is the exaltation of self, which is why the greatest test of all is when we are praised. The answer to the flesh is not to grovel in self-loathing, which is in fact the favourite disguise of the flesh; the answer is to die daily, and if necessary hourly. We do this by trading the shallow pleasures of self-indulgence with the pure joy of surrender to the Holy Spirit. Living from our own resources, we can never overcome sin. Once we discover the secret of letting go our lives, our hearts are bathed with the radiant light and joy of Jesus, and all the praise and glory will be only His forever.

~~~~~~~~~~~~~

October 16

"Then I beg you, father, send Lazarus to my family ... Let him warn them, so that they will not also come to this place of torment." Abraham replied, "They have Moses and the Prophets... If they do not listen to them, they will not be convinced even if someone rises from the dead."
(Luke 16:27-31 NIV)

God has complete faith in the power of His word to reveal Himself. In fact, He designed the human race and knows best how to reach the inner sanctuary of our will. It must also be stated that Satan, too, believes in the power of the Bible. In communist and Muslim countries the Bible is frequently banned, indicating that someone in authority fears the power and influence of this book to change its readers. Doreen Irvine rose to a high rank in the temple of Satan in London before she came to Christ. She describes in her life story how vehemently they were warned never to read the Bible or visit a church.

One might wonder what would happen if all who profess Christ had the same awe of opening these sacred pages. Jesus taught in the parable of the rich man and Lazarus that the most powerful tool to impart faith is the reading and teaching of God's word.

The word of God is living seed, which has the power to produce all the qualities of its own life in anyone who receives it. Many people pray for an outpouring of the Holy Spirit, but the Spirit needs the presence of living seed to be germinated in our hearts. No farmer will simply pray for rain, but will sow good seed so that the rain will not fall on lifeless soil. The book of God is a key to all moves of the Spirit. It is the message of the Creator, specifically designed and targeted to restore God's image in our damaged lives. Turn the key, lift the latch. The effects will always be more than we ever imagined possible.

~~~~~~~~~~~~~~~~

October 17

Behold, thou desirest truth in the inward parts.
(Psalm 51:6 KJV)
Above all else, guard your heart, for everything you do flows from it. *(Proverbs 4:23 NIV)*

Psalm 51 is David's prayer of repentance after his sin with Bathsheba. Augustine said: "David's fall should put all on their guard who have not fallen, and save from despair all those who have fallen." In fact, David's prayer is quite astonishing. He realised that there was no provision for his sin under the law. He deserved stoning both for adultery and murder. Yet he realised with powerful prophetic insight that God had made provision to dispel his inner darkness and restore the worst sinner. This is what underlies the gospel message with all its redemptive power of grace.

The great lesson, which is so easy to miss, is that David's sin was a symptom of things that were wrong in him. If only he had realised this earlier, he would have avoided the painful events that engulfed him. But through his fall, he came to the conviction that he needed to be changed so that his inward parts were truth.

The heart is the invisible counterpart of the face and it is vital that the heart be right before God. If the symmetry of the face is disturbed even a little, it is a disfigurement that is obvious to all. If one eye is an inch out of place, it might even be considered a deformity. David had discovered that his heart needed to be readjusted in the presence of God, with cleansing and renewing. Put quite simply, he needed to embrace truth at the centre of his being. Jesus Christ is the truth that we must embrace. Our heart is only right when it is a throne for Him and for His presence. Once that is established, we will be strengthened with might in our inner man. Christ in me is God's great cure for all the deformities of the soul. This is the glory and power of the New Covenant, and we are to walk in this with loving attention to the rule of Jesus Christ in our heart.

October 18

For God, who said, "Let light shine out of darkness," made his light shine in our hearts to give us the light of the knowledge of God's glory displayed in the face of Christ.
(2 Corinthians 4:6 NIV)

John Lennox, an Oxford mathematician who has a fervent faith in Christ, was once visiting a young Christian friend dying of cancer. Lennox asked him what he would like preached at his funeral. The young man answered "Tell them to read the word of God together, discuss it, think about it, pray about it and wait on God till His face appears."

This encapsulates, in a phrase, the whole purpose of prayer and Bible study. It is a reaching out through every faculty given to us to know the person behind the book. This is precisely the wonder of the Scriptures that we never know what may happen when we read them. They are a deep mine full of precious stones. The treasures are the gift of faith and a transformed character.

The face that shines through the pages is sinless and we have never seen such a beautiful countenance on earth. There are no petty grudges, no hard edges, no mean eyes or impatient glare. In Him, there is no regret of the past nor fear of death or of anything in the future. There is absolute incontestable authority. The most beautiful quality that shines through is grace, which is love that forgives and washes us completely. To see this face is to be saved and prepared for anything that may come. There is inspiration to be tireless in the face of disappointments and hopeful in the direst circumstances. There is motivation to rise and live and be part of the great adventure of discovering God and sharing Him with others. The revelation of God through the Scriptures imparts the same breath-taking beauty into our own hearts. To neglect the Bible is the greatest folly. To take it up and bathe in its pages is the greatest wisdom.

∽∽∽∽∽∽∽∽∽∽∽∽∽

October 19

"The LORD has declared today that you are a people for his treasured possession... and that you are to keep all his commandments, and that he will set you in praise and in fame and in honour high above all nations ···, and that you shall be a people holy to the LORD your God."

(Deuteronomy 26:18-19 ESV)

Peter refers to this promise when he says in his letter that we are "His own special people" (1 Peter 2:9). The purpose of God's people is to be a witness to the greatness of God and His kingdom. Often we think of our testimony as being how we first came to faith in Christ. While that is a vital part of our message, the greater part is our demonstration of another way of life.

The people of Israel in the Old Testament ceased to be His special people because they compromised with foreign gods and so lost their uniqueness. The same is true of many Christians today, that the moment they lose their distinctive qualities, they cannot be true witnesses. The church is not merely to show forth a more moral lifestyle, though that is essential to its credibility, it is to be an expression of the kingdom of God in the power of the Holy Spirit. If we will rid ourselves of the mixture of worldly goals and attitudes, then we will be free to partake of the river of life that flows from the throne and waters the whole kingdom.

When Jesus said, "Seek first the kingdom of God and His righteousness", He was teaching the foundational truth that as believers we must allow the Holy Spirit to make us single-hearted. Paul said "this one thing I do" (Philippians 3:13). Jesus said of Mary "one thing is needed." He said to the rich, moral, religious, young ruler: "You lack one thing" (Luke 18:22). The distinctive nature of the kingdom is that it is all centred on the person of Jesus Christ. It is our loving relationship with Him that sets us apart from mere morality. Through Him, there is a powerful, clear and pure expression of God and His rule in our lives. That is what makes us His special people.

~~~~~~~~~~~~~

October 20

Manasseh led the people ... to do even more evil than the pagan nations ...The Assyrian armies took Manasseh prisoner, put a ring through his nose, bound him in bronze chains, and took him to Babylon. But while in deep distress, Manasseh sought the LORD his God and sincerely humbled himself .... And when he prayed, the LORD listened to him and was moved by his request. So the LORD brought Manasseh back to Jerusalem and to his kingdom. Then Manasseh finally realised that the LORD alone is God! (2 Chronicles 33:9-13 NLT)

God cannot close His ears to the prayers of even the worst human being. Manasseh was an evil man who had filled Jerusalem with innocent blood. Yet even this man was heard when he turned to God for mercy. Incredibly, God not only forgave him but restored him to his throne. God's heart was even touched by the prayers of the wicked kings Ahab (1 Kings 21:27-29) and Nebuchadnezzar (Daniel 4) when they repented. These examples are to give us comfort and hope that there will be many in heaven whose hearts turned in their last moments to ask for a drop of grace. No-one but God sees them and He is the One who holds the eternal destiny of all in the palm of His hand.

History is replete with examples of what happens when people turn to God in prayer. Between 1873 and 1877 the mid-western USA was plagued by swarms of locusts that even hindered the migration of settlers westwards, leaving many on the brink of starvation. On April 26, 1877, Minnesota residents observed a state-wide day of prayer led by Governor John Sargent Pillsbury. In the next two days, warm weather caused millions of grasshoppers to hatch and sceptics to scoff; but a plunge in temperature on the fourth day froze and killed them all. A chapel was built at a town called Cold Spring to commemorate the miracle.

God cannot close His ears to anyone who humbles themselves to seek His mercy. It is as if He is melted by the cries of penitent people. This is the bedrock of the universe: that there is a God in heaven who is waiting to be invited to act on our behalf. It is the most basic message of all: God hears and answers prayer.

∼∼∼∼∼∼∼∼∼∼∼∼∼

October 21

These all died in faith, not having received the promises, but having seen them afar off, were assured of them, embraced them and confessed that they were strangers and pilgrims on the earth. *(Hebrews 11:13)*

The Christian is a pilgrim who has set out on a journey from one world to another. The believer's attention has changed from earth to heaven, from time to eternity, from accumulating bank accounts to gaining heavenly rewards. This world is passing away; it is temporary and gives only the illusion of permanence.

The astonishing thing about the Old Testament believers was that they never received the great promises that are the privilege of followers of Jesus Christ. They saw the promises afar off, and renounced their cultural context to live for a heavenly city. Now we are privileged to have a colossal down payment in the person and work of the Holy Spirit. The promise of the New Testament is to put a deposit of eternity deep into the lives of whoever will believe. This means that Christians are to be active explorers of the kingdom of God. This is not pie in the sky when we die, it is an invitation to partake in a banquet around the table of the great king right now.

We still live in a broken, dying world, but in our spirits we have begun to partake of a world of light. Saints of old saw but the gleam of the new creation. Now we sit at a table set with the very substance of God Himself. We eat His flesh and drink His blood. We partake of the essence of what makes God who He is. We receive His love and share in His joy. The same principle still holds, that only those who bid this world adieu can explore the wonders of Christ and His new creation. As we live our lives with our gaze fixed on the kingdom of God, we become a window through which people can glimpse the coming glory.

~~~~~~~~~~~~~~~

October 22

By faith Abraham obeyed. (Hebrews 11:8 KJV)

Every benefit that can ever be received from the person and work of Christ is to be received by faith. Faith is not imparted by clever arguments but by revelation of the extraordinary presence and character of God revealed through Jesus Christ.

There are three different types of faith. The first is mere intellectual persuasion of a truth. The Bible says that "Even the demons believe--and shudder!" (James 2:19 ESV) This is certainly not saving faith!

The second kind of faith is persuasion of the reliability of a person's character. If a friend said he would meet us at 4 pm, it would be the worst insult if we replied "I don't believe you!" This is the faith that God requires, that we believe that He is the most trustworthy being in the universe, worthy that we stake our all on the fact that He cannot lie, He cannot break His word and He cannot disappoint anyone who trusts in Him. The Bible says that "Those who trust in me will never be put to shame." (Isaiah 49:23 NLT)

The third level of faith is to entrust oneself entirely into someone's keeping. This is what Paul spoke of when he said, "I know whom I have believed, and am persuaded that he is able to keep that which I have committed unto him against that day. (2 Timothy 1:12 KJV). When Abraham went out of Ur of the Chaldees, not knowing where he was going, he was entrusting his entire future to God. It was belief combined with entire surrender to God's faithfulness. Saving faith is like one side of a coin. The other side is obedience. The great challenge is not only about what we believe, but whether we will dare to let it affect us in every area of our life.

∼∼∼∼∼∼∼∼∼∼∼∼∼∼∼

October 23

Has God forgotten to be gracious? ... But .... I will remember the works of the LORD; surely I will remember Your wonders of old.... Your way was in the sea. (Psalm 77:9-19)

Asaph, the chief musician of David, was passing through a deep trial when he wrote Psalm 77. He was so despondent he wondered if God had changed and ceased to be loving. He could see no flicker of interest in his problems and he could not imagine any way in which God could help him.

The turning-point came when he remembered songs he had written about the wonders the Lord had performed. He particularly thought about the crossing of the Red Sea, when the people were being pursued by Pharaoh's armies and were trapped between the enemy and the sea. Humanly speaking, God's people were doomed. But God made a way through the sea. God is never without a way forward. He is never without an answer. It may be completely invisible and inconceivable but when it comes, it will be straightforward and breathtakingly simple. God simply opened a way where there was no way.

It takes time for faith to rise in our hearts. Like Asaph, we pass through the dark nights of wondering, of reaching out and sinking into despair. We cannot fix things and we cannot imagine how God can fix them. At such moments we are to remember God's faithfulness of old. Asaph remembered a song that he had sung and probably had written for the benefit of others. Now he had to apply what he believed to his own circumstances. Ruth Bell Graham was a student at Bible college when she went through a deep crisis of faith. She confessed to a counsellor that she was losing her faith. No, said the counsellor, you are not losing your faith, you are in process of making it yours. We all know so well how God has dealt with His people in times of old, allowing them to be hemmed in on every side. Well, now it is our turn to prove that God has not changed. He is about to open up the waters and reveal a path that was completely hidden from our view.

~~~~~~~~~~~~~~

October 24

But you, do not be called `Rabbi'; for One is your Teacher, the Christ, and you are all brethren. Do not call anyone on earth your father; for One is your Father, He who is in heaven.
(Matthew 23:8-9)

Jesus cut to the heart of true and false religion with searing precision. He denounced all who by their title or practice take the place of Christ in any person's life. No-one has any right to be the final authority in teaching over any person. There are two great areas where God must be supreme, as Father and Teacher.

The essence of the Christian gospel is the life of God in the soul of man. We must be born from above and such a birth cannot be given by any teacher or preacher. God may use preachers, but only in as much as they introduce people to God Himself. The Father is the begetter of life in us by His word and by His Spirit. Without this, all religious practice is meaningless.

Similarly, once life has been imparted, Christ is the inner teacher and guide of every believer. This is because He is not merely instructing but imparting. Jesus did not merely say "I teach." He said, "I am the truth." If Christ is presented to any person, whether sinner or saint, then they immediately find themselves in the presence of transforming truth.

The essence of Christianity is our personal submission to Christ in us. If He is the life of God in our soul, then we must fellowship with that life. All external conduct is to be based on the impulse of Him within. In all we do, and every attitude we cultivate, the compelling force must be our direct relationship with God through Christ. This is the path of inner beauty and power. There is a fragrance rising in the heart of everyone who has received Him as their life and then looks to Him as the inner light in matters of conscience and conduct. Let Christ be your teacher today and every day.

∾∾∾∾∾∾∾∾∾∾∾∾∾

October 25

To me, who am less than the least of all the saints, this grace was given, that I should preach among the Gentiles the unsearchable riches of Christ. (Ephesians 3:8)

There is a huge paradox in this verse which lies at the heart of the Christian life. Paul's estimation of himself was that he was the very least of all believers. Yet at the same time, he was the object of the greatest grace. This principle is written large over the whole Bible. There is no editing out of the weaknesses of its heroes. Rather, their flaws are portrayed in all their horror. Moses, David and Paul were all murderers. Abraham and Isaac lied to save their own skins in dangerous situations. Peter vehemently denied the Lord with curses and oaths. And so the list goes on and on.

Does this mean that we will be more blessed if we sin more? God forbid. It rather means that we had better get off our high perches or we are heading for a fall. The reason these men all fell so deeply was because of their mistaken belief in their own abilities. It takes the full power of the Scripture and the crucible of life to teach us that God only requires our weakness combined with faith in Him. Grace is the amazing riches of God extended to powerless individuals. The reason some receive so little grace is because they feel they don't need it as much as some others.

Faith in God is in direct relationship to our realisation of our own spiritual bankruptcy. If we will only come in deep persuasion of our unworthiness, we will be struck by the heavenly hosts praising God's mercy and welcoming us. Heaven was not waiting for us to be great spiritual stars by our own exertions. They were waiting with bated breath for us to grasp that we are less than the least, and that is precisely the trigger for God to impart the unsearchable riches of Christ.

∾∾∾∾∾∾∾∾∾∾∾∾∾

October 26

They have no root in themselves, but are for a time: then, tribulation arising, or persecution on account of the word, immediately they are offended. (Mark 4:17)

This verse from the parable of the sower explains the great need for deep roots if we are to bear fruit for God. The result of having shallow roots is that we are easily offended when things go wrong. Bearing fruit is all about setting our hearts to cooperate with God through the difficult days as well as the easy ones. A deep foundation is laid when we settle it that we will praise Him and trust Him in the storms that shake us on our journey.

The Bible holds several examples of fruit-bearing through adversity and none more inspiring than that of Joseph. He was sold as a slave by his own brothers. This was a life sentence to poverty. He was falsely accused and unjustly imprisoned and laid in chains to await death in prison (Psalm 105:18). Yet each time, he embraced his low estate and became a blessing to others through his fellowship with God. Everything he touched was blessed. Both Potiphar and the keeper of the prison recognised God's hand in Joseph's life: "Because the LORD was with him; and whatever he did, the LORD made *it* prosper." (Genesis 39:23). Joseph was not looking for light at the end of the tunnel, because by faith his tunnel was filled with the light of God's presence. He was looking for God's hand in the waiting.

It is easy for us to think it was easy for Joseph because we know the end of the story. The truth is that Joseph could easily have sunk down in despair, thinking God had abandoned him and was not hearing his prayers. But he found God at every stage of his journey. There is no whiff of offence in his life. Perhaps he had days when he felt the stirrings of resentment and quickly repented. Through the trial, he kept a sweet spirit of confidence in God, producing a willingness to help and serve others. Joseph was not waiting for a future date when he would be free to bear fruit. He was bearing fruit in the midst of his trials regardless of the future, and a greater than Joseph is now living in us.

~~~~~~~~~~~~~

October 27

They also took Lot, Abram's brother's son who dwelt in Sodom, and his goods, and departed. ... Now when Abram heard that his brother was taken captive, he armed his three hundred and eighteen trained servants who were born in his own house, and went in pursuit as far as Dan. (Genesis 14:12-14)

The story of Abraham and Lot is the acting out of the parable of the lost sheep. Lot followed the God of Abraham but not with the same zeal. He was drawn to the wealth of Sodom and needed rescuing not once but twice. First when Abraham led his small army to deliver him by force of arms, and then again when he interceded before God for the city of Sodom (Genesis 18). Lot was saved because Abraham loved and cared for this weak believer who was living in the twilight zone between the full light of God and the darkness of an evil world.

Abraham was astonishing in his reckless courage, risking his own life for this bothersome nephew. It seems as if Abraham gave little or no thought to his own safety. Like Paul, he did not count his own life dear to himself (Acts 20:24). It is the heart of the Saviour Himself, unafraid to die for sinners who rejected him. Abraham was infused with the spirit of Calvary, ready to die for love's sake. There is a battle to be fought for lost sinners whether they are relatives, neighbours, colleagues or total strangers.

The great missionary to the South Sea islands John G. Paton had a successful ministry in Scotland when he felt God's call. His parents supported his decision, affirming "they had long since given me away to the Lord." His friends and fellow ministers urged him to stay, fearing he would die as a martyr, since several others had already died in the attempt to win the islands for Christ. One old friend, Mr. Dickson, pleaded with him: "You will be eaten by cannibals." Paton replied with characteristic humour: "Mr. Dickson, you are advanced in years and soon to be laid in the grave, there to be eaten by worms. I confess that if I can live and die serving and honouring the Lord Jesus, it will make no difference to me whether I am eaten by cannibals or worms!" Paton proved to be a powerful and effective witness – a messenger of the cross who had already lost his life before he ever left his home country.

October 28

"Not one sparrow falls to the ground apart from your Father's will... Do not fear therefore; you are of more value than many sparrows." (Matthew 10:29 & 31)

It was 1944 and three members of the Ten Boom family had been betrayed and taken prisoner by the Nazis for sheltering Jews in Amsterdam. 10 days later, Corrie's father Caspar Ten Boom died in Scheveningen prison. Corrie Ten Boon and her sister Betsy were still in a prison in Holland. Their names were suddenly called out, giving them hope that they were about to be released. They went out into the prison yard, where they were joined by about 15 male prisoners. "Can anyone here pray?" came the desperate cry of one of the prisoners. "Why?" said Corrie, "are we not about to be released?" "No," came the alarming response, "and we had better pray that we are not all killed this day." Betsy Ten Boon prayed for God's mercy, and then, incredibly, raised her voice in song. They never found out what happened to the men but Corrie and Betsy were spared and sent to Ravensbruck concentration camp, where during the war 130,000 women were imprisoned, of whom some 97,000 died.

Some time later, Corrie came down with a cold, and was embarrassed because she had no handkerchief. "Let's pray," said Betsy and prayed: "Lord, please give Corrie a hankie as she has caught a cold. Amen." Seconds later, Corrie heard her name called and she ran to a window, where a friend who worked in the camp hospital had come to see her. The prisoner explained that she had found an old sheet and had cut out a piece of material and made a handkerchief, and as she sewed it, a voice said in her heart: "Take the handkerchief to Corrie Ten Boom."

The first prayer was one of life and death, the second for a handkerchief. We are to spread our lives before the Lord and share everything with him from the most mundane to the most grim. God listens and cares for sparrows, so how much more for us His children?

~~~~~~~~~~~~~~

October 29

Who shall not fear You, O Lord, and glorify Your name? For You alone are holy. (Revelation 15:4)

It is a remarkable truth that God alone is holy. This is not merely purity. It is rather the presence of God, a quality that is uniquely divine. For a person to be holy, they must have a relationship with God, and have allowed Him to inspire a quality of life that is devoted exclusively to Him and lived out before Him.

There are different levels of purity. A street may be clean but no-one would eat their dinner from it. A knife and fork may be clean but no surgeon would accept the hygiene of the cutlery drawer for the tools used in the operating theatre. These different levels are to do with the exclusion of dirt and bacteria. But holiness is of an even higher level of purity. It has to do with the stamp of the divine ownership on our lives. To be holy is to be set aside for God's pleasure and use.

When Isaiah was touched with burning coals from the altar (Isaiah 6), the result was to bring his life into line with a conscience under God's searching gaze. It is impossible to be truly holy and hypocritical. Every person who is more holy in public than in private has never grasped the true meaning of the word. Holiness, by definition, is to be gripped by the inner consciousness of the divine. The result is a moral awareness that outshines all the legal requirements of outward law. The person breaking the speed limit slows down as soon as they see a police car. But the person who is holy has the policeman as a passenger sitting beside them. The divine presence is not a constant badgering to do better, it is rather the inner pleasure of a Father sharing His delight with His own child. God alone is holy but he loves to share Himself with us. It is as we surrender to Him from the deepest part of our being that this beautiful, miraculous quality of holiness is ours.

~~~~~~~~~~~~~~~

October 30

"The lad and I will go yonder and worship." (Genesis 22:5)
"Now I know that you fear God, since you have not withheld your son, your only son, from Me." (Genesis 22:12)

It is surprising that God said that He was pleased that Abraham feared him. One might have expected the word "love" rather than "fear". The Bible bids us constantly not to fear, yet at the same time God seeks to instil in our hearts this godly fear. We 21st century people easily assume that to love God is to be chummy with Him. But the key element of loving and worshipping God is reverence.

The first aspect of this reverence is precisely the depth of love we feel for God. Imagine a young man in love who discovers that the girl he is trying to win is allergic to cats. If he has a dozen beloved cats at home, they would all be sold to new homes before their paws could touch the ground. The house would be fumigated and cleansed and, if need be, sold in order not to offend the one he loved. We are to esteem God as infinitely more valuable than any other relationship or possession. Abraham proved that he prized his covenant of love with God above even his son. A casual attitude to sin is proof that a person has no true love for God and no deep experience of worship. The first mention of worship in the Bible is here in this chapter, as Abraham's hushed and uncompromising love for God is revealed.

The second aspect of the fear of God is awe and amazement at His greatness. Worldly throne rooms are lavishly opulent and guarded by stern, disciplined soldiers in perfectly presented uniforms. Visitors are intimidated by the grandeur. The splendour of the King of kings is infinitely more breath-taking. True worship is not craven fear but the adoration of hearts aflame with reverential love and wonder.

~~~~~~~~~~~~~~~

October 31

And whatever things you ask in prayer, believing, you will receive. *(Matthew 21:22)*

I was in the Canadian Arctic waiting for my flight home. We could hear the small plane approaching, but as so often happens in that hostile climate, a "white out" suddenly descended over the remote valley and the plane couldn't land. We heard the sound of the engine retreating as the snow fell in persistent flurries. I went to the one desk in the small one-room airport, where I was told that I was not on the waiting list for the next three daily flights. I was on the waiting list for the fourth and fifth days, and I had a seat reserved six days later, if the weather didn't force more cancellations.

Next morning I trudged down through the snow to the airport and presented myself to the sceptical staff. As the minutes ticked by, a plane managed to land. I wasn't on the waiting list, but I stood resolved to see what would happen. 15 minutes before the departure, I approached the desk. The agent had a fixed expression and said if no-one came to claim it in the next ten minutes, there was one seat free for me. Those ten minutes seemed to me ten hours. But at last he smiled and handed me a boarding pass, and I was first out of the shed and on to the plane.

There were so many in my position but I was the only one who asked and waited persistently for the answer. My earnestness did not move the staff, nor my pleading. I had no soul power to move them to give me a place. I had asked, and could simply watch and wait for the outcome.

Prayer is simply asking. We cannot influence the outcome by anything other than believing that we have been heard. Prayer is not an accumulation of soul power that is affected by intensity or numbers. The power of prayer is simply measured by the greatness and authority of the one we are talking to. Nothing and no-one can resist His will. When He decides a thing, it is done. Ask – watch – wait for His smile and your boarding pass.

November 1

No king is saved by the multitude of an army; A mighty man is not delivered by great strength. (Psalm 33:16)
Do not fear, for those who are with us are more than those who are with them. (2 Kings 6:16)

It is an astonishing fact that a single believer is more than a match for the strongest armies of earth. David's victory over Goliath was as magnificent as it was humanly impossible. It may seem that the USA is invincible, with its huge army and its state-of-the-art equipment. But the truth is that no power of flesh is of any influence whatsoever against the strength of God. Mary Queen of Scots is reputed to have said "I fear the prayers of John Knox more than all the assembled armies of Europe", and she was right in her assessment.

The fact is that the legions of darkness are terrified of the prayers of the righteous. As soon as a person aligns himself with God and His purposes, he joins the ranks of heavenly hosts that are unconquerable. If Jesus Christ were our only ally, then we would still be assured of victory, since He is infinitely greater than the universe He created and more powerful than the millions of angels that came into being through His word. Since God is infinite and all His enemies are finite, the difference between these two worlds is immeasurable.

The weakest believer is defended by an invisible and impenetrable wall. So the only battlefield is in fact the mind. Satan's only stratagem is to attack the mind and intimidate the believer into believing what he can see with his eyes rather than what he perceives through the written word of God and the witness of the Holy Spirit.

Some may object that it is presumptuous to claim such power for believers. The opposite is true: it is the utmost folly to think for a single second that any threat will ever have any effect on God. It is the greatest vanity of all for any human being to believe that he can defend himself by force of arms or prevail against the will of God by force of personality. "He who sits in the heavens shall laugh" (Psalm 2:4). It is not the laughter of derision, but the laughter of the Almighty at the sheer incongruity and emptiness of the bravado of powerless human beings, who cannot even guarantee their next breath. Dwell on the unassailable serenity that surrounds God and let it seep into your heart and shape your mind.

~~~~~~~~~~~~~~~

November 2

Christ Jesus made himself nothing, taking the form of a servant, being born in the likeness of men.
(Philippians 2:7 ESV)

When Jesus Christ came into this world, He had no means by which to succeed in His mission other than faith in His Father. He had none of the resources that most people rely on to achieve their ends. He had no wealth but was born into a poor family. He had no advanced level of education but accepted the career of a carpenter. He grew up in Nazareth, a despised backwater of the Roman province of Palestine. He had no title or position from which to exercise influence. He was neither a rabbi from a religious school nor a prince in a palace.

His achievements were all through the means of trusting in His Father to lead Him, empower Him and provide everything He needed. His faith was tested as all faith must be. In the wilderness, the underlying reality was His trust in His Father where there was no bread to nourish Him, no miracle to attract attention and no position of power and influence to change the world. The truth is that the weaker we are in human resources, the stronger we can be in the things that really matter.

The path of the cross is lonely and barren but rich in access to the courts of heaven. A soul in communion with God is richer than all the millionaires of earth and more powerful than all the assembled armies of men. Everything of earth that we trust in detracts from our faith in God. The plan of God is to wean us from every teetering human support till we rest on the One that will never fail. No-one who trusts in the Lord will ever be ashamed.

∼∼∼∼∼∼∼∼∼∼∼∼∼∼∼

November 3

Looking carefully lest anyone fall short of the grace of God; lest any root of bitterness springing up cause trouble, and by this many become defiled. (Hebrews 12:15)

To be bitter is a sure sign that we are drifting away from grace. In the same way, a heart that is abiding in grace is always thankful and positive. The Bible is constantly challenging us to keep our hearts, since the heart is the fountain from which all life springs. The most important goal is to keep our hearts sweet, in an attitude of loving praise to God for the place and conditions in which we find ourselves right now.

To fall short of grace is to lose the inner strength to endure. Grace is an inner fragrance that softens the mind, enabling constant forgiveness and love. We so easily diagnose our problems in a superficial manner. Many problems that afflict us are simply symptoms of a deeper malaise. Cain's anger was the symptom of a graceless soul. King Saul's descent into vicious resentment towards David was the sign of a man who had no inner touch of God's love. Saul was a chosen and blessed vessel, supported and advised by Samuel, a godly friend and spiritual father. Yet He lost everything by neglecting the inner refreshings that come to those who constantly humble themselves before the Lord.

The word "grace" in Greek can be translated "thanks", rather like the Italian word "Grazie". Once we begin to thank God for the difficult things in our lives, we will discover an open channel for the beautiful supply of kindness to flow into our parched hearts. It may not be easy but it will always bear rich fruit. We do not have to thank God *for* everything but we must thank Him *in* all things. Positioning our soul to be thankful is to hold up the vessel of our heart to be filled with abounding grace.

~~~~~~~~~~~~~~~~

November 4

Bring all the tithes into the storehouse, that there may be food in My house, and try Me now in this," says the LORD of hosts, "if I will not open for you the windows of heaven and pour out for you such blessing that there will not be room enough to receive it. (Malachi 3:10)
Oh, that You would rend the heavens! That You would come down! (Isaiah 64:1)

There are two large bodies of water in Israel: the Sea of Galilee and the Dead Sea. They could not be more different. One is full of life, teeming with fish and with orchards and olive groves all around it. The other is dead, with hardly a bird or an insect stirring the heavy air above the lifeless waters.

The difference is simply in the fact that one receives and passes on what has been given, while the other has no outflow at all. The Bible reveals quite simply that the windows of heaven can be opened through simple, believing prayer. But the Bible also makes known that those same windows will be firmly shut if the blessing is not passed on. There is a deep and powerful relationship between my hand open to receive and my hand open to give. The two are firmly linked and we have power to open and close heaven by our generosity to others in our use of time and money.

This truth is repeated over and over as a foundational principle of life. *"Blessed are the merciful, for they shall obtain mercy." (Matthew 5:7.) "Give, and it will be given to you: good measure, pressed down, shaken together, and running over will be put into your bosom. For with the same measure that you use, it will be measured back to you." (Luke 6:38) "And forgive us our debts, As we forgive our debtors." (Matthew 6:12).*

We have been introduced to a wonderful world of mercy, truth, love and light. But if we become selfish in our spiritual walk, we will turn the Garden of Eden into a desert and the heavens will be as brass. God hears our actions much more clearly than our words. God has solemnly and firmly promised that if we will indeed obey His word, we will discover that we cannot contain the blessings that will be poured out.

∾∾∾∾∾∾∾∾∾∾∾∾∾

November 5

The kingdom of heaven is like a certain king who arranged a marriage for his son. *(Matthew 22:2)*

The kingdom of heaven is manifest in a group of people who are allowing the kingship of Jesus to shape their lives in actual relationships. The kingdom of heaven is here likened to a great feast, with music, feasting and rejoicing. This feast is in the context of love. We are to allow the rule of God in our lives to shape us to this enjoyment of God and His delightsome ways. The old hymn put it well when it declared "Him serve with mirth!" That is always the outcome of enthroning Christ in our lives, in our homes and in our churches.

In the parable, the wedding invitation provoked many reactions including violent hostility and rejection. But the most grievous reaction was indifference marked by lame excuses. The enthronement of Christ is to be a daily reality and it is to be our daily delight to rejoice in Christ and in His goodness. We may have believed in Christ but are we daily feasting at His table with Him in His kingdom?

Every day the table is set with love, kindness and abundant joy. There is no stuffy religious atmosphere at this celebration. We must throw off all excuses, repenting of the indifference that makes us procrastinate. Open the Bible, sing praises to the King of love and let it dawn on you that you are not invited to the feast merely as a guest but as one of the central figures. We are the bride at this wedding, the apple of God's eye and the object of His loving-kindness through all the unfolding ages to come.

"Rejoice, the Lord is King:
Your Lord and King adore!
Rejoice, give thanks and sing,
And triumph evermore.
Lift up your heart,
Lift up your voice!
Rejoice, again I say, rejoice!" (Charles Wesley)

November 6

The LORD has appeared of old to me, saying: "Yes, I have loved you with an everlasting love; therefore with lovingkindness I have drawn you." (Jeremiah 31:3)
Perhaps for a good man someone would even dare to die. But God demonstrates His own love toward us, in that while we were still sinners, Christ died for us." (Romans 5:7-8)

God's love is astounding. There are so many verses that celebrate His great heart of love. Unsurprisingly, it is not possible for us to fully grasp the extent of His love because we always measure it by our own love, which is so often weak and poor. We love the lovely and the good, but God loves sinners. God's love of righteousness caused Him to slay His Son, but He did not slay love. In fact, He magnified it in that matchless act of supreme love.

God is like a father who has a child given to a life of immorality or crime. Perhaps a daughter became a prostitute or a son became a drug-pusher. The father may grieve deeply for the chaos and destruction wreaked upon his offspring, but he never ceases to love them because he remembers them as little children full of promise. God looks into the heart of the worst sinner and still believes that He can restore that broken vessel to the very image of God Himself.

We have all lost the right to be loved by God by the dark thoughts and deeds that have marred our lives. But the word of God bids us throw off all doubts and fears and return to Him in brokenness, trusting in His mercy and His matchless grace made manifest in Christ. God is amazing and His wonderful love calls out to every human being to throw themselves in absolute surrender into His loving arms.

~~~~~~~~~~~~~~

November 7

Yet indeed I also count all things loss for the excellence of the knowledge of Christ Jesus my Lord, for whom I have suffered the loss of all things, and count them as rubbish, that I may gain Christ. (Philippians 3:8)

It is a most simple fact of spiritual logic that those who give up most for Christ love and enjoy Him most. Paul had reduced his whole life to "one thing" - the pursuit of God. Philippians chapter 3 is the personal testimony of a man whose soul is ablaze with love for God.

There are four things that Paul reached out for:
"That I may win Christ………….." (v.8)
"That I may know Him ………." (v.10)
"That I may attain the resurrection……….." (v.11)
"That I may apprehend/fulfil the reason I was created …" (v.12)
Paul's whole personality was active in one direction, which was to know Christ. The relentless activity of the Holy Spirit is to strip our lives from the pursuit of worthless baubles and to energise our whole being in the discovery of why we were created.

Mark Twain said the two most important days in any person's life were the day they were born and the day they discovered why. Deliverance from sin is a vital step in our salvation. But it is the discovery of why we were set free that truly causes the soul to burst into life.

I remember seeing a jet aircraft in Zimbabwe that had been converted into a restaurant. It must have been a great place to meet up and it no doubt provoked much interest and conversation. But the plane was made to fly. The soul of a man is like a caged eagle, restless and only half alive, until he glimpses the wonder of Jesus Christ. He is a door, a window into another world of beauty and infinite love. Many achievements of earth will be utterly forgotten, but the soul that knows and loves Jesus is journeying out of shadows into the brightness of eternal life.

ᴎᴎᴎᴎᴎᴎᴎᴎᴎᴎᴎᴎᴎ

November 8

And he said unto him, What is thy name? And he said, Jacob. And he said, Thy name shall be called no more Jacob, but Israel: for as a prince hast thou power with God and with men, and hast prevailed. *(Genesis 32:27-29, KJV)*

Jacob wrestled with God and pressed through till his inner strength was broken. Jacob was still clinging to God despite the pain and his inner turmoil. God then renamed him Israel: literally "A prince of God". Jacob had entered into an honoured company of people of whom God declares He is their God.

We too are invited to be part of this company. God is not encouraging us to embark on the quest for some great title. Rather, it is that we may bear the distinguishing marks of God's kingly character. We should not compete to be the most generous person on the planet, but we may certainly desire to belong to the ranks of reckless givers who are prepared to risk all for love's sake.

A prince with God has passed into the courts of eternity. He has been transformed by the shocking of God, who dared to call Himself the God of Jacob. God has stooped to boldly and proudly associate Himself with us! How then can we be anything other than full of joy at the scandalous grace of God? We are to firmly refuse to sit as beggars at the gates of God's kingdom, when those very gates stand open wide and a joyous host are singing praises to Christ the Redeemer and beckoning us inside.

We waste so much time fretting over our unworthiness. The truth is that all of God's princes have been raised from the dust of disaster and clothed with the royal robes of the Lion of Judah. Peter had reason to meditate on his disqualifying denial of the Lord. Moses could rightly fret over his impetuous murder of the Egyptian. But every soul that turns to God will always find a vast and warm embrace welcoming him into the heart of the Father.

∾∾∾∾∾∾∾∾∾∾∾∾∾

November 9

"Your Father knows." (Matthew 6:8 NIV)

He Himself knew what He would do. (John 6:6 KJV)

The fact that God is all-knowing is one of the most comforting of God's attributes. Believers need to think long and hard about this wonderful bedrock of the universe. It means that He knows all the trials through which we pass and He already knows what He will do to solve them. God's knowledge is absolute - there is nothing that escapes His gaze.

If God is not all-knowing, then our trials might take Him by surprise and He may not know the outcome. We tend to think that the only good outcome is the intervention of God making our circumstances trouble-free. But that is not the case. Stephen was able to pass through an unjust trial and the frenzy of mob violence by trusting that God knew the outcome. We always think of death as a bad outcome but for Stephen it was a door from a world of irrational evil into the world of eternal light and love. God knows the day of our departure from this world and it will not come by some chance happening or by the whim of some evil schemers. Our days are in the hands of our loving heavenly Father.

We may freely live in joyful anticipation of the outcome of each day. Whether we are enjoying easy days of freedom and health or imprisonment and affliction, each day is part of a great plan and purpose. Let the underlying foundation of each day be "My Father knows."

~~~~~~~~~~~~~~~~

November 10

In this is love, not that we loved God, but that He loved us and sent His Son to be the propitiation for our sins. (1 John 4:10)

God demonstrates His own love toward us, in that while we were still sinners, Christ died for us. (Romans 5:8)

Love is irrational and needs no reason to explain itself. Pascal said: "The heart has its reasons, of which reason knows nothing." So to love is a matter of the heart and has a power quite beyond the force of logic.

There are many astonishing facts about the love of God. His love is unconditional and is lavished on the good and the bad in equal measure. Moreover, He loves before a response is guaranteed. There is nothing we can ever do to make God love us more, and there is nothing we have ever done that can stop Him loving us. Salvation is conditional upon our response, but God's love is absolute and immeasurable.

God so loved fallen humanity that He stooped in total identification with our sinful condition. He made Jesus to be sin on the cross in order to release us from the guilt and power of evil. There is no greater humiliation that can be imagined, no greater act of sacrifice than the love of God revealed at Calvary.

Love is the reason that the background noise of the universe is the singing of myriads of angels and people that are objects of His breath-taking love. Love is the foundation of all, the mind that created all things, the source of beauty and the very melody that made and redeemed humanity. To be loved by God is to be invited to a wedding feast at which we are the bride. It is because of love there is hope and because of love we may dare to believe. God is love and this means that His love is enthroned forever and can never fail. The Bible is the story of God's universal, all-conquering love and we were made to receive and enjoy the floods of that love for all eternity.

∼∼∼∼∼∼∼∼∼∼∼∼∼∼

November 11

I will lift up my eyes to the hills- from whence comes my help? My help comes from the LORD, who made heaven and earth.
(Psalm 121:1-2)

Then David said to Saul, "Let no man's heart fail because of him; your servant will go and fight with this Philistine."
(1 Samuel 17:32)

A preacher was once praying for a small amount of $75. In his prayers, he helpfully suggested a dozen ways by which God could answer his request, including prompting someone to post him a cheque or finding the money in an old coat pocket. At day's end, he had his $75, but God had not used any of the methods suggested.

When Israel faced the army of the Philistines, no-one would have suggested sending out a boy in his early teens, with no sword or armour, clothed like a shepherd and armed with 5 stones and a sling. God's answer was completely out of proportion to the scale of the need, and so it will always be. God's answers will always come, and they will come from unexpected quarters. God's ways are designed to confound the proud ways of man.

No-one expected Hezekiah to survive a siege by the mighty Assyrians. No-one expected Gideon and his 300 to win against the Midianites. No-one expected a boy with a basket of loaves and fish to feed five thousand men plus women and children. No-one expected God to rain manna down on the congregation to feed millions of people. Moreover, when the same circumstances repeated themselves, no-one could see how God could provide any help. The reason is because our faith is so limited by what we can see and measure.

It is only with a supreme conscious focusing of our eyes on God that we may dare to believe. We are incapable of imagining how He will do it. But He will do it. We may sweat and fluster but that will not improve or hinder the outcome. God can no more forget His children than an earthly father can when the children are crying out with hunger. We may look to the hills, but our help will come from the Lord who made them.

~~~~~~~~~~~~~~~~

November 12

Then He taught, saying to them, "Is it not written: 'My house shall be called a house of prayer for all nations." (Mark 11:17)

Jesus quoted this great prophetic declaration by Isaiah minutes after He had entered the temple in Jerusalem and had cleansed it. The temple area was constantly echoing with prayers, but they were not prayers from the heart, just repeated ritualistic prayers. Before God the temple was spiritually dead.

The great heart and centre of all that God is about is communion with His people. Many projects can grow a church, but these things must always be separate and secondary to the very purpose for which we have been saved. If a church is not in communion with God, through prayer, it is soul-less and spiritually colour-less. Prayer is the aortic artery that allows God's presence to be pumped throughout the courts of our hearts. Once there is connection with God at the centre, there will be an invisible attraction that draws people to be touched by the divine presence. Nothing can replace this and we must be deeply persuaded that this is God's way with us.

The most important room in a house is the kitchen, where the food is prepared. Without a kitchen the inhabitants will all die. Yet the food strengthens people to go out and work, and live, to serve their generation. Prayer is the source of sustenance among God's children and by it we are empowered to fulfil our calling. We are not to be obsessed with prayer any more than we are to be obsessed with food. But we must attend to nourishing our souls just as much as we cherish our bodies.

The calling of the church is to know God and to make Him known. This is His plan not ours. He will see to it that people are saved and blessed if we will focus on fulfilling the great destiny for which we were created.

~~~~~~~~~~~~~

November 13

Then Jesus said to them, "Follow Me, and I will make you become fishers of men." (Mark 1:17)

The gospel is summed up in these two words: "Follow Me." Jesus never challenged the disciples to follow an experience but to set out on a journey of faith, trusting in Him, in His character and faithfulness. There is always a subtle temptation to replace Jesus Christ with something that He gives, such as salvation, baptism with the Holy Spirit or healing. Sometimes we may even hear people claim that so and so has got 'it'.

Though this change is subtle, it is nevertheless disastrous. Occasionally, one may hear of someone talking about "prayer" or "revival" as if these were the great keys to power and transformation. Jesus did not say "prayer" is the way, the truth and the life. There is a relentless focus of the Holy Spirit on knowing Jesus Christ.

Meditation is another means religions use in their quest for peace and tranquillity. But all such methods are deceptive until there is deep inward surrender to the lordship of Jesus Christ. "Follow Me" demands that we cease to follow any other path and requires that our confidence is in relating to Him moment by moment.

This path of knowing Him comes with a promise that God will make something of us as we follow Him. He will make us into evangelists, teachers, people of prayer and/or ministers of healing. The deep underlying result will be that we will love people, since following Christ is to follow and be taught by love. As we forsake every other 'way', we will become living embodiments of His teaching. This can never be the result of following a book or a doctrine. Such things never challenge the heart as do the rigours of maintaining a living relationship with Christ. Methods will disappoint but knowing Jesus Christ leads to an eve-increasing brightness of hope as we leave shadows behind and discover the wonder of His luminous personality.

~~~~~~~~~~~~~~~

November 14

As He sat at the table, a woman came having an alabaster flask of very costly oil of spikenard. Then she broke the flask and poured it on His head. (Mark 14:3)

This is one of the greatest expressions of love for Jesus in the gospels. The flask would have been a large bottle of expensive perfume. The room would have been flooded immediately with a fragrance that no-one could ignore. This is what happens when believers worship Jesus in total surrender of their inner being to Him. Love is an inner fragrance that must be expressed and all of heaven is filled with singing, with beauty and with fragrance.

Jesus Christ is God's alabaster box. The Father broke open His Son when Jesus surrendered His life into the hands of God on Calvary. The contents were poured out onto a sinful humanity and the centurion directing the crucifixion was immediately astonished at what he witnessed. The words of Jesus expressed the meaning of this extravagant act of love. There was forgiveness and salvation as Christ reached out to a fallen race.

The full power of the costly oil was poured out on the day of Pentecost as Jesus anointed and filled His church with the Holy Spirit. The scent of God's love is as fresh today as when the Holy Spirit was first poured out. The power is just as real and new in all believers who open their hearts to God in full surrender. There is cleansing and transformation, coming through the outpouring of God's innermost being on those who love Him. Wherever the gospel is preached, these same scenes are re-enacted as God pours out Himself on sinners and incredulous sinners respond by pouring their hearts out to God. It is vital that we grasp the enormity and power of this great act of God. It is essential that the church respond with constantly renewed love poured out on Christ. He receives worship, which pleases Him. Outpouring is His way of life and He yearns to find the same joyous abandon in His people.

~~~~~~~~~~~~~~

November 15

And no one puts new wine into old wineskins; or else the new wine bursts the wineskins, the wine is spilled, and the wineskins are ruined. But new wine must be put into new wineskins. *(Mark 2:21-22)*

Jesus taught by this parable that the Old Covenant of Moses is completely incompatible with the New Covenant. By it, He described His desire to fill people with the Holy Spirit and form in them His own life and nature. It is a disaster to try and patch up the old life, even at its religious best. What is required is a new start and a new foundation.

This parable teaches how this is possible. To get a new wineskin, a farmer would select a goat and slaughter it. He would remove the skin and take it straight to the fire to burn out the remnants of the flesh. Then he would sew up the skin, seal it and immediately fill it with the freshly-pressed grape juice. The skin is still flexible and as the wine ferments and expands, the skin will take the shape dictated by the wine within it.

In the same way, if we are to be people of the New Covenant, constantly allowing the Holy Spirit to form Christ in us, we must go to the cross and surrender our lives into the hands of God. It is the master-plan of God to create a death by which the power of the flesh is put to death and we are enabled to receive the Spirit and cooperate with Him. This is a death by faith, not by nails and wood. It is painless to us, but it was not painless to the One who opened the path for us to follow. For us this death is full of joy since by it we lose the heavy baggage of a self-centred life and are set free to know and love Jesus in the power of a renewed inner life. Habit and familiarity harden us and so we must be constantly on the watch to guard our inner life by turning to the Father, who will skilfully and tenderly renew us by applying the power of His Son's cross in us. By the inner cut of the master-surgeon, we are kept alive and fresh in the love of God and are being renewed in the image of His beloved Son.

~~~~~~~~~~~~~~

November 16

You shall also make a covering of ram skins dyed red for the tent, and a covering of badger skins above that.
(Exodus 26:14)

"Pray to your Father who is in the secret place." (Matthew 6:6)

We have access to the secret place of fellowship with God. This place is within us by the Holy Spirit and it is the very presence of God. Jesus Christ is not in the Holy of Holies - He *is* the Holy of Holies.

God gave instructions for thick fur-skins to be the covering of the tabernacle and the effect would have been to soundproof it. There would have been a deep hush in the Holy of Holies and this is an indication of the profound tranquillity that is in the Spirit. This is to be our conscious experience when we turn to God in prayer. His presence immediately drowns out the voices that clamour for our attention. More important still is the inner calm that rises as our anxieties fall away and disappear as we enter the awesome place of prayer.

It is vital that we grasp that prayer is a place not primarily a cerebral exercise. If we intellectualise prayer, we become obsessed with information and easily begin to lecture God on what He should be doing and why. Once we understand that prayer is a secret place, then we begin to enjoy the marvellous atmosphere that is imparted to us as we pray. It is a secret place, and impossible to explain to those who have never experienced the Holy Spirit. Prayer is the place of knowing God and of allowing God's inner states to become mine. The delight of this place is the realisation of the beauty of God's being. As the sounds of earth fade, we become aware of joyful holiness and unquenchable love. God is so wonderful that as we draw near we love Him and the attributes that make Him a living jewel. Loving God is not a duty but the uprising of the heart to adore and enjoy Him. The door is open - enter in and let all that He is be within you.

November 17

You have become estranged from Christ, you who attempt to be justified by law; you have fallen from grace. (Galatians 5:4)

We most often associate the phrase "fallen from grace" with some serious moral lapse in a person's life. But Paul is not referring to a moral lapse but a spiritual one. He describes the subtle shift in a person's walk with God from trusting in the indwelling Spirit to trusting in ourselves. Walking in the flesh is all about the place from which we live. A man or woman of the Spirit is utterly convinced of their inability to produce a spiritual character without the presence of God through the Holy Spirit.

There is a rest and poise in the heart of a person walking in the Spirit. They are what they are by grace and so have no ambition to be better than others or excel as though the Christian life were competing against one another. The disastrous consequence of walking in the flesh is boasting, as if one were to boast in George Muller rather than the God of George Muller. It would be to brag about praying as if our prayers were the source of blessing and not the channel.

The shift is subtle but fundamental. The choice is between trusting in God or believing in ourselves, between resting in God's love or striving to attain an intensity that is as impossible as it is unreal. It is for this reason that we are not trying to make ourselves extraordinary Christians, we are simply allowing the Holy Spirit to shape us into the unique person that God has destined us to be. It is as if a swan were striving to be a humming-bird or an eagle were striving to be a sparrow. God has called us by His grace, and will equip and empower us by that same grace to reach the goal each day that He asks us to attain. Through grace, we are free to be children of God, liberated to discover that we are not battling a life-long war to get right with God. We are right with Him now by faith and filled with all the spiritual resources that we need to please Him.

November 18

Abraham did not waver at the promise of God through unbelief, but was strengthened in faith, giving glory to God, and being fully convinced that what He had promised He was also able to perform. (Romans 4:20-21)

God is a promise keeper. God does not speak lightly nor does He speak according to how easy it may be to keep His promises. When God promised a son to Abraham, He knew that Abraham's body would grow old and that Sarah was barren. God knew all the obstacles that lay in His path but disregarded them as if they did not exist. His firm intention is, in itself, the power to make things happen and His promise means that it will happen, though heaven and earth may be shaken in the process.

God has promised to provide for us, His people. He has promised never to abandon or forsake us. He has promised to be with us to the end of our lives and make us partakers of His glory. Faith is all about grasping that God has spoken and that therefore it will surely come to pass.

Reflect for a moment on what God has already promised and fulfilled. He promised to send His Son to save the world by bearing our sins away. He carefully made this promise through the prophets and the patriarchs. He even had Abraham offering Isaac, foreshadowing the act of redemption two thousand years before it happened and on the very spot where it would take place. God has promised to save us from the guilt and power of sin and has fulfilled this to the letter. All who believe in Him may rest in the deep, unshakable confidence that our eternal salvation is as sure as the word spoken from eternity and fulfilled in time. God, who cannot lie, has promised to present us faultless before Himself in perfect love. All we have to do is look long and hard at the record of God's faithfulness in the written word and simply believe that He is the unchanging God.

November 19

And one cried to another and said: "Holy, holy, holy is the LORD of hosts; the whole earth is full of His glory!"
(Isaiah 6:3)

Holiness is unique to God. People without God may have moral standards but holiness is always and only through the impact of God on our lives. It is for this reason that prayer and holiness are so bound together. People who would be holy must look on God and cry "holy" from the depths of their heart.

The same is true of love and joy, which are always expressed in worship. These things are all by-products of looking at God, and sensing the burning purity and beauty of His being. These things must be released through verbal expression and there is an increase of knowing God as we take the time to put into words the marvellous things that are present in the Godhead. It is as we cry "holy" that we are touched with the burning coals that are upon the altar of God's person.

It may be easily grasped, even by a casual observer, that holiness has nothing to do with rules and codes of conduct. It has rather to do with the glory of God's being, washing in waves over His people. Holiness is as the light and heat radiating from the sun. It sustains spiritual life, imparts the knowledge of God and transforms the character of the one gazing on God. It is no more possible to be holy without prayer than for our physical life to continue without breathing. The words "Holy Spirit" can be translated "holy air or breath". The miracle of the work of the Holy Spirit is the constant imparting of God's own life to sustaining His people and keeping them in spiritual health and wholeness. There is no carnal intensity in God's holiness, but rather a quiet sanity and normality, resulting in spirituality without strain. How blessed are those who know God and cry "Holy, Holy, Holy."

November 20

For we do not wrestle against flesh and blood, but against principalities, against powers, against the rulers of the darkness of this age, against spiritual hosts of wickedness in the heavenly places. (Ephesians 6:12)

Prayer is to engage in warfare with unseen hosts that afflict the souls of men. The battle begins at the lowest levels of the conflict and the feelings of lethargy and discouragement are the first blows struck by the enemy. To be an effective participant in this war, we must first join the army. The enemy will whisper in our ears about the faults and weaknesses of our fellow-soldiers. He will discourage us and point out how weak we all are compared to great heroes of the faith such as Gideon, David or Hudson Taylor. The fact is, we must wrestle with these thoughts and overcome them by steadfast resistance.

The war will be won as we simply defy the hosts of darkness, whether with a weak, trembling voice or with a great shout of confidence. All soldiers must overcome their fears on the eve of battle, and so it is with Christians. We must join hand in hand with others, realising that this is the purpose of God: to form a company of people who will exercise the authority of Christ. When Jesus said the gates of hell would not prevail against the church, He was referring to the loving fellowship of believers.

This battle is not for the faint-hearted. There will be moments of intense feelings of disqualification and of abject spiritual impotence, but these are all the fiery darts of the evil one. He is the father of lies and fights with a fixed purpose to deflect us from our great calling as men and women of prayer. Raise the shield of faith and remember: "You *are* a chosen generation, a royal priesthood, a holy nation and His own special people, so that you may proclaim the praises of Him who called you out of darkness into His marvellous light; who once *were* not a people but now *are* the people of God." (1 Peter 2:9-10) We are a people of prayer by the very nature in our hearts imparted through new birth. We don't have to make ourselves overcomers, we must simply take our place and discover that that is what God has already made us.

November 21

Hear my cry, O God; attend to my prayer. From the end of the earth I will cry to You, when my heart is overwhelmed; lead me to the rock that is higher than I. (Psalm 61:1-2)

If we ask anything according to His will, He hears us. And if we know that He hears us, whatever we ask, we know that we have the petitions that we have asked of Him.
(1 John 5:14-15)

The Psalmist was overwhelmed with grief and had the sensation of being far from God. Such moments will afflict all of us at some point and then we face a choice: we can anaesthetise our grief and turn to some form of emotional escapism, such as the shallow entertainments of the world, or we can turn to God in prayer.

Our first steps in prayer will be filled with the consciousness of the greatness of our problems and our pain. But we are to press through these and to allow the Lord to unfold to us that He is greater than all our difficulties. There is "a rock that is higher than I", and from that vantage-point I will see everything in a new light. Prayer is the means by which God's power is brought to bear on impossibly dark situations, and it is also the means by which faith is imparted to the heart of the one praying. Through prayer, the people we pray for are changed, but at the same time we are also touched at the deepest level of our being.

We become conscious of the supreme unassailable lordship of Jesus Christ. When we approach Him, we may be anxious and fearful, but as we turn and look upon Him our hearts will be filled with peace. Prayer is sharing all that burdens our hearts with the omnipotent King of all. Once the matter is in His hands, we can rest with a calm that passes understanding. The answer may be minutes or years in coming, but to the praying soul, the answer is already secure because we know He has heard our cry.

~~~~~~~~~~~~~

November 22

The earth is the LORD'S, and all its fullness, the world and those who dwell therein. *(Psalm 24:1)*

The ships travel through the sea, and over here swims the whale you made to play in it. *(Psalm 104:26 NET)*

As human beings, it is completely understandable if we think that the earth belongs to us. After all, we built all the roads, bridges, factories and airports. We buy and sell the land, along with its agricultural produce and mineral wealth. But the truth is that we are squatters on property that belongs to someone else. It only truly becomes ours when we turn back to God and become His beloved children.

The whole planet belongs to God. He made it and created all the thousands of creatures that live in it. He sustains the life of growing and living beings. It is such a relief to grasp this simple fact. It suddenly makes one realise that though proud individuals are strutting around making loud claims about their own importance, they are actually only a detail to the grand daily display of God's glory. The world is a vast stage on which multitudes of creatures bring constant pleasure to God. The immense majority of earth's beauty is only seen and enjoyed by the Creator. There are millions of flowers blooming in remote valleys, millions of fish and birds that will never be seen by human eyes. Not to mention the vast reaches of the universe with its uncharted wonders. These are all made by God for His own delight.

As God's children, we are leaving this mad world of darkness and sin and returning to the Creator, to live in the majestic world He made for Himself and for His loved ones. It is a step out of confusion into the calm, ordered world of God's glory. He owns it. He rules it. Disobedient humanity merely grasp and misuse it, placing it under false constraints called money and armies. We are to return and recapture the ability to wonder at our Father's world.

∾∾∾∾∾∾∾∾∾∾∾∾

November 23

For who has despised the day of small things?
(Zechariah 4:10)
For where two or three are gathered together in My name, I am there in the midst of them. *(Matthew 18:20)*

It is a common human mistake to confuse big things with greatness. The truth is that it is the small things that matter most. A ship without a compass is in great danger and if it has no rudder, it is crippled. It may not matter where a car is parked, or how wide a window is fitted in a room, but move an eye one centimetre and the whole face is disfigured.

In the same way, the most significant part of a church is the fellowship of the mystery between an individual and Jesus Christ. Zechariah prophesied this of Zerubabel, who was seeking to rebuild the temple in Jerusalem. Zerubabel was despised and belittled, but what he was doing was of immeasurable importance. In the same way, church life is not experienced in large meetings or in great preaching. It is most known by those who agree in one Spirit and are able to pray together. This heart unity implies a breaking down of every barrier, whether racial, social or financial. There is a unity and a love between believers that transcends everything and unites us with Christ in the eternal mystery of the love of God.

The early church gathered in homes, as it has often done in communist Russia and China. It is from such homes that vast empires have been transformed. We are never to despise the day of small things for it is in the beauty of Christ revealed in quiet moments of prayer that the kingdom of God is built and that strongholds of darkness are destroyed. Guard the quiet places of the heart for the King. One day we will be astonished at what eternal destinies were changed in the transactions that took place there.

~~~~~~~~~~~~~~~

November 24

Jehoshaphat appointed those who should sing to the LORD, and who should praise the beauty of holiness, as they went out before the army and were saying: "Praise the LORD, for His mercy endures forever." Now when they began to sing and to praise, the LORD set ambushes against the people of Ammon, Moab, and Mount Seir, who had come against Judah; and they were defeated. (2 Chronicles 20:21-22)

Jehoshaphat was one of the greatest kings of Judah. His exultant faith was most clearly demonstrated when he placed the singers in the forefront of his army to praise and worship the Lord. The best song is produced in a person who is relaxed enough to delight in this most heavenly of human activities. A world or a home without song is desolate, for singing releases the fragrance of love and creates a beautiful setting for God's presence. Heaven is filled with singing and so should churches and Christian homes be also.

Imagine the scene. The enemy is drawing near with its most fierce and callous soldiers at the front uttering their bloodcurdling cries to dishearten the opposing army. They are armed to the teeth with swords and spears, bows and arrows. But the army they face is looking upward to heaven, with faces alight with joy and confidence that God is with them. The battle was settled at that moment, for no army has power to defeat the people of God when their hearts are right with Him and their mouths filled with praise.

The lesson is simple: we are to face the hardest battles with songs of faith that will make our hearts soar. The battle is won when we set our sights to get into step with heaven. Singing and worshipping God in the Spirit are the Christian's most powerful weapons, for they paralyse the hosts of darkness and fix us firmly in the impregnable fortress of God's presence.

November 25

Death and life are in the power of the tongue, and those who love it will eat its fruit. (Proverbs 18:21)
A word fitly spoken is like apples of gold in settings of silver. (Proverbs 25:11)

The power to touch other lives is in our tongue and the open secret is that words can build up or destroy. The tongue is an ever-flowing well of water continually releasing what is in the heart. The gift of speaking with new tongues is most evidenced when we speak in our native language, not in an unknown tongue. If we have really been touched in the depths of our being, we will speak faith, hope and love to others.

The writer of Proverbs compared a good word to solid gold in settings of pure silver. This is because it is not possible to calculate either the harm or the good that is done by a single word. God spoke the world into being at creation. He spoke our salvation and redemption when He uttered prayers of love from the cross. We in turn must speak words that create and redeem because it is given to us to do so. When we align ourselves with the love of God, we will find our words are a conduit for the Holy Spirit. When we allow bitterness to define us, we are a channel for darkness.

The first person to feel the impact of our words is our self. We shape our own inner universe by the things we utter. If we are tempted to say negative things, then we must quickly and heartily repent. Words are like cool, refreshing waters in a thirsty land. They are like the sweetest fragrance in the midst of the rancorous stench of conflict. Our words will heal our own hearts and bring healing to others. To forge a new way of speaking will require patience, frequent repentance and, on occasions, confession to others. The results will come slowly because we are sowing to the Spirit, but we will be overwhelmed by the rich harvest that comes from words of life.

~~~~~~~~~~~~~~

November 26

Moreover, as for me, far be it from me that I should sin against the LORD by ceasing to pray for you.
(1 Samuel 12:23)

Samuel assured the people that he would keep praying for them, and maintained it would be a sin if he stopped. It is a simple fact of spiritual life that we are not saved by the level of holiness to which we have attained. Most of us measure our holiness by the things we do not do rather than the things we do. But the Bible teaches that holiness is not the absence of sin, it is much rather the active life-giving presence of God expressed in loving care for others. It is precisely for this reason that no-one is able to assess how holy they are.

Holiness is marked by the child-like enjoyment of God. It is not some stuffy legalistic attention to some detail as trivial as jewellery or clothing. There is a delight in the heart of the person who has discovered that we are to take pleasure in loving God and entering into His magnificent courts.

Praying for others is a sure indication that we have passed from the carnal self-preoccupation of worldly souls. The person who has suffered some painful illness and then been cured will automatically think of those who need that same medicine. To attain the beautiful presence of God is to be infused with such a depth of joy unspeakable and full of glory that we are beside ourselves. Yet, like Samuel, we continue to live amongst a fallen race, whose afflictions we deeply understand. It would be criminal not to reach out to God for those who are perishing around us. Our discovery of God must always be combined with a care for the lost or it will become the worst form of selfishness. Love and holiness are two sides of the same coin. Love will never minimise holiness and true holiness cannot slay love. They flourish together and are revealed as one on Calvary, when love poured out perfect intercession to reconcile a guilty world with a holy God,

November 27

For God knows that in the day you eat of it your eyes will be opened, and you will be like God, knowing good and evil.
(Genesis 3:5)

Satan is the originator of unbelief. In conversation with Eve, he targeted the character of God and imputed base intentions to God. All unbelief is based on ascribing something to God's character that is not there or on taking something away from God that is there. The moment we think God could forget us, or think He could in any way be unkind, we stumble in our faith.

Unbelief is a grievous prison that leads to despair and sorrow. But the answer always lies within our reach: we can choose to believe the word of God and the perfect faithfulness of the One who spoke it. Unbelief seeks to undermine the foundations of the universe since it rests on God's unchanging goodness and love. Faith is the foundation of our inner life and the source of strength and stability. We are weakened whenever we entertain any notion that is not true about God. Our ability to work and pray is undermined. But the moment we realise what is happening, we are released from that dark dungeon and refreshed.

God is love. He is the very definition of faithfulness. He has never broken a promise or said anything that He did not mean. He is faithful to hear our prayers and we must hold fast to the power of His promises. Faith must be tested if it is to grow and there will be days when it seems as if the foundations of the universe are being shaken. The fact is that the universe is built on God's immutable kindness. I am connected to that foundation through faith and I must declare my trust whether in perfect sunshine or in the teeth of a tempest. The fiercest storms come when His face is hidden, but wait a while and the clouds will depart and we will see that He has not changed and He cannot change.

November 28

For through Him we both have access by one Spirit to the Father. *(Ephesians 2:18)*

Towards the end of the American Civil War, a dejected confederate soldier was sitting outside the grounds of the White House. A young boy approached him and asked him why he was so sad. The soldier told how he had repeatedly tried to see President Lincoln. He wanted to tell the President that his farm in the South had been unfairly taken away by the Federal soldiers. But each time he tried to enter the White House, the guards crossed their bayoneted guns in front of the door and turned him away. The boy motioned to the soldier to follow him. When they approached the guarded entrance, the soldiers came to attention, stepped back and opened the door for the boy. He proceeded to the library, where the President was resting, and introduced the soldier to his father. The boy was Tad Lincoln, the President's son.

The miracle of the cross is that the enmity between God and man has been abolished. The way back to God is wide open through the Son. We may find ourselves in a terrible state and feel completely disqualified from ever entering the holy presence of God. But the moment we put our trust in Christ, we are ushered into that life-transforming atmosphere that pervades the Father's house. We can never be worthy of ourselves, which is why Jesus taught us to pray for the forgiveness of sins. It is only by grace that we enter, but we enter with full confidence that we are loved and accepted. Moreover, the way is continually open, since by coming we are adopted into the family of God and have continual access to the Father's heart. The Bible does not bid us come timidly but boldly to claim the blood-bought gift of knowing God for ourselves.

November 29

Ascribe greatness to our God.   (Deuteronomy 32:3)
But even if our gospel is veiled, it is veiled to those who are perishing, whose minds the god of this age has blinded.
(2 Corinthians 4:3-4)

The people of God were about to enter a period of intense conflict as they began to possess the promised land. Moses here spoke to the people his exhortation for the coming battles. His first word was that they should ascribe greatness to God.

The simple truth is that we must choose to whom we grant the place of power and greatness. We do this often without conscious decision. Fear is itself an unconscious act of attributing power and authority to negative forces in our lives. We must recognise that we are bowing to these threatening voices and allowing them to rob us of peace and of the blessings that God has promised. It is often only when we realise how we have allowed problems to take centre stage that we realise what an awful insult this is to God. God is standing right there, declaring His power and inviting us to trust Him. The moment we refuse to allow sickness or difficulties to be lord, we enter into another world. The mists depart and we see clearly. When problems are lord, the mists descend and we lose our way.

Hold a flimsy piece of paper before your eyes and it will block out Mount Everest. Satan would have us fix our eyes on the things that trouble us, and then they block out the glory of God and impede the unspeakable promises of God. Satan has no ability to throw a blanket over God; his power is limited to the eyes of our heart. The moment we push his hand aside, we see the majestic Son of God with immeasurable power and authority.

We have a choice to allow problems to block our vision or let God take centre stage and see our problems shrink. The god of this age is theatrical and he will pout and stamp his feet, he will threaten and cajole. He will hold a magnifying glass to problems and turn molehills into mountains. God waits for us to hear His quiet, untroubled voice of authority and so awaken us to the real world where God is Lord and God alone.

November 30

"For there is hope for a tree, if it is cut down, that it will sprout again, and that its tender shoots will not cease. Though its root may grow old in the earth, and its stump may die in the ground, yet at the scent of water it will bud and bring forth branches like a plant." (Job 14:7-9)

Job felt that human beings had less hope than a tree, but actually this image of the tree is a lesson in God's ability to bring life and redemption into the most desperate of human circumstances. The marvel is that at the merest scent of water a tree revives and buds again. It is at the merest touch of grace that a soul awakens from its deep sleep to realise that there is hope. God's touch may come through a word, an action or a mere whisper, but when it does, the dark clouds roll away and the sun comes out.

The year was 1815 and 18-year-old Jane Lucretia D'Esterre was standing by a deep lake in Scotland preparing to cast herself into the dark waters. A few weeks earlier, she had lost her husband John D'Esterre, who had died in a duel with Daniel O'Connell in Ireland. She was suddenly aware of a young man whistling and ploughing a straight furrow on the other side of the lake. This touched a deep chord in her life and she determined to live with a purpose as simple and straight as that of the ploughboy. Two weeks later she gave her life to Christ and later married into the Grattan-Guinness family. Subsequent generations of this family served the Lord, teaching and preaching the word of God and bringing revival to Ireland.

God reached out and touched her with the mere scent of purpose and grace and it turned her soul around onto the path of life. There are many lessons from this event; firstly, that God is able to reach down and stir hope in the darkest hour of any life; secondly, we are to be as cheerful and true as the ploughboy and focus on guarding a heart of faithfully keeping our hand on the plough. The most insignificant moments of our lives may be the scent of water that reaches some trembling onlooker who we may never meet again.

December 1

For this commandment which I command you today is not too mysterious for you, nor is it far off. It is not in heaven, that you should say, 'Who will ascend into heaven for us and bring it to us, that we may hear it and do it?' Nor is it beyond the sea, that you should say, 'Who will go over the sea for us and bring it to us, that we may hear it and do it?' But the word is very near you, in your mouth and in your heart, that you may do it. (Deuteronomy 30:11-14)

There are times when the Holy Spirit lifts us to great heights of wonder at the mysteries of Christ and His work in our soul. But we are not to forget that God is also incredibly practical when it comes down to the foundations of our salvation. This is most relevant in days when we seem to be unable to rise above the mundane, commonplace feelings of everyday life. Or, worse, we might be passing through some trials in which we completely lose our awareness of the divine presence.

At such times it is vital to return to the basic facts of salvation: Christ died for me, my sins are forgiven and I believe it. To reach out for some feeling or experience is to make my salvation depend on an emotion rather than God's unchangeable and unbreakable covenant promise. God has never broken a single promise; He has never abandoned a soul that believes in Him. It is so simple that it seems too easy. But watch Jesus handling the soul of the prostitute in Luke 7:50: "Your faith has saved you. Go in peace." He extended His sceptre, spoke the royal command and it was done. This is not a temporary foundation - it is as permanent and unshakable as God Himself.

Let this faith be the bedrock of joy, both in days of exultation and in days when clouds obscure the sun. Speak from the heart, speak aloud with your mouth the unshakable truth. There are uncountable varieties of human personality, and there is a large spectrum of different feelings through which each individual passes, some very vivid and strong. But through it all, the anchor of God holds secure: God has said it, I believe it, and that settles it.

~~~~~~~~~~~~~~

December 2

Before I was afflicted I went astray, but now I keep Your word.... It is good for me that I have been afflicted, that I may learn Your statutes. (Psalm 119:67 & 71)

They ... strengthened the souls of the disciples, exhorting them to continue in the faith, and saying, "We must through many tribulations enter the kingdom of God." (Acts 14:22)

When we ask God to take control of our lives, to be the Lord of every part of our being, we scarcely know what we are praying for and we certainly have no inkling what is involved to answer that prayer. God will answer this prayer with heights of joy as He reveals Himself, but there will also come days when the fires of affliction will burn fiercely, melting the hard, resistant parts of our souls.

We must recognise this simple fact, that there are lessons that can be learnt from studying the Bible, and there are other lessons that can only be learnt in the white heat of trouble. Paul strengthened the disciples with this teaching, having himself just passed through a deep trial, having been stoned and left for dead by the people of Lystra.

It is through difficult times that our hearts are sifted. Attitudes come to the surface that surprise us, but they are not caused by affliction, they are simply revealed by it. We need a deep adjustment of our inner life if we are ever to display the glory of God. A right attitude to suffering is vital if we are to have healthy minds and pass on to a positive outcome. For this reason, we are to keep a praising heart turning the heaviness to solemn but genuine joy. We are to identify deeply with others whose suffering we may not have noticed. We are not to narrow down our interests, but to enlarge them to include others, praying for those whose faith may be weaker.

"No discipline is enjoyable while it is happening - it's painful! But afterward there will be a peaceful harvest of right living for those who are trained in this way." (Hebrews 12:11 NLT.) Above all, recognise that it is the loving hand of God on your life, faithfully working out His amazing plan.

December 3

Truly my soul silently waits for God; from Him comes my salvation ... My soul, wait silently for God alone, for my expectation is from Him. *(Psalm 62:1 & 5)*

Silent meditation before God is practised by many religions, but there is a key difference in the Christian's approach to stilling their soul before God. The believer approaches God to be cleansed from sin and delivered from the power of self through the cross. Without this, the mind will wander into silence for its own sake and fall short of knowing God.

The cross is God's power to still all the wayward chatter of our mind and establish peace and the exquisite consciousness of God. For this reason it is through faith that we enter in, not through meditation. The moment we believe, we enter into another world where God is revealed in His holiness, love and beauty. To find this, there must be a loss of self-importance, a relinquishing of striving to be something and a contentment to be a spectator of the great magnificence that is God. Jesus is beautiful and a few seconds in His presence silences our questioning mind till we find the deep reverent hush that fills all eternity with the awe and the joy that are the marks of His presence.

The blood of Jesus in us is the constant elimination of our proud selves, which hinder us from knowing the reason we were created. The blood is the equipping of our souls to meekly take our place in the ranks of beings that are privileged to behold God in His breath-taking qualities of being. It is only by faith that we can enter these hallowed halls. As our self-consciousness is diminished, we become as nothing before Him. Then the miracle of eternal life is triggered and our lives become as a mirror to display the glory of God. Yet not an inanimate mirror, rather a living companion, a soul mate, a worshipper, a friend and eternal partner of the living God.

December 4

Day unto day utters speech, and night unto night reveals knowledge. There is no speech nor language where their voice is not heard.   *(Psalm 19:2-3)*
The law of the LORD is perfect, converting the soul.
(Psalm 19:7)

The Psalmist begins his meditation by considering the universal word of the Lord spoken through the creation. This word is understandable by all humanity and needs no translator. The Psalmist then moves on to consider the law of the Lord, with its power to convert and confer wisdom. It is easy to miss the force of the earlier part of the Psalm, that God is speaking constantly through the power and beauty revealed in beautiful sunsets, or in the beauty of birdsong.

The point is that so many of us are too hurried to even pause and consider that God desires to impact our soul by the world around us. God made a garden in Eden and there He placed His beloved children to walk with Him and to commune with Him. God is not in a tree or a flower, but through them He does speak to the listening soul. "Consider the lilies of the field... look at the birds of the air..." (Matthew 6:26 & 28).

Reflect, slow down and allow God to interpret His world to you. As we do so we recognize that the act of considering is part of the message. We pray for God to speak and suddenly realise that we were waiting for a verse, while God was seeking to remove the strain and stress from our souls. We believe that earnest study is the way to find God's truth and slowly it dawns that that is only a part of God's self-revelation. It is God's plan to cause us to sit with Him and partake of His unhurried delight in all He has made:

Drop Thy sweet dews of quietness
Till all our strivings cease.
Take from our souls the strain and stress
And let our ordered lives confess
The beauty of Thy peace.

Speak through the heat of our desire
Thy coolness and Thy balm,
Let sense be dumb, let flesh retire,
Speak through the earthquake, wind and fire,
Thou still small voice of calm.

∼∼∼∼∼∼∼∼∼∼∼∼∼∼

December 5

For I determined not to know anything among you except Jesus Christ and Him crucified.   *(1 Corinthians 2:2)*

Paul preached this message on three levels: firstly as the doctrinal foundation of salvation, that we are saved by grace alone through the redeeming sacrifice of Jesus Christ.

Secondly, he preached the cross of Christ as a doorway of power through the baptism with the Holy Spirit. Paul proclaimed that by a transaction of faith, believers are to be united with Christ through His death and resurrection. This is a place of surrender to the fact that when Christ died, I also died. While for some this is accompanied by a vivid experience, it is vital that this is not the focus. It is rather a foundational revelation fact, to be embraced by a definite act of faith. The outworking of this is to lead to a Christ-centred life and to the boundless joy of being dead to sin and self and alive to God.

Thirdly, Paul preached the cross as a life-style. Through salvation and the power of the cross, believers have the power to take the lowest path and to serve others without selfish ambition. Of all the mysteries of the gospel, the greatest is that we have the nature of the cross imprinted into our instincts. There is a gentle urge in believers to let go rather than grasp, to honour others more than themselves and to seek the blessing of others rather than themselves.

This is the supernatural power of God in us: to live like Christ. It is not automatic and believers face a daily choice to follow the passion of the Spirit within us. The Holy Spirit loves Jesus and loves to make our lives a setting for Him, that He be exalted and glorified. When we follow this path, we sense the joyous backing of all the hosts of heaven and all the delight of God Himself.

~~~~~~~~~~~~~~

December 6

The people refused to enter the pleasant land, for they wouldn't believe his promise to care for them.
(Psalm 106:24 NLT)
For He makes His sun rise on the evil and on the good, and sends rain on the just and on the unjust. *(Matthew 5:45)*

The goodness of God is like the sun in the sky: it radiates warmth and light, dispelling the darkness and conquering all in its majesty. Yet unlike the sun, it is not visible to the physical eye, it is only visible to the eye of faith. Unbelief doesn't change who God is, nor can it diminish His marvellous qualities of character. Unbelief simply robs us of the spiritual benefits of His unspeakable goodness.

Whether we like it or not, we have a daily choice to believe in God's love and care or to soldier on alone through a wilderness that is the product of our mean minds. God is generous, lavishing His love and care on all mankind. Yet the majority of the human race remain unaware of Him and don't acknowledge or thank Him.

We are to believe His promise to care for us and so enter the pleasant land. This land is a state of heart where we are partaking of the constant upward flow of the currents of God's own being. The kingdom of God is an irrepressible inward rising to meet the challenges of each day. It is an unshakable belief that God will work all things together for good. It is the supreme consciousness that God is on our side and that therefore all our enemies are terrified of us. The pleasant land is a world of conquering love that will never cease but will sweep aside all its enemies.

Our faith may be tiny, but it is equally effective no matter its size. Faith is the conduit through which our conscious minds are infused with God's delight in His children. Choose to believe and choose to act on that faith by thanksgiving and praise. It is by this that we rejoice in the Lord and become partakers of His eternal kingdom.

~~~~~~~~~~~~~

December 7

Therefore the ungodly shall not stand in the judgment, nor sinners in the congregation of the righteous.   (Psalm 1:5)
Let God be true but every man a liar.   (Romans 3:4)

It is often the lot of the believer to be out of step with the world around him. He is shunned in the midst of the unrighteous. He is looked down on by the worldly man who is familiar with compromise. But a day of great reversal is coming when the ungodly will be the odd ones out and will hang their heads in shame and confusion at the radiant joy of those who have kept their faith and followed their conscience, swimming against the tide of temptation.

To walk with God sometimes requires us to suffer misunderstanding and rejection, and we do well not to forget that there is a day of joy coming for those who love God. To follow the crowd is the easy way but it is a delusion. The crowd will disappear on the days that really count. We will stand alone before God on the day of judgment, and on that day the voice of the majority will be silenced before the brightness and clarity of God's righteousness.

The battle of each day is to keep our heart in step with God's heart. Others may feel free to follow an easy path but we may not disturb the peace of a heart in tune with the Spirit within us. Spiritual greatness is not produced in great meetings but is forged in the white heat of a quiet consciousness that God is asking me to walk out of step with those around me. The fires are hottest when we must walk a different path to those we love most. In many parts of the world, water baptism is a simple matter of choice. But in some cultures, to be baptized is to reject the whole culture and world view of those around you. In some countries it must be practised with care and sometimes even secrecy or it will result in riots or even death. We are to so live now that we may one day be part of the great company who would hazard all to follow the Son of God.

~~~~~~~~~~~~~

December 8

Then Jacob asked, saying, "Tell me Your name, I pray."
(Genesis 32:29)

When Jacob prayed this prayer, he had just passed through the deepest crisis of his life and he still had to face his brother Esau, who was on his way to meet him with an army of 400 men armed to the teeth. Jacob had wrestled his way through to a face-to-face encounter with God in which all his selfishness had been exposed and swept aside. His problems were wholly a product of his own selfish scheming, but now the awful burden had been loosed from his back.

The first and most wonderful fruit of his liberty was that he had hunger for God Himself: Jacob wanted to know God's name. This prayer was now possible because he had room for God. Liberty from self is a door of opportunity and through it will flood the beautiful perfume of the sweetness of knowing God. Jacob looked up and for the first time realised that God was smiling on Him with loving tenderness.

Looking up into the face of God, we become aware of a kindness that melts our stubbornness. We receive a sense of awe that completely dissolves our cynicism. We lose all dread of things to come under the powerful consciousness that God is watching over us. The only thing that changed in Jacob's night of wrestling with God was his awareness of God. His problems hadn't changed, but Jacob had. He had become a different man simply because his outlook was now focused on the wonderment at the amazing God who is the true and living God. Whether it is just an upward look, or a night of wrestling in prayer, turn your gaze away and upwards and the effect will be life-changing and permanent.

December 9

But indeed, O man, who are you to reply against God? Will the thing formed say to him who formed it, "Why have you made me like this?" (Romans 9:20)

There are many questions we put to God on our life's journey. Perhaps the worst question is to ask God why He made me to be as I am. It is only human beings who frequently have this disquiet. The truth is that God makes all things beautiful in their time (Ecclesiastes 3:11). It is the fall that has made us uncomfortable in our own skins and made us wish we were somebody else. This disease is common to a huge proportion of the human race and afflicts even the rich, the famous and the powerful. It is as if the humming-bird turned to God the moment he was created and said: "I would prefer to be a flamingo!"

Once we belong to God we slowly grasp that every human being is a unique and outstanding work of art. Each person has a beauty waiting to be displayed. God has designed us with skill and amazing qualities, many of which are dormant and hidden. The gospel grants us freedom from the guilt and power of sin and then liberates us to be the wonderful person God has made us.

You cannot be anyone else and no-one else can replace you. It is a great release when we turn to God and say: "Thank you for making me who I am." We may know others who have talents we will never possess. But each of us is a masterful combination of qualities that make us bearers of a unique aspect of God's greatness. When placed in the great orchestra of God's people, we produce a symphony of such depth and power that it causes God's heart to skip with joy and delight in His handiwork. God created you for this and the sooner you realise what an amazing person you are, the sooner God will be glorified and you will discover your amazing destiny.

~~~~~~~~~~~~~~

December 10

Because you are sons, God has sent forth the Spirit of His Son into your hearts, crying out, "Abba, Father!" (Galatians 4:6)

There are two words in the Greek New Testament for father, just as there are two in the English language. "Father" is the more formal word, that one can imagine a Victorian boy calling his father after returning from a long spell at boarding school. The other word "Abba" has no perfect English equivalent, but the closest is "dad" or "daddy" for very young children. However, the English word "dad" has a familiarity that the word "Abba" does not have and there is no perfect English equivalent to this precious word.

If we are to grasp the greatness of being children of God, then we must dare to call God our father and we must invest into that word our deepest love, affection and reverence. This will change our mind more deeply than we realise. There is absolutely nothing formal about our heavenly Father. A dad is a child's biggest fan. He is full of the warmest feelings of love towards his offspring. He will follow his children into endless trails through parks and woodlands, playing games and never tiring. Dad's greatest delight is to identify with his children and to surprise them with little parcels of treats that are as unexpected as they are frequent.

God the Father cares for His children with infinite tender love and we are to allow that love to reach the deepest level of our hearts. As we dare to call God "Father", we are at the same time releasing an inner consciousness of our true identity. God is melted as we love Him and our hearts are melted as we confess the truth of who God has made us. To be a child of God is to be protected, to be cared and provided for - in short, to be loved. God wants to adopt every human being into His family, and He wants those who He has already adopted to fully grasp the wonder of what has happened. The Holy Spirit in us is strongly urging us to cry out "Abba, Father!"

~~~~~~~~~~~~~

December 11

Immediately the father of the child cried out and said with tears, "Lord, I believe; help my unbelief!" (Mark 9:24)

The man who prayed this prayer was filled with total honesty, driven by strong desire. The comfort of this event is that the Lord took what the man had and used it. God will always take an open heart and enter into whatever He finds there and bring healing and power.

The great preacher F.B. Meyer attended a Keswick convention and became deeply convinced that there was a deeper work that God needed to do in his heart. But he found things in his heart that conflicted with his desire for a deeper victory. He prayed: "Lord, I am not willing, but I am willing to be made willing." God took this open door and ushered him into a fullness that transformed his life and ministry.

Discipleship is never about pretending or striking a pose. It is about radical honesty of heart. God sometimes has to allow circumstances to humble us and press a prayer out of our lips that allows God to enter at the deepest level into our hearts. The man in Mark 9 was conscious of the inadequacy of his faith but that was not a hindrance, rather it was the basis for God to work. Prayer is not about making ourselves holy or believing, it is about presenting ourselves in the raw reality of who we are. Prayer is definitely not about striking a pose before God, it is about speaking from the heart. What we say may have much about it that we are ashamed to admit, but it is the only way to get through to God.

God is seeking people who will worship Him in Spirit and in truth. The word 'truth' is a word that could just as easily be translated 'reality'. A doctrinally polished prayer may be true but totally lacking in reality. The moment we speak to God from the heart, we get His attention and He is walking alongside us.

December 12

You will find a colt tied, on which no one has sat. Loose it and bring it. And if anyone says to you, 'Why are you doing this?' say: 'The Lord has need of it,' and immediately he will send it here. (Mark 11:2-3)

There are several astonishing details revealed in this verse about the entry of the Lord into Jerusalem. Firstly, the Lord needed a donkey to carry Him into the city. It is truly amazing that God needs a vessel to bear Him to situations where He can work. It may sound very pious to say: "The Lord doesn't need me," but it is completely untrue. The gospel never reached any city on planet earth until a human being took it there.

Secondly, the donkey was wild and unbroken. If transferred to a human context, it would mean that God uses people who are far from perfect but have a readiness to do His will. There were surely many believers in Israel more sophisticated than Peter, the impulsive fisherman, but they were not willing to respond to the call of God. As soon as we respond to the call, the Lord enters in and tames our wayward character. This donkey might have protested by bucking and rearing up against the Lord. But the peace of God in Christ subdued the wildness without a moment's fuss.

Thirdly, the donkey was bound and needed loosing. God will free us from fears and worries about the future at the very moment we respond to His call. Yes, we are complicated people but the moment we respond to the call of God we will find a liberty and a power flowing through our lives that make us different. The call of God is not about service, it is about offering up our insignificant lives to be a vessel for that majestic, magnificent Son of God. To let Him live through us is the heart and centre of why we even exist.

We may say "Surely there is someone else more qualified than me", but the truth is that each person is utterly unique and irreplaceable. God needs me, and the moment I stop fussing and arguing and let Him help Himself to me, I will find the peace, the majesty and the dignity of that royal life rubbing off on me. Being ridden by Jesus must have been the best day of that donkey's life.

December 13

And he showed me a pure river of water of life, clear as crystal, proceeding from the throne of God and of the Lamb. In the middle of its street, and on either side of the river, was the tree of life, which bore twelve fruits, each tree yielding its fruit every month. The leaves of the tree were for the healing of the nations. (Revelation 22:1-2)

John saw the river of life, the Holy Spirit, flowing from the throne. If an engineer saw this sight he would automatically look behind the throne to see where this vast river was coming from. This is because in nature there must be a cause and effect to all things. Something cannot flow from nothing. But God has no cause. He is Himself the source of all things. No matter how great the flow, God is never diminished, nor does He grow weak or weary. God is self-renewing and inexhaustible.

The river of life is clear and pure and makes all things live wherever it flows. This is no ordinary river, for in the midst of its flow and on either side there are trees of life bearing twelve kinds of fruit and giving a harvest each month all year round. The leaves themselves have nourishing and healing properties. Certainly all the wounds and scars of life are healed forever in that life-giving atmosphere. More than that, the leaves will be for the "healing of the nations"; the imparting of positive health and well-being. Just as vitamins impart health, so too the leaves of the tree bestow wholeness to all.

The tree of life was in the Garden of Eden and the way to it was barred after the fall. Now the way is open and all may eat of its fruit. The tree of life was placed within the reach of every sinner when Christ died on the cross and poured out His life as an offering for sin. All who go to the cross and partake of His flesh and blood are eating of the tree of life. In the New Creation, the tree of life will be fully available but then without a cross of wood, without nails and a crown of thorns. Here we have the taste, but then we will feast on the fullness at God's table in paradise.

~~~~~~~~~~~~~~~

December 14

And Esau said to Jacob "Please feed me! ..." But Jacob said: "Sell m your birthright." (Genesis 25:31)
Then Jacob made a vow, saying, "If God will be with me, and keep me ... and give me bread, then the LORD shall be my God... and I will pay to God a tithe. (Genesis 28:20-22)

Jacob must have believed he was doing God an enormous favour by believing in Him and even giving a tithe back to God. Jacob was such a trader that he seemed to believe he could even pull the wool over God's eyes. Jacob was suffering from the affliction of an enormous ego. He saw himself as the centre of the universe and God was there for him.

The truth is that Jacob did not realise that there was a monster within, which twisted everything for his own benefit. He saw nothing in the light of how it affected others. He tricked his twin brother into giving him his birthright. He fooled his father into giving him the blessing of the first-born. And now he even believed he could flatter God and con Him into blessing his life. He never considered how his actions and words might affect others.

The deepest blessing is to be shifted from a self-centred life to one that is Christ-centred. This means that we no longer ask "What's in it for me?" We are released from that millstone and begin to ask whether a matter will bring glory and delight to God. The cross is the key to blessing because the alternative is to enthrone selfishness. Jacob's life was a flight from the cross and his past kept catching up with him until he faced himself and allowed God to break that 'selfish gene' that was ruining his life. Blessing does not lie in having more of anything. It lies in the bliss of being dead to self and alive to God.

∾∾∾∾∾∾∾∾∾∾∾∾∾

December 15

They shall see His face.   *(Revelation 22:4 KJV)*
We shall see Him as He is. And everyone who has this hope in Him purifies himself, just as He is pure.   *(1 John 3:2-3)*

Believers shall see God face to face. In the gospel of John, the key word is to believe. In John's epistles, the key word is to know. In Revelation, the key word is to see. Believing turns to inner knowledge and in the New Creation we shall see with our eyes all that we have believed. The sight of God's face will be the sweetest and most awesome moment of our existence. In that face God's holiness and love are bathed in depths of pulsating life. We shall look and look and be forced to cover our faces at the brightness of inexpressible and unapproachable glory. We shall know as we are known but there will always be riches of personality and beauty that are beyond our gaze.

"Out of Zion, the perfection of beauty, God will shine forth." (Psalm 50:2.)

The depths of the Godhead are not like any three-dimensional sight we have ever seen. To gaze on God is to gaze on an infinity of transcendent beauty. As we behold God in His unveiled splendour, the riches of His tranquillity of being, the heights of His love and the power of His holiness will be poured into our being. Believers already have access to this place by faith and many have experienced a foretaste of this bliss in rare moments of prayer, when the soul has taken flight and soared into the presence of God. Here we have but glimpses, but then we shall have the fullness of knowing God as we are known.

Night will have passed away, eternal day will have come and as God shares His being with His beloved children, so He will share His authority and they shall reign with Him forever. All who have this hope are strengthened and purified to reach this unspeakable prize.

∼∼∼∼∼∼∼∼∼∼∼∼∼

December 16

I have come that they may have life, and that they may have it more abundantly. (John 10:10)
And he who had died came out bound hand and foot with grave clothes, and his face was wrapped with a cloth. Jesus said to them, "Loose him, and let him go." (John 11:44)

The mark of life is to have healthy, active sensory perception. We see, hear, touch, smell and taste and we interact with our environment. For the person who is without hearing or sight or touch they are trapped in their conscious mind as in a tomb. This is a description of the deadness of the human spirit without God. Our spirit is the most important dimension of life and if we are dead in that realm then we are like a car without an engine or a bird without wings. The Bible says that we were "dead in trespasses and sins" (Ephesians 2:1) and that we were "having no hope and without God in the world". (Ephesians 2:12).

Now God has called into our depths and His voice has called us back to life. His voice awakens the dead and gives abundant life. We are alive from the dead and we are able to interact with God for the first time. But so often we are encumbered with the habits of death and the smell of the tomb. Lazarus was alive but hampered by his grave clothes. We are to set aside the old man with all the habits and ways of the old life. Jesus came that we might have joy and that our joy might be full. His gift is not existence, but eternal life. This life is the awakening of all our spiritual senses to be conscious of God and to interact with Him.

We do not become alive through morbid praying or mournful longing or endless Bible study. We are to throw off the clinging, suffocating unbelief that would muffle our voice and hamper our steps and to fling aside the doubts and fears and step boldly into His beautiful presence with singing and everlasting joy.

December 17

But the woman was given two wings of a great eagle, that she might fly into the wilderness to her place.   (Revelation 12:14)

But those who wait on the LORD shall renew their strength; they shall mount up with wings like eagles, they shall run and not be weary, they shall walk and not faint.   (Isaiah 40:31)

God has a special place prepared in the Spirit for His people to escape and be nourished from the face of the enemy. But this place can only be reached on the wings of an eagle.

This place cannot be reached by study, nor by force of striving or intellect. It can only be reached by unfolding the wings of faith and worship and waiting on the Lord. The discipline of waiting on the Lord is the art of stilling the clamour and chatter of our minds till we become conscious of the divine presence in our hearts. The touch of the Holy Spirit awakens our souls to soar and sing. The more we are conscious of God in His perfect beauty and splendour, the more our hearts rise in confidence to His throne.

Believers may be caged in prisons, but no-one can stop believers from rising above every situation and escaping to a secret place, where we eat secret food that the world knows nothing of. The eagle does not flutter like a butterfly with fragile wings, nor does it strain like a bee with tiny wings that keep it aloft by intense beating. The eagle has wide wings that catch the upward thermals of rising air and enable it to fly with effortless ease. The eagle cannot travel by walking, it must fly, and so it is with Christians. We must spread our wings of faith and catch the ministry of the Spirit. We must march to a different drum beat and so escape the floods of evil that proceed from the mouth of the dragon.

~~~~~~~~~~~~~~~

December 18

And He put all things under His feet, and gave Him to be head over all things to the church.   (Ephesians 1:22)
Christ is head of the church.   (Ephesians 5:23 NASB)

The kingdom of God functions on the direct rule of Christ in the hearts of His people. Christians may be strongly encouraged to part with their money, giving sacrificially of their substance. But Christ is not satisfied with offerings of mere possessions and wealth. He wants the hearts of His people. True peace of heart begins here and springs from the depths of a person who has personally and directly touched the feet of Jesus and known the kingdom of God established in the inner sanctuary of the heart.

This is not as common an experience as may be assumed. In salvation the authority of Christ is experienced. When we repent and believe, we are accepted into His kingdom and have all the rights associated with this transfer of our citizenship. However, the surrender of the inner sanctuary of the heart is a much deeper transaction. It will involve the willingness to let go of everything in order to know His loving rule. The result will be an immediate change in the note of our lives. There will be a deeper peace and an inner cessation of striving. Worry will vanish from the mind as the realisation begins to take hold that Christ is Lord of all our circumstances and that under Him we are secure. It does not mean that Christians are not secure until we surrender all, but it certainly means we need to surrender consciously to Him to experience the full wonder of the safety and security that are ours. Find the place of surrender, and renew it every day whether storms are raging or the sun is shining.

~~~~~~~~~~~~~~~

December 19

Now when Jesus looked at him, He said, "You are Simon the son of Jonah. You shall be called Cephas" (which is translated, A Stone). (John 1:42)

Whenever God looks at any person, He sees two people: the person we are, and the person we can be. Jesus called Simon "a stone" referring to the fact that he would be strong, reliable and faithful. Simon was anything but reliable in his character, but God saw what he could be and called into his life to make him what he would be by God's grace.

The difference between these two may seem small at first, but the truth is that there are two vastly different paths before us, one ending in decay and grief, the other ending in the limitless joys of God's majestic presence. Once we hear God's call into our lives, we must allow it to dislodge all the shifting sand of our natural abilities. Peter is in some measure representative of all humanity. By nature we may be brave and fearless, but when it comes to spiritual excellence, there is simply no virtue to be found in us at all. Humanity is weak, ignorant and spineless in the great realms of spiritual warfare, where our need is not for a stiff upper lip but rather for revelation and understanding from another world. Jesus looked at Peter and saw a rugged fisherman who was completely at a loss in the world of the Spirit. He called into his life and awakened God's original plan for him, to be a man of spiritual power and faith.

We look at ourselves and realise that we fail so comprehensively in the spiritual disciplines of life. We are weak and ineffectual and we grasp that that only God can call into us and make us into a royal priesthood, a people of prayer in the likeness of Jesus. Once God's grace has touched us and we glimpse the person we are becoming, we can never look on any human being the same again. Like God, we also see two people: an alcoholic and an evangelist, a prostitute and a mother in Israel, a liar and a preacher of truth. Once God begins to get a hold of us, we are the product of His prophesying power to change us, and we begin to prophesy and speak in believing prayer to the sin-sick world around us.

∼∼∼∼∼∼∼∼∼∼∼∼∼∼

December 20

Now let it be that the young woman to whom I say, 'Please let down your pitcher that I may drink,' and she says: 'Drink, and I will also give your camels a drink'- let her be the one You have appointed for Your servant Isaac. And by this I will know that You have shown kindness to my master. (Genesis 24:14)

When Abraham's servant was seeking a bride for Isaac, he prayed that above all else the woman would be extravagantly generous and unselfish. It's one thing to dip a cup in a bucket and fill it with water for a man to drink. But to slake the thirst of camels is an arduous task. A thirsty camel can drink more than 100 litres in three minutes! And Abraham's servant had more than one camel.

The Holy Spirit is God's servant sent out to find and prepare a bride for the Son of God. He seeks a bride whose reputation is that she will welcome and love all with the same extravagant love and generosity of heart as her Master. If a bride is tight-fisted and mean she can never bring honour and glory to her husband.

All over the world Christians are rightly known by their love for the outcast. Among the first Christians in Nepal were many lepers who nobody else wanted to care for. All around us are people who need our help. German pastor Jonathan Paul was once walking along the sidewalk with some friends deep in conversation. They suddenly realised that he wasn't with them and looked around to see him on the other side of the road carrying the bags of an old woman. Everyone who knew him remembered not only his powerful Spirit-filled preaching, but a life full of random acts of loving-kindness. Love is the one and only true mark of the bride of Christ.

~~~~~~~~~~~~~~

December 21

Now may the God of hope fill you with all joy and peace in believing, that you may abound in hope by the power of the Holy Spirit. *(Romans 15:13)*

We may always be filled with joy and peace at the moment we believe and at no other. Anxiousness is the sign that we are not believing. If we think we will have peace as soon as we hear good news, then we are deceiving ourselves. If we only have peace when things are going well, then all we are doing is postponing everything till the next crisis. Seeing is not believing and it is definitely not trusting.

The heart of peace is to trust God and rest in His love. We are to commit our tomorrows and our problems into His loving hands. There is always a potential disaster waiting round the corner if we allow our minds to stray off course. The centre of the kingdom of God is trusting in the invisible. We are to write the words "I TRUST YOU" in bold large letters on the inside of our heads and whenever we are afraid, we are to read them and defiantly declare them to the winds and storms that beat over our fragile lives.

Once we have peace, joyous anticipation will soon follow, which will in turn produce hope. Peace, joy and hope are all by-products of believing. In the same way, anxiety, depression and despair are all by-products of unbelief. We are to attend to one thing: developing an attitude of quiet trust in God's word. Choose to believe when everything screams give up. When darkness presses in, rise up and hold fast to what God has said. Walking through a long, dark tunnel will reach a mid-point, the darkest section. We will automatically walk slower and strain to catch a gleam of light. Let the word of God be the lamp to your feet and so keep you pressing forward into the light at the end of the tunnel. Enjoy the light today while waiting for great light tomorrow.

~~~~~~~~~~~~~

December 22

Pharaoh summoned Moses and said, "Go, worship the LORD. Even your women and children may go with you; only leave your flocks and herds behind." But Moses said, "Our livestock too must go with us; not a hoof is to be left behind."
(Exodus 10:24-26 NIV)

Pharaoh was a stubborn negotiator. He kept bargaining with Moses to try and limit the losses he would suffer when the Israelites left Egypt. He simply would not surrender to Moses and to the Lord. It is absolute surrender that God requires and He is no negotiator.

The reason that God requires this is that He can only do His work in our hearts at the point at which we yield everything to Him. God can only cleanse what is given over to Him. What is kept back will remain unsanctified. We might rationalise our position and argue that we have only kept back a very small percentage of the whole. But on closer examination, it is the smallest part that is the most important. Give someone a car but keep back the keys. Build a massive ship but leave off the rudder. Pharaoh was simply maintaining his control and seeking to put God firmly under his thumb. We are to bring everything to the feet of Jesus as the basis of our relationship with Him. We are to constantly renew this foundation of totally ceding ownership of our whole being - body, soul, spirit, money and possessions - to God alone.

It is possible to offer God other things rather than surrender, including praise and worship. When Wellington defeated Napoleon at Waterloo, the French generals began by expressing their esteem of the Iron Duke and of his courage and wisdom in battle. But Wellington still had his eye on the main issue and said: "I appreciate your admiration, but gentlemen, this is a surrender. Yield to me your swords!" God loves to hear the songs of His people, but He never overlooks for a single instant the central concern of His heart. He has given His all and the only thing that is worthy of such a great being is the entire surrender of His people to Him in love.

December 23

You thought that I was altogether like you.   (Psalm 50:21)

Perhaps the most subtle weakness of the human heart is to attribute to God qualities that are in our own flawed personality. The truth is that God is bigger, deeper and wider in His character than we can ever grasp. We know that God is loving, but we think there are limits to His love because our love is so limited. We slowly realise that our doubts and fears about life and the future are all linked to our view of God. Will life crush us like some implacable machine? Will we be disappointed? All these things are expressions of our own mind, not God's.

The walk of faith lies in developing the skill of discerning the difference between the god who is a projection of my own personality and the true and living God of the Bible. God is an indescribably wonderful Father. He is compassionate and caring. He is never hard-hearted or difficult to approach. The only barriers between a human being and God are in the heart of that individual. God cannot be cold and He cannot be any other than good. If God could ever be cruel, even for a moment, then He could never be described as good. The heavens are friendly and there is a great divine conspiracy to bless and do good to every person who ever lived.

The father of the prodigal son never ceased to longingly reach out with open arms to his lost son. When the son returned to those arms from the madness of living for sensual pleasures, he discovered what God felt and thought about him through all the long years of separation. God is good, He has no flaws and He only has plans to bless and do us good.

~~~~~~~~~~~~~~~~

December 24

And the word became flesh. (John 1:14 NASB)

Of all the things that God ever did this is one of the most mysterious and amazing. Yet this mystery of God becoming man is continued in the equally astonishing fact that Jesus Christ lives in us His followers. The truth is that humanity was created with the intention that God and mankind be blended into one. A human being without God in them is unable to function as God first intended. No-one can fulfil their destiny until Christ lives in their heart.

There is a side to humanity that can only be fulfilled by the presence of God in us. Without this supernatural empowerment, we are like a bird without wings. Now an eagle can fly from London to Bristol in a few hours, but if it has to walk, the poor creature will almost certainly die before achieving this goal. In the same way the simple things that God has designed us to accomplish are only possible with the divine indwelling. Only through Christ can we love, be holy and commune with God.

In this light the incarnation is the most obvious step for God to take, since He has united Himself with us by His own eternal plan and design. God's commitment is so breath-taking because He agrees to enter even the most sinful and degraded human life with the aim of restoring it to His original plan. God has limitless faith in what can be done in a human life if only we will make room for Him. Of course, He cannot be given a secondary place in our hearts - He must be acknowledged as Lord. But into the chaos of a soul broken by sin, God will enter and then begin to speak the beautiful order of His own mind and character into us. Through Christ in us, the divine word will again become flesh.

December 25

You shall call His name Jesus, for He will save His people from their sins. *(Matthew 1:21)*

Among all the tinsel and stories of shepherds and angels it is easy to forget the true simple meaning of Christmas: Christ Jesus came into the world to save sinners. The wonder of Jesus is seen whenever a sinner bows and receives Christ into their cold, dark, unclean heart and they are changed forever.

It was 10 August 1950 and a man named Fred Lemon was in Dartmoor prison for violent crime. That night, in solitary confinement, he had a vision of Jesus and angels. Jesus simply told him that he must "drive the hatred from his heart if he wanted to be a Christian". Fred was elated at the vision and began to change but struggled with the word that pierced his heart. Months passed and Christmas Day 1950 came and Fred was in his cell getting ready to attend a Christmas service in prison. He was suddenly overwhelmed at the realisation of the love of God and prayed:

"Lord, it's Christmas! And I can't give you anything except my heart, so I give you that for the rest of my life. Come and cut this lump of hatred out of it, will you? Tell me how I can forgive the prison warders…" There in his cell, he felt the lump melt from his heart like warmed snow. In Fred's own words:
"In my ugly, cheerless cell, it was as if the Christmas angels sang again their joyous timeless message:
"Glory to God in the Highest,
On earth, peace,
Goodwill toward men."

Fred was completely transformed by the love of God in Jesus Christ. That is Christmas.

∾∾∾∾∾∾∾∾∾∾∾∾∾∾

December 26

If you then, being evil, know how to give good gifts to your children, how much more will your Father who is in heaven give good things to those who ask Him! (Matthew 7:11)

Most parents take extreme delight in watching their children open their gifts on Christmas Day. They will have spent days planning carefully to surprise them as an expression of deep love. Imagine then their disappointment if their offspring merely shrugged their shoulders and watched TV rather than open their presents. Imagine their dismay if the gifts remained permanently untouched and unopened.

The truth is that God has purchased unspeakably wonderful gifts for His children through the blood of His Son. Yet many believers are easily satisfied with a few blessings. Imagine our own amazement to find unopened packages bearing our name when we get to heaven. There are heights and depths of faith and love waiting to be imparted. These gifts will lead us to pray prayers that we might have thought unreachable at one time. God has supernatural wisdom, prophetic power and insight to impart. Yet many amazing promises of the Bible remain unclaimed, like dusty, forgotten books in the attic.

The key is to realise that it is when God is glorified and delighted that we in turn will find our true inner poise and well-being. Most children, when they have received an amazing gift, will embrace their parents with joy and pleasure. That is the parents' reward. God, too, is watching for the look of love, the spontaneous surge of praise. God is a cheerful giver. It is an essential characteristic of His being. He expects us to receive and share the swelling joy with Him and all those we meet.

~~~~~~~~~~~~~~

December 27

Then Jacob awoke from his sleep and said, "Surely the LORD is in this place, and I did not know it." And he was afraid and said, "How awesome is this place! This is none other than the house of God, and this is the gate of heaven!"
(Genesis 28:16-17)

Jacob dreamed about a place of supernatural power, where angels communicated God's power, but most importantly where God Himself dwelt. Jacob had slept in the very gate of heaven and had not known it.

Human beings are like sleep walkers. We carry on doggedly with such limited vision and understanding because we walk by sight and not by faith. To behold the physical universe is to see only one half of reality, and the lesser half at that. It is like watching a movie of a man dying in a desert and willingly forgetting that the man is surrounded by cameras and abundant food supplies. The visible world is made up of shadows and mirrors that can easily deceive us.

The greatest tragedy is that many believers do not believe their own beliefs. Christians so easily minimise the importance and power of the church. The church is, of course, only such a wonderful place because Christ is there. Often He is hidden behind the inflated egos of church members. It is for this reason that the cross is the door between the physical and the spiritual world. It is as we lay our lives down and become nothing that we suddenly realise that we have lived in wilful ignorance of the majesty and power that is at our disposal when we gather with God's people.

Many farms in the mid-western United States went bankrupt in the 1930s. Many farmers sold their land for a pittance, only to discover subsequently that there were vast reserves of oil waiting to be discovered below the surface. They had lived as paupers when they could have been millionaires. Believers are joint heirs of Jesus Christ and have all the power and spiritual riches of His life at our disposal. Multitudes in the world are searching for meaning and answers. If believers will rise up and exchange their deep sleep for the astonishing truth of Christ in us, then the church itself will become a blazing door of glory into the world where angels sing and Christ is adored.

~~~~~~~~~~~~~~~~

December 28

A merry heart does good, like medicine, but a broken spirit dries the bones. *(Proverbs 17:22)*

Praise the LORD! For it is good to sing praises to our God; for it is pleasant, and praise is beautiful. *(Psalm 147:1)*

When a person is sick, they will turn to their medicine cupboard and take the treatment appropriate for the illness. But by the far the most important area that needs addressing is the mind. It is our mental attitude that will determine our well-being. The most important matter is our inner joy.

Joy and happiness are two very different things. Happiness is a word from the Old English word "hap" meaning "luck." Happiness then depends on our circumstances, but joy depends on inner attitudes. An individual may lack money, physical health or even liberty. Even in prison, even under harsh deprivation, Christians may draw joy from the inner wells of the Holy Spirit.

Praise will always shape the mind and soothe our pain. Suffering will always be affected by the way we approach it. For this reason, we are to always begin our day meditating on the innumerable reasons we have to praise God. Focusing on God will always lift the heart to bathe in the light of His goodness. Praising God will allow the Holy Spirit to bathe us in the glow of God's glory. Exalting God is a choice and it is for this reason that the Lord commands us to rejoice. Sorrow and mourning flee before the presence of God and are replaced with everlasting joy. Believers may be trapped in a prison, a hospital or a wheel chair, but none of these things can stop the spirit from soaring above the clouds into the throne room of the universe and joining with the hosts to celebrate the majesty and goodness of God. This medicine not only works wonders in our body, it gives a wonderful flavour to the soul's palate.

~~~~~~~~~~~~~~

December 29

At that time the disciples came to Jesus and said, "Who then is greatest in the kingdom of heaven?" ² And He called a child to Himself and set him before them, ³ and said, "Truly I say to you, unless you are converted and become like children, you will not enter the kingdom of heaven. (Matthew 18:1-3 NASB)

It is so vital that we grasp this word since it is one of the absolute, uncompromising utterances of the Lord. Unless we change and become as children, we shall "by no means" enter God's kingdom. Adults fear loss of face and are defensive, building walls and nursing hurts and often pouting with self-importance and pride. Children on the contrary do not expect to be taken seriously at every moment, nor do they take themselves too seriously. If they fall or hurt themselves, they feel no great depths of shame but run into the arms of their father or mother to receive the comfort they believe they will always find there.

Children do not have the pride of believing they know everything. They are vulnerable and weak and ready to be taught, to be corrected. They have none of the complexity of a long history of sin and they are full of hope, believing that something better is just ahead.

They have no sense of the importance of money, wealth and possessions. They therefore do not feel sorry for themselves if they lack certain things since they have not learned to believe they have automatic rights to everything. It is touching to watch an African child bereft of all toys and possessions. I have seen a child take a wire coat hanger and make it into a toy car or an airplane. Their delight is so total and absorbed that such a child will be unconscious of its rags and lacks but will play happily for hours.

The biggest challenge then is to lose our stiff posturing and become vulnerable and weak, running into those big arms of love and finding the inner spring of wonder bubbling up again in our souls.

~~~~~~~~~~~~~~

December 30

God is light. (1 John 1:5 KJV)
God is love. (1 John 4:16 KJV)
Let your light shine before men in such a way that they may see your good works, and glorify your Father who is in heaven.
(Matthew 5:16 NASB)

It is easy to fall into the trap that polishing our Bible knowledge is the primary activity that pleases God. The simple truth is that God is a God of love and of action. He is ceaselessly involved in inspiring His people to touch lives with His love. If we are truly illuminated within, then that light must first be the light of love and it is deeds of love that most glorify God.

"You have not lived today successfully unless you've done something for someone who can never repay you." John Bunyan.

It is staggering to realise how easily we make the Christian life an intellectual exercise rather than an outpouring of love to God and those around us. We pray correct prayers, we bristle at minor doctrinal deviations, we strain out a gnat from our perfect cup of tea and swallow a camel by our indifference to some hurting soul.

The challenge is to turn all that God has done in our lives into an outpouring of love to God and an eagerness to give a cup of cold water to the parched and dying world around us. When love becomes active, faith will always rise with it. When we are on the watch for opportunities to express God's love, we will be praying for all those we meet. We are indeed to get our minds immersed in the Bible so that we can catch the upward surges of the heart of God, who delights to give rain to the just and the unjust. God is not a university professor, He is a Shepherd seeking to reach and touch a lost world, and His method is to do it through us.

"Do all the good you can
To all the people you can
In all the ways you can
For as long as you can." D.L. Moody.

December 31

Who then is the faithful and wise slave, whom the master has put in charge of his household, to give the other slaves their food at the proper time? Blessed is that slave whom the master finds at work when he comes. (Matthew 24:45-46 NET)

On 19th May 1780 in Connecticut USA, a dense fog combined with dust to produce an unusual darkness that the inhabitants had never witnessed before. One hour the sun was shining, the next everything was plunged into the darkness of night at midday, making it impossible to read. The Connecticut State Council was in session and members were convinced it was the day of judgment and requested an adjournment so they could go home and get ready to meet their Maker. One member, Abraham Davenport objected: "I am against an adjournment. The day of judgment is either approaching, or it is not. If it is not, there is no cause of an adjournment; if it is, I wish to be found doing my duty. I wish therefore that candles may be brought."

The truth of the second coming should be the source of a hope and a purpose that spurs believers to serve their Master to the full. Each day should be lived as if it were the last. This is the joyous anticipation of the Saviour's welcome into the courts of eternity. Let candles be brought in the darkest hour and let believers be found serving their King, loving and caring for those who have no certain hope and praying for the interventions of God in the lives of those who do not know Him. As another year ends and a New Year begins, let us settle our hearts to serve each day for the coming King.

~~~~~~~~~~~~~~~

A Closer Walk

THEME AND NAMES INDEX

Abiding	Feb 28
Abundant life	Dec 16
Access to God	Nov 28
Accountability to God	Oct 2
Acts of Kindness	Dec 30
Akhari, J.S.	Sep 25
Altar	Feb 24
	Aug 6
Anderson, Sir Robert	Mar 9
Anointing	Mar 21
Applying truth	Jun 27
Assurance	Sep 23
Auschwitz	Apr 3
Authority	Jul 13
Babylon	Oct 1
Baptism with the Spirit	Feb 29
Beauty of God	Dec 15
Bible	Jul 22
Bridge, W.	Jul 22
Brokenness	Feb 27
	Nov 8
	Jan 31
Bunyan, John	Dec 30
Call of God	Dec 12
	Dec 19
Cameroon,	Jan 16
	Feb 7
	Feb 21,
	Apr 30
	Jun 17
Captain of our salvation	Apr 30
Caring for others	Sep 13
Carmichael, Amy	May 29,
	Aug 29
Character of God	May 28
Child-likeness	May 12
	Dec 29
Christ crucified	Aug 25
	Dec 5
Christ the gospel	Aug 7
Christmas	Dec 25
Church	Jul 10
Church, bride of Christ	Sep 5
Churchill, W	Jun 30
Comfort	Jan 10
Comforter	Aug 26
Coming of Christ	Apr 4
	Aug 1
	Aug 4
	Dec 31
	Oct 11
	Sep 11
Communing with God	Mar 14
Communion	Mar 9
Compassion	Mar 8
Complacency	Mar 2
Complaining	Feb 2
	Jul 2
Confession	Mar 25
	Oct 10
Conscience	Aug 28
Cornerstone	Jul 24
Corrie Ten Boom	Mar 20
	May 10
	Jul 3
	Sept 17
	Oct 28
Cross	Mar 4
	Aug 23
	Jun 12
	Jun 26
	Sep 7
Cross bearing	May 8
	May 2
D'Esterre, J.L.	Nov 30
Danger of Ignorance	Feb 20
Dead to sin	Jun 15
Death	Aug 16
Death to self	Feb 18
Depression	Jan 13
	Sep 2
Discernment	Oct 6
Discouragement	Apr 1
Distraction	Sep 15
Distress	Feb 4
Eagles' wings	Dec 17

A Closer Walk

Eisenhower, Pres.	Jul 31	Flesh	Oct 15
Elizabeth II	Sep 15	Following Jesus	Nov 13
Endurance	May 14	Foreknowledge of God	May 1
	Sep 25		Apr 28
Entire Surrender	Feb 29		May 31
Expectation	Feb 6	Forgiveness	Jul 20
Eye of the needle	Jul 30	Franklin B.M.	Mar 10
F B Meyer	Dec 11	Frazer, J.O.	Jul 15
	Dec 11	Free will	Jan 30
Fabian, G.L.	Jun 9		Oct 4
Failure	May 9		Oct 7
Faith	Mar 5	Freedom from self	Dec 8
	Apr 15	Freedom's limits	Sep 16
	Feb 14	Friendship with God	Aug 15
	Feb 22	Fulness of God	Sep 4
	Feb 23	Fulness of the Spirit	Sep 3
	Mar 11	Generosity	Dec 20
	May 21		Nov 4
	Jan 11	Gentleness of Christ	Apr 3
	Jun 23	Genuine Faith	Mar 26
	Jun 5	Gift of prophecy	Aug 12
	Jun 8	Gifts of God	Dec 26
	May 19	Glory of God	Jun 28
	Nov 11		Oct 13
	Nov 2		Oct 8
	Oct 22	God of Now	Jul 15
Faith of Abraham	Aug 21	God the centre	Sep 28
Faith of God	Apr 9	Good Shepherd	Mar 29
Faith's perspective	Nov 29	Goodness of God	Dec 6
Faithfulness	Jan 25	Gospel	Apr 20
	Jul 7	Grace	Mar 16
Faithfulness of God	Aug 8		Mar 19
Falling from grace	Apr 10		Nov 3
	Nov 17		Oct 20
Fatherhood of God	Dec 10	Graham Billy,	Apr 8,
Fear	Feb 7		Jul 21
	Jul 29	Graham, Franklin,	May 31
	Jun 17	Guidance	Jan 8
Fear not!	Sep 9		Jun 14
Fear of God	Jun 3	Gypsy Smith	Feb 16
	Oct 30	Habits	Jun 4
Fellowship	May 4	Hardship	Jul 21
Fellowship with God	Nov 16	Heart	Mar 6
Fervency	Feb 12	Heaven	Apr 8

A Closer Walk

Heaven on earth	Jul 3	Kindness	May 18
Hidden riches	Dec 27	Kingdom of God	May 15
Holiness	Jan 14	Knowing God	Dec 23
	Jan 21		Jul 4
	Nov 19	Knowing Jesus	Nov 7
	Oct 29		Oct 18
Holy Spirit	Apr 5	LaGuardia Mayor	May 6
	Feb 13	Lampstand	Jul 27
	Mar 15	Lemon Fred	Dec 25
	Dec 13	Lennox, John	Oct 18
	Jan 9	Life of God in us	Oct 24
Honesty in prayer	Dec 11	Light	Jan 18
Honour	Jul 23	Limits of Liberty	Jul 14
Hope	Mar 3	Lincoln, Pres.	Nov 29
	Aug 19	Locust plague	Oct 20
	Jan 12	Lordship of Christ	Dec 18
	Nov 30	Love	Feb 3
	Sep 10		Jul 1
Hudson-Taylor	Jul 14,		Jul 11
	Jul 28	Love for Jesus	Nov 14
Hughes Howard	Jan 26	Love of God	Apr 18
Humility	Apr 27		Apr 17
	May 25		Feb 8
	Jun 6		Aug 11
Hyde J	Mar 7		Aug 30
Identification	Apr 14		Jan 19
	May 16		Jul 31
Identity	Dec 9		Nov 10
Idolatry	Feb 5		Nov 6
	Mar 22	Love of the world	Aug 9
	May 13	Loving God	Jul 6
Immutability of God	Sep 19		Sep 30
Importance/small things	Nov 23	Majesty if God	May 11
Incarnation	Dec 24	Masai	Jun 24
Indwelling of Spirit	Mar 12	Matthews, Stanley	May 2
Inuit	Jan 18	Mephibosheth	Aug 20
Jesus Christ	Jan 17	Mercy	May 6
Journey of faith	Sep 18	Meyer, F.B.	Dec 11
	Sep 20	Mind of Christ	Jun 30
Joy	Feb 10	Miracles	Jan 6
	Jan 27		Jan 7
	Dec 28	Moody, D.L.	Dec 30
	Nov 5	Mueller G.	Apr 22
Kindness	Jul 5	Nature of Christ	Aug 13

A Closer Walk

Nee, Watchman	Jun 15	Prayer	Oct 31
New Covenant	Feb 9		Sep 17
	May 17		Jan 2
	Nov 15	Prayer, unanswered	Jun 7
	Oct 21	Presence of God	Mar 17
Niemoller, Capt.	Oct 13		Aug 27
Nixon, Patricia	Aug 16		Apr 2
Nixon, Pres.	Aug 16		Jul 17
Obedience	Jul 16		Jun 19
Offence	May 5		Sep 26
Offences	Apr 12	Pride	Apr 29
	Jan 28	Promised land	May 10
Omniscience of God	Nov 9	Promises of God	Nov 18
Passivity	May 7	Purity	Apr 23
Patience	Apr 22	Pursuit of God	Feb 21
Patience of God	May 22	Quiet heart	Aug 14
Paton, John G.	Oct 27	Ravenhill L	Mar 6
Paul, Jonathan	Dec 20	Remembrance	Jun 2
Peace	Jan 15	Repentance	Apr 6
	Jan 22		May 29
	Jul 12		Feb 16
Persecution	Oct 12	Rest	Apr 11
Perseverance	Sep 22	Resurrection	Mar 24
Peter's restoration	Aug 10		May 26
Pleasures of God	Nov 22	Revelation	Jan 26
Power in Prayer	Feb 15		May 23
Power of God	Aug 3	Risk of Faith	Oct 27
Power of grace	Oct 17	Roberts, Evan	Oct 13
Power of praise	Nov 24	Roots	Oct 26
Power of prayer	May 20	Roseveare, H.	Aug 27
Power of the tongue	Nov 25	Salvation	Jan 16
Power of the word	Apr 24		Sep 21
	Oct 16	Scriptures	Feb 11
Practical faith	Feb 25	Self denial	Mar 27
	Dec 1	Self-control	Jul 8
Prayer	Apr 19	Selfishness	Apr 13
	Jan 20		Jul 18
	Jan 29		Jun 20
	Jun 22		Dec 14
	Mar 31	Sin	Mar 18
	Nov 12	Singing	Feb 17
	Nov 21		Aug 31
	Nov 26	Small things	Mar 20
	Oct 3		Oct 28

A Closer Walk

Solzhenitsyn A.	Aug 16	Trials	Sep 1
Sovereignty of God	Jan 3		Sep 12
Spafford, Horatio,	May 3		Oct 23
	Jul 6	Tribulation	Jan 10
Special people	Oct 19	Trust	Jun 9
Spiritual exercise	Jun 25	Trusting God	Dec 21
Spiritual warfare	May 30	Twain, Mark	Nov 7
Spiritual warfare	Aug 22	Unbelief	Nov 27
	Jun 13	Unity	Jul 9
	Jun 18		Jun 10
	Jun 24	Veil	Sep 27
	Nov 1	Vertebrates	Jul 25
	Nov 20	Victorious faith	Apr 26
	Oct 9	Victory over Satan	Jul 19
Stalingrad	Sep 21		Jun 29
Suffering	Jan 5	Vietnam war	Feb 3
Sufferings	Aug 29	Voice of God	Sep 29
	Sep 24	Voltaire	Oct 14
Sundar-Singh	May 30	Waiting on God	Mar 1
Surrender	Dec 22		Dec 3
	Oct 14		Mar 30
Talantov, Boris	Oct 5	Walk in the Spirit	Aug 18
Telugu	May 26	Walking with God	Apr 7
Ten Boom Corrie	Mar 20		Dec 7
	May 10		Jan 24
	Jul 3	Warfare	Mar 23
	Sept 17	Washington G	Feb 11
	Oct 28	Weakness	Jul 28
Testimony	May 27		Oct 25
Throne of God	Apr 16	Wellington, Duke of	Dec 22
	Aug 5	Wilderness	Aug 24
	Feb 19	Wilderness	Sep 6
Timing of God	Jun 16	Will of God	Jan 23
Today	Jul 26	Willard D.	Apr 26
Tongue Power of	Feb 26	Wisdom	Jun 21
Transformation	Jun 1	Witness of the Spirit	May 3
Trials	Apr 25	Witnesses	Sep 14
	Mar 13	Word of God	Aug 17
	Feb 1		Aug 2
	Mar 10		Mar 28
	Dec 2		Dec 4
	Jun 11	Worry	Apr 21
	May 24		Jan 1
	Oct 5	Worship	Mar 7

A Closer Walk

Worship	Jan 4	Zimbabwe Mar 18, May 18
	Sep 8	
Wurmbrand, R.	Oct 2	

SCRIPTURES INDEX

Old Testament

Genesis 1:26	May 4	Judges 3:1-2	Oct 9
Genesis 2:21-23	Aug 23	Judges 6:12	Apr 9
Genesis 2:9	Jan 30	Ruth 1:1	Jul 5
Genesis 3:5	Nov 27	1 Samuel 2:8	Aug 3
Genesis 4:7	Mar 18	1 Samuel 12:23	Nov 26
Genesis 6:9	Apr 7	1 Samuel 17:32	Nov 11
Genesis 14:12-14	Oct 27	1 Samuel 22:8	May 19
Genesis 15:13-15	Jan 24	1 Samuel 22:8	Oct 10
Genesis 15:5-6	Aug 21	1 Samuel 30:6	May 19
Genesis 15:6	Jun 9	1 Samuel 30:6	Oct 10
Genesis 21:19	Jan 26	2 Samuel 9:6-7	Aug 20
Genesis 22:5 & 12	Oct 30	2 Samuel 11:1	Mar 2
Genesis 22:5-6	Mar 24	2 Samuel 23:10	Aug 17
Genesis 24:14	Dec 20	1 Kings 8:27	Jan 4
Genesis 25:31	Dec 14	1 Kings 14:6	Aug 12
Genesis 28:16-17	Dec 27	1 Kings 18:33	Aug 6
Genesis 28:20-22	Dec 14	1 Kings 19:9	Sep 2
Genesis 28:20-22	Jul 18	1 Kings 19:11-12	Sep 29
Genesis 32:24	Apr 13	2 Kings 2:2	Apr 1
Genesis 32:27-29	Nov 8	2 Kings 2:9-10	Mar 31
Genesis 32:29	Dec 8	2 Kings 6:16	Nov 1
Genesis 42:36	Jun 5	2 Kings 6:17	Sep 14
Exodus 10:24-26	Dec 22	2 Kings 18:5	Feb 25
Exodus 12:7	Jan 14	1 Chronicles 29:1	Jun 28
Exodus 13:21	Sep 20	2 Chronicles 1:7	Jan 20
Exodus 14:22	Jan 14	2 Chronicles 9:3-4	Mar 1
Exodus 15:22-24	Jun 2	2 Chronicles 20:6-12	Oct 3
Exodus 20:12	Jul 23	2 Chronicles 20:21-22	Nov 24
Exodus 20:20	Jun 3	2 Chronicles 32:30	Feb 25
Exodus 20:41	May 13	2 Chronicles 32:31	Oct 7
Exodus 25:31	Jul 27	2 Chronicles 33:9-13	Oct 20
Exodus 26:14	Nov 16	Nehemiah 8:10	Jan 27
Exodus 26:33	Jan 14	Nehemiah 9:5-6	May 11
Exodus 33:11	Jun 22	Esther 5:2	Sep 5
Leviticus 26:8	Jul 9	Job 13:15	Jul 6
Numbers 17:7-8	Jul 1	Job 14:7-9	Nov 30
Numbers 21:5-9	Feb 2	Psalm 1:5	Dec 7
Deuteronomy 4:7	Jul 10	Psalm 4:3	Jul 31
Deuteronomy 6:23	Feb 21	Psalm 9:9-10	Aug 11
Deuteronomy 6:23	May 10	Psalm 19:2-3	Dec 4
Deuteronomy 11:21	Jul 3	Psalm 19:7	Dec 4
Deuteronomy 26:18-19	Oct 19	Psalm 23:4	Feb 7
Deuteronomy 30:11-14	Dec 1	Psalm 23:5	Jun 13
Deuteronomy 32:3	Nov 29	Psalm 24:1	Nov 22
Joshua 1:8	Jul 22	Psalm 27:4	Jun 19
Joshua 6:9-10	Aug 14	Psalm 32:8-9	Jun 14
Joshua 10:12-13	Jun 8	Psalm 33:16	Nov 1
		Psalm 37:4	Jan 20
		Psalm 42:11	Jan 13
		Psalm 46:10	May 28
		Psalm 46:2 & 10	Jul 29

A Closer Walk

Psalm 50:15	May 22	Ezekiel 10:18	Oct 13
Psalm 50:21	Dec 23	Ezekiel 36:26	Mar 6
Psalm 50:21	Sep 19	Ezekiel 37:10	Jun 18
Psalm 51:6	Oct 17	Daniel 4:35	Jan 3
Psalm 61:1-2	Nov 21	Daniel 6:3	Oct 1
Psalm 62:1 & 5	Dec 3	Hosea 2:14-15	Sep 6
Psalm 68:1	Aug 3	Hosea 2:19-20	Aug 30
Psalm 73:16-17	Apr 2	Obadiah 1:17	Mar 26
Psalm 77:9-19	Oct 23	Micah 6:8	Jan 23
Psalm 84:1-3	Jul 17	Habakkuk 2:4	Feb 23
Psalm 84:2 & 10	Sep 26	Haggai 2:19	Mar 28
Psalm 86:11	Jun 10	Zechariah 4:10	Nov 23
Psalm 95:1 & 7- 8	Mar 7	Malachi 3:1	Feb 6
Psalm 102:26-27	Feb 4	Malachi 3:3	Apr 23
Psalm 102:6-7	Feb 4	Malachi 3:6	Sep 19
Psalm 104:26	Nov 22	Malachi 3:10	Nov 4
Psalm 106:15	Jan 29		
Psalm 106:24	Dec 6	**New Testament**	
Psalm 118:24	Feb 10		
Psalm 119:105	Aug 2	Matthew 1:21	Dec 25
Psalm 119:67 & 71	Dec 2	Matthew 3:14	Apr 27
Psalm 121:1-2	Nov 11	Matthew 4:19-20	Jul 21
Psalm 130:5-6	Mar 30	Matthew 5:16	Dec 30
Psalm 145:5-6	Aug 11	Matthew 5:45	Dec 6
Psalm 147:1	Dec 28	Matthew 6:3, 5, 16	Jun 25
Proverbs 4:23	Oct 17	Matthew 6:6	Nov 16
Proverbs 17:22	Dec 28	Matthew 6:6-8	Nov 9
Proverbs 18:21	Feb 26	Matthew 6:7	Jun 22
Proverbs 18:21	Nov 25	Matthew 6:10	Jul 3
Proverbs 25:11	Nov 25	Matthew 6:34	Jan 1
Ecclesiastes 7:1-4	Aug 16	Matthew 7:11	Dec 26
Ecclesiastes 11:4-6	May 7	Matthew 8:16-17	Apr 24
Song of Sol 2:8-12	Aug 31	Matthew 8:8-9	Jul 13
Song of Sol 2:15	Jan 25	Matthew 10:29-31	Oct 28
Song of Sol 2:16	Jul 31	Matthew 10:30-31	Apr 17
Isaiah 6:3	Nov 19	Matthew 11:1	Apr 6
Isaiah 6:10	Oct 4	Matthew 11:6	Jan 28
Isaiah 7:14-15	Oct 6	Matthew 11:11	May 17
Isaiah 30:18	Jun 16	Matthew 11:12	May 29
Isaiah 30:18	May 22	Matthew 11:28-30	Apr 11
Isaiah 35:1-2	Aug 24	Matthew 11:29	May 25
Isaiah 40:31	Dec 17	Matthew 12:20	Apr 3
Isaiah 41:10	Jun 17	Matthew 12:30	May 30
Isaiah 43:1-2	Sep 9	Matthew 13:3	Mar 28
Isaiah 45:22	Sep 21	Matthew 13:8	Mar 28
Isaiah 64:1	Nov 4	Matthew 14:16	Sep 13
Jeremiah 9:23-24	Jul 4	Matthew 14:29-31	May 21
Jeremiah 29:11-	Mar 3	Matthew 15:26-28	Mar 11
Jeremiah 31:3	Nov 6	Matthew 16:21-23	Jun 20
Jeremiah 31:15-17	Aug 19	Matthew 16:24 & 26	Oct 14
Ezekiel 1:28 - 2:1	Oct 8	Matthew 17:20	Jun 23

A Closer Walk

Matthew 17:27	Mar 20	Luke 17:1	Apr 12
Matthew 17:4-8	Feb 5	Luke 18:1	Apr 19
Matthew 18:1-3	Dec 29	Luke 18:8	Apr 19
Matthew 18:19	Jul 9	Luke 18:16	May 12
Matthew 18:20	Nov 23	Luke 19:5	Apr 29
Matthew 18:24	Jul 20	Luke 19:5	May 25
Matthew 18:28	Jul 20	Luke 21:28	Oct 11
Matthew 19:19	Feb 3	Luke 22:15	Feb 8
Matthew 19:24-26	Jul 30	Luke 22:61-62	Feb 27
Matthew 19:30	Apr 10	John 1:14	Dec 24
Matthew 20:11-12	Jul 2	John 1:18	Aug 13
Matthew 20:32	Mar 5	John 1:42	Dec 19
Matthew 21:2	May 31	John 2:5-8	Jan 7
Matthew 21:22	Oct 31	John 2:9	Sep 7
Matthew 22:2	Nov 5	John 2:11	Jan 6
Matthew 23:8-9	Oct 24	John 3:2-3	Dec 15
Matthew 24:3	Sep 11	John 3:30	Mar 27
Matthew 24:45-46	Dec 31	John 4:24	Jul 11
Matthew 25:40	May 18	John 4:35	Jul 15
Matthew 26:34	May 9	John 5:21	May 13
Matthew 27:51	Apr 2	John 5:44	Oct 15
Mark 1:12	Aug 24	John 6:5-6	Apr 28
Mark 1:12	Sep 6	John 8:7-9	Aug 28
Mark 1:17	Nov 13	John 8:12	Jan 18
Mark 2:21-22	Nov 15	John 9:25	May 27
Mark 3:14-19	Sep 22	John 10:4	Sep 20
Mark 4:17	Oct 26	John 10:10	Dec 16
Mark 5:22	Feb 1	John 10:9 & 11	Mar 29
Mark 8:34	May 8	John 11:6	Mar 13
Mark 9:1	Jul 16	John 11:11	Aug 15
Mark 9:1-2 & 9:7	May 15	John 11:32-35	Sep 10
Mark 9:23-24	Apr 15	John 11:33 & 35	Mar 8
Mark 9:24	Dec 11	John 11:33-35	May 16
Mark 10:46-52	May 20	John 11:39-40	Apr 26
Mark 11:17	Nov 12	John 11:44	Dec 16
Mark 11:2-3	Dec 12	John 13:38	Feb 27
Mark 13:35-37	Aug 1	John 14:6	Aug 7
Mark 14:15	May 1	John 14:6	Feb 9
Mark 14:3	Nov 14	John 14:13-14	Jun 7
Mark 14:37-38	Jan 31	John 14:15	Jul 16
Mark 16:6-7	Aug 10	John 14:27	Jan 15
Luke 4:3-4	Aug 17	John 14:27	Jan 22
Luke 6:26	Oct 15	John 15:5	Sep 7
Luke 7:23	Apr 12	John 15:7-8	Feb 28
Luke 7:37-38	Sep 30	John 15:11	Jan 15
Luke 10:35	Sep 13	John 15:16	Feb 8
Luke 11:9	Jan 29	John 16:8	Aug 26
Luke 11:13	Apr 5	John 17:24	Sep 4
Luke 11:17	Jun 10	John 18:10	Feb 26
Luke 15:25-26	Jul 2	John 20:21	Aug 12
Luke 16:27-31	Oct 16	John 20:22	Sep 3

A Closer Walk

Reference	Date	Reference	Date
John 21:19-21	Sep 15	1 Corinthians 15:31	Jun 15
Acts 2:37	Jun 27	2 Corinthians 1:10	Jan 16
Acts 2:42	May 4	2 Corinthians 1:3-4	Jan 10
Acts 4:13	Sep 22	2 Corinthians 3:14-16	Sep 27
Acts 4:32	Aug 9	2 Corinthians 3:18	Mar 17
Acts 9:4	Apr 14	2 Corinthians 3:18	Mar 14
Acts 10:20	Jan 11	2 Corinthians 4:3-4	Nov 29
Acts 14:22	Dec 2	2 Corinthians 4:6	Mar 17
Acts 14:22	Mar 10	2 Corinthians 4:6	Oct 18
Acts 17:28	Aug 27	2 Corinthians 4:8-10	Sep 12
Acts 18:24	Feb 11	2 Corinthians 4:17	Sep 24
Acts 18:24-28	Feb 12	2 Corinthians 5:5	Mar 15
Acts 19:2	Feb 13	2 Corinthians 6:2	Jul 26
Acts 19:11-12	Feb 14	2 Corinthians 11:25	Apr 25
Acts 19:15	Feb 15	2 Corinthians 12:10	Jul 28
Acts 19:18-20	Feb 16	Galatians 2:15	Jun 4
Acts 21:12-14	Jan 8	Galatians 3:23-25	Jul 25
Acts 24:15-16	May 5	Galatians 4:6	Dec 10
Romans 1:16	Apr 20	Galatians 5:4	Nov 17
Romans 3:4	Dec 7	Galatians 5:22	Jul 11
Romans 4:20-21	Nov 18	Galatians 5:22	Jul 12
Romans 5:7-8	Nov 6	Galatians 5:22	Jul 7
Romans 5:8	Nov 10	Galatians 5:23	Jul 8
Romans 6:3	Feb 20	Ephesians 1:3-4	Mar 16
Romans 6:5	May 26	Ephesians 1:15-19	Jan 26
Romans 6:19	Sep 16	Ephesians 1:16-18	May 23
Romans 7:11	Mar 18	Ephesians 1:22	Dec 18
Romans 8:5-6	Aug 18	Ephesians 2:1-6	Jan 2
Romans 8:16-17	May 3	Ephesians 2:3-5	Feb 22
Romans 8:18	Sep 24	Ephesians 2:10	May 1
Romans 8:18-19	Aug 29	Ephesians 2:14-16	Sep 23
Romans 9:20	Dec 9	Ephesians 2:18	Nov 28
Romans 10:6	Mar 25	Ephesians 3:8	Oct 25
Romans 10:9	Mar 25	Ephesians 3:19	Sep 4
Romans 12:1-2	Feb 24	Ephesians 5:8	Jun 1
Romans 12:12	Jan 12	Ephesians 5:18	Jan 9
Romans 14:5	Mar 26	Ephesians 5:18	Sep 3
Romans 14:7	Jul 14	Ephesians 5:23	Dec 18
Romans 14:12	Oct 2	Ephesians 6:12	Nov 20
Romans 14:21	Jul 14	Ephesians 6:12	Mar 23
Romans 15:13	Dec 21	Philippians 2:5	Jun 30
Romans 16:20	Jun 29	Philippians 2:7	Nov 2
1 Corinthians 1:12	Jun 26	Philippians 3:10-11	May 26
1 Corinthians 1:23-24	Aug 25	Philippians 3:7-8	May 2
1 Corinthians 2:2	Dec 5	Philippians 3:8	Nov 7
1 Corinthians 2:16	Jun 30	Philippians 4:6-7	Apr 21
1 Corinthians 6:19	Mar 12	Philippians 4:7	Jan 22
1 Corinthians 8:1	Jun 21	Colossians 1:13	Feb 21
1 Corinthians 8:6	Jul 19	Colossians 3:1-3	Apr 8
1 Corinthians 10:13	Aug 8	1 Thessalonians 4:3	Jan 23
1 Corinthians 11:26	Mar 9	1 Thessalonians 5:17	Sep 17

A Closer Walk

Reference	Date	Reference	Date
I Thessalonians 5:18	Jan 23	1 Peter 2:17	Jul 23
2 Timothy 2:3-4	Mar 23	1 Peter 3:7	Jul 23
2 Timothy 2:3-4	Jul 21	1 Peter 4:12	Jun 11
2 Timothy 3:12	Oct 12	1 Peter 5:5-6	Jun 6
2 Timothy 4:8	Oct 11	2 Peter 3:10-11	Aug 4
Hebrews 2:9	Jun 12	1 John 1:5	Dec 30
Hebrews 2:9	Mar 4	1 John 1:5	Jul 11
Hebrews 2:10	Apr 30	1 John 2:14	Jun 24
Hebrews 2:10	Sep 28	1 John 2:15	Aug 9
Hebrews 2:13	May 12	1 John 2:27	Mar 21
Hebrews 4:7	Jul 26	1 John 4:4	Jul 19
Hebrews 4:12	Aug 2	1 John 4:8	Jul 11
Hebrews 4:15	May 16	1 John 4:10	Nov 10
Hebrews 6:12	Apr 22	1 John 4:16	Apr 18
Hebrews 6:12	May 14	1 John 4:16	Dec 30
Hebrews 9:14	Feb 29	1 John 4:16	Jan 19
Hebrews 10:19-22	Jan 21	1 John 5:11	May 27
Hebrews 10:20	Sep 27	1 John 5:14-15	Nov 21
Hebrews 10:36	May 14	1 John 5:21	Mar 22
Hebrews 11:6 & 8	Sep 18	Revelation 1:11	Aug 5
Hebrews 11:8	Oct 22	Revelation 1:13-14	Jan 17
Hebrews 11:13	Oct 21	Revelation 1:17	Feb 18
Hebrews 11:21	Sep 8	Revelation 2:7	Aug 22
Hebrews 11:35-38	Oct 5	Revelation 3:17 & 21	Mar 19
Hebrews 12:1-2	Sep 25	Revelation 4:1	Aug 5
Hebrews 12:5-6	Sep 1	Revelation 4:1-2	Feb 19
Hebrews 12:11	Jan 5	Revelation 5:9-10	Feb 17
Hebrews 12:15	Nov 3	Revelation 5:11-12	Apr 16
James 1:2-4	May 24	Revelation 12:14	Dec 17
James 2:13	May 6	Revelation 15:4	Oct 29
James 3:13	Jun 21	Revelation 18:4	Oct 1
James 4:7	Jun 24	Revelation 22:1-2	Dec 13
James 5:8	Apr 4	Revelation 22:4	Dec 15
1 Peter 1:6	Jun 11		
1 Peter 2:6	Jul 24		

A Closer Walk

A Closer Walk

Printed in Great Britain
by Amazon